THE WORD HAS DWELT AMONG US

THE WORD HAS DWELT AMONG US

EXPLORATIONS IN THEOLOGY

Guy Mansini, O.S.B.

Sapientia Press
of Ave Maria University

Sapientia Press
of Ave Maria University
5050 Ave Maria Blvd.
Ave Maria, FL 34142
888–343–8607

Cover Design: Eloise Anagnost

Cover Image: *The Life of St. Benedict* (fresco) (detail), Signorelli, L. (ca. 1441–1523) and Sodoma, G. (1477–1549)
© Monte Oliveto Maggiore, Tuscany, Italy
The Bridgeman Art Library

Printed in the United States of America.

Library of Congress Control Number: 2007938205

ISBN: 978-1-932589-45-0

Table of Contents

SECTION II: Ecclesiology and Sacramental Theology

PREFACE

THE ESSAYS in this volume treat mainly either of Christ and his work or of his presence in the Church through the sacrament of Orders. Taken together, the essays on Christ and his work constitute a call to return to the Christology of St. Thomas and the soteriology of St. Anselm.

The first essay, "A Short Christology," though relatively informal, presents a quick overview of the Christological framework supposed by the other essays, but with special attention to relating the classical to the more contemporary senses of "person" and personal identity. The second essay, " 'Christology': What's in a Word," addresses some of the implications of taking Christology as a part of theological *scientia* in the strong, Aristotelian sense of the word.

The next two essays, "Quasi-formal Causality" and "Theodramatic Enrichment," take up the problem of change in the divine nature, both in Christology narrowly, and with respect to the economy of salvation more comprehensively. They address, respectively, the two most influential though very different proposals within Catholic theology for a modification of the ancient consensus on the immutability of God and indeed on the relation of the divine persons to the economy, those of Karl Rahner and Hans Urs von Balthasar. In both cases, what seems the narrow and technical issue of immutability serves as an entrance to the more comprehensive and fundamental theological claims of these thinkers.

The next essay, on Christ's human knowledge of his divine identity and divine nature, tries to provide a way to recover in St. Thomas, and with the help of Bernard Lonergan, the once common Catholic theological position on Christ's immediate vision of God. The last two essays of section one, "St. Anselm, *Satisfactio*, and the *Rule* of St. Benedict" and "Rahner and Balthasar on the Efficacy of the Cross" reclaim the traditional soteriological doctrine of Christ's satisfaction, first in the original Anselmian context, and next in the contemporary theological context whose parameters are once again taken to be set by Rahner and Balthasar. Balthasar is enlisted against Rahner to make of the Cross a deed and not only a message, but Rahner is enlisted against Balthasar to confine this deed to the economy.

In section two, after an essay on the ecclesiology of communion, "On the Relation of Particular to Universal Church," the essays move to the theology of Orders. The first two engage the question of the ordination of women. The justification of the Church's exclusion of women from presbyteral orders requires two things: confidence in asserting dominical authority for the exclusion, and insight into the intelligibility of the exclusion. "On Affirming a Dominical Intention of a Male Priesthood" addresses the issue of authority; "Representation and Agency in the Eucharist" addresses what sense the exclusion can be seen to make within the theology of the Eucharist.

The next two essays take up the seemingly ever problematic question of the "character" imparted by orders, that is, the "indelible character" that was once commonly understood in Catholic theology to be one effect of ordination. They are written in the conviction that what has played an important part in the theology of orders for many years cannot simply be ignored or consigned to an historical footnote. "Episcopal *Munera* and the Character of Episcopal Orders" addresses the especially complex issue, both historically and speculatively, of how we might think about the character of *episcopal* orders. "Sacerdotal Character at the Second Vatican Council" combs through the *acta* of the Second Vatican Council for what the council fathers thought of sacramental character, both presbyteral and episcopal, and stumbles upon a seemingly quite accidental moment of conciliar history wherein the representative and iconic stature of priest and bishop with respect to Christ was asserted with a strength and comprehensiveness novel for such a magisterial text. The last essay, "The Durable Synthesis of *Presbyterorum Ordinis*," written in conjunction with Lawrence J. Welch of Kenrick Seminary, depends centrally on this happy moment of conciliar labor, and undertakes to defend the coherence, theological classicism, and providential nature of the conciliar teaching on the priesthood, especially in light of post-conciliar controversies. We think the conciliar view of priesthood cannot reasonably be dismissed as a failed compromise or incoherent pastiche of contrary views.

If there are any unifying threads to these essays, they are, first, the idea that theology has guidelines and boundaries in the dogmatic teaching of the Church, and that theology makes its way most handily by consciously appropriating the metaphysical realism implicit in that same Catholic dogmatic tradition. In this way, although he does not appear prominently, except in the essay on the knowledge of Christ, all the essays are indebted to Bernard Lonergan, S.J.

I wish especially to thank Matthew Levering of Ave Maria University for his help and unfailing encouragement in bringing these essays to light once again.

SECTION I

Christology

CHAPTER 1

A Short Christology

W HEN WE BEHOLD the risen Christ on Easter morning, we see two things. First, we see a human body once subjected to the ravages of sin but now glorious. Second, in seeing this first thing we see also . . . the Son of God. It is one of the achievements of contemporary Christology to have hit things off just so, to have articulated in just this way the relation between person and nature in the way they are displayed to us. For, of course, the Son is a "person." And the human body of this person is what is visible of a human "nature," an instance of humanity. It is not that there is manifested to us first the nature, and then afterward the person; rather, we have the person only in and with and through the nature. Moreover, and second, the person is given in the nature because it is given in terms of a history—"*once* subjected to sin, *now* glorified"—that the nature makes possible. The body of that nature forever bears the marks of the story enacted by that Person.

Putting things this way, if we think of the Church's summary formula for Christ, "one person in two natures," we might think that the divine nature is also shown to us in that the human nature is glorified, that is to say, deified. But while it is true that the humanity is made to share in the prerogatives of divinity, to participate in the divine nature as much as possible, strictly speaking, we do not see the divinity. We see a divine Person, but not the divine nature. We see a human nature as the instrument of a divine person. But at Easter, as ever, divinity remains incommunicable to us in our present condition of life, and a space is granted us in which we can choose, or not, to follow the Lamb.

We can appreciate how it is that Christ manifests himself to us, how he reveals his person to us, if we think first of how it is that anyone is revealed to us. How is it that we know a person, any person, a self, any self? Here, a host of contemporary philosophers and thinkers and theologians, from Max Scheler to Karol Wojtyla to Charles Taylor, tells us the same thing, that personal identity is constituted by moral decision, and so we know the person in knowing a moral journey, a moral journey that just is the history of the constitution of a personal identity. We need only think here how it is that we identify people. When we ask who someone is, the answer will relate circumstances that call for a moral response, and it will narrate the morally significant actions the person has taken, the morally significant actions of others the person has been a target of, the morally significant and abiding relations the person has entered into. These things are one's personal identity. The ensemble of these morally significant relations is what we mean when we speak of "selves" and "persons" today. We can, if we like, identify people by street address or social security number. But this is to treat persons like interchangeable items in a store inventory. The proper identification of persons goes on in sometimes short, but always morally loaded because story-laden, conversations:

"Who is Jack?"

"You remember; he joined the Peace Corps after college; he married George's sister."

"Who is Sally?"

"The woman whose son was assaulted in jail and who sued the city for negligence."

"Who is Steve?"

"The man who started to work at the soup kitchen after his wife died."

Now in one sense, we identify Christ in no other way. We consider his preaching of the Kingdom, his compassion for sick and sinner, and his restoration of the poor and outcast to the people of God awaiting the Kingdom. We recall such moments as his conduct in the synagogue at Capernaum and his meeting with Zaccheus, and we note the moral transactions going down, all of which give us different slants on the person whose identity we are learning. Most especially, we look to his death, since often enough the definitive moral determination of a person's identity is accomplished or at least sealed there. But while our native wit is sufficient to determine the personal identities of the people we ordinarily encounter, it is not sufficient to grasp the personal identity beheld in Jesus' preaching the Kingdom, in his miracles, forgiveness of sins, and inauguration of the community of the redeemed, and most of all, in his atoning death. Such apprehensions of his person as we summarize in calling him Messiah, Lord, Savior, and Son do not take place unless, as he said to Peter, the Father reveals them. They do not take place without faith, and for the very good reason that to understand that a man is anointed with the Holy Spirit, has a divine mission, is the Son of

God, exceeds the capacity of "flesh and blood," that is, of our natural power of understanding. Still, there is this continuity with our ordinary perception of persons, in that we behold the person's identity in the person's story. It is just that, in this case, the story is divinely plotted, divinely directed, and divinely enacted, and so, the human acts of preaching, healing, calling, forgiving, and dying reveal a divine identity, the person of the Son of God.

As Hans Urs von Balthasar has it, in Jesus' obedient fulfillment of the Father's mission, we see the Son who proceeds from the bosom of the Father before the foundation of the world. Moreover, his mission, and so his obedience to the Father, and so the manifestation of his person, come to a climax in his death for our sakes and on account of sin; for it is a death died because of a love of us first founded in an obedient love for the Father whence he proceeds. In this light, the humility and obedience of Christ, of which St. Paul speaks to the Philippians, turn out to be the keys to the identity of Jesus. Here, the lowly form of a servant bespeaks in the created order what uncreated sonship looks like; his obedience unto death is a transcription, in a sinful order, of what hearing the word of forgiveness, repeating that word to sinful men, and being this Word under the shadow of the valley of death, looks like. The Resurrection is nothing but the light that focuses this death for us, so that we see it as the death of the Second Adam, and not one more death that does nothing except repeat the pattern of the death of the First Adam.

Another way to put this is to say that the human acts of understanding that take place in the human mind of Christ, the human acts of love placed in his will, are all of them the temporal translation of an eternal identity, which itself consists in an eternal act of understanding and love, the divine act of love and knowledge that is one with the divine act of being. Only, as Son, this act of being and knowing and loving is the one single divine act as begotten by the Father, and in common with the Father, as breathing forth the Holy Spirit.

We have in Jesus' human acts of love and understanding, embodied in his flesh and making a perfect and wholly human history—we have these human acts as manifesting a divine act of knowing us and loving us and transforming us that proceeds and is begotten and is spoken. So, a human mission to save his people from their sins communicates an eternal proceeding; a human humility communicates an eternal filiation; a human hearing-obedience matches an eternal being spoken, being the Word. In this way, moreover, the humanity of Christ, but most especially his morally significant, humanly registered acts of knowing and loving, shows forth a person not only in the modern sense, but also in the ancient sense of Chalcedon, classically expressed by Boethius, for whom a person is a distinct and subsistent individual of an intellectual nature. For the eternal Son, because generated from the Father, is distinct from the Father, another "individual." And because the Son is nothing except the infinite act of understanding and love that divinity is, in common with Father and Spirit, he is most truly "of an intellectual nature." And because this act of understanding is one with the divine act of being, he is "subsistent."

What difference is there compared to us? As to the fullness and perfection of his humanity, none. And we can say if we want that the ensemble of his human acts of knowing and loving make a "person" in the modern sense. Only, they do not make a person in the ancient sense, as neither do *our* acts of understanding and loving fulfill the Boethian definition. No, for us, as for Jesus, these human acts do not subsist; they rather have their existence in what does subsist. And that is the "person" in the ancient and Chalcedonian sense. But for Christ, these human acts of understanding and loving, which do not subsist, reveal an understanding and loving that *does* subsist—the understanding and love that is one with the being of the eternal Son. While our acts of understanding and loving reveal and *constitute* our personal identities, the human acts of Christ reveal an *already* eternally constituted, because eternally begotten personal identity, the Son's.

The ancient quarrels over Christ are easy to express in this light. Modalists thought the humanity of Jesus bespeaks one who is indistinguishably both Father and Son. But the Church observed that one does not pray to oneself or obey one's own commands or send oneself. Father and Son are distinct. The actions of Jesus identify one distinct from the Father.

Next, Arius supposed the actions of Jesus to be within the capacity of a created person to accomplish. But the Church pointed out that salvation is a divine work, and that therefore the Son, though really distinct from the Father, must be divine in the same way the Father and Spirit are divine. Arius made of Christ something above the human and beneath the divine, and took the Scriptures to be speaking of him always in the same way, a third, middle way between God and man. But Athanasius said rather that, while the Scriptures speak always of one and the same Christ, one and the same personal agent, they speak of him sometimes as divine with the same divinity as the Father's, and sometimes as a man like us in all things but sin, and liable to death.

Third, Apollinaris supposed the actions of Jesus to be divine, not only as belonging to and manifesting a divine personal identity, but also as accomplished in virtue of the divine nature; therefore, he had it that there was neither need nor possibility for a human mind and a human heart in Jesus. But the Church thought rather that, though the effect of the work is divine in its scope, being nothing less than our salvation, we see a human mind and a human decision, a human heart and a human response, at work in the life of Jesus. His divinity, like the divinity of the Father who dwells in unapproachable light, remains incomprehensible. To the contrary, the actions of Jesus are comprehensible because of a human kind, our kind, and therefore they are imitable by us, as they could not be were they actions of a divine nature. We can become conformed to Christ in our own acts of minding and loving; therefore, there is a human mind, a human will, a human consciousness in Jesus.

Fourth, Nestorius's idea of what makes a person is remarkably similar to the modern idea of what makes for personal identity. If, together with the nature, there is an ensemble of human experiences, relations, knowings, lovings—Nestorius called all these things the *idiomata*—then for him there is a human "person" there as well. The Church observed that while those things that Nestorius says are present really are there, there is but one agent in Christ, one person in the Boethian sense, and that is the divine Son. Again, the acts of knowing and loving we see Jesus make in the Gospels do truly belong to him in virtue of his assumption of flesh from Mary the Virgin; but while they manifest him, they do not make him who he is. Rather is it that they make his mission to be accomplished in time, as showing us a person constituted from before the foundation of the world.

Last, in the seventh century, in guarding Chalcedon against various attempts to ignore or compromise the fullness of the humanity of Christ, Maximus Confessor worked out just the relation between the human actions of Christ and his divine person that has become so important for contemporary Christology. It is not only that what he wills by his human will for our salvation is the same thing that he wills through his divine nature in common with Father and Spirit, but also that what distinguishes Christ from other men—namely, the humility and obedience with which he discharges his mission—this very thing shows us what distinguishes him from Father and Spirit. It is this line of thought that one finds again variously taken advantage of in Balthasar, Herbert McCabe, and Bernard Lonergan.

What this way of understanding the ancient formula does for us is to return us, as every dogmatic formula should, to the Scriptures whence it proceeds. The person of Jesus is disclosed in his history, especially his passion and death. It is therefore to the Bible that we return again and again to know him, first in the expectation of those who awaited his coming, and then in the memory of those who beheld his glory and who in the breaking of the bread taught us to proclaim his death until he comes again.

There is also an important implication for understanding our own persons. As Balthasar has pointed out, our conformation to the image of the Son is a matter of sharing in his mission, and so imitating his story. Our conformation to the pattern of his life is the guarantee that he will know us on the last day when he sees us, and that beholding his glorious wounds, we shall recognize in him the truth of our own personal identities. Then the Father will see in us what he sees and loves in Christ.

2

"Christology": What's in a Word

YES, CHRISTOLOGY is the *logos* or science of the Christ. But science is the invention of the Greeks, and while *Christos* is Greek, too, it does duty here for "Messiah." The word contains the encounter of Jerusalem and Athens that has been the sustaining event of the whole of Western culture, the only word that, as a "culture" (so with a *cultus*), the West has to speak to Arabia and India. Even prior to those dialogues, however, just for us and within the West, it is a difficult word, maybe a weasel word. What does it mean to say Christology bespeaks an "encounter" of two "cultures"? Does not Athens then bid fair to make of Jerusalem just one more collection of human conventions and *nomoi*? In that way, the one culture has absorbed the other. But if we say that "Christology" signifies the destruction of proud arguments *(logismoi)* and the capture of every thought unto the obedience of Christ (see 2 Cor 10:4–5), then it may be thought that *logos* can no longer recognize itself here, and that Jerusalem has triumphed over Athens.

Or maybe this meeting of Jerusalem and Athens inscribed in "Christology" is just a confusion. "Messiah," originally a title, here means the Messiah, Jesus of Nazareth, and functions as a proper name. So Christology is the science of an individual man. According to the most thoughtful of the Greeks, however, there can be no *logos*, no science, no *episteme*, of the individual as such.[1]

Neither for us moderns is science of the individual as such. Chemistry may be about radium, but it isn't about *this* radium atom. It's about the nature of radium, and so tells you about this atom insofar as it has the

---

[1] See Thomas Aquinas, *In I post. anal.,* lect. 42, nos. 5ff.

common nature. But it doesn't give you the history of this atom, or that one, or any one. With Christology, however, we are surely concerned with a one and a unique. How then is there a science, a *logos* of him?

Where we are concerned to know an individual human being, we ordinarily write a kind of history. Anthropology is about man. But not about this or that man. There is one anthropology for all men insofar as they are men. But insofar as they are many individuals, distinct from one another, we have to have many biographies. Not *logos*, but *graphie-writing* about, not science of, the individual. There is biography of Harry Truman or of Winston Churchill. There may be "Churchilliana." But there isn't a Churchillology. What would that even mean? There is no treatise on Trumanitas. We tell his history, his story. Why is there not, then, a Christography? How can there be a Christology?

And how can followers of a Jew have a science of a Jew? Israel tells a narrative. It is Greece that writes a treatise. Israel pursues a historical understanding of herself and the nations, an understanding achieved in terms of identifying agents, motives, actions—those of God and of Israel herself. Greece pursues a contemplation of all things in the light of being. To gain a science is to bring something into the light of being, to measure it against the horizon of being; that is what gaining a universal is—seeing how this thing stands in the light of being.

All this is familiar enough. And we can say that the Church inherits and pursues both these paths of reflection when thinking about Christ. First and immediately, reading Christ against the background of Old Testament narrative, seeing in him the continuation of God's agency, the fulfillment of Old Testament promises, the Church follows the path of Israel. This way of proceeding is productive of the New Testament itself, but one should think also of the scriptural theology of the Fathers. The second way is productive of conciliar Christology—the understanding of Christ produced at Nicaea, Ephesus, Chalcedon—and finds an especially convincing expression in the Christology of St. Thomas. Here, the Church contemplates Christ, no longer with the practical contemplation of Hebrew sapiential tradition, but with the theoretical contemplation of Greek philosophy, and asks how he is "in himself." The effort is to understand Christ against the background of being, and it inserts discourse about Christ into the philosophical discourses of the Greeks.[2]

It is sometimes thought that there is an easy way to dismiss the second way in the name of the first. But it is not so. In the first place, the second way of proceeding is not entirely extra-biblical. Just as Hellenistic thought-forms and expressions are already taken up in the latter parts of the Old

---

[2] See Hans Urs von Balthasar, *The Glory of the Lord* VII (San Francisco: Ignatius, 1989), 104ff.

Testament, so too in the New Testament. And anyway, what does the decision of the Church to preach Christ to Greeks without requiring them first to become Jews mean, if not that the word of God in Christ can be heard, not only as completing the history of salvation of which the Jews were heirs, but also as speaking that word about being which it was the glory of the Greeks to devote themselves to bring to speech? How else fulfill the dominical command to preach the gospel to the whole world, including Greeks? So, evidently, the attempt in some sense to make Christ intelligible in terms of Greek culture and philosophy is perfectly legitimate.

All this is familiar enough. Or is it? As long as we think these two paths proceed on parallel tracks, the familiarity is soporific. But it is the force of the one word, "Christology," to keep us awake. The point of the one word is that here, if not elsewhere, the *logos* is the *logos* of a history, and that this history cannot be itself unless the "science" of it is articulated.

But it might be that we are mistaken to think we ought to take these two "ways" in any way, either by themselves or—in some unimaginable sense—together. Perhaps Christology is to be fitted into neither path. Maybe it is something by itself.

> For Jews demand signs and Greeks seek wisdom, but we preach Christ crucified, a stumbling block to Jews and folly to Gentiles, but to those who are called, both Jews and Greeks, Christ the power of God and the wisdom of God. (1 Cor 1:22–24)

The first part of this passage seems to block access to Christ from either Athens or Jerusalem. Christ, in his unsurpassable uniqueness, seems to stand over against both ways. He does not quite fit into the series of public, political, divine acts of power recorded in the Old Testament, nor does his death exemplify any recognizable philosophical wisdom. But there is the second part of the passage as well. "Standing over against" has meant not a simple abandonment of the attempt to understand Christ in the two ways, but a more elaborate path, according to which Christ is apprehended as a power and wisdom that, if not anticipated by Jerusalem or Athens, at least yet rightly bear those names. "Standing over against" generates an understanding of Christ by contrast, a subsequent criticism of the inherited paths of understanding, and the possibility of a final sublation of these now criticized paths.

As to the Old Testament, then, Christ is not simply one more prophet. He is the last prophet, the completion of prophecy. The word of God does not come to him; he brings it in his person. "Of old God spoke to our fathers in the prophets, but now he speaks to us through his Son." Further, the God who speaks is now Father, since Christ is his Son, and our Father as well according as we are in Christ. Further, the mighty deeds of power of the Old Testament, the signs and wonders prayed for in Psalm 77, are laid aside. The powerlessness of the weakness of the cross, because it is the instrument of God's love, is more powerful than ordinary power. Once refined in this crucible, however, we apprehend God's power in the Resurrection in some continuity with "power" even ordinarily understood. So, the realities' of the Old Covenant are not just *gramma*, the dead letter opposed to the living spirit, but also *typos* and *skia*, type and shadow of the realities of the New.[3]

As to philosophy. For the Greek there is no agent or person who is responsible for all of being. All persons, even the gods, are within being. And the philosophic life consists in conforming oneself to the exigencies of a majestic but impersonal order. But no longer. Christ is Son of the creator, and creation is in Christ. If created being reveals God and has inscribed in it principles of life and conduct, still, conforming to them we conform ourselves ultimately to the love of a Person, an Agent. And that Love could be the intelligibility of being is not suspected by the Greeks. This love may prove to be wise, but if so, it is an unseen and unheard of wisdom, not conceived by the heart of man.

This means that, in pursuing the second path, more light is shed on being than on Christ, just as, in the first way, reading Christ against the Old Testament, we understand the promises better for what they are in themselves than before. As in the first way, where the deadly letter passes into spiritually understood type, so in the second, there is worked out an analogy of names.

To say, then, that there are two ways to proceed in the effort to think the Christ, the way of reflection on the Old Testament and the way of reflection on being, is by no means to say that Christ turns out to be a function of the Old Testament, or a function of philosophy. The Old Testament and philosophy provide categories to think with, yes. But the categories do not remain unscathed.

Or one can think of it this way, as did the Apologists. The subject of Christology is God's Word, the Father's subsistent Son and Image, who is made flesh. The Incarnation of the Word in our flesh does really give us words with which to speak him and declare him, found in the words of the Old Testament and of Greek thought, which are all of them, after all, but diminished forms of the Eternal Word. So to speak, he has prepared these words for himself beforehand: in the words of Old Testament prophecy, in the creation of that speakable being that the Greeks brought to speech. But if these words are to be true of him, they will have always to be perceived in their distance from the incomparable Word of the

---

[3] For the progression in St. Paul from *gramma* to *skia*, see Henri de Lubac, *The Sources of Revelation* (New York: Herder & Herder, 1968), 43.

incomprehensible God, who is the source of all prophecy, as well as the creator of being.

One can indeed say that the fundamental problem of Christology is how to speak God's Word in our human words. The problem, insoluble for us, is however first and fundamentally God's problem, and it is he who "solves" it. The trick of Christology is simply to be attentive to the way in which he has done this.

He has solved it, not only by preparing words for himself in the Old Testament and in philosophy, but also by enlarging our capacities to perceive, so that in and through human words, we can hear the Word. This is a matter of giving us new ears, ones that can hear the Word in human words, and new eyes, ones that see the Image in earthly images, because they are organs of a heart that is moved by a love that, while it surpasses understanding, also bears it up. This means that the condition of Christology is essentially something that God himself provides, namely faith, the chief exercise of which is prayer and worship.

But all this is not yet to see how the ways call to each other, need each other. First, Christ is not so much inserted into the history of Israel, so as to be within it, as he defines the end of it. The eschatological prophet makes us think the end of history, the whole of it. If there is but one history, moreover, a history of the whole, and if being does not so encompass history as to provide for an infinity of eternal recurrences, then history must be commensurate with being. Eschatological thought has to become metaphysical thought.

And the other way around, too? Must metaphysics become historical? A first way to answer, with some of the ante-Nicene Fathers and Hegel, is to take the Incarnation as an adequate ground upon which to assert that creation is part of the history of God himself. But then, I think, the distinction between God and the being qua being that is the subject of Aristotle's metaphysics collapses. Classically, the way to answer is, if successful, more difficult.

To see this, we can return to the question: How can there be a science of an individual human being? Ordinarily there is no such science, remember, because science grasps the universal, and each life is unique. If we mean by a human person, or personality, the psychological reality constituted by acts of knowing and loving, then this is an unrepeatable reality, for the acts in question are intrinsically conditioned by place and time (a function of "materiality"). There is no science of the individual for the same reason that there is a gap between every moral principle, no matter how refined, and *this* my moral action, a gap that is bridged by prudence alone.

However, it is not that there cannot be a science of a person as such— as long as the person is not a human person. There is a science of the three-personal God; it is called theology. Because our science is suited first of all to the abstract natures of material things, this science will be for us analogous, imperfect, and strictly dependent on revelation. But just so, as a personal reality that can be the subject of a science, God has no history, either. He makes history, and he can be the agent effective of events within history. But since he is the creator of all times and places, of every condition of every action of every agent, he is himself conditioned by none of them. Therefore, unconditioned by places and times, he can be the subject of a science; his action is himself, and his prudence is the same as his wisdom.

This suggests that if there is to be a science of a person who is also a human being, that person must be divine. The human acts of Christ will belong to a divine agent. They will bespeak a wisdom of infinite intelligibility, of which we can have an analogous, imperfect, but still very fruitful understanding. Christology will be, as a science, a kind of theology.

And yes, it will have to be a kind of history as well, though not in Hegelian fashion, because the divine agency will be available only in the humanly constituted acts. What is wanted is a new skill, the knack of finding a sort of divine and unconditioned personal intelligibility in human and humanly conditioned acts. For instance, in the obedience of Jesus to his Father and unto death, we shall intuit his prior "hearing," and the Father's prior "speaking," that is the eternal begetting of the Son. In Christ's love of us, we shall behold the Love in which Father and Son surpass themselves in the ecstasy of the Holy Spirit.

CHAPTER 3

Quasi-formal Causality and "Change in the Other": A Note on Karl Rahner's Christology

MONG THE MOST characteristic and prominent of the claims made by Karl Rahner about the Incarnation are the following three:

1. Only the Logos, the second Person of the Trinity, and not the Father or the Holy Spirit, can be incarnated.[1]

2. Granted there is to be a mission *ad extra* of the Logos, what comes to be is the hypostatic union of the Logos with some created nature, and indeed, with a human nature and a human nature alone.[2]

3. The Logos, immutable in himself because identical with the divine nature, is mutable in the "other" of the human nature that he assumes hypostatically.[3]

I am concerned in this essay with how these three claims are related to a fourth, more generally theological, claim of Rahner's, namely:

---

[1] "Current Problems in Christology," *Theological Investigations* (hereafter *TI*), vol. 1, trans. Cornelius Ernst (Baltimore: Helicon, 1961), 183; "On the Theology of the Incarnation," *TI*, vol. 4, trans. Kevin Smyth (Baltimore: Helicon, 1966), 106, 115; "Nature and Grace," ibid., 176; "The Theology of the Symbol," ibid., 236; Karl Rahner, *The Trinity*, trans. Joseph Donceel (New York: Seabury Press, 1974), 29, 84, 86.

[2] "Current Problems," 197; Theology of the Incarnation," 116; "Theology of the Symbol," 237–38; Rahner, *The Trinity*, 27, 32–33, 89–90.

[3] "Current Problems," 175–82, esp. 181n3; "Theology of the Incarnation," 112–15.

4. The supernatural self-communication of God to what is not God must be understood as a kind of quasi-formal causality exercised by God on the creature.[4]

In Christology, this fourth claim means that the Logos is quasi-formally related to the humanity of Jesus. More particularly, just as uncreated grace is quasi-formally related to the just so that created sanctifying grace is its dispositive formal effect, really distinct from it,[5] and just as the divine essence is quasi-formally related to the created and beatified intellect so that the *lumen gloriae* is its dispositive formal effect, really distinct from it,[6] so the divine *esse* of the Logos is quasi-formally related to the humanity of Jesus so that the *esse secundarium* of Christ spoken of by St. Thomas is its dispositive formal effect, really distinct from it.[7] In all three cases, and in Maurice de la Taille's words, some created reality, though not informed by Uncreated Act, is actuated by it. In each case, some created actuation— sanctifying grace, the light of glory, the *esse secundarium*—disposes created reality to quasi-formal union with Uncreated Act.[8]

Indeed, the substantial identity of the positions of Rahner and de la Taille on the supernatural is here assumed. This assumption is justified on two grounds, beyond Rahner's own recognition of the identity of his position with de la Taille's.[9] First, like de la Taille, Rahner expressly distinguishes between a form and its actuation.[10] Second, just as de la Taille's analogy for the union of the Word and the human nature of Christ is the union of soul and body, so is it Rahner's.[11]

---

[4] "Some Implications of the Scholastic Concept of Uncreated Grace," *TI*, vol. 1, 329–33, 334ff.; "Nature and Grace," 175; Rahner, *The Trinity*, 36.

[5] "Uncreated Grace," 341.

[6] Ibid., 332–33.

[7] Cf. Rahner's remarks as reported in the "Rapport Patfoort," in *Problèmes actuels de christologie*, ed. H. Bouëssé and J.-J. Latour (Paris: Desclée de Brouwer, 1965), 414–15. For St. Thomas, cf. his disputed question *De unione Verbi incarnati*, a. 4.

[8] Cf. Maurice de la Taille, S.J., *The Hypostatic Union and Created Actuation by Uncreated Act* (West Baden, IN: West Baden College, 1952), especially 30, 32–35. This booklet contains a translation of de la Taille's "Actuation créé par acte incréé," which first appeared in 1928 in *Recherches de science religieuse*.

[9] Rahner, "Uncreated Grace," 340.

[10] Ibid., 331n1: "It is usual today to distinguish two senses of 'forma' by speaking of 'actus *informans*' and 'actus *terminans*': thus, 'forma' (the determination) in the first sense is that which in itself arrives at reality and perfection in virtue of the act of determination; in the second sense it is that which in itself is and remains a perfect reality in spite of and prior to the act of determination."

[11] Rahner, "Theology of the Symbol," 237–39, 246; for de la Taille, cf. *Hypostatic Union*, 21, 34.

Apropos of this second ground, it is important to remember for what follows that, despite the distinction between act and actuation, and despite the prefix "quasi," the basic category with which to understand God's supernatural relation to what is not God is, for Rahner, formal causality. God is related to what is not God somewhat as the soul is related to the body, form to matter, or act to potency.

Now, if one thinks for a moment of what it might be said that it is immutable in itself but that it changes in the other, one sees at once why Rahner might want to make, and why he might feel confident in making, the third claim listed above, namely that the Logos, while immutable in himself, changes in the other. For it is precisely of a *form* that we might say that, although it is immutable in itself, it nonetheless changes in the "other" (of matter).

Thus, consider the form of humanity. Like all forms, it is immutable in itself. For it to change is for it not to be itself. It is not itself a subject of change, but rather a principle of what is a subject of change, namely some man. But once it is considered as being "in the other," once it is considered as composed with matter, which is the principle of mutability and the ultimate subject of substantial change, then indeed we might want to say that it changes *in* this other. Thus, humanity is sometimes grammatical or musical, and sometimes not, according as these accidents do or do not determine some man. Even so, "in itself," humanity does not change: for it is precisely a man that becomes musical from being unmusical, and if it is a man that perdures as a man throughout this change, then the form of man—which is just what it is in itself and no other nor capable in itself of being other (what would that mean?)—abides "in itself" unchanged throughout the change whose subject is the man. If humanity be said to change, we must hasten to add that it does so not in itself, but only "in the other" of matter.

And indeed, Rahner says as much about forms as we have just indicated, that, unchangeable in itself, a form changes in the other of matter. This seems very clear from *Spirit in the World.*

> With regard to its form, an existent cannot in principle suffer *(erleiden)*, in the sense of receiving an inner-worldly influence. Consequently, if a being is to receive in this sense, then that is conceivable only under a two-fold presupposition: (1) The external influence strictly as such cannot already be a determination of the patient itself. . . . (2) Nevertheless this external influence must already be in the patient, otherwise it would have no relation to the patient at all. But these two presuppositions are conceivable only if a real principle of absolute indeterminateness belongs to the constitution of the patient. . . . [T]he patient cannot be merely form. For otherwise the

> form as such would have to be the medium of the emanating influ-
> ence [of some agent] as such.[12]

That is, a form "as such" cannot suffer or change, but only as composed with a principle of indeterminateness, matter. Again:

> The material cause does not "produce" an effect "in" the form, that is, it does not bestow on it a determination which would be different from itself or the form. Such a notion would destroy the concept of material-formal causality. The matter does not give the form a deter-mination, but bestows itself upon it. Or, vice versa and better expressed: the form enters into the otherness of its material cause, gives itself away to it. In this act of information, which the form itself is, the form does not produce something different from itself, but the form itself taken as itself is the actuality of matter, and as such an actuality producing itself as the actuality of matter, the form is determined by the matter, and not by an efficient process from the side of matter.
>   . . . Thus the form "suffers" in the strictest sense only by the fact that it actively informs, since it is nothing more than the act of matter.[13]

And because the form "suffers" in this strictest and most fundamental sense, it can actively "suffer" different, contrary accidental determinations.[14] In fact, the form can be said to realize itself in the active "suffering" of these accidental determinations.[15]

Thus, for Rahner, a form, immutable as such and in itself, changes in the other of matter. And the Logos, immutable in himself, changes in the other of the human nature of Christ, for he is related (quasi) formally to this nature. I am suggesting that it is this systematic, theoretical position about quasi-formality that controls Rahner's thinking, and not a simple and straightforward embrace of Cyrilline Christology, according to which

---

12 Karl Rahner, *Spirit in the World,* trans. William Dych, S.J. (New York: Herder, 1968), 341.

13 Ibid., 354–55.

14 Ibid., 350: "[W]ithin the limits of its own substantial content of meaning, the form can be the ontological, productive ground for many different, contrarily opposed, determinations of itself. . . . where there is question of a 'passible quality' as opposed to a 'passion' in the narrowest sense, this quality, in its being which remains even after the influence from without, must be produced by the substan-tial ground of what is determined by it." But the ultimate ground for this capacity to "suffer" accidental determinations is the "suffering" of the form in its informa-tion of matter.

15 Ibid., 351, 353–54, 357.

the impassible Logos suffers in the flesh, from which, after all, Rahner rather distances himself.[16]

Once it is granted that the Logos is quasi-formally related to human nature in the hypostatic union, then the second claim of Rahner's listed above seems to follow as well. For it is not just any proximate matter that a form can inform, and when a human soul informs primary matter, it is the human body that appears.

Indeed, as we have said, the relation of the soul to the body is Rahner's analogy for the relation of the Logos to the human nature of Christ. Just as the body is the "real symbol" of the soul in the "other" of *materia prima*,[17] so Christ's humanity is the real symbol of the Logos.[18] Just as the body is intrinsically and essentially related to the soul, human nature is "intrinsically and essentially" related to the Logos.[19] Just as one can say that when one sees the body one sees the spirit of a man,[20] so one can say that when one sees the humanity of Christ, one sees the Logos.[21] When the soul expresses itself in what is not itself, matter, there we have the human body;[22] and when the Logos expresses himself in what is not himself, there is the humanity of Jesus.[23]

The underlying reason, however, why it is unthinkable that the Logos assume any other created nature than human nature should be clear. As it is unthinkable that the human soul expresses itself by any body other than a human body, since it is formally related to the body, so it is impossible that the Logos express himself in any other than a human nature, since he is quasi-formally related to this nature.

Again, it seems that some light is shed on the first of Rahner's claims listed above. It is true that the remarks Rahner usually offers in support of the claim that only the Logos can be incarnated bear on the nature of the Logos as Word and Image and Expression of the Father. If the Father is to express himself outside of himself, it cannot be otherwise, Rahner urges,

---

16 For the contrary opinion, see Thomas G. Weinandy, *Does God Change?* (Still River, MA: St. Bede's Publications, 1985), 163–74, who thinks that Rahner is simply upholding the truth of the communication of idioms. For Rahner's idiosyncratic understanding of the communication of idioms, as also for what he understands to be the indeterminateness of the principle of unity in Christ, see *Foundations of Christian Faith: An Introduction to the Idea of Christianity*, trans. William V. Dych (New York: The Seabury Press, 1978), 290–92.

17 "Theology of the Symbol," 246–47.

18 Ibid., 237–38.

19 Ibid.

20 "The Body in the Order of Salvation," *TI*, vol. 17, trans. Margaret Kohl (New York: Crossroad, 1981), 84.

21 Rahner, *The Trinity*, 32.

22 "Theology of the Symbol," 246–47; "The Body in the Order of Salvation," 86.

23 "Theology of the Symbol," 239; Rahner, *The Trinity*, 31 *n* 27, 89.

than through his interior expression of himself, namely his Son, the Word; thus, only the Logos can be incarnated.[24] However, I think it important to see that, if one knows that the Logos is incarnate, and if one knew that the relation of the Logos to the assumed humanity were quasi-formal, then one would also know that, if it be a question of a hypostatically assumed *human* nature, only the Logos could assume that nature. For just as it is inconceivable that a human body be informed by anything other than a human soul, so it would be impossible that human nature be quasi-informed, if such were to happen, by any other divine Person than is in fact incarnate, namely the Logos.[25]

It should be clear from the foregoing that if it is wrong to conceive of the Logos as quasi-formally related to the human nature of Christ, then it will be difficult to make sense of the claim that the Logos changes in the other of human nature, and it will be difficult to defend the truth of the claims that only the Logos can be hypostatically united to a created human nature, and that only human nature is able to be assumed by the Logos.

It will be difficult to make sense of the claim that the Logos changes in another, for there will be no analogy for it bearing precisely on the understanding of change. If the Logos is not quasi-formally related to the humanity of Jesus, then he does not change in this humanity in the way that a form can be said to change in matter. It would be hard to avoid Dom Illtyd Trethowan's conclusion that Rahner's dictum lands us in a straightforward contradiction in which God is affirmed to be both mutable and immutable.[26]

But second, it will be difficult to maintain the truth of the uniqueness claims examined above ("*only* the Logos;" "*only* human nature"). For apart from an argument for them that depends on the quasi-formal relation of the Logos to the humanity of Jesus, it is hard to follow Rahner's argument.

For the second of these claims, that only human nature can be assumed by the Logos, Rahner suggests that somehow this would follow from the unity of spirit and matter, which includes a relation of the angels to the world of matter, and from the fact that the grace of the angels is also in fact the grace of Christ.[27] But he does not argue this fully and in detail. Of course, we may agree that if the Logos "decides to step outside of himself" into *our* world, the human world, then doubtless what appears is the humanity of

---

24 Cf. for example "Theology of the Symbol," 235–36.

25 One can note, Rahner, *The Trinity*, 31–33, the strictness of the relation between the claim that only the Logos can be incarnated and the claim that only human nature can be assumed.

26 Cf. Dom Illtyd Trethowan, "A Changing God," *Downside Review* 84 (1966): 247–61.

27 Rahner, *The Trinity*, 90.

Christ. But Rahner seems also to say that if the Logos decides to "step outside of himself" at all, then what appears is the humanity of Jesus. This is a much stronger claim; it is the claim we are concerned with. It seems that if it were to be established along the lines Rahner suggests, one would have to establish, as a necessary if not sufficient condition of knowing its truth, that any possible world must be a world that includes prime matter, and that a world of separated substances just by itself is impossible. I do not know of any way to establish this.[28]

For the first of these claims, that only the Logos can be incarnate, Rahner often urges, as has been mentioned, that this follows from the fact that the Logos is the expression of the Father within the divinity, and that therefore, if there is any expressing to be done *ad extra*, then it is perforce the Logos that is going to do it. In this way, he thinks expressly to take up the pre-Augustinian, pre-Nicene view of "invisibility" as a property of the Father (cf. 1 Tim 6:16).[29] But Rahner does not show how this fits with Nicaea.[30] And indeed, it does not seem that visibility and invisibility, or accessibility and inaccessibility, indicate relations of opposition. But if they do not indicate mutually opposed relations, they do not indicate personal properties.[31]

Rahner says that we ought not to conclude from the fact that the Logos can be incarnated to the possibility that any Person can be incarnated, and indeed, without further ado, we should not so conclude.[32] But if the fact of the Incarnation of the Logos does not provide all by itself sufficient grounds for concluding to the possibility of the incarnation of other Persons, neither does it by itself require us to deny that possibility. And this seems to be all that Rahner's sole attempt (to my knowledge) to argue at any length for his position amounts to. We turn now to this argument.

In *The Trinity*, Rahner says that the claim that any Person could be incarnated is not only not demonstrated, but false.[33] For, he says, if this claim were true, we should have to know two things: (1) that hypostasis is univocally said of the three divine Persons and (2) that no difference in a

---

28 Doubtless, there is the argument that the great distinction and inequality of creatures, from angels to minerals, represent the divine goodness better than a simpler universe would (cf. *Summa theologiae* I, q. 47 aa. 1 & 2). But this is an argument *ex convenientia*, showing what intelligibility there is in the actual universe, with its great distinction and inequality of creatures. It does not show the necessity of creatures composed of matter for any creation whatsoever.

29 Cf. Rahner, *The Trinity*, 41, 60n10; "Theology of the Symbol," 236.

30 Apropos of Nicaea, it is perhaps worthwhile to observe that it is Arius who thinks that, as between Father and Son, it is only the Son who can be incarnate.

31 *DS* 1330 (Council of Florence, Decree for Jacobites).

32 Rahner, *The Trinity*, 29.

33 Ibid.

divine hypostasis (no personal property) could prevent it from being incarnated. Of these two presuppositions, he remarks, "the former is false and the latter is by no ways demonstrated."[34] However, it can be observed that, though the latter presupposition may not be demonstrated, for Rahner really to know that only the Logos can be incarnated, he must show that this presupposition as well is false (not merely undemonstrated). In the absence of that, it seems that the question is begged.[35]

It may be thought that I am ignoring the main argument that it is the burden of Part III of Rahner's *The Trinity* to provide and that for the purposes of this essay can be cast as follows:

1. Suppose man is called to a strictly supernatural end; that is, suppose God decides to communicate himself to man.

2. Man is such, however, that his historicity and his transcendentality are both (a) irreducible one to another or to some common term and (b) inseparable from one another in that they mutually condition one another in a kind of "perichoresis."

3. Thus, if *man* is to receive God's self-communication, both his historicity and his transcendentality must be addressed by God as God is in himself.

4. Behold (factual premise), we see that the mission of the Son, in which God communicates himself as Truth, addresses man's historicity and that the mission of the Spirit, in which God communicates himself as Love, addresses man's transcendentality.

5. But if God can address man and call him to a strictly supernatural end only by addressing his historicity and his transcendentality, which are distinct but inseparable, then the missions that constitute God's self-communication to man must likewise bespeak distinct yet consubstantial modalities within God, granted that he communicates *himself* to man, and that the missions are not some sort of charade played out in the economy, but not really expressive of God himself as he is in himself communicating himself to man.

6. Thus, God is immanently Trinitarian, just as he is economically Trinitarian.

---

34 Ibid.

35 Rahner says (ibid., 30) that "should it be true [that any Person can be incarnate] . . . it would create havoc with theology. There would no longer be any connection between 'mission' and the intra-trinitarian life." It seems rather safer to say that there would not be the same connection there is in fact, but not that there would be no connection.

7. Hence, it appears that man is created in the first place with just that nature (historicity and transcendentality) that is required of a recipient of God's self-communication. In other words, if God decides to communicate himself to something outside of himself, man appears as the appropriate recipient, and creation is merely the first moment of this self-communication of God.

8. Thus, *only* human nature can be assumed by the Logos.

9. And since it is God's Truth that must address man's historicity only the Logos can be incarnated.

This line of reasoning, however, does not get off the ground *unless* it is tacitly supposed that the relation between God and a supernaturally elevated creature must be quasi-formal. This supposition is made in (3), above. For what that premise really means is that since there are two formalities in man (historicity and transcendentality), they must be addressed distinctly by God if man is to be supernaturalized, so that we can conclude from that distinction to a distinction within God himself. But why must both be addressed, and addressed distinctly? Because they are to be addressed quasi-formally. And in this way, they argue to two distinct "formalities" in God. Indeed, Rahner is quite forthright about the importance of this supposition for the argument of his *The Trinity*.[36]

To resume: It seems to me that Father Rahner would have an argument for the claim that only the Logos can be incarnated, as he would for the claim that only human nature can be assumed, if the Logos were quasi-formally related to the humanity of Christ.[37] However, I think Bernard Lonergan convincingly argues that this is not the case. And although Lonergan does not expressly address Rahner, he certainly does address de la Taille.

In his *De Verbo Incarnato*, Lonergan presents three very cogent arguments against de la Taille's position on the quasi-formal relation of the Logos

---

[36] Ibid., 36.

[37] Strictly, he would have an argument *either* for the first or for the second of the three claims we listed at the beginning of this essay. That is, if one knew that the Logos alone can be incarnate, and if one knew his relationship to the assumed nature was quasi-formal, then one would know that only human nature (the actually assumed nature) can be assumed by the Logos. Or: If one knew that only the human nature could be assumed by a divine Person, and if one knew the relationship was to be quasi-formal, then one would know that only the Logos (the Person actually assuming) can assume human nature. But if all one knew was that the relationship between a divine Person and an assumed nature was to be quasi-formal, one could conclude neither the first nor the second uniqueness claim.

to the humanity of Christ. First, the position seems to locate the hypostatic union, not in the Person of the Logos, but in a created intermediary, namely the created actuation it is held to effect, the *esse secundarium*.[38] This means that the union is not, in fact, hypostatic.

Second, the distinction between an act and its actuation is illusory.[39] If what can be known by experience, understanding, and rational affirmation is the real and the real is what is known by experience, understanding, and rational affirmation, then the ultimate composing causes of finite material being are material potency, form, and act.[40] If actuation is real, it is therefore to be asked whether it is potency, form, or act. The actuation of both potency by form and form by act are nothing in addition to these three, but are the three as composed and constituting a finite material being.

If the distinction between act and actuation is illusory, however, then there is nothing to the "quasi" of "quasi-formal causality" but the name. But then, we have formal causality simply speaking. God, however, cannot be formally related to finite reality really distinct from and in potency with respect to him, for potency limits act, and the Infinite Act is not limited.[41]

Third, and generally, Lonergan denies that there is any created analogy to the hypostatic union in the composition of finite beings, and precisely because form is limited by potency, and act by form.[42] But the Logos, who as God is infinite act, though united with a human nature in the Incarnation, cannot be said to be limited.

For Lonergan, if the divine *esse* of the Logos cannot be quasi-formally united to the humanity of Christ, it is nonetheless the *principium quo* of the union.[43] *What* is united to the humanity of Christ is indeed the Person of the Logos, and for this contingent truth to be true, there is required a contingent, finite, created reality, really distinct from God, as a consequent condition ensuring that the contingent truth of the statement "the Word became flesh" *is* true.[44] This is the *esse secundarium*, a substantial act, strictly supernatural, a

---

38 Bernard Lonergan, *De Verbo Incarnato* (Rome: Gregorian University Press, 1960), 344.

39 Ibid., 344; cf. Lonergan, *De constitutione Christi ontologica et psychologica*, 3rd ed. (Rome: Gregorian University Press, 1961), 32–33.

40 *De constitutione Christi*, 27–33, 35; cf. Lonergan, Insight, 3rd ed. (New York: Philosophical Library, 1970), 431–34.

41 *De Verbo Incarnato*, 340; *De constitutione Christi*, 64.

42 *De Verbo Incarnato*, 339–42, 344; *De constitutione Christi*, 64; Lonergan, *Divinarum personarum conceptionem analogicam*, 2nd ed. (Rome: Gregorian University Press, 1959), 208.

43 *De Verbo Incarnato*, 336–39, 352; *De constitutione Christi*, 69, 71–72; *Divinarum personarum*, 213.

44 *De Verbo Incarnato*, 345–63; *De constitutione Christi*, 73–80.

created resemblance of the divine paternity, and thus relating the human nature of Christ to the Son,[45] ensuring, as well, that *a* human nature is assumed, and not *all* human nature.[46]

Still, the *esse secundarium* is a created reality, as is the humanity of Christ. As created, it is the production of the three Persons in common. Further, just as God understands contingent realities by understanding himself, and just as he wills contingent realities by willing his own infinite goodness, so if Father, Son, and Spirit understand and will that the Son be a man, then the Son is this man, a contingent reality, by the infinite divine *esse* itself, which is not distinct from the divine understanding and will.[47] And this is to say nothing except that the divine *esse* is the *principium quo* of the hypostatic union. But if the divine *esse* is common to the three Persons, and it is, then it follows necessarily (on *this* ground, that of the *principium quo*) that any of the divine Persons can become incarnate.[48]

The point of the foregoing criticism of Rahner is not to maintain that the possibility of the Incarnation of the Father or the Spirit and the possibility of the hypostatic assumption of an angelic nature are important theological propositions. With regard to the first and second claims of Rahner listed at the beginning of this essay, the point is to argue for more modesty in theology. It may be that only the Logos could become incarnate, and that only human nature could be assumed. But we do not see those necessities.[49] Often enough, Rahner proceeds as did St. Anselm, seeking necessary reasons for the facts of the economy of salvation where St. Thomas sought merely the intelligibility of the facts. Rahner's project is therefore ambitious. However, to set for theology the standard of *rationes necessariae*, and then to suggest that they have been found when they have not, is to risk an inflation of theological currency.

---

[45] *De Verbo Incarnato*, 353–63; *De constitutione Christi*, 75–80; for the *esse secundarium* as a created similitude of paternity, cf. *Divinarum personarum*, 214.

[46] *De Verbo Incarnato*, 358.

[47] Ibid., 345–46; *De constitutione Christi*, 70, 72; *Divinarum personarum*, 208, 215.

[48] *De constitutione Christi*, 59, 72. If the divine *esse* of the Logos is the constitutive cause of the union, then it is the capacity for union. But if the *esse* of the Logos is common to the three Persons, the capacity to be incarnated in common to the three.

[49] On the other hand, the denial that we see the necessity that it be the Logos that is incarnated is not a denial and does not imply the denial that it is only the incarnate Logos that in fact appears in the theophanies recorded in the Old Testament, as John Behr is on the brink of asserting, *The Nicene Faith*, Part 1 (Crestwood, NY: St. Vladimir's Seminary Press, 2004), 3.

With regard to the third and fourth claims of Rahner, the point of this essay is easier to state. There is no great theological project that does not come into close quarters with the question of the transcendence and therefore the immutability of God. Certainly Rahner's project was great. Whether it comes away unscathed by the encounter is another question.

CHAPTER 4

Balthasar and the Theodramatic Enrichment of the Trinity

THE *THEO-DRAMA* of Hans Urs von Balthasar is the middle section of his theological trilogy. It is the section about the Good, following the one about the Beautiful and preceding the one about the True. *The Glory of the Lord* studies the form and splendor of revelation, its perception *(aisthesis)* in and across and beyond the forms and splendors of the world, its reduction to an inner-Trinitarian form and splendor. The *Theologik* studies the truth of this same revelation, leading it back to a truth within God. But the *Theo-Drama* studies how revelation is manifested, and how its truth is constituted, in action, in a dramatic encounter between God and man, an encounter that also in its turn leads back to a prior and inner-Trinitarian one.[1] If we de-italicize the word, then, Theodrama is the drama between God and man reflecting the inner-Trinitarian drama of Father, Son, and Spirit.

Is the drama between God and man also constitutive of the inner-Trinitarian drama? The aim of this essay is to think about Balthasar's answer, his affirmative but subtle answer, to that question. He would have it not only that there can be no true drama between God and man if there is not an inner-Trinitarian drama to be manifested, but also that there can be no

---

[1] See "Dramatic Theory between Aesthetics and Logic," in *Theo-Drama: Theological Dramatic Theory*, vol. 1 (San Francisco: Ignatius Press, 1988), 15–23. *Theo-Drama* vols. 1–5 (San Francisco: Ignatius Press, 1988, 1990, 1992, 1994, 1998), are hereafter *TD* 1, 2, 3, 4, and 5, which correspond to *Theo-Dramatik*, vol. I, *Prolegomena*; vol. II/1, *Die Personen des Spiels: Der Mensch in Gott*; vol. II/2, *Die Personen in Christus*; vol. III: *Die Handlung*; and vol. IV: *Das Endspiel* (Einsiedeln: Johannes Verlag, 1973, 1976, 1978, 1980). Hereafter, parenthetical references, with roman numerals for volume numbers, are to the German edition.

drama between God and man unless it really and truly can be said to constitute the inner-Trinitarian drama.

In order to see the novel way Balthasar has discovered to express the way in which the world matters to God, we will compare him at a key point to St. Thomas.[2]

The Aim of the *Theo-Drama*

The second edition of *Mysterium Paschale* contains a preface written after the *Theo-Drama*, in which Balthasar offers a short statement of the theological issue that the much larger work addresses. He draws two positions into opposition, that of the "older dogmatics" and that of certain moderns. Moderns assert the pain of God (K. Kitamori), have God develop (process theology), or constitute the Trinity in dependence on the economy (Hegel and J. Moltmann).[3] To the contrary, the older dogmatics affirms the immutability of God and relegates the effect of the kenosis of the Son of God to the human nature of Christ, "the divine nature remaining inaccessible to all becoming or change, and even to any real relationship with the world."[4] In so doing, Balthasar tells us, it runs the risk, paradoxically enough, of both Nestorianism and monophysitism at once. By relegating suffering to Jesus, this dogmatics courts a Nestorianism in which an immutable Son of God must be distinct from the suffering Jesus. On the other hand, in restricting suffering to the lower faculties of Christ's soul, it suggests a monophysitism of the "higher faculties," which enjoy the vision of God just as does God.

The way forward, according to Balthasar, "relates the event of the Kenosis of the Son of God to what one can, by analogy, designate as the eternal 'event' of the divine processions."[5] For this, Balthasar takes as a clue the scholastic assertion of the divine processions as the condition of the possibility of creation. The upshot is twofold, one in the order of manifestation or revelation, and the other in the order of being. In the order of revelation, we understand that the economy, and within the economy especially the Cross, simply manifests modalities of love already enjoyed eternally among the Persons. In the order of being, while it is true that

---

[2] In this way, we attempt to further the inquiry into the relation of St. Thomas and Balthasar that James Buckley called for, and the difficulties of which he called attention to in James J. Buckley, "Balthasar's Use of the Theology of Aquinas," *The Thomist* 59 (1995): 517–45.

[3] *Mysterium Paschale* (Edinburgh: T&T Clark, 1990), vii. *Mysterium Paschale* is the translation of Chapter 9 of *Mysterium Salutis*, ed. J. Feiner and M. Löhrer, vol. III/2, *Das Christusereignis* (Einsiedeln: Benziger Verlag, 1969).

[4] Ibid., viii.

[5] Ibid.

God does not change by dependence on the world such that without the world there would be something in him there is not, it is nevertheless the case that he does change, with a change already forever "included and out-stripped in the eternal event of Love."[6] It is this solution, though not always so compactly expressed, and with an appeal to the same clue, that Balthasar develops at length in the *Theo-Drama*.[7]

The foregoing puts the issue in terms at once of the history of Christian thought and of "theology," where the term denotes a doctrine of divinity, the divine nature. But the *Theo-Drama* has several ways of casting the issue.[8] A favorite and only slightly different way of stating the problem, a way that a "theodrama" suggests by its very nature,[9] is that of the dilemma of choosing between the God of the philosophers and the God of myth.[10] A God who is involved in the world and who reacts as an actor within a drama that includes him and the world is mythic. But a transcendent divinity, a divinity acceptable philosophically, seems religiously inadequate. Again, Balthasar expresses the issue from its anthropological pole, as a question regarding finite freedom in a world created by absolute freedom. In such a world, is finite freedom really real? And does it count for anything if it has no impact on absolute freedom?[11] Otherwise expressed, and in terms of Trinitarian theology, how shall we express the relation between the immanent and the economic Trinity in a non-Hegelian way?[12] And yet again, in the Christological specification of the Trinitarianly expressed question, how shall we find a position between, or above, those of Karl Rahner and Jürgen Moltmann on the relation of the Cross to

---

6 Ibid., ix.

7 For the processions as the condition of creation in the *Theo-Drama*, see *TD* 5:61–65, 75–76 (IV:53–57, 65–66).

8 For a brief overview of the *Theo-Drama*, see Gerard O'Hanlon, "Theological Dramatics," in *The Beauty of Christ: An Introduction to the Theology of Hans Urs von Balthasar*, ed. Bede McGregor and Thomas Norris (Edinburgh: T&T Clark, 1994), 92–101, and idem, *The Immutability of God in the Theology of Hans Urs von Balthasar* (New York: Cambridge University Press, 1990), 110–36. Both of these texts deal with the central argument of the *TD*. See also Edward T. Oakes, *Pattern of Redemption: The Theology of Hans Urs von Balthasar* (New York: Continuum, 1994), Part 3; and especially Part 2 of Thomas G. Dalzell, *The Dramatic Encounter of Divine and Human Freedom in the Theology of Hans Urs von Balthasar* (New York: Peter Lang, 1997).

9 O'Hanlon, "Theological Dramatics," 94.

10 *TD* 1:131 (I:118); TD 2:9, 125, 191–94 (II/1:9, 112, 172–75); *TD* 4:322–23, (III:300); Hans Urs von Balthasar, *The Glory of the Lord*, vol. 4 (San Francisco: Ignatius, 1989), 216–19; Dalzell, *Dramatic Encounter*, 55, 162.

11 *TD* 1:255, 495–96 (I:236, 465–66); *TD* 2:72 (II/1:64–65); *TD* 4:328–29, 377ff. (III:305–6, 352ff.).

12 *TD* 1:69, 131 (I:64, 118).

the Trinity?[13] To understand Balthasar is in large part to see how for him all these questions are aspects of one central issue.

The constantly reexpressed dilemma, this one central issue, is brought to a final—and one cannot help saying, climactic, expression—in the eschatology with which the *Theo-Drama* concludes. What does God gain from the world?[14] Is God plus the world more than God alone? If one chooses the "God of the philosophers," and says no, then the world is ultimately illusory. If one says yes, then one will also say that God needs the world. What is the way between, or above, these alternatives, which present us with but an "apparent contradiction?"[15] In fact, the world plus God is "more," but on the understanding that the world is enfolded into the relations, the relations of gift-giving, of the Trinitarian Persons.

The way forward is thus a Trinitarian way, just as the assertion of the Trinity is originally the way between the One of the philosophers and the many gods of paganism.[16] The Trinitarian relations, the exchanges between the Persons, would of course occur even without the world. Thus Balthasar can write:

> The whole thrust of this book has been to show that the infinite possibilities of divine freedom all lie within the trinitarian distinctions and are thus free possibilities within the eternal life of love in God that *has always been realized.*[17]

Having the world's response to God occur within the Trinitarian relations is the way to overcome the dilemma of choosing between myth and philosophy. Balthasar thinks its advantages significant. First, the gratuitousness of creation is grounded in the ever greater gratuity of Trinitarian life.[18] Second, where the "participation of creatures in the life of the Trinity becomes an internal gift from each Divine Person to the other," the appearance of a kind of divine solipsism, as if God made the world for his extrinsic glory, is removed.[19]

---

13 *TD* 4:322 (III:300); and *TD* 2:49 (II/1:44–45), closely related to the issue of myth.

14 *TD* 5:508 (IV:464–65).

15 *TD* 5:508 (IV:464).

16 O'Hanlon, *Immutability,* 110. See Gregory of Nyssa, *Cat. Orat.,* no. 3.

17 *TD* 5:508 (IV:465): "Der ganze Denkzug dieses Buches strebte dahin, zu zeigen, daß die unendlichen Möglichkeiten der göttlichen Freiheit alle *innerhalb* der trinitarischen Differenzen liegen, somit freie Möglichkeiten innerhalb eines immer *verwirklichten* ewigen Liebeslebens Gottes sind."

18 *TD* 5:507 (IV:464).

19 *TD* 5:507 (IV:464): "von der *gloria Dei* in der Schöpfung aber wird jeder Verdacht eines göttlichen Solipsismus abgewehrt: die innere Teilnahme der Geschöpfe am trinitarischen Leben wird zu einem inwendigen Geschenk jeder göttlichen Person an

It is just this "inclusion" of the world within the Trinitarian relations that will explain how the world matters to God. This, Balthasar's most original move in the *Theo-Drama*, will be taken up below, but we need first to present at least some attempt at a comprehensive sketch of how Balthasar executes the aim of the *Theo-Drama*.

The Argument of the *Theo-Drama*

The following sketch of what I call the argument of the *Theo-Drama* is not a summary of the *Theo-Drama* just as such; that would be something fuller and more difficult than anything that could be attempted here. It would be fuller, for it would retail the properly dramatic resources that Balthasar brings to his work and the theological transformation he works on them.[20] It would be more difficult, for the transformation just mentioned involves questions of theological method, and these would need to be addressed in detail. I propose here a statement only of the dogmatic theological argument of the work, at the inevitable risk of distortion and for the purposes and convenience, as it were, of those still beholden to what Balthasar labeled "theological epic."[21]

The more modest project is ambitious enough. It is an attempt to present the chief and all-informing theological intelligibility of the work. Given the place of the *Theo-Drama* in the oeuvre, this is tantamount to grasping the central argument of Balthasar's work as a whole.[22]

The chief axis of understanding on which the *Theo-Drama* as a whole depends is the relation between the Cross, which reveals the Trinity, and the Trinity, which founds the Cross.

1. The Cross reveals the Trinity.[23] For Balthasar, it does so in a way than which no greater could be thought, for the greatest imaginable distance, that between sin and the Holy God, is discovered to be outdistanced, and encompassed, by the distinction between Father and Son.[24] No greater way of revealing the Trinity in the created order could be thought, for the opposition between the sinner and God is seemingly the greatest imaginable. It supposes the infinite distance between creature and Creator, and then multiplies that distance by the factor of rebellion.

---

die andere, womit jeder Anschein einer bloß äußerlichen 'Verherrlichung' überwunden wird."

[20] See here especially Dalzell, *Dramatic Encounter,* Chapter 4.
[21] See *TD* 2:43 (II/1: 39).
[22] See O'Hanlon, "Theological Dramatics," 93.
[23] See, for example, *TD* 5:120–24 (IV:104–7).
[24] *TD* 4:325–27, 333–34 (III:302–4, 310–11).

And yet, as Balthasar has it, this "distance" is outdistanced by the distinction between Father and Son—meaning that the distance between sinful creature and holy God can be "contained" and so rendered neutral by the greater distinction within unity of Father and Son.[25]

Dramatically, this point can be expressed by saying that the economic drama between Christ and God reveals the immanently Trinitarian play between Father and Son.[26]

The Cross reveals the Trinity, of course, in that the Trinity is the ground of the Cross and enables the Cross; that is, it enables precisely this form, the crucified Christological form, of the redemption of sinful humanity, this form of the reconciliation of finite and infinite freedom.

More pointedly and exactly expressed for Balthasar, the Trinity is ground of the Cross in that the Cross happens and could happen only within the personal relations defined by the Trinity. It is not just that, since Christ offers himself to God in the Spirit, and since in that same Spirit God raises Christ, therefore we learn that the one who offers himself and is raised must be distinct from the one to whom he offers himself and who raises him, as also from the one in whom he offers himself and in whom he is raised. Rather, the very offering is a manifestation of the relation of Son to Father; it is an economic mode or extension of it.[27] The economic drama between Christ and God can take place only within the personal transactions already and eternally actualized in the Trinity.

As the ground of the Cross, however, the Trinity is not also at the same time constituted just as such by the Cross. That the Cross not only manifests, but manifests because it constitutes the Trinity, such that without the Cross there would be no Trinity, is the position of Hegel and Moltmann, and Balthasar rejects it.[28] The absolute, "immanent" Trinity is eternal and is not constituted as such by the economy or any event within it. And yet, there is another form of constitution of which one can speak, as we shall see.

2. While it is true to say, then, that God would be triune even were there no creation by the Word and no created world to redeem by the Incarna-

---

25 See Dalzell on the "distance" metaphor, (*Dramatic Encounter,* 146–51); swallowing up the distance of sin in the greater distance between Father and Son who are yet united by the Spirit means the offer of the Spirit to the sinner, in virtue of which his heart is transformed.

26 *TD* 1:20, 129 (I:19–20, 116–17); 2:72 (II/1:64–65); 4:322–25, 327 (III:300–303, 304); Dalzell, *Dramatic Encounter,* 114.

27 *TD* 3:157 (II/2:143–44); 4:326 (III:303).

28 *TD* 5:224–27 (IV:202–4) (Hegel); 5:227–29 (IV:205–7) (Moltmann).

tion of the Word and the descent of the Holy Spirit, the Cross neverthe-less "enriches" the Trinity.[29]

This is something distinctively Balthasarian. That the event of the Cross reveals the Trinity, its ground, is not distinctive. And that Balthasar wants to deny that the Cross constitutes the Trinity is nothing except Nicene Christianity. But that nevertheless the Cross "enriches" the Trinity—this is proper to Balthasar; it is how he thinks to insert modern concerns into the framework of the ancient dogmatics.

The modern concern is to make the world matter to God, and to ensure the truth of this by making the world really change God. The modern concern would have finite freedom make a difference not only to God, but in God. Of course finite freedom matters to infinite and immutable Love—what we do is either in accord with or contrary to God's will, and it "matters" to him in this sense. But the modern concern wants God to be different than he would have been because of finite freedom.

On the other hand, Balthasar's thesis can be said to maintain the ancient framework for three reasons. In the first place, the "enrich-ment" in question is predicated of the Persons, not of the Divinity. In the second place, Balthasar wants to say that this is not a becoming like an earthly becoming, not a passage from potency to act, but rather a matter of a supra-worldly Trinitarian "event."[30] In the third place, the enrichment is a gratuitous enrichment; that is, it is so to speak a contingent means by which the Persons glorify one another, a means enfolded in an eternal conversation, glorification, and enrich-ment that takes place among the Persons, and would take place, whether the world existed or not, and whether the world was redeemed in the way that it in fact is or not.[31] We will return to this most important point.

3. Further, and on the strength of the view of the relation of the econ-omy to the Persons just outlined, Balthasar thinks to have a Trinitar-ian overcoming of a supposed dilemma generated by the doctrine of creation: Does the world "add" anything to God or not? If not, then the world seems to be not really real. If so, then God cannot be immutable.[32] But if the Persons glorify and enrich themselves through the economy, then the world really does matter; it is no charade. On the other hand, and for the reasons already given just above, we remain with a God of whom nothing greater can be conceived, the

[29] *TD* 5:514–15 (IV:470–71).
[30] *TD* 5:512 (IV:468); see Dalzell, *Dramatic Encounter,* 178, 207.
[31] *TD* 5:507–9, 514–15 (IV:463–65, 470–71).
[32] *TD* 5:508 (IV:464–65).

transcendent and absolutely perfect God of classical theism. This is
the cardinal point, with which, if Balthasar can really have it, he has
all the rest. It is the topic of the next section.

Before that, however, it would be good to illustrate the claim that the
intelligibility expressed above in (1) through (3) informs the entire *Theo-
Drama*. I shall pick out two important points where this can readily be seen.

First, the economic revelation of the Trinity is given particularly pointed
form in the characteristically Balthasarian Christological position that the
Person of Christ is his mission. Already, given what was said in (1), above,
we have it that the mission is the economic manifestation of the Person, and
so of the procession (since the Son is his being generated and so is his proceeding from the Father). The idea that the Person of Christ is his mission is
a function not simply of the dialogical conception of the person to which
Balthasar is indebted,[33] nor alone of the identity of person and role-mission
that dramatic theory makes possible, nor again of the Thomist thesis of the
identity of mission and procession, nor of all three together. Rather, it is the
notion of person that the Trinitarian resolution of the dilemma between
mythology and philosophy needs. It is the notion of person that the Trinitarian resolution of the question of creation's "addition" to God requires. For
it is maintained that just as purely immanently Trinitarian exchanges would
enrich and ever more fully constitute the Persons, so now in fact do economic exchanges enrich and ever more fully constitute the Persons. These
"economic exchanges," however, are simply matters of the missions. The
enrichment and continuing constitution of one Person by another via the
economy occurs through the missions. This is to say, then, that the mission
is the Person, and the Person is the mission. The missions turn out to be the
vehicle by which the Persons in fact enrich one another.

Second, there is Balthasar's soteriology. Why is it that St. Thomas's theology of satisfaction is wanting, according to Balthasar? The fundamental
reason is not that St. Thomas asserts the continuance of the *visio beatifica*,
nor that Christ does not sufficiently take on our sin, for Balthasar himself,
when pressed, confines the Son's "becoming sin" to taking on the effects of
sin.[34] He finds St. Thomas's soteriology lacking because it confines the
effects of Christ's passion and death to the economy. The "wonderful
exchange" is so profound for Balthasar that the passion is taken into the
modalities of the Trinitarian relations—it "enriches" them.[35]

---

33 *TD* 1:626–43 (I:587–603); see also Hans Urs von Balthasar, "On the Concept of
    Person," *Communio* 13 (1986): 18–26.

34 *TD* 4:337–38 (III:314).

35 For an exposition of Balthasar's soteriology, see G. Mansini, "Rahner and Balthasar
    on the Efficacy of the Cross," in this volume.

The governing theological intelligibility of the *Theo-Drama* may be summed up, then, as follows. If creation is really to count and add something to God, if created freedom is to be in real dialogue with God, if the event of the Cross is really to matter to the interior life of God, then the reality of God must be such as to be an ever more increasing event of Trinitarian exchanges. We must locate the world not outside of God, and relative to the immutable and eternal divinity of God, for in that way it will never be made good that the world matters to him in the relevant way. Rather, we must locate the world not in the divinity just as such (Hegel), but within the Trinitarian relations. For only so can we say that the economy really effects something in God, and yet at the same time maintain that, since there would be this effect anyway, God remains transcendent in the way philosophy, as Balthasar understands the term, requires.[36]

The Economic "Enrichment" or Constitution of the Trinity

In order to appreciate the key and unprecedented solution Balthasar offers to the manifold dilemma that is its point of departure, it is helpful to compare two series of texts within his final treatment of the central question of the *Theo-Drama*; that is, within the concluding section of the last volume, titled "What Does God Gain from the World?" The citations all occur within a few pages of one another, and this is important to remember. A first series declares that God does not need and is not affected by the world, which is related to him as manifesting, not constituting, him. A second series seems straightforwardly to contradict this in asserting that the world affects God and changes him. The resolution is to see that God's being affected by the world, or rather the result of this, is something that would happen even did it not happen through the agency of the world. It is a result that would occur simply in virtue of the relations of the Persons of the Trinity themselves, although *in fact* they act toward one another

---

[36] I put it this way since it is just as arguable that it is revelation that requires such transcendence, and not philosophy. See Robert Sokolowski, *The God of Faith and Reason* (Notre Dame, IN: University of Notre Dame Press, 1982). I note as well that for Sokolowski the Christian distinction is not understood by contrast to modern philosophy and paganism, but by contrast to ancient philosophy and paganism. For him, distinctive to Christianity is that God is out of the world completely, which is true neither for myth nor for philosophy. Balthasar seems rather to situate Christianity relatively to an already contaminated philosophy—that is, a philosophy contaminated by Christianity. But then, he thinks that it is pre-Christian philosophy that is contaminated by grace and the supernatural, and only Christian theology that can construct a philosophy not so contaminated; see Hans Urs von Balthasar, *The Theology of Karl Barth* (San Francisco: Ignatius Press, 1992), 280.

through the world and in such a way that it really is true to say that the world changes God.

The first series runs as follows. Already above, we read of "free possibilities within the eternal life of love in God that *has always been realized.*" And continuing: "This eternally realized love in God, therefore, does not require the positing—in a Hegelian manner—of these free possibilities."[37] Quoting Adrienne von Speyr: "In the Christian context, sacrifice, suffering, the Cross and death are only the reflection of tremendous realities in the Father, in heaven, in eternal life." [38] Here, then, the economic realities are but reflections, manifestations. So also are they where we read that the "economic" sacrifice of Father and Son reflects eternal, Trinitarian sacrifices.[39] Again, Adrienne von Speyr: "In God, becoming is a confirmation of his own Being. And since God is immutable, the vitality of his 'becoming' can never be anything other than his Being."[40] And Balthasar, in his own voice again: "Primarily, what we have said about heaven is meant to show that neither creation nor incarnation necessitates a change in God and his eternal life. In fact, the concept of eternal life 'cuts off all possibility of positing a change in God' "[41] And Christ "simply expresses in the *oikonomia* what he has always expressed anew in the eternal, triune life: his complete readiness to carry out every one of his Father's wishes."[42] Of Christ's forsakenness, we learn that it is "the revelation of the highest positivity of trinitarian love."[43]

Then there is the second series. "We must also bear in mind that infinite richness is rich in freedom and can enrich others (and hence itself) in ways

---

37 *TD* 5:508 (IV:465): "freie Möglichkeiten innrhalb eines immer *verwirklichten* ewigen Liebeslebens Gottes . . . welches somit nicht—hegelisch—der setzung jener freien Möglichkeiten innerhalb bedarf."

38 *TD* 5:511 (IV:467): "Opfer, Leiden, Kreuz und Tod sind christlich betrachtet nur die Widerspiegelung von gewaltigen Wirklichkeiten im Vater, im Himmel, im ewigen Leben."

39 *TD* 5:510 (IV:466–67).

40 *TD* 5:512 (IV:468): "Das Werden in Gott ist Bestätigung seines Seins. Auch weil Gott unveränderlich ist, kann die Lebendigkeit seines 'Werdens' nie etwas anderes sein als sein Sein."

41 *TD* 5:513(IV:469), quoting von Speyr at the end: "Diese Aspekte von unten nach oben sollen aber hier vor allem beweisen, daß weder Schöpfung noch Menschwerdung eine Veränderung Gottes und seines ewigen Lebens notwendig machen. Durch den Begriff des ewigen Lebens 'wird die Möglichkeit abgeschnitten, eine Veränderung in Gott anzunehmen.' "

42 *TD* 5:513 (IV:469): "er drückt innerhalb der *oikonomia* nur aus, was er im ewigen dreieinigen Leben immer neu ausgedrückt hat: seine völlige Bereitschaft, jeden Willen des Vaters zu erfüllen."

43 *TD* 5:517 (IV:473): "in der Kreuzesverlassenheit wird . . . die höchste Positivität der trinitarischen Liebe offenbar."

that are ever new."[44] It is "enriching itself"; it is growing. And this: "Eternal life, as the word itself says, is not a complete state of rest, but a constant vitality, implying that everything is always new."[45] Novelty, the changed, and so change, are asserted. Quoting von Speyr: The unchangeability of God is not something "static" but is "the movement of all movements."[46] And this most important sentence: "We must think of this in such a way that the work of the *oikonomia*, which is 'not nothing' either for the world or for God, actually does 'enrich' God in a particular aspect, without adding anything that is lacking to his eternal life."[47] Quoting von Speyr again: "[T]he Trinity is more perfected in love after the Incarnation than before," which fact "has its meaning and foundation in God himself, who is . . . an eternal intensification in eternal rest."[48] So, the economy perfects God, who is ever intensifying anyway. And last: "We need not be shocked at the suggestion that there can be 'economic' events in God's eternal life. When the Father hands over all judgment to the Son, 'something happens in God.' When the risen Son returns to the Father, 'a new joy arises after the renunciation involved in the separation. This new joy . . . perfects the Trinity in the sense that the grace that is to be bestowed becomes ever richer, both in the world into which it pours forth and in God himself, who is willing to bestow it.' "[49]

How can we read both series together, and always on the supposition that Balthasar means what he says?[50] Because of the Trinitarian involvement

---

44 *TD* 5:509 (IV:465): "Man muß somit gelten lassen, daß das unendliche Reiche sich aus dem Reichtum seiner Freiheit immer neu bereichern (lassen!) kann"; earlier, *TD* 2:259 (II/1:234–35).

45 *TD* 5:511 (IV:467): "Ewiges Leben ist, wie das Wort es schon sagt, kein Stillstand, sondern immerwährende Lebendigkeit, was ein Je-Neu-Sein einschließt."

46 *TD* 5:511 (IV:467): "die Bewegung aller Bewegungen."

47 *TD* 5:514 (IV:470): "Das muß so zusammengedacht werden, daß das Werk der *oikonomia*, das wie für die Welt, so auch für Gott keinesfalls nichts ist, selbst Gott in einer bestimmten Hinsicht 'bereichert', ohne seinem ewigen Leben etwas ihm Fehlendes hinzuzufügen."

48 *TD* 5:514 (IV:470): "daß die Trinität nach der Menschwerdung vollendeter is als vorher, hat also seinem Sinn und Grund in Gott selbst, der keine starre, sondern eine immer neu in der Liebe zusammenschlagende Einheit ist, eine ewige Steigerung in der ewigen Ruhe."

49 *TD* 5:515 (IV:471), with quotations from von Speyr: "Man braucht deshalb vor einer Aussage nicht zu erschrecken, die ein ökonomisches Ereignis in das ewige Leben Gottes einschreibt. Wenn der Vater das ganze Gericht dem Sohn übergibt, so 'geschieht etwas in Gott.' Wenn der auferstehende Sohn zum Vater zurückkehrt, 'entsteht eine neue Freude nach dem Verzicht der Trennung und vollendet die Trinität im Sinne eines Je-reicher-Werdens der zu spendenden Gnade, sowohl in der Welt, in die sie ausströmt, wie in Gott selbst, der sie zu schenken bereit ist.' "

50 For a good discussion of how to take Balthasar's language, as metaphor or analogy, see Dalzell, *Dramatic Encounter*, 169–71, 186–91.

in it, the world enriches God, but not as adding anything lacking to God. For the Persons are in themselves and eternally always enriching one another, and would do so without the world. But in fact, the economy enfolds the world into this ever increasing exchange of love and glory. "From all eternity the divine 'conversation' envisages the possibility of involving a non-divine world in the Trinity's love."[51] The concluding paragraph of the *Theo-Drama* should be quoted.

> What does God gain from the world? An additional gift, given to the Son by the Father, but equally a gift made by the Son to the Father, and by the Spirit to both. It is a gift because, through the distinct operations of each of the three Persons, the world acquires an inward share in the divine exchange of life; as a result the world is able to take the divine things it has received from God, together with the gift of being created, and return them to God as a divine gift.[52]

As a father gives his child the wherewithal to provide him a Father's Day gift, so does the Father bestow this on his children—not only his Son, but also us, as inserted into the Son's return of himself to the Father. As Thomas Dalzell explains, commenting on this same passage:

> What he is saying is that in the finite's being drawn into the trinitarian life, God receives not only the [finite being's] createdness, itself a gift of God, but also an additional [*zusätzliches*] gift which is to be understood as its ever-greater giving back to God the gift of God's own love which it receives in taking part in the divine conversation. But since this additional gift is in fact a divine gift, any increase implied by its being given to God by created freedom is situated by him within the eternal increase in God, and specifically within the increase due to the Son's ever-greater self-gift to the Father.[53]

Therefore, the world does not just express an eternally complete God, for God is not eternally complete. Or perhaps we should say that part of being complete is always to grow. As the world expresses precisely that

---

51 *TD* 5:509 (IV:466): "Zunächst ist die Möglichkeit der Einbeziehung einer nichtgöttlichen Welt in die trinitarische Liebe von Ewigkeit her im göttlichen Gespräch."

52 *TD* 5:521 (IV:476): "Was hat Gott von der Welt? Ein zusätzliches Geschenk, das der Vater dem Sohn, aber ebensosehr der Sohn dem Vater und der Geist beiden macht, ein Geschenk deshalb, weil die Welt durch das unterschiedliche Wirken jeder der drei Personen am göttlichen Lebensaustausch innerlichen Anteil gewinnt und sie Gott deshalb, was sie Göttliches von Gott erhielt, mitsamt dem Geschenk ihres Geschaffenseins auch als göttliches Geschenk erstattet."

53 Dalzell, *Dramatic Encounter,* 210.

fact, it is a contingent, non-necessary, gratuitously chosen means of accomplishing this free eternal exchange, which would happen anyway.[54]

Does God really depend on the world? Yes. Does God depend on the world such that he would be different did he not? No.

Criticism

Balthasar might be said to have the best of all possible or at least all prior positions. With the "older dogmatics," God does not need the world, and the classical philosophical requirement of transcendence seems to be met. With Hegel, the world constitutes the Trinity—only contingently so, and only a Trinity that exists independently of the world process, it is true; still, the Trinity is affected by world process. With modern process thought, growth and novelty become metaphysically privileged and find a place in the Absolute. The categories of "event" and "self-giving" *(Ereignis, Er-gebnis)* provide an opening to postmodern philosophy.[55] Most of all, we have a religiously satisfying way of taking those texts in sacred Scripture that suggest dialogical, mutual relations between God and the world. The rest of this essay is concerned with only one of these prior positions, and with whether the requirements of transcendence installed in the older dogmatics really are met.

Comparison with Aquinas on the Divine Understanding of Created Reality

One might think that what Balthasar is proposing is not unlike what St. Thomas offers by way of explaining how we can say that God truly knows and loves us, we who are really not God, and yet do so without prejudice to his transcendence.

St. Thomas's understanding of this is as follows. The primary object of the divine understanding, which is an infinite act of understanding, is the divine intelligibility, an infinite object. Finite intelligibility is a partial imitation of the divine intelligibility. In understanding himself, God necessarily understands all possible ways he can be and is imitated. And such

---

54 Ibid., 208: "But if the worldly response is to be thought of as meaning something to God, Balthasar has to approach the hypothesis of God being 'enriched', so to speak, in such a way that there is no suggestion of that response adding something to the eternal life of love which was missing. In other words, he has to hold together the idea that finite freedom can make a meaningful contribution to the inner-divine conversation *and* the idea that there is already in God an ever perfect giving and receiving of love."

55 See the discussion of Heidegger in *The Glory of the Lord*, vol. 5: *The Realm of Metaphysics in the Modern Age* (San Francisco: Ignatius, 1991), 429–50.

understanding adds nothing to what he already understands—himself; nor would the absence of such understanding deprive God of anything he in fact has.[56]

It might appear, therefore, that just as for St. Thomas God's understanding of the contingent world is enfolded within his understanding of himself, so for Balthasar the Father's gift of creation to the Son is already enfolded in his always-surpassing-itself gift of himself to the Son, which is the generation of the Son. Therefore, again, just as for St. Thomas, if God did not understand the world (on the supposition of its non-existence), there would be no diminution of what it is that God understands, so if the world did not exist there would be no diminution of the ever increasing richness of the personal exchanges within the Trinity. Thus, the world is a non-necessary way that the Persons in fact actually increase one another—with an increase that would happen even if the world did not exist. Perhaps it is helpful to write out the parallels as follows.

1. As the divine mind understands finite intelligibles in understanding the Infinite Intelligible,

2. as the divine will wills the finite good in willing the Infinite Good,

3. so the Father generates (or creates?) the world in generating the Son,

4. and so Father and Son give the world to each other in giving themselves to each other.

The formal similarity of Balthasar to St. Thomas consists in integrating a divine act relative to a finite reality into a divine act relative to a divine reality. Again, there is a formal similarity in the concern to express the fact that nothing external to God operates on God—at least, for Balthasar, independently of God.

But the differences emerge, also. The point of (1) and (2) is to show how it can be true that God understands and wills something not himself and yet is not dependent on what is not himself and is not different from what he would be did he not understand and will something not himself. The point of (3) and (4), however, is to show how the world can really contribute to the divine glory and goodness, and yet, in such a way, that, did it not, there would be no diminution of the divine glory and goodness.

---

[56] For the infinity of the divine understanding, see *Summa theologiae* (hereafter *ST*) I, q. 7, a. 3; q. 14, a. 4; for the infinity of the primary object of God's understanding, see *ST* I, q. 14, aa. 2 and 3; for the relevant infinities of will and object willed, see *ST* I, q. 19, a. 1, c, and ad 3, q. 20, a. 1, ad 3. A nice statement of this argument is found in Bernard Lonergan, *De constitutione Christi ontologica et psychologica* (Rome: Gregorian University, 1961), nos. 55–56.

The problem with (3) and (4) is that while it is possible to understand that the divine will and the divine understanding can have a finite as well as an infinite object, it is more difficult to understand how the first procession can have a finite as well as an infinite product. And the gift, insofar as it names a product of inner-Trinitarian commerce, is the Holy Spirit, Proceeding Love. We could sum up the position as follows: The world relative to the Father is not in an opposed relation of origin, such that, without the world, there is no Father (as, without the Son, there is no Father). Neither can Father and Son be who they are without breathing the Spirit; but they can be without the world.

Balthasar indeed knows that the world is not necessary for God. But in (1) and (2), we see how the world can be distinct from God, and yet known and loved by God. Knowing and loving can have objects distinct from the knower and lover. In (3) and (4), on the contrary, we do not see how the world can be distinct from God, and yet generated, or given by God, within the first or second processions. The processions serve to distinguish Persons within a single nature, but not distinct natures. If the world is "in" the first procession, it would be the Son, or, if it is "in" the second, it would be the Holy Spirit. Or else Son and Spirit are created.

What does account for the distinction of the world from God? Not that it be generated within the generation of the Son, distinct from the Father, or given, within the mutual gift of Spirit, but that it be understood and willed to be so distinct. This knowing and willing are common to the three Persons. This does not prevent St. Thomas from finding an exemplar of the procession of creatures from God in the procession of the Word from the Father and of Love from both, as the texts adduced by Balthasar report.[57] Thus, St. Thomas's teaching does not suggest the note of efficiency that Balthasar's solution trades on.

An Ever Growing God

Even so, we have not yet broached the most obvious problem with Balthasar's position, which is that whether the world contributes to God's increase or not, still, there is increase. But from what? With what? At the end of the day, Parmenides will have his say. If the increment comes from what is, it already is and does not come to be; and if it comes from nothing, it does not come to be, for nothing comes from nothing. There can be no additions to God, therefore; whatever he is, he is. This is so, at least, unless one wishes to deny the priority of act to potency.

Again, growth is a kind of becoming or change. Becoming is the actualization of the potential insofar as it is potential. Becoming requires passive potency in the becoming subject; it requires an agent or principle of

---

[57] See *TD* 5:61–62 (IV:53–54) for the texts in question.

actualization really distinct from the principle of potency. It requires time, which is nothing but a measure of becoming. Therefore, if there is growth in God, the divinity is potential, non-simple, and not eternal.

There are, it would seem, two ways Balthasar's position might be saved. It will be rejoined, in the first place, that the addition in question is predicated of the Persons and not the nature. But this does not avoid the problem. Where the Persons are distinct from one another but not from the nature, growing Persons would seem to imply a growing divinity. One would have to restrict the "growth" in question and conceive it as in some way belonging to the Persons alone. The growth would have to be a growth, for example, in the very relationality of Father and Son, such that the "addition" means the Father is more Father, and the Son more Son, and this as not touching what they possess in common, which cannot change. But growth predicated of the relation would seem to be a relation of a relation, and relations of relations are relations of reason only. Therefore, the growth in question would be not real but only a manner of speaking, nothing except a pointed and arresting way of indicating the richness of the Trinitarian relations.

Nor does it help, in the second place, to urge, as Balthasar does, that this is becoming in another sense, not an earthly sense, and that the time in question is a kind of supra-time.[58] Of such things as wisdom, goodness, or understanding, we say that what they are in God is not like what they are in creatures. But we do not say this of change or becoming, because change is constituted by potency and imperfection. Perfection is act. Becoming requires potency; it requires being imperfect.[59]

This is not a matter of the Thomistic and Aristotelian account of change versus some other possibility of thought. There is no other analysis of change besides that of Aristotle. There are denials of change from Parmenides to (in his own way) Hume. There are assertions that some kinds of change are really other kinds of change, as with the reduction of qualitative to quantitative change in materialism. There are assertions of novelty with no ground or cause, with Nietzsche and Bergson. There are reversals of the priority of act to potency, with Hegel. But there is no *analysis* of change, a location of the principles of change, except that of Aristotle.

It is hard to see how the invocation of a change in God such as one that is not in our earthly experience, therefore, can be anything more than

---

58 For example, *TD* 5:67 (IV:59) (no ordinary becoming); 5:92 (IV:81) (time); Dalzell, *Dramatic Encounter,* 178, 207 (a becoming not like ours); idem., 168*n*3 (a time above our time).

59 See here the exchange of papers on passivity in God, beginning with David L. Schindler, "Norris Clarke on Person, Being, and St. Thomas," *Communio* 20 (1993): 580–92; Steven Long, "Divine and Creaturely 'Receptivity': The Search for a Middle Term," *Communio* 21 (1994): 151–61; and David L. Schindler, "The Person: Philosophy, Theology, and Receptivity," *Communio* 21 (1994): 172–90.

words. Change requires passive potency; it requires composition in the subject of change. To speak of change that is not like this, that does not involve a passage from potency to act, is not to speak of anything at all.

What does Balthasar want? The liveliness of an "event" as opposed to substance? But substance is nothing except what is in itself and not in another. If the Balthasarian event exists in itself, it is a substance in the required sense.[60] If one wants to think of such an "in itself" as a pure event, as a pure liveliness, then what is wanted, it would seem, is a sort of pure act—a line of thought already well developed in the history of Western theology and metaphysics.

Conclusion

Much earlier, in *The Theology of Karl Barth*, Balthasar called strenuously for a theology that is not antecedently measured and confined by philosophy.[61] Does the foregoing criticism fail to meet that standard, and so fail to appreciate a theology whose inspiration is wholly from revelation? To the contrary and to repeat, to invoke the Aristotelian analysis of change is not an invocation of something peculiarly, narrowly Aristotelian. It is to invoke the only analysis of change that human thought has produced. The *Physics*, at this point, is strong. It is strong with the strength of reason, and so of nature, itself. To say that revelation, as read by Balthasar, trumps Aristotle here is not to preserve revelation and therefore the autonomy of theology; it is to say that grace does not complete but rather destroys nature, that faith kills and does not perfect reason.

It is in that same earlier work on Barth that Balthasar takes such pains to defend an analogous naming of God and the world. If the analogy of names were the point of departure for an answer to the question of the *Theo-Drama* as to whether the world adds anything to God, the answer would most certainly be no. Nor would this denial imply that the world is therefore illusory—to the contrary, in two ways. First, and obviously, participated being, for all that it cannot add anything to the being (God's being) of which it is a participation, is not therefore unreal.[62] Second, if

---

60 On the other hand, if we are supposed to hear Heidegger in the talk of a Trinitarian "event," and if this means that we are in the order of manifestation and appearance, and not of constitution, then the problem disappears. Evidently, I do not think this is the way to take things in Balthasar.

61 See Balthasar, *The Theology of Karl Barth*, trans. Edward T. Oakes (San Francisco: Ignatius Press, 1992 [Ger. 1951]), 264–65, for criticism of St. Thomas in this vein. See also ibid., 267ff., for the delimitation of a *theological* concept of nature.

62 Balthasar's fear about the world seeming illusory next to the God who need not create seems to suppose some field of being in which the divine nature would compete with worldly natures. Sokolowski, *The God of Faith and Reason*, is especially valuable in warding off intellectual vertigo of this kind.

infinite Love loves a finite good, that is to make that finite good "matter" both infinitely and, since infinite Love is immutable, unchangeably. This is to find a sense of what it means to "matter," furthermore, that is instructed by the manifestation of the God than which nothing greater can be thought.

It is this answer that alone seems congruent with the classical theology Balthasar intends still to preserve in the *Theo-Drama*. The *Theo-Drama* itself, so promising in the prospect of a properly theological and indeed Trinitarian reconciliation of modern concerns with the "older dogmatics," appears to be yet another demonstration of the impossibility of such a project, if indeed, as it seems, the Trinitarian overcoming of the impasse there proposed rather destroys than preserves the classical part of the material it seeks to integrate.

CHAPTER 5

Understanding St. Thomas on Christ's Immediate Knowledge of God

THE INTERNATIONAL Theological Commission's 1985 state-ment on "The Consciousness of Christ Concerning Himself and His Mission" undertakes to state what by faith Christians hold about the knowledge of Jesus. Jesus of Nazareth knew: First, that he was the Son of God, and that he possessed divine and not merely prophet-ical authority; second, that his mission was to preach the Kingdom and die for the salvation of all; third, that he was founding a Church. Fourth and last, since he knew he was dying for all, he knew the "all" he was dying for in such a way as to enable each Christian to say truly "he died for me" (see Gal 2:20). Beyond this, the bare statement that Jesus was con-scious of his identity and mission, the Commission declines to go, and expressly avoids "theological elaborations calculated to give an account of this datum of faith."[1]

The traditional account of this datum is, of course, the theory of Christ's immediate (or "beatific") knowledge of God, and usually as elabo-rated by St. Thomas. It is an approach to precisely this "account" of St. Thomas's that I will outline in the second part of this essay.

---

[1] "The Consciousness of Christ Concerning Himself and His Mission," in *Interna-tional Theological Commission: Texts and Documents, 1969–1985*, ed. Michael Sharkey (San Francisco: Ignatius, 1989), 307. Again, the Commission "rules out any *a priori* philosophical terminology" (307). Hence I take the liberty of using "knowledge" where the Commission speaks of "consciousness." The Commission characterizes the cognitional state of affairs it imputes to Christ merely as a "pres-ence" of the knowing-conscious subject to itself in its "heart." I take it that the Commission means to avoid being specific with regard to any distinction between conceptual and non-conceptual modes of knowledge, and that this is the reason it prefers "consciousness" to "knowledge."

There are three things especially that seem to stand in the way of approaching St. Thomas's account today. First, there is some difficulty in seeing it precisely as that, an account of what the Commission calls the datum of faith. Second, a key distinction upon which St. Thomas's account depends, that between faith and knowledge, tends to be obliterated in contemporary analytic epistemology, where knowledge is described as "justified true belief." This makes it hard to see the difference St. Thomas supposes there is between the cognitive state of Christians, on the one hand, and that of Jesus, on the other. Third, some modern biblical theology discovers Jesus himself as the exemplar of Christian faith. Thus, even supposing we have kept the distinction between faith and knowledge, the required application of the distinction becomes impossible.[2] I will be unable to deal at any length with these last two difficulties, but will advert to them briefly within the outline of an approach to St. Thomas's account that I mean to give here.[3]

St. Thomas's Position as an Account of the Datum of Faith

The first difficulty, however, is to be addressed at the outset and at some length. It arises from the way in which St. Thomas presents his teaching on the knowledge of Christ in the *Summa theologiae*. But also, it is magnified by a common explication and defense of St. Thomas's position by some of his contemporary friends that seems to me to be without foundation in the texts. I will first dispatch this erroneous explication, and then address the question of the order of the *Summa*.

The reason St. Thomas affirms Christ's immediate vision of God, we are sometimes told, is that he thinks this follows as a metaphysical necessity from the fact of the hypostatic union.[4] Thus for instance Luigi Iammarrone:

---

2 Another cause of confusion as to what St. Thomas means by Christ's immediate knowledge of God might be said to be the popularity of Karl Rahner's "Dogmatic Reflections on the Knowledge and Self-Consciousness of Christ," *Theological Investigations,* vol. 5 (London: Darton, Longman and Todd, 1966), 193–215, where Rahner conflates consciousness and knowledge in a context where they need to be distinguished. This has been nicely sorted out by Raymond Moloney, "The Mind of Christ in Transcendental Theology: Rahner, Lonergan and Crowe," *Heythrop Journal* 25 (1984): 288–300.

3 There is also the difficulty for this question of modern exegesis, a difficulty mentioned by the International Theological Commission. But this is a difficulty for the original apprehension of the datum of faith itself rather than for understanding St. Thomas.

4 Karl Rahner suggests this course in "Dogmatic Reflections," 204–5. However, he claims but to argue broadly from "thomistic axioms." The claim that the knowledge of vision follows from the hypostatic union is at least as old as Matthias Scheeben; see Rudolf M. Schmitz, "Christus Comprehensor: Die 'Visio Beatifica

In the *Commentary on the Sentences* and in other writings, the Angelic Doctor affirms categorically that the beatific vision was due to Christ not only as something fitting, but *as a result of the hypostatic union*: "From the very fact that the soul of Christ *was personally conjoined to God*, the union of fruition was due to it, and was not made due to it through any operation."[5]

Iammarrone notes St. Thomas's argument in the *Summa* that, by reason of the personal subject of the grace of Christ, this grace could not be increased. Such consummate grace implies enjoyment of the beatific vision.[6] Thus, as St. Thomas says in the *Compendium*, "it was necessary that the Word of God incarnate be perfect in grace and in the wisdom of truth."[7] The necessity of the vision as following metaphysically from the hypostatic union is affirmed again by St. Thomas, according to Iammarrone, where he writes: "Christus ex hoc quod fuit Deus et homo etiam in sua humanitate habuit aliquid prae caeteris creaturis: ut scilicet statim a principio esset beatus."[8]

It is not necessary to follow every text Iammarrone adduces. As to the text from the *Sentences*, I think it evident that it affirms exactly and only a *convenientia* and not a necessity. As to the *Summa*, it is true that St. Thomas thinks the fullness of the grace of Christ, which cannot be increased, implies vision. But it is not true that he deduces this fullness of grace as a necessary metaphysical consequence of the union. He says indeed that "to the extent something receptive is nearer to the influencing cause, the more it participates in its influence."[9] God is the cause of grace; the union of the soul of

---

Christi Viatoris' bei M. J. Scheeben," *Doctor Communis* 36 (1983): 347–59. Schmitz does not, however, seem to think that Scheeben is following St. Thomas at this point (354).

5 Luigi Iammarrone, "La visione beatifica di Cristo Viatore nel pensiero di San Tommaso," *Doctor Communis* 36 (1983): 303–4: "Nel *Commento alle Sentenze* e in altri scritti l'Angelico afferma categoricamente che la visione beatifica a Cristo era dovuta non solo per convenienza, ma *in forza dell'unione ipostatica*: 'Ex hoc ipso quod anima Christi *erat Deo in persona coniuncta*, debebatur ei fruitionis unio et non per operationem aliquam ei facta debita.'" See *In III Sent.*, d. 18, q. 1, a. 4, q. 4, c. The emphases are his.

This whole fascicle of *Doctor Communis* is devoted to Christ's beatific knowledge. Luigi Bogliolo, "Strutture antropologiche e visione beatifica dell'anima di Cristo," makes the same claim as Iammarrone (345).

6 Ibid., 304. See *Summa theologiae* (hereafter *ST*) III, q. 7, a. 12.

7 C. 213.

8 Iammarrone, "La visione," 305; see *ST* III, q. 34, a. 4, ad 3: "From this very fact that Christ was God and man he possessed in his humanity as well something beyond other creatures: namely, that he was at once from the beginning blessed."

9 *ST* III, q. 7, a. 1: "Quanto enim aliquod receptivum propinquius est causae influenti, tanto magis participat de influentia ipsius."

Christ to the Word is personal; therefore what? "Et ideo maxime fuit *conveniens* ut anima illa reciperet influxum divinae gratiae."[10] As to the argument from the *Compendium*, the necessity in question is a function of Christ's role as the cause of beatitude in us, not of the hypostatic union itself in its metaphysical structure.[11] As to the last quotation in the above paragraph, it can be read as asserting what is true of the soul of Christ as much by fitting reasons as by metaphysical necessity.

Moreover, St. Thomas is fairly clear that the immediate knowledge of God does not exist in the soul of Christ merely as a result of the union. He asks in Book III of the *Sentences*, d. 14, qu. 3, whether the soul of Christ knew the Word through some mediating habit or not. The first objection:

> Nothing is required for knowledge except that the knowable be united to the knower. But the Word is not united to the soul of Christ by any mediating habit. Therefore, it does not know the Word through any habit.[12]

And the reply:

> It must be said that it is not the same union by which the Word is united to the soul of Christ in person, and by which it is united to it as the seen to what sees, for it is united to the body in person, but it is not seen by the body. And therefore, although there is no medium in that union by which the soul is united to the Word in person, it does not follow that there is required no medium for vision—I do not say a medium in which it is seen, as a mirror or species, but a medium under which it is seen, as light.[13]

---

10 Ibid.: "And therefore it was in the highest degree fitting that that soul received the influx of divine grace."

11 Iammarrone, "La visione," 395, seems indeed to be partly aware of this. But he says: "il nesso necessario cioè metafisico tra l'unione ipostatica e la visione beatifica si manifestava sotto due aspetti," the second of which is the role of Christ in the economy. How is this a manifestation of *metaphysical* necessity?

12 "Ad cognitionem enim non requiritur aliud nisi ut cognoscibile cognoscenti uniatur. Sed Verbum unitum est animae Christi non mediante aliquo habitu. Ergo Verbum cognovit non per aliquem habitum."

13 "Dicendum quod non est eadem unio qua unitur Verbum animae Christi in persona, et qua unitur ei ut visibile videnti; quia unitur corpori in persona, non tamen videtur a corpore. Et ideo licet in illa unione qua unitur anima Verbo in persona, non cadat aliquod medium; non tamen opportet quod in visione non cadat aliquod medium—non quidem dico medium sicut in quo videtur, ut speculum vel species; sed sicut sub quo videtur, sicut lumen."

The required medium, of course, is the light of glory.[14] Does the light of glory follow as a necessary result of the union? This is nowhere to be read.[15]

St. Thomas does not affirm Christ's immediate vision of God on the basis of some swift metaphysical deduction. Why does he affirm it? One can get the impression that the main reason St. Thomas imputes an immediate knowledge of God to the human mind of Christ is on the ground of a so-called principle of perfection. Thus, for instance, Engelbert Gutwenger and Liam Walsh argue that because of the dignity of the Person of Christ, it is fitting for the humanity of Jesus to be endowed as perfectly as possible commensurate with the requirements of his mission.[16] And indeed, we find St. Thomas arguing in just this way in *Summa theologiae* III, q. 9, a. 1.

It is seriously misleading to take this as the whole story, however, and for two reasons. First, the more exact reason St. Thomas gives in q. 9, a. 2, for positing an immediate knowledge of God in the humanity of Christ turns on the end of the Incarnation. The humanity of Christ is the instrumental cause by which God brings us to the vision of God. But a cause ought to be more potent than the caused; therefore, the soul of Christ enjoyed the immediate knowledge of God. The same argument is repeated in the *Compendium theologiae*, chapter 213. This should alert us to the fact that the profound reason for the theorem of Christ's immediate knowledge, like that of the Incarnation itself, is economic, and the argument depends on thinking out what it takes in the humanity of Christ if that humanity is to have the desired effect.

There is a second reason it is misleading to suppose that what leads St. Thomas to posit an immediate knowledge of God in Christ is some "principle of perfection." This has to do with the order of the *Summa* itself. What is this order? St. Thomas indicates in the Prologue that he will lay things out according to the *ordo disciplinae*. He means by this that he will lay things out beginning with what is last known to us but more intelligible in itself and proceeding to what is first known to us but less intelligible in

---

14 See also *Quaest. Disp. de Veritate*, q. 20, a. 1, c.

15 Iammarrone appeals expressly to Rahner's "Dogmatic Reflections," where there is talk of the "actuation" of the soul of Christ in virtue of its union with the Word. See "La visione," 307–8. For a criticism of "actuation" as something distinct from act, the great thesis of M. de la Taille, see Bernard Lonergan, *De constitutione Christi ontologica et psychologica,* 3rd ed. (Rome: Gregorian University Press, 1961), no. 27.

16 Engelbert Gutwenger, "The Problem of Christ's Knowledge," in *Who Is Jesus of Nazareth?* Concilium (English), vol. 11 (New York: Paulist, 1965), 91; Liam Walsh, the Introduction to *Summa Theologiae*, vol. 49: *The Grace of Christ* (New York: McGraw-Hill, 1974), xxii–xxiii. Walsh recognizes as well that St. Thomas asserts Christ's immediate knowledge of God on economic grounds.

itself.[17] That is, he will proceed as much as possible from real causes of being to the effects of these causes, or from the prior theological reason to what is controlled by that reason.[18] With the question of Christ's immediate knowledge, we have an instance of both. Thus, from the fundamental reason for the Incarnation, namely the salvation of humankind, he argues to what the assumed humanity must be like in order for the Incarnation to do the job it is intended to do.[19] As to causes, it should be noted where the treatment of the grace (qq. 7–8) and knowledge (qq. 9–12) of Christ fall in the *Summa*. It comes after a treatment of the hypostatic union, and after a treatment of the soul of Christ, for these things are causally prior to the properties of that soul. However, it comes before a treatment of the mysteries of the life of Christ—the actual doings and sayings of Christ—for these operations of Christ are causally dependent on the properties in question.

Thus, to continue this last point, it is no accident that the knowledge of Christ is treated long before the questions on such things as the manner of life (q. 40) and the teaching of Christ (q. 42). The perfections of the soul of Christ are *explanatory* of these things. Correlatively, these things, the things first known to us and most easily known by us, the things recorded in the Gospels, are the *data* whose theoretic intelligibility, an

---

17 For example, consider the order of topics in the *Prima pars*. What is closest to us is God's actual ordering and governance of the universe (qq. 103ff.). But this is treated last. What is first treated are the principles that enable us to understand that order and governance in its causes: (1) proximately, the parts of the universe, spiritual, material, and composite (qq. 50–102); (2) remotely, the creation of these parts (qq. 44ff.); (3) more remotely, the creator of these parts, God (qq. 2–26). The power (q. 25), will (q. 19), intelligence (q. 14) of the Creator are similarly ordered: What is closest to creating and governing is the power of God; the principles of this are the will and wisdom of God; the final principle of all is simply the divine being (qq. 3–13). I am not trying to determine all of the many questions raised as to the organization of the *Summa*, but I maintain that the ordering principle identified here is indeed operative in the organization of the *Summa*. See Bernard Lonergan, *Divinarum personarum conceptio analogica* (Rome: Gregorian University, 1959), 20–28; *De constitutione*, no. 46.

18 For since God is not reduced to causes, the order of topics in the *Summa* is not always according to prior causes, but sometimes insofar as one truth is the reason of another; see Lonergan, *De constitutione*, nos. 43–45. So in the preceding note, the divine understanding and will and power are not really distinct from the divine essence; still, what is concluded about those things has its reason in what is said about the divine essence.

19 Strictly, this too is a matter of causal ordering: final cause as determinative of means. But if we say that God's decision to save mankind is the reason for his decision to endow the humanity of Christ in such and such a way, then we are in the order of reasons, not causes, for the "decisions" of God are distinct neither from one another nor from God, and yet there is still to be discerned an order of reason as comprehended by the divine mind.

intelligibility that gives an account of the data in terms of causally prior factors, has already been outlined in such considerations as are devoted to the grace and knowledge of Christ.

In fact, if one turns to q. 42, on the teaching of Christ, one will look in vain for an expression of the kind of connection I have just indicated. This question takes up various aspects of the manner and circumstances of the teaching of Christ. Still, I point to article 1 of q. 40, on whether Christ should have lived a life of contemplative solitude rather than associating with men.

> I answer that Christ's manner of life had to be in keeping with the end of his incarnation, by reason of which he came into the world. Now he came into the world, first, that he might publish the truth. . . . Second, he came in order to free men from sin.

And by this point in the proceedings, we have already had it explained to us how it is that Christ has been rendered capable of publishing the truth. What a man can teach depends causally on what he knows,[20] and prior to considering his teaching, we have indeed considered his knowledge. So also for redemption, we have already considered the grace of Christ.

Still, one would like to see that St. Thomas concludes to the immediate knowledge of God in Christ simply from the *content* of Christ's teaching. And for this, one must forsake the *Summa* and turn to St. Thomas's commentaries on Scripture. Even here, however, things are not plain sailing. Thus, in the *Lectura* on the Gospel of John, there are quite explicit affirmations of Christ's human knowledge as *comprehensor*, at 4:45 and 6:14, where Thomas explains in what sense Christ is and is not a prophet.[21] In these places, Christ is said to have the prophet's kind of imagination, and so is *viator*; the light of his intellect, however, is beyond any prophetic light and without defect, for he is *comprehensor*. He does not, alas, fill in any argument as to how one can conclude to the existence of this light, this knowledge, in the first place. That is, he does not lay out for us the *via inveniendi*, the path that leads us from the first and easily known data of the Gospel to the human knowledge of Jesus as explanatory of that data.[22]

We get a glimpse of how the immediate knowledge of God in the soul of Christ works as an account of the datum of faith only by putting certain

---

[20] *Quaest. Disp. de Veritate*, q. 11, a. 2, c.

[21] *Lectura super Evangelium S. Ioannis* IV, 6 (no. 667); VI, 2 (no. 868). Paragraph numbers refer to the Marietti edition of 1952; they are the same for the English translation by J. Weisheipl and F. Larcher, *Commentary on the Gospel of John* (Albany, NY: Magi Books, 1980).

[22] See also at 1:14, *Lect.* I, 8 (no. 189); 1:18, *Lect.* I, 10 (no. 211); 3:11, *Lect.* III, 2 (no. 462); 13:31, *Lect.* XIII, 6 (no. 1830); and 17:8, *Lect.* XVII, 2 (no. 2201).

scattered things together. The bare assertion of the human knowledge of Christ as *comprehensor* as above is only one of these things. Two more things are needed. First, there is the principle that, as God, Christ is the Truth, but as man, the one who testifies to the truth before men.[23] And second, it is important to see that what St. Thomas concludes from the *teaching* of Jesus in John is commonly and in the first place the more fundamental truth of faith that Christ the Word is the Truth, that is, that he is the consubstantial Son of the Father.

As to the last, commenting on 7:29 ("I know him [the one who sent me] because I am from him, and he sent me"), St. Thomas argues as follows. A thing is known according as a similitude of it is in the knower. The perfect knowledge of the Father, however, can be based on no created similitude; such perfect knowledge can be grounded only on the perfect similitude that the Son is, as proceeding from the Father and as of the same essence as the Father. So much Christ tells us, when he says he is from him, the one who sent him, "as it were, having the same essence of nature with him by being one in substance with him."[24] The claim of Christ to know what he knows leads to an assertion of his divinity, since such knowledge is proportionate to the divine intellect alone. But of course, it is as a *man* that Christ says to us "I know him" and so on, and for this is required a human knowledge: "so also because of this, that the soul of Christ is united to the Word in a singular way, it has a singular and more excellent knowledge of God, beyond that of other creatures."[25]

Sometimes St. Thomas inserts the human knowledge of Christ as the required medium between his divine knowledge and his preaching, as at 17:8, where the two knowledges explain the mediatorship of Christ.[26] Other times, however, he does not, but simply presupposes it. At 17:25–26, he moves from the divine knowledge of Christ to the transmission of this knowledge through the exterior word of Christ's teaching.[27] At 15:15, likewise, he moves from the divine knowledge of Christ to the disciples' sharing of this knowledge, in that what Christ knows perfectly as the consubstantial Son, the disciples know imperfectly by faith.[28]

I think the foregoing explains what can otherwise disconcert, namely that in the *sed contra* to *Summa theologiae* III, q. 9, a. 2, establishing the fact of the human knowledge of Christ as *comprehensor*, St. Thomas adduces John 8:55, while in the commentary on that passage, St. Thomas argues

---

23 At 3:32, *Lect.* III, 5 (nos. 533–34), and at 4:45, *Lect.* IV, 6 (no. 667).

24 *Lect.* VII, 3 (no. 1065). And see the *Lectura super Evangelium S. Matthaei* XI, 3 (nos. 965–66).

25 *Lect. super Evang. Ioannis* VII, 3 (no. 1065).

26 *Lect.* XVII, 2 (no. 2201).

27 *Lect.* XVII, 6 (nos. 2267, 2269–70).

28 *Lect.* XV, 3 (no. 2017–18).

only to the divine knowledge of Christ—what he knows as the consubstantial Word—and nothing at all is said of his human knowledge.

In any case—and this is the point I wish to establish—the *ordo cognoscendi* is clear. What we know in faith we know because of the preaching of Christ. From that content, we may conclude to what he knows as man, in his human soul. But since that content either asserts or implies the identity of Christ as the Word of the Father, we conclude at last both to this identity and to the divine knowledge of Christ as God. And in this order of things, the theorem of the man Christ's immediate knowledge of God becomes evident as what it is: an account (part of the account) of the datum of faith, precisely as the datum is handed to our faith from the human preaching of the human Christ. Thus, St. Thomas knows Christ's beatific knowledge because it is required to explain the fact, recorded in the Gospels and grasped by faith, of what our Lord knows and tells us. The "principle of perfection" is not the reason St. Thomas knows the beatific knowledge of Christ. That principle is merely the theological glue of an argument *ex convenientia*, and in the absence of a metaphysical deduction, that serves as a bridge in the *ordo disciplinae* between a consideration of the soul of Christ and a consideration of the properties of that soul.

In what now follows, I want to show in relatively brief compass and an informal manner what line of questioning can lead us today to an appreciation of St. Thomas's account of the datum of faith that the International Theological Commission spells out. This itinerary is in part contained in Thesis XII of Bernard Lonergan's *De Verbo Incarnato*.[29] But I think it is important today to start the itinerary in the Synoptics rather than in John. Because of the common opinion as to the already heavily interpreted and theologized character of John, Lonergan's treatment has lost some of its persuasive character. This character, however, is easily restored.

A Contemporary Path to St. Thomas's Position

Suppose we ask the following questions:

Did Jesus know who he was?
Did Jesus know what he was doing?

where the answers to the questions:

Who was Jesus?
What did Jesus do?

already known to us as Christians and by faith, are:

---

[29] *De Verbo Incarnato* (Rome: Gregorian University, 1964).

He was the Son of God, the Second Person of the Trinity; and
He saved us all from sin by his passion and death and opened for us
the gates of heaven.[30]

Did Jesus know about himself what we know about him by faith? If we
put it like that, as I shall argue, the answer has certainly to be Yes.

Notice that we are not asking whether Jesus, who is the Logos, the
Second Person of the Trinity, knows by the divine nature with which his
person is identical who he is and what his mission as incarnate was. The
Logos, one in being with the Father (Nicaea), is also one in understanding
with the Father. And just as the Father knows all things, especially, his own
infinite intelligibility (which is the intelligibility of infinite being), and
knows this by an infinite act of understanding not distinct from himself,
nor from his infinite being, so also does the Logos.[31] The persons of the
Trinity are not distinct according to being, understanding, or will, for they
are the same infinite act of being, the same infinite act of understanding,
the same infinite act of willing.[32] They are distinct only according to the
opposed relations of Paternity-Filiation (the distinction of Father and Son)
and Breathing and Breathed (Father and Son distinct from Spirit).

Notice also that we are talking about the pre-Paschal Jesus. We are not
asking about what he knows through his fully glorified humanity after the
Resurrection, but what he knew while he lived his life, before he died.

So, we are not asking about the knowledge of Jesus qua divine, but
about the knowledge of Jesus qua human (and indeed, where the humanity of Jesus is not yet fully glorified). That is, we are asking whether the
Logos knows the things in question, not only through his divine nature,
but through his human nature. Does the human mind of the Logos (of
Jesus) know the things in question? Does Jesus know the things in question humanly, through (or in) his human understanding? As I say, the
answer to the question must be Yes. Why?

The International Theological Commission answers the questions
affirmatively on the basis of an "ecclesiastical-dogmatic" reading of the
New Testament, but one that, given the brevity of the statement, is not
indifferent to "historical-critical exegesis."[33] Another starting point there
cannot be, but it will be worth while to focus on a more particular ques-

---

30 There is also a third question that can be added to the first set of questions: Was
    Jesus conscious of himself, where consciousness, the internal experience of oneself
    prior to understanding, is something distinct from knowledge, and the self is the
    divine self that is the Logos? See Lonergan, *De Verbo Incarnato,* Thesis X.
31 *ST* I, q. 14, aa. 1–4.
32 *ST* I, q. 28, a. 2; q. 39, aa. 1 and 2.
33 "The Consciousness of Christ," 306–7.

tion embedded therein, namely, the question as to how we know who Jesus is and what he did.

How do we know these things? By faith, of course, the faith that comes from hearing (Rom 10:17). Nor does it do to stop with what we hear from the apostles and the inspired writers. For they know the answer to the questions only by faith, too. And whence was their hearing? Who spoke to them? I mean to suggest that we (and the apostles and whoever is a Christian) know these things only because Jesus himself so talked and so acted as to give it out that he was the Son of God, and was in the business of saving us. These are not the sorts of things we could know unless someone told us them.[34] He, Jesus, communicated these things to us.

Of course, he did not necessarily communicate these things to us in these terms.[35] But I rely here on the common fundamental theological reading of the New Testament, and especially on the sort of historical work of the "New Quest" exegetes, according to which we can discern in the words and actions of Jesus an, at least, implicit claim to be divine.[36] And I advert briefly to the most common and most historically defensible way of establishing this, namely Jesus' preaching of the nearness of the Kingdom of God.[37] If it is true that Jesus tells us that the Kingdom of

---

[34] For the same point, see Brian Davies in "Why Should We Believe It?" *New Blackfriars* 69 (1988): 365–66. See also Michael Dummett, "Unsafe Premises: A Reply to Nicholas Lash," *New Blackfriars* 68 (1987): 562–63; and John Lamont, "The Nature of Revelation," *New Blackfriars* 72 (1991): 335–45.

[35] Nor am I claiming that he did. This should go without saying, but some of the responses to Michael Dummett's "A Remarkable Consensus," *New Blackfriars* 68 (1987): 424–31, make it evident that it does not. For a list of responses and replies, see *New Blackfriars* 69 (1988): 544–45.

[36] See, for example, Hans Conzelmann, *Jesus* (Philadelphia, PA: Fortress Press, 1973), 49–50: "In deed and teaching, [Jesus] confronts the amazed people *directly* with God through himself. In his figure one can find traits of the prophet as well as of the rabbi. . . . The concepts of prophet and rabbi, however, express only a partial aspect and not exactly the core of the matter. Jesus understands himself as the one who makes the *final* appeal. His place is unique, since after him nothing more 'comes'—but God himself."

[37] See for what follows W. Kasper, *Jesus the Christ* (New York: Paulist, 1976), 100–104; J. Moltmann, *The Crucified God* (New York: Harper and Row, 1974), 121–22; W. Pannenberg, *Jesus—God and Man,* 2nd ed. (Philadelphia, PA: Westminster Press, 1977), 58–60. For recent exegetical treatment of Jesus' preaching of the Kingdom, see G. R. Beasley-Murray, *Jesus and the Kingdom of God* (Grand Rapids, MI: Eerdmanns, 1986), esp. his "Conclusion," with which I think my remarks are congruent.

I mean to suggest here that it is mistaken to look for the New Testament evidence that leads to the assertion of Christ's immediate knowledge of God in the way, say, that André Feuillet does in "La science de vision de Jésus et les Evangiles," *Doctor Communis* 36 (1983): 158–79. Feuillet pretty much reads off the immediate knowledge of Christ which has been traditionally recognized from a few Johannine

God is near, and if it is true that he expects his hearers to accept this in faith, and as guaranteed by his preaching it and by his presence—if, that is, he associates himself personally with the object of his teaching, the Kingdom, as the authoritative herald and guarantor of the presence of the Kingdom—then he is making a claim to be an eschatologically significant person. The anticipation of an eschatological event within time, namely his own Resurrection, confirms both his claim and his own importance in relation to that claim. And for the purposes of this essay, I shall assume that it is a short step from "eschatologically significant person," or "uniquely eschatologically significant person," to "divine Person," divine in the same sense that the God of the Old Testament is divine. What sort of person, after all, could so guarantee the presence of the Kingdom by his own word and presence so as to justify not only faith in that word, but such faith as has him, himself, for its object, as we see to be the case in the call of the disciples?[38] All this, or something like it, must be granted.

What it is necessary to dwell on for the purposes of this essay, however, is the following; namely, that some such at least implicit claim on the part of Jesus seems to be required for the reasonability of our faith. This can be seen if we put it like this: If we can tell on the basis of his words and actions who he was, what he was up to, how could Jesus not know? Could we know this if he did not make a claim to be who he is? And if he in no way knows the "implicit claim" he is making, then he is not making any claim.

The situation seems to be as follows: He talks and acts in such a way that we see he must be divine and our savior. He does not say he is divine. But we see that the intelligibility of his talk and action is such. We "see" this in the way only of reinterpreting what he is claiming in his words and actions, as couched in the categories of the Old Testament and of intertestamental theology, in other, and sometimes non-scriptural and systematic categories, as when we read the scriptures across Nicaea. Could it be that Jesus gave out this intelligibility of his talk and action unintelligently, as it were, unconsciously? Is it that we are claiming to understand him better than he understood himself? He did not really know who he was, but we

---

passages (1:18; 3:11–13) as well as Mt 11:27. It is not so much that this is wrong as it is misleading. We may conclude in such a way to what the Gospels teach about what Jesus knew, but to conclude to the immediate knowledge of God such as this is traditionally understood requires a theory about what knowledge is. If one is working strictly as an historian, one will conclude only to that datum of faith described by the International Theological Commission. It is like trying to find the homoousios in the New Testament. It is there in a way, and not there in another way. If it were there in the way that a historian could find it, Nicaea would have been unnecessary.

38 For the call of the disciples, see Kasper, *Jesus the Christ*, 102–3; Moltmann, *The Crucified God*, 54–55.

know? He did not really know what he was doing, but we do? No; it is more like someone's saying *X* and *Y* to us, and our responding, "I get it; what you are really saying is *Z*." It is not that we are inferring something about him that he did not know; we are rather changing categories, interpreting what he gave out in his speech and actions in other categories. Where he says "Son of man" (or whatever), we say "divine Person."

In other words, he did not communicate these things to us the way a drunk communicates to us that he is drunk (he may not know he is drunk, he may deny it), or the way a paranoid schizophrenic communicates to us that he is a paranoid schizophrenic (he does not think he is crazy). It is not that the words and actions of Jesus are pieces of data, "behavior," of which we seek an intelligibility unknown to Jesus himself. Rather, his words and actions are formally communicative of who he is, what he did. It is not that we infer Jesus' identity and mission from his words and actions; we learn them from his words and actions because that is their meaning, and he is the mean-er of this meant. It is not like deducing that the butler did it from the clues that he unintentionally left behind; it is like knowing the butler did it because he told us he did it.

Again, consider that Jesus' saving us was a moral act. Moral acts are intelligently done. If his saving us was a moral act, then he did not perform it without knowing what he was doing. Did he save us mechanically—without the engagement of his mind and heart? Did he do things like a robot?

If we think of things in this way, then the answer has to be that he knew the answer to the questions of who he was and what he was doing, else he could not have acted and spoken in such a way that we know the answers to these questions. Are we to suppose he thought he was doing something else than saving us, but that, as the unintended consequence of his action, that is what happened? But then, in an important sense, he did not save us, and his action is not correctly described by saying he did. His saving us becomes like somebody's accidentally "doing" something. I reach for the sweater on the hook and I knock down the lamp. "I knocked down the lamp." On the other hand, this is not what I intended: I intended to get the sweater—that was my action. But I was clumsy and also knocked down the lamp. This is quite different from knocking down the lamp because I am tired of looking at the ugly thing and want to break it. I am blamed for knocking down the lamp differently according to the two situations. And in fact, we might say, if Jesus saved us unintentionally, without really meaning to, unconsciously, then we can blame him for our salvation, but we cannot really thank him the way we do.

Consider, finally, that if God does not save us from sin through Christ insofar as Christ acts consciously, intelligently, like a human being operating at the highest level of human operation, with what is proper to a human being, then why the Incarnation? Why pick the "instrument" of the human-ity of Jesus, if it is not really going to be used for what it is?[39]

⸭ ⸭ ⸭

Now, if it must needs be that we know who Jesus is and because he knew, then the question to ask is:

How did he know? In what manner? with what kind of "knowledge"?

But we should once more think of ourselves: How do we know who he is and what he did?

According to the foregoing, we know because he told us. That is, we know by what is called faith, where faith is "taking something as so on some-one's word that it is so." And indeed, we can say that we know by *divine* faith, where divine faith is "taking something as so on a divine Person's word that it is so." What is it that we are taking as so? That Jesus is divine, and that he saved us. And we are taking this on his word. We take this on his word, moreover, precisely as it is the self-authenticating word of God, of Jesus apprehended as God. So, we have what we are taking to be so by divine faith; that is, we believe that Jesus is who he is, that he did what he did.

We must now ask whether Jesus himself knows what he knows by faith, divine or human, or in some other way. Our language is sometimes confusing at this point. We can speak of "knowing by faith," and this is perfectly good usage. Sometimes, however, it is useful to distinguish knowledge and faith, and that is what we shall do in what follows. Faith is taking something on someone's word; knowledge is a matter of understand-ing the thing and knowing the truth of it "on one's own," so to speak. It is the difference between knowing the Pythagorean theorem because one has proved it for oneself—understood it, and verified the equation—and tak-ing it on a geometer's word. We will keep *faith* for the latter, and *knowl-edge* for the former.[40]

Thus, to rephrase: Did Jesus have it that he was who he was and did what he was doing by faith or by knowledge?

The only way to answer this question is to examine the New Testa-ment. In the Gospel of John, the answer is perfectly and abundantly plain: He knew; he did not have the things in question on faith. Rather, faith is what he asks of men—and he asks it on the ground that he knows, and is telling them so in a manner worthy of their credence.[41]

---

[39] See *ST* III, q. 9, a. 1, c, 2nd arg.

[40] See *ST* II–II, q. 1, aa. 4 and 5.

[41] For faith on the part of those who hear Jesus, have faith in him, and believe that he is the Son of God, see Jn 3:15, 16, 18, 36; 6:29, 35, 40, 47; 7:38, 39; 8:24; 11:25, 26; 13:19; 14:10, 11, 12. For Jesus as knowing, see Jn 3:11; 6:46; 7:28, 29 (and

Some people do not like to rely on John for such things. What is asserted in these Johannine formulations, however, finds expression in the Synoptics, in such places as those where it is remarked that Jesus teaches with authority, not like the scribes.[42] Jesus does not act like one who believes, or one who is a prophet, in the Synoptics. In the Sermon on the Mount, he does not say, "Thus saith the Lord," but "I say."

This is only what we should expect. We are the sick; Jesus is the physician. We are sinners; Jesus is sinless and saves us from sin. We are disciples; Jesus is the master. We have all gone astray like sheep; he is the Lamb of God who takes away the sins of the world. Or, we are sheep; but he is the Good Shepherd. We are branches; he is the vine. We are the hungry; he is the Bread of Life. So also, we are the ones who have faith; he is the one who knows. And after all, as Bernard Lonergan remarks, "where all believe and no one knows, no one believes reasonably."[43] Someone must know, or belief is vain.

Of course, there are also all those passages in John where our Lord says that he has "heard" or "received" all that he has from the Father. St. Augustine, when he reads the Gospel of John, says that certain things must be understood of the divinity, and other things of the humanity of Christ.[44] He takes these passages in John as referring to the divinity. That our Lord has "heard" from the Father all that he speaks is a matter of his being from the Father, being the Son, having his whole reality in being generated and spoken by the Father.[45] However, as Lonergan remarks, one ought not suppose that the author of the Fourth Gospel applies the distinction between Christ qua God and Christ qua man, intending in this way to demarcate the subject of his predications, since this distinction is the work of patristic reflection.[46] Therefore, where these predications can be understood both of the Second Person of the Trinity and of the man Jesus Christ, they ought to be. Therefore, while St. Augustine's interpretation ought to stand, it is incomplete, and we must say also that Christ as a man, and in his properly human knowledge, "hears" and "receives" all he knows from his Father. And since faith also seems to be a hearing and a reception, this should make us think once again whether what Christ holds as true is not a matter of faith rather than of knowledge.

5:37); 8:38, 54, 55; 10:15. See Lonergan, *De Verbo Incarnato*, 386–387; J. Alfaro, *Esistenza Cristiana* (Rome: Gregorian University, 1979), 55–66.

[42] See, for example, Mk 1:22, 27; 6:2; 9:23, 24. And see Mt 11:27.

[43] *De Verbo Incarnato*, 391.

[44] *Homilies on the Gospel of John* XXI, 7; XXXVI, 2; XCIX, 1; CVI, 5; CVII, 5. Section numbers are as in the Oxford translation.

[45] Ibid. XVIII, 9–10; XX, 8; XXI, 4; XL, 5; XLVII, 14, CVI, 7. See also St. Thomas, for example, *Lect. super Evang. Ioannis* III, 5 (no. 534).

[46] *De Verbo Incarnato*, 388.

This brings us to the third difficulty in approaching St. Thomas's position mentioned at the beginning of this essay. For indeed, it seems that it is just this very character of what our Lord holds as received that induces some modern interpreters to impute faith to Christ, and to find in him the model of our faith. So, for example, Gerhard Ebeling, in a remarkable passage on Jesus' use of "amen," ordinarily a word of response to something that is heard, concludes to the faith of Christ.[47] Moreover, since trust and fidelity are important elements of New Testament *pistis*,[48] and since we are to recognize in Christ a trust in and obedience to his Father, there seems all the more reason to discern in Jesus the model of the faith of Christians, and this in spite of the fact that nowhere in the New Testament is faith explicitly imputed to Jesus.[49]

Neither of these arguments, however, is coercive. Christ's knowledge would not necessarily preclude trust in and obedience to God.[50] That is, the trust and obedience of Christ do not mean that, in the required sense of "taking something that one does not see to be the case on the word of another." He is in our position of believing, and not in the position of one

---

[47] Gerhard Ebeling, "Jesus and Faith," in *Word and Faith* (Philadelphia, PA: Fortress, 1963), 236–38. Thus in part, Jesus' use of "amen" gives expression "to the fact that Jesus understood his statements, and wished to have them understood, as statements made before God, in which God himself is the Guarantor of what is said . . . [as well as] to the fact that Jesus identifies himself entirely with his words, that in the identification with these words he surrenders himself to the reality of God, and that he lets his existence be grounded on God's making these words true and real. That means, he is so certain of these words that he stakes his whole self on that certainty. And this absolute certainty that puts his whole existence at stake is so much the decisive thing in Jesus' proclamation that he sometimes begins with *amnv* as a sort of slogan to mark the tenor of the whole."

[48] Alfaro, *Esistenza Cristiana*, 2–24.

[49] This is commonly recognized, even by those who wish to impute faith to Jesus. See Jacques Guillet, *La Foi de Jésus-Christ* (Paris: Desclée, 1980), 15. Guillet rounds up all the passages that seem to impute faith to Jesus. For the most important, where we have the Pauline *pistis Christou*, see p. 17: "Christ" designates the person of Jesus not as the object of faith, nor as exercising faith, but as evoking and inaugurating faith. See also G. E. Howard, "Notes and Observations on the 'Faith of Christ,'" *Harvard Theological Review* 60 (1967): 459–65, for whom this *pistis Christou* is the faithfulness of Christ.

[50] For Lonergan's solution to this problem, see *De Verbo Incarnato*, Thesis 15, the sixth part of the argument: Since Christ's knowledge of God extends only to the actual economy of salvation, but does not encompass the whole of what it is possible for the divine wisdom to order and the divine power to effect, Christ can be truly obedient to his Father with that kind of obedience that does not see why the command is the best command in the circumstances. See *ST* III, q. 10, a. 1.

who knows.[51] So also with the character of what our Lord holds as true as something received. This is to be admitted. However, what is granted to the human mind of Christ concerning his identity and his work can be just that, something granted. This does not mean that what is granted is not granted in its evidentness. Further, then, as to the very receptivity or passivity of faith, Christ can still be recognized as the model of faith, notwithstanding that he knows, for perhaps it is the case that what he knows as a creature depends on a greater receptiveness, a greater passivity before the always greater God, than does our faith.[52]

If we stop at this point, then we stop just about where the statement of the International Theological Commission leaves us. Indeed, we have gone one small step beyond the statement, by distinguishing knowledge from faith in the section just preceding, for the Commission leaves it quite open as to how to characterize the "consciousness" of Christ. Still, it is really only our next question that moves us into the "theological elaboration"

---

51 For a resolution of matters along these lines, see L. Malevez, "Le Christ et la foi," in *Pour une théologie de la foi* (Paris: Desclée, 1969), 159–216, esp. 170–71, 175–77. However, Malevez thinks that the freedom and trust of Jesus require a real not-knowing on the level of objectivated knowledge, notwithstanding a real "vision" of something at least of his role in the economy of salvation that is unthematic and, as with Rahner, an immediate ontological effect of the hypostatic union. The faith-trust of Jesus is his existentielle ratification of the ontic abandonment of the human nature of Christ, which lacks a created act of existence, to the divine act of existence.

52 For St. Thomas, there is an important sense in which God is the only teacher. So in the *Lectura super Evangelium S. Matthaei* XXIII, 1 (no. 1848): "It must be said that he is properly called teacher who has his teaching from himself, not he who spreads a teaching received from someone else to others. And thus there is only one teacher, namely God, who properly has a teaching; but ministerially, there are many teachers." Thus, even Christ, knowing God in his humanity, is a teacher only ministerially, and teaches only what he receives in his human mind from the vision of God vouchsafed him. Further, it should be noted that the light of glory, for which see below, is a perfection of the possible intellect, as St. Thomas says in the *Quaest. Disp. de Veritate*, q. 20, a. 2, ad 5. Every act of understanding is a perfection of the possible intellect, however, and understanding is a *pati*, as Lonergan never tired of pointing out. But for those sciences proportioned to the human intellect, the sciences of material things, these things are in a way made intelligible for us by the light of the agent intellect—that is, by our active and strenuous inquiry. No matter that we are receiving the intelligibilities of things that are intelligible only as similitudes of God, human science thus has the character of something achieved, accomplished, *made* by us. But if what our Lord holds as true has none of this character of the acquired, achieved, made, this does not mean that it ceases to be *scientia*—according as knowledge here means understanding the thing in itself in its own intelligibility—and is rather to be described as faith.

that the Commission resolutely avoids. The further question is as follows. If Jesus has the things he does by knowledge, and not by faith, how shall we think of this knowing of his? It is at this point that the nature of the objects known as well as the nature of knowing itself become crucial.

Let us take up that last point first, and face the second difficulty in appreciating St. Thomas's position listed in the introduction to this essay. If we think of knowledge as "justified (evident, warranted) true belief," then we are pretty much thinking of knowledge as the justified holding of a proposition as true.[53] If we do this, as with Alvin Plantinga and other proponents of so-called reformed epistemology, then there will be no good reason to distinguish faith and knowledge as we did in the previous section.[54] If I am justified in taking the word of my geometer friend that Pythagoras was right, then we shall have to count both the geometer and me as knowers. And we shall likewise be unable to distinguish Jesus as a knower from his disciples as believers.

If we are going to be able to distinguish, we shall have to continue to think of knowing as understanding the object known. And we shall have to try to think what this knowledge, as understanding, *is,* which is by no means an easy thing to do. Aristotle tried to do this when he said that knowledge is the identity in act of knower and known.[55] To know some-

---

53 For an introduction to the early stage of the contemporary analysis of knowledge as justified true belief, see Michael D. Roth and Leon Galis, eds., *Knowing: Essays in the Analysis of Knowledge,* 2nd ed. (New York: University Press of America, 1984).

54 See Alvin Plantinga, *The Twin Pillars of Christian Scholarship* (Grand Rapids, MI: Calvin College and Seminary, n.d.), 41–56. Plantinga knows the distinction between faith and knowledge such as I have outlined it above, but thinks it vicious, since granting it means that very little of what we hold as true is knowledge (58–60). The implication that very little of what we hold as true is to be counted as knowledge pure and unalloyed with faith (human or divine) is to be granted. There is also, of course, a sense of "knowledge" according to which we know what we reasonably and responsibly believe. This is the sense of St. Thomas's *cognitio* as distinct from *scientia* in, for example, *ST* I, q. 12, a. 13, ad 3: "fides cognitio quaedam est, inquantum intellectus determinatur per fidem ad aliquod cognoscibile. Sed haec determinatio ad unum non procedit ex visione credentis . . . et sic . . . deficit a ratione cognitionis quae est in scientia."

55 *De anima,* 430a3–5. There is, however, a path from "justified true belief," the third definition of knowledge in the *Theaetetus* (201C–D), to "identity in act of knower and known." First, the third definition of the *Theaetetus,* and where the "justification" or "account" of the thing known is said to be its difference from all else (208C), is rejected because Socrates introduces a learning paradox with regard to knowledge, and where the object is a sensible, material individual (209A–210A). The conclusion ought to be that such things are not the object of knowledge. Congruently, Aristotle's definition is for "objects which involve no matter." Second, something prior to belief, propositionally expressed, is to be recognized. This is suggested by *Theaetetus* 191C–D, where the mind is compared to

thing is to be that something. It is not to be it as it is under all the conditions of its own existence. But it is to be it "formally;" that is, it is to be
the thing by giving existence to its "idea," to its intelligibility, in oneself.
Predicates of propositions report this intelligibility as lived by the knower,
but they are posterior to it. Moreover, it is to be wondered whether, if
what we know depends on our being able to report it in propositions,
there are some things that cannot be known.

Indeed, the question of the kind of thing we are supposing our Lord
to know is just as crucial as what we think knowing is. For how is it with
the things we are saying that Jesus knew? It would seem that their nature
is strictly supernatural, where the nature that these things are said to surpass is not only human nature but any created nature whatsoever. The
things known, in other words, are things naturally proportioned to the
divine mind alone.

We must think briefly of just what these things are. Jesus knows who
he is. And he is the Son of God. We can rephrase this by saying that for all
intents and purposes Jesus knows the mystery of the Trinity—and does
not simply believe, as we do, that God is Triune. When we believe that
God is Triune, the propositions in which we express this belief do duty for
the Idea of the thing, for perfect identity in act with the intelligibility of
the Triune God.[56] Our holding these propositions as true is justified if we
think that a divine person has given them to us to hold as true. That he
has told us is sufficient justification for our holding them. However, we
are at the point where we want to say that Jesus did not hold them by
faith, as we do, but knew of what he was speaking.

To know such a thing as the Triune God—meaning, to understand it
in itself and properly—and where knowing is being one in act with the

---

a block of wax on which ideas are imprinted, and which becomes Aristotle's writing tablet (430a1–2), the mind that is potentially all things. To become something, however, to think the definition of something, is to think its constitutive
essence (430b27–28); but essence is especially form, which it is the point of *Metaphysics* Z to sort out in its two careers, in that, introduced into matter, it is the substantial principle of the individual material substance; introduced into mind, it is
the principle of knowledge.

The point of this note is that criticism of the contemporary career of "justified
true belief" is not criticism of Plato. Plato and Aristotle are far closer on what knowledge is than Lonergan sometimes suggests.

56 For the proposition as a substitute for intuition or idea, see Joseph Maréchal, *A
Maréchal Reader*, ed. Joseph Donceel (New York: Herder & Herder, 1970), 156ff.
The implicit affirmation of being as real and intelligible implied in every judgment
is the substitute for the intuition of being that is the end of our intellectual
dynamism. This is most evident, however, where the affirmation is of some analogically understood predicate of God, for there the particular judgment has itself to
do expressly, and not just implicitly, with absolutely intelligible Being.

object known, would seem to require an infinite act of understanding, proportioned to the infinite reality of the object understood. It seems therefore impossible to attribute knowledge of such a thing to Christ, for the reason that our minds, all created minds, including the human mind of Christ, are finite. Human minds are first of all only potentially identical in act with what they know. They become actually one with what they know only according as they receive some representation of the object known (St. Thomas's "similitude" or "species"). By definition, however, there can be no finite representation that properly represents something infinitely intelligible.[57] Therefore, there is no naturally infinite act of understanding that a finite mind can enjoy.

We should also think of the basic and original content of Jesus' preaching: "The Kingdom of God is at hand." If he asks us to believe this, but himself *knows* it, how could he know such a thing except knowing what is in the divine mind and wisdom for the salvation of men? How can someone know this unless for all intents and purposes he knows in just the way the divine mind does? How could he *know* this decision (and not just believe it or have information about it) unless he sees it in the ordering wisdom of God?

"In just the way the divine mind does." How can a human mind, for our question is of Jesus' human knowledge, know "in just the way the divine mind does"? If it cannot, then there is nothing more to be said here, and there must be some mistake in our preceding considerations.

It is just here that we arrive at very subtle point in St. Thomas's account of the human knowledge of Christ. How can a human mind know in the way the divine mind does? St. Thomas does not think we really know the answer to this question. To know this we should have already to be knowing in the divine way, and as long as we are in this life, we are not doing that. We are walking by faith, not by sight. We have the promise of eternal life, and suppose that it consists in knowing both the Father and Jesus Christ whom he has sent (Jn 17:3). But we do not understand any of this yet in a full and adequate way. The idea that we, and our Lord in his humanity, can know God in God's way of knowing himself is just as much an object of faith as is what our Lord tells us, such things as we collect in the creed and give such names as "the doctrine of the Trinity."

"Knowing God in God's way," the end state of our knowledge as Christians, a state St. Thomas imputes to Christ in his earthly life, is what is called "the beatific vision." By this is meant an immediate knowledge of God as he is in himself, the finite mind's sharing in the infinite act of understanding the infinite intelligibility that God is. That such a thing could happen, however, is not known except to faith, and the idea of it is

---

57 *ST* I, q. 12, a. 2.

therefore just as much a sort of limit or "analogical" idea—indeed an "ana-gogical" idea—as is the idea we have of God, or of the Trinity, or of the Incarnation. All St. Thomas really has to say about it is this: That if no cre-ated similitude of God could really give us knowledge of him as he knows himself to be, then this knowledge does not happen by way of a created similitude; rather, the divine being itself is what is immediately present to the created mind.[58]

The idea of such a state of affairs is an odd one. We can talk about the "light of glory" modifying our mind if we wish, but to mention it is noth-ing more than to say that we trust God so to arrange things that, whatever it takes to get a finite mind ready to be immediately present to God, he manages to do. On the other hand, there does not seem to be anything expressly contradictory about the state of affairs in question.[59] And to sup-pose that such a state of affairs exists, and exists for the earthly Jesus, solves the problem of how he can know the things he tells us. Or rather, it sim-ply expresses the datum of faith in a context where some thought has been given to the nature of knowledge.

If the immediate presence of God to the human mind of Christ is the only condition under which he could know such things as he told us in his life, then it follows that he enjoyed this same immediate knowledge of God as we hope to enjoy in heaven. That is the whole point of talking about his "beatific knowledge" of God while he was on earth.

Certain difficult questions immediately suggest themselves, however. When we talk about the immediate knowledge of God, we are talking about something that is non-propositional, non-conceptual, and, in that respect, ineffable. For we can say—speak—only that for which we have ideas for. And yet we are supposing that our Lord delivers this knowledge to us, insofar as it can be delivered to us, in human terms. He speaks what is unspeakable. How, then, are we to think the relation between these two kinds of knowledge?

It is because of what Jesus the man communicates to us, and communi-cates to us authoritatively, we have said, that we are led to say that he knows these things. The things turn out to be things that cannot be known by a human mind unless that mind "sees God"—that is, share in the infinite act of understanding by which God himself in his divine nature understands and knows all things. But then, it turns out that knowing things in this way is to know them non-conceptually, ineffably. So, the question arises, even if, as a man, he did know the things in ques-tion by sharing in the understanding of the divine mind, what good

---

58 Ibid.
59 For the defense of this, see especially the *Summa contra Gentiles* III, c. 51.

would it do? How could this ineffable knowledge get put into speech, so as to be communicated to us?

It is important here to stress the ineffability of what our Lord might know in his human mind by that mind's sharing in the understanding of the divine mind. For a man to understand something effably—speakably—is to have conceptual knowledge of it. Our concepts, properly, are suited to dealing with the sensible things of this world. By them, we distinguish one thing from another, relate one thing to another. Because they are expressions of the intelligibilities of sensible things, they can themselves have expression in sensible words. But God's understanding of himself is an understanding of an infinite intelligibility; such understanding is not suitably expressed in concepts that are fitted to the expression of finite things that are what they are only by not being other things. God is not what he is by not being other things—he would be what he is and as he is even if all the other things that are were not. Again, the intelligibility of God is not the intelligibility of a sensible thing.[60]

Of course, in one way, there is no problem. It is not as if our Lord tries to communicate to us what God is in himself. His giving out to us who he is, and his giving out to us that the Kingdom is present (with all that means) is not a giving out of the essence of God. It is a giving out of certain facts about God concerning his Tri-Personal life and concerning the plan of salvation, such facts as cannot be known, fully understood, unless one sees God. But simply to affirm that God is Triune (which we imperfectly understand but nonetheless affirm in imperfectly understanding but yet affirming who Jesus is, the Son of the Father, united with him in one Spirit) is not to understand what God is. Simply to affirm that the Kingdom is at hand is not to understand what God is either. Nor is it to see the infinite wisdom of the plan of God of which the presence of the Kingdom at Jesus' time, in Jesus, is a principal part. It is ("merely") to affirm that our destiny is intimacy with God; it is to affirm that God forgives the sin that would otherwise impede us from reaching our destiny; it is to affirm that we share in this intimacy even now according as we repent and believe in the Gospel. Furthermore, an analogical understanding of God and his decision and action is sufficient understanding for our ability to affirm these things.

So, it is not as if what our Lord communicates to us is, *per impossibile,* the Idea of God.[61] Still, there is a problem. If our Lord knows all these things as a man in an act of understanding God (and the decisions and

[60] Lonergan, *De Verbo Incarnato,* 334. For God as not what he is by not being other things, see Robert Sokolowski, *The God of Faith and Reason* (Notre Dame, IN: University of Notre Dame Press, 1982), the first four chapters.

[61] See *ST* I, q. 12, a. 11.

actions of God—the decisions and actions of the three Persons), and if this understanding as such is strictly inexpressible in human concepts and language, then how does what our Lord understands by sharing in the understanding of God get into expressible, analogical form, so as to be communicated to us?

There are other questions to be asked, as well. If our Lord knows all things already in seeing God, does this not count against his "being like us in all things but sin"? For then how does he know things the way we do, and how could he learn anything? That is a second question. And third, since this knowledge is supposed to make one perfectly happy, how could he suffer anything?

The last question is more easily dealt with than is sometimes thought. One of the reasons for speaking about our Lord's human knowledge of God as immediate and not beatific is precisely to avoid the imputation that, as perfectly happy, he could not suffer anything. Still, the problem is not to be got rid of by a terminological device. The immediate knowledge of God is, one supposes, something that, as a super-perfection of our humanity, and of our intellectual desire, makes us happy.

However, posing of the question in the abstract—How can one be happy and sad at the same time?—has the unfortunate consequence of deflecting attention from our own sometimes quite complicated experience. Are we not in fact sometimes happy and sad at the same time? Am I not both happy and sad at the same time to send my friend off to Europe? I am happy in the prospect of his education and enjoyment; I am sad to think I cannot share the common life of friends with him for the next months. It would be very mistaken to think happiness and sadness here are an alternation of acts; no, it is the abiding presence at the same time of two affective states. And lovers, after all, sometimes claim to experience at the same time what in the abstract can only be described as contradictory affective states. Furthermore, it is sometimes the very presence of our happiness in the possession of some good that increases our sorrowfulness over some evil. This is something well within our ordinary experience.

Thus, is it really so strange to hold that our Lord's identification with the experience of our alienation from God as sinners, which is partially, at least, what it means to say he loves us while we are still enemies of God (Rom 5:8), and which it is the concern of many moderns to impute to him, should coexist with his beatifying immediate knowledge of God? It is rather because of Christ's abiding love for his Father—a love the human perfection of which is radically a function of his immediate knowledge of the Father— he can be all the more sorrowful unto death at the sin for which he dies, at sinners for whom he dies, and at the consequences of sin, even the most interior, that he bears in identifying himself in love with sinners.[62]

As to the second question. How can Jesus learn anything if he enjoys the immediate knowledge of God, in whom the intelligibility of all created things is already contained? The answer would seem to be that he cannot, if learning means discovering an intelligibility that is not already possessed in the mind. However, it is to be denied that "perfect in manhood" implies sharing in the imperfect states and processes that lead to what a supernaturally perfected humanity consists in, one of which is the knowing in not-knowing of ordinary learning.

Moreover, this does not mean that no learning whatsoever is to be attributed to our Lord. That our Lord knows God immediately does not automatically mean that he can say what he knows. And yet, the point of the Incarnation is precisely that: to say to us what he knows. If he cannot learn what to say, he must still learn how to say it. This kind of learning, moreover, is not something wholly outside our experience, as anyone who has tried to explain something in a foreign language is well aware of.[63]

But then, we are returned to our first question: how to think more exactly the relation between the immediate and ineffable knowledge of our Lord and that knowledge by which he can say to us, analogically, what he knows. It is this problem that especially concerned Bernard Lonergan, for on its solution depends our ability to conceive the human subjectivity of Christ as something ordered and unified, rather than as a collection of unrelated knowledges (and volitions), beatific and acquired.[64]

His solution depends on a prior identification of the principle of unity in ordinary human subjectivity, and on a prior identification of the principle of unity in Christian subjectivity. What are these principles? For created human subjectivity, this principle is the "light of the agent intellect." For Christian subjectivity, this principle is the "light of faith." As the light of the agent intellect is a created participation in the First Light, God, so the light of faith is an increased, but supernatural, participation therein. The limit of such increased supernatural participation is, of course, the "light of glory" that renders the mind able to see God.

> Therefore, what the natural light of the intellect and the light of faith
> do in us, that is what the immediate knowledge of God did in Christ
> the man. What is ineffable in us, the expression of which is our life,
> is that light in which all knowledge is originally impressed on us, by

---

[62] Lonergan, *De Verbo Incarnato,* 340.

[63] Ibid., 342–44.

[64] Ibid., 405ff. Here, if anywhere, I think, Lonergan might be said to go beyond anything St. Thomas says.

which we naturally desire to have an essential knowledge of being, and therefore of God.[65]

This requires some comment, for we will understand the analogy only according as we understand what the light of the agent intellect is. The natural light, then, is in the first place the native and consciously operative intellectual desire in virtue of which we ask discrete questions as to the intelligibility of this or that thing, as to the truth of this or that judgment. In Lonergan's formulation, it is the intention of being as intending,[66] where being is what is known by understanding and judgment, where to speak of the intention of being as intending indicates the tension that the human mind is, its stretch from desire that is originally empty to a fullness of possession that would understand the whole of the real, the way stations on the way to which are our understandings of now this, now that, now the other being or limited region of the real. He indicates in the text just quoted that this light is "ineffable," because what is effable, speakable, are the discrete realities that we sense and understand and affirm in virtue of the light. The "light" itself, however, is our intention of the complete intelligibility of all that is. As intention, the light is prior to expression, which is accomplished in concept and language. Further, just as in this life we lack the ability to express the object of this intention completely and adequately, so, with regard to the very intending itself, we are reduced to speaking about it analogically. "All knowledge is originally impressed on us" by this light, for it is the principle of our knowing whatever it is we do come to know. Lonergan continues:

> But what was ineffable in Christ the man, the expression of which was the human life of Christ, was the divine Word itself, immediately known. Therefore, where we operate by moving from the intention of the end unto the end to be attained, Christ the man, from the end that was possessed, seen, and loved, shared out goodness; which sharing out, indeed, was in the first place his human and historical life itself, and in the second place included all those things that Christ did through his life.[67]

Thus the basic analogy Lonergan offers is as follows. As in our lives the principle of their unity insofar as they are truly human, that is, intelligently lived lives, is the light of the agent intellect. As in a Christian life the principle of its unity, insofar as it truly is and becomes ever more truly Christian, is the light of faith, so in Christ the unity of his life is the ineffable and immediate knowledge of God, which seeks not to know, but to

---

[65] Ibid., 406.
[66] *De constitutione Christi*, no. 3.
[67] *De Verbo Incarnato*, 406.

find expression, for our salvation's sake, in the words and deeds of a complete human life.

Of course, the basic analogy is only that, a foundation. One will understand more exactly and concretely (but still imperfectly) what the relation is between Christ's knowledge of God and his action and preaching according as one has some understanding of the relation in us between the light of the agent intellect and the innumerable discrete acts of inquiry and verification that are the instruments of the fulfillment of our intellectual desire.

> Still, you will ask how Christ the man proceeded from the ineffable to the effable knowledge. But in the first place, one must ask how the scientist proceeds to understanding, how the philosopher proceeds to truth, how the saint proceeds to a holy life; for he who seeks understanding does not yet understand, he who seeks the truth does not yet possess it, he who still has to achieve a holy life is not yet a saint; all of whom, however, already know in a certain way what they desire and so can recognize it when they attain to it. To which men Christ was in a certain way similar, and in a certain way not. For he was not like them insofar as, having already gained the end, he immediately knew God; but he was like them insofar as all his human powers and capacities—as it were, a vacuum to be filled—strove to that point such that they might render effable what was possessed in an ineffable way within the same consciousness.[68]

It is time to conclude. Why is St. Thomas's account of the datum of faith important? Evidently, the International Theological Commission is concerned simply to affirm the datum of faith: Jesus knew who he was and what he was doing. Why, beyond that, is it important to attribute to Christ in his humanity an immediate knowledge of God? One answer is simply to advert to the relative necessity of systematic theology, of faith seeking understanding, a necessity relative only to those who ask about the conditions of the possibility of what faith grasps. Not all believers ask systematic questions. On the other hand, the Roman magisterium does not enter idly into questions of systematic theology. And it has entered into this question.[69]

Even so, what is the religious import of St. Thomas's account? Here, we must think what it means to call Christ "Teacher." "You have one Teacher, the Christ" (Mt 23:10).

Socrates, our other teacher, claimed to know only that he did not know. He taught by asking, but not answering, questions, the cumulative

---

[68] Ibid., 407.

[69] For example, *DS* 3433–35 (*Lamentabili*, 1907); *DS* 3646–47 (Decree of the Holy Office, 1918); *DS* 3812 *(Mystici Corporis)*.

import of which practice was simply to commend to us the philosophic—but basically human—task of commending ourselves in wonder to the mystery of being, and to the mystery of ourselves as both open to but never perfectly possessed of being.

Is our Lord like Socrates? Is that the way in which he is a teacher? What is the same about them is that they are both men. But what is different about them is to be found in comparing the *daimon* of Socrates to a Father who is not hoped or wished for, not hypothesized nor intended across some absence, but known.[70]

---

[70] See the great comparison between Christ and Socrates as teachers in Kierkegaard's *Philosophical Fragments*, where the contrast is between remembering what we already in some way know and hearing something new that we have never known.

CHAPTER **6**

St. Anselm, *Satisfactio,* and the *Rule* of St. Benedict

LTHOUGH a general influence of monastic thought and practice upon the thought of St. Anselm of Canterbury has been asserted by historian R. W. Southern,[1] Hans Urs von Balthasar is to my knowledge the only theologian who has convincingly related this monastic consciousness to a significant part of Anselm's theological work, namely his theology of satisfaction.

"Anselm's aesthetic reason," Balthasar writes, "which considers the mystery of salvation, is ultimately monastic reason."[2] Just as monastic obedience is owed to God because freely vowed, but is not required as a true debt on the basis of a divine command, Balthasar explains, so for Anselm were Christ's suffering and death owed because freely willed by Christ, yet were not required because not strictly speaking the payment of a debt.[3] Thus, Christ renders satisfaction to God for sin; he does not unwillingly undergo the consequences of sin—that is, he is not punished.[4]

---

[1] R. W. Southern, *Saint Anselm and His Biographer* (Cambridge: Cambridge University Press, 1963), xi, 30.

[2] Hans Urs von Balthasar, *The Glory of the Lord: A Theological Aesthetics,* vol. 2: *Studies in Theological Style, Part 2: Clerical Styles,* trans. A. Louth et al. (San Francisco: Ignatius Press, 1984), 251.

[3] See the summary statement in *Cur Deus homo* (hereafter *CDH*), II, 18, in *S. Anselmi Cantuarensis Archiepiscopi Opera Omnia,* ed. F. S. Schmitt (Edinburgh: Thomas Nelson, 1946), 2:129: "debuit [Christus] facere quod fecit, quia quod voluit fieri debuit; et non debuit facere, quia non ex debito." And cf. *CDH,* I, 9 and 10. Schmitt's edition of Anselm's works is hereafter cited as Schmitt, with volume, page, and line numbers.

[4] *CDH,* I, 19; Schmitt, 2:85.28–29.

For his monastic interpretation of satisfaction Balthasar relies on Anselm's discussion of the meaning and excellence of monasticism as preserved in the *De similitudinibus*. He does not confront Anselm's soteriology directly with the *Regula Monachorum* of St. Benedict. Nor, to my knowledge, has anyone done this. It is what I propose to do in this essay.

Studies of St. Anselm's monastic and ascetic doctrine there have been.[5] And Dom H. de Sainte-Marie has examined the influence of the *Rule* on Anselm's letters.[6] Again, some relation between the *Rule* and the medieval penitential discipline of the Western Church is generally admitted.[7] And the relation of the latter to Anselm's notion of satisfaction has been often suggested.[8] Still, in view of the prominence in the *Rule* of the notion of *satisfactio*, it would seem valuable to compare Anselm and the *Rule* directly.

In fact, I think it can be rather easily shown that the notion of satisfaction such as Anselm employs it in the *Cur Deus homo* is substantially the same notion of satisfaction to be found in the *Rule*. The following, then, is yet another attempt to locate the provenance of Anselm's notion of satisfaction. As is well known, historians of dogma have in the main been of two minds on this issue: (1) Anselm's notion of satisfaction is that of the *wergeld* of Germanic feudal law; (2) Anselm's notion is borrowed from the penitential theory and practice of the Church.[9] The following is thus a

---

5 See the studies of Jean Leclercq, Jean-Marie Pouchet, and P. Salmon in *Spicilegium Beccense*, 1, *Congrès international du IXe de l'arrivée d'Anselme au Bec* (Paris: J. Vrin, 1959).

6 H. de Sainte-Marie, *Les lettres de saint Anselme de Cantobéry et la Règle bénédictine*, in *Mélanges bénédictins* (Paris: Éditions de Fontenelle, 1947), 259–320.

7 See, for example, Bernhard Poschmann, *Penance and the Anointing of the Sick*, trans. and rev. F. Courtney (New York: Herder & Herder, 1964), 120–21, 129–30; Paul Anciaux, *The Sacrament of Penance* (New York: Sheed and Ward, 1962), 60–63; and Monika Hellwig, *Sign of Reconciliation and Conversion* (Wilmington, DE: Michael Glazier, 1982), 45–57.

8 For a good summary, see Robert S. Franks, *The Work of Christ,* 2nd ed. (Edinburgh: Thomas Nelson, 1962), 113–18.

9 German scholarship (H. Cremer, A. Ritschl) has upheld the first hypothesis; cf. Franks, *Work of Christ,* 137–38; Louis Richard, *The Mystery of the Redemption,* trans. J. Horn (Baltimore: Helicon, 1966), 179ff. The great French historian of soteriology, Jean Rivière, has upheld the second hypothesis; see esp. his "Sur les premières applications du terme 'satisfactio' à l'oeuvre du Christ," *Bulletin de littérature ecclésiastique* 25 (1924): 285–97, 353–69, as well as his "De la 'satisfactio' du Christ chez saint Ambroise," *Bulletin de littérature ecclésiastique* 28 (1927): 160–64. Perhaps the finest summary in English of the state of the question is still to be found in John McIntyre, *St. Anselm and His Critics* (Edinburgh: Oliver and Boyd, 1954), 82–89. McIntyre, moreover, argues forcefully for the recognition of St. Anselm's originality as to the content of the notion of satisfaction. Of course, the two hypotheses are not necessarily exclusive at every point, and if the notion of satisfaction is not sought for in Germanic law and custom, the notion of the commutation

refinement of the second hypothesis. The provenance of the notion is the penitential theory and the practice of the Church, indeed. But this is not so "in general"; it can be located quite specifically in Benedictine *monastic* theory and practice.

I will proceed under the following heads: (1) a brief statement of Anselm's notion of satisfaction as in the *Cur Deus homo*; (2) verification of this notion in the *Rule* of St. Benedict and as it is applied to monastic life; (3) demonstration of Anselm's acquaintance with the notion within its properly monastic context; and (4) demonstration of the importance of this notion for his understanding of the monastic life as a whole.

The Notion of Satisfaction in the *Cur Deus Homo*

For St. Anselm, sin consists in not rendering to God what is due him,[10] namely justice or rectitude of will—that is, willing what God wills us to will, and so honoring him.[11] This disturbance of the order and beauty of the universe, God's "external honor,"[12] is repaired by either satisfaction or punishment[13] It is repaired by punishment when God exacts a penalty of the sinner whose will has not returned to God.[14] It is repaired by satisfaction when the sinner himself willingly repays to God the honor he has taken from him by sin.[15] As Bernard Lonergan remarks, therefore, the teaching of St. Anselm on satisfaction "is practically contained" in the disjunction,

---

of penance (satisfaction) ought perhaps to be located there; see P. Anciaux, *Penance,* 62. One has the impression that the first hypothesis is kept alive by those who wish to dismiss the theology of satisfaction; cf. for example John C. Dwyer, *Son of Man and Son of God* (New York: Paulist Press, 1983), 161, and William M. Thompson, *The Jesus Debate* (New York: Paulist Press, 1985), 348–49. One should rather consult Jaroslav Pelikan, *The Christian Tradition,* vol. 3: *The Growth of Medieval Theology (600–1300)* (Chicago: University of Chicago Press, 1978), 143: "Although historians have looked for the origins of this idea of satisfaction in Germanic customs such as 'wergild', . . . or in feudal law, the most obvious and immediate source of the idea would appear to be the penitential system of the church, which was developing just at this time."

[10] *CDH,* I, 11; Schmitt, 2:68.10: "Non est itaque aliud peccare quam non reddere deo debitum."

[11] *CDH,* I, 11; Schmitt, 2:68.14–21.

[12] *CDH,* I, 15; Schmitt, 2:72.29–73.9. All translations unless otherwise noted are mine.

[13] *CDH,* I, 15; Schmitt, 2:74.1–2: "necesse est ut omne peccatum satisfactio aut poena sequatur."

[14] *CDH,* I, 15; Schmitt, 2:73.19–20; and cf. *CDH,* I, 14; Schmitt, 2:72.8–12.

[15] *CDH,* I, 16; Schmitt, 2:73.14–22; and cf. *CDH,* I, 19; Schmitt, 2:85.28–29: "sine satisfactione, id est sine debiti solutione spontanea."

"either satisfaction or punishment."[16] But in addition, it is not sufficient merely to return to God the honor that was taken from him; because of the insult to God, satisfaction must consist in giving back more than was taken away, that is, in giving God something not already owed him.[17]

The conceptual content of *satisfactio* is thus as follows.

First, the context in which it makes sense may be said to be the restoration of the due order, or due relation, between persons, that is, the order in relations of honor, which consists in conforming one's will to the will of another.

Second, granted the above context, satisfaction may be said to be the appropriate means, employed by the one who has disturbed the due order between persons by his offense, of seeking forgiveness from the offended party.[18]

Third, then, satisfaction is the *willing* acceptance on the part of the offender of the consequences of his offense, the willing acceptance of whatever it takes to restore the due order between the persons that has been disturbed by the offense. This restoration consists on the part of the one offended in pardoning the offender. But on the part of the offender, satisfaction is distinguished from punishment, which is unwillingly bearing the consequences of one's offense, unwillingly bearing whatever it takes so that the disturbed order be rectified. In this way, it is an alternative to punishment: *aut satisfactio aut poena*. This means that according as satisfaction is rendered, punishment is remitted by the one offended.

Fourth, on the part of the offender, what it takes to restore due order is to render to the one offended something not already owed him according to the previous order of the relation. Satisfaction must be supererogatory.

According as the above four notes are verified in the notion of satisfaction contained in the *Rule of Benedict*, therefore, we can assert that Anselm's notion of satisfaction is that of the *Rule*.

Satisfaction in the *Regula Monachorum*

Satisfaction plays a large role in the public penitential discipline envisaged in the *Rule* of St. Benedict.[19] Of course, the language of satisfaction was

---

16 Bernard Lonergan, *De Verbo Incarnato* (Rome: Gregorian University Press, 1960), 602.

17 *CDH*, I, 11; Schmitt, 2:68.22–27. It is because sinners have nothing additional they can render to God that it not already owed, of course, that it is necessary for a God-man to die in order to make satisfaction of our sins; cf. *CDH*, I, 20, and II, 11.

18 See *CDH*, I, 12; and I, 19 (Schmitt, 2:85.28–86.7). See also Lonergan, *De Verbo Incarnato*, 613–16.

19 For a discussion of non-public penitential discipline in the *Rule*, see A. Santantoni, "La confessione dei pensieri e delle colpe segrete nella *Regula Benedicti*," in *San*

already familiar to Benedict both from the penitential theory and practice of the Church at large (from at least the time of Tertullian)[20] and from previous monastic tradition (for Benedict, notably the *Regula Magistri* and John Cassian). The question of the *Rule's* originality will be broached after an exposition of the notion in the *Rule* as it stands, together with some brief remarks on *emendatio* in the *Rule*.

Satisfactio *in the Rule*

1. First, then, *satisfactio* occurs nine times and *satisfacere*, "to satisfy" eight times in the *Rule*.[21] This leads us to suspect that it is not at all a marginal notion in the *Rule*.

2. Second, the grammatical subject of forms of *satisfacere* in the active voice is always the monk or monks at fault.[22] Again, while the one at fault is said to "incur" *(incurrit)* the "punishment of murmurers" *(poena murmurantium)*,[23] or "be subjected to" *(subiaceat)* the "punishment of excommunication" *(poena excommunicationis)* or "amendment" *(emendatio)* or "corporal punishment" *(corporalis vindicta)*,[24] he does not "incur" or is not "subjected to" *satisfactio*; rather, it seems that satisfaction is something he performs, does, executes as an active subject. This is clear enough for the following uses of the noun: A murmurer should make amends "with satisfaction" *(cum satisfactione)*; one excommunicated is to be provoked "unto the satisfaction of humility" *(ad humilitatis satisfactionem)*; one late to vigils repents by a "public satisfaction" *(publica satisfaction)*.[25] All the uses of the noun in chapters 43, 44, and 45, in fact, seem (like the last just cited) to refer to prostrations performed by the one at fault as the way of making satisfaction,[26] with possibly one exception—the last use in chapter 43 seems to mean

---

Benedetto agli uomini d'oggi, ed. Lorenzo De Lorenzi (Rome: Abazzia de S. Paulo fuori le muri, 1982), 647–80.

20 See P. Galtier's article, "Satisfaction," in the *Dictionnaire de théologie catholique*, vol. 14, 1, c. 1129–1210, and Auguste Deneffe's work also remains very useful, *Zeitschrift für katholische Theologie* 43 (1919): 158–75.

21 I rely on the *Concordantia Verborum* in the edition of the *Rule* by Philibert Schmitz, *Regula Monachorum*, 2nd ed. (Maredsous Namur, Belgium: Éditions de Maredsous: 1955).

22 *Regula S. Benedicti* (hereafter *RB*), 11.13, 43.12, 44.t, 44.8, 44.9, 46.3, 71.8, and cf. 44.3. References are according to chapter and the Neufville-de Vogüé versification.

23 *RB*, 5.19.

24 *RB*, 23.4, 46.4, 71.9.

25 *RB*, 5.19, 27.3, 43.6.

26 *RB*, 43.11, 44.8, 45.1; cf. 44.8, prostration as satisfaction.

simply bearing the imposed penalty of eating alone and without wine.[27] This leaves the use of the noun in chapter 24, where *satisfactio* seems similarly to mean bearing the imposed penalty either of eating alone or of abstaining from public leadership of prayer.

3. Third, there is the question of who it is who is offended and so is satisfied by the one at fault. Once, God is the one satisfied by the offender, when because of his late rising, all arrive late to vigils.[28] God is supposed to be offended at this, it may be urged, because the divine office is a service the monks owe God.[29] Once, we are given to understand that it is the abbot or one of the monks senior to the offender who is satisfied.[30]

    What of the other cases? Judging from the first case above, we could perhaps say that satisfaction for faults connected with the oratory is to be thought of as rendered to God.[31] Judging from the reasons for excommunication in chapter 23—stubbornness, pride, disobedience, murmuring, defiance of seniors, breaking the *Rule*—then the five uses of satisfaction in chapter 44 ("How the excommunicated are to make satisfaction") might indicate: (1) that individual monks (seniors) offended by the one at fault are to be thought of as receiving satisfaction;[32] or (2) that the entire community, bound to the good order of the *Rule*, is to be thought of as satisfied; or again (3) that God, who is served by the monks "fighting under a rule and an abbot,"[33] is to be offered satisfaction for disobedience and infractions of the *Rule*. These alternatives are not necessarily exclusive.

4. In any event, fourth, satisfaction is rendered formally for offense—*culpa, delictum, vitium* (guilt, crime, fault).[34] But there is no offense unless *someone* is offended; satisfaction takes place in a context of personal relations. That this is so is indicated, as well, by the fact that it is the abbot's

---

[27] *RB*, 43.16.

[28] *RB*, 11.13.

[29] *RB*, 16.2 and 18.24. See also the honor and reverence given to God in RB, 9.7 and 11.3. Honor is by no means a notion foreign to the *Rule*; the West did not have to wait until the advent of feudalism to discover it.

[30] *RB*, 71.6,8.

[31] Thus for *RB*, 43.6, 43.11 and 12, 45.1.

[32] See *RB*, 71.6–7, where the abbot or some senior is disturbed by a junior.

[33] *RB*, 1.2; cf. Prol. 3, 40, and 45.

[34] *Culpa: RB*, 24.1–3, 44.1, 44.9, 45.3; *delictum*: 46.3; *vitium*: 43:14. For *neglentia* as reason for satisfaction, see *RB*, 43.14, 45.2, 11.13, and 43.5. For the material determination of those things for which satisfaction must be made, see *RB*, 23 and 44 (excommunicable offenses), and 43 (tardiness), 45 (mistakes in reading), 46 (other faults, for example, breakage), and 71 (angering or disturbing a senior).

part to judge the seriousness of faults and so the corresponding measure of *disciplina*,[35] which seems to include both excommunication, which is a *poena*, and satisfaction.[36]

5. In the fifth place, satisfaction is distinct from pardon or forgiveness *(venia)*. It seems rather to be the fitting means to obtain pardon—"until by a fitting satisfaction he may pardon" *(usque dum satisfactione congrua veniam consequatur)*.[37]

6. Sixth, the fittingness of *satisfactio* to obtain pardon results from its expressing, being an act of, or consisting in humility. Prostration, of course, which is the common way of making satisfaction, is calculated to signify humility in a striking and original way, since it is the natural embodiment of *humilitas* as "nearness to the ground" *(humus)*. Thus, the prostration-satisfaction in chapter 45 is expressly the act of the humbled offender: "unless he should have humbled [himself] there before all by satisfaction" *(nisi satisfactione ibi coram omnibus humiliatus fuerit)*. Pride *(superbia*—from *super*, "above, over") is one of the faults for which excommunication is imposed and satisfaction therefore expected.[38] And in chapter 27, the *senpecta*—a secret consoler—is sent to provoke the excommunicated monk "unto the satisfaction of humility" *(ad humilitatis satisfactionem)*.

7. Seventh and most important, satisfaction is quite distinct from punishment, where punishment is taken strictly as unwillingly bearing the privation of some good because of offense. This point has already been anticipated above in (2), but is especially clear from three texts, and will be even clearer when the *Rule*'s use of *emendatio* can be explored.

    In chapter 5, we read that the monk who obeys while murmuring in his heart obtains no reward *(gratia)* for such obedience, but "rather incurs the punishment of murmurers, if he should not make amendment with satisfaction" *(immo poenam murmurantium incurrit, si non cum satisfactione emendaverit)*. Bearing punishment and amending with satisfaction are here alternatives; either one or the other will follow the fault in question.

---

[35] *RB*, 24.1.

[36] *RB*, 23.4, excommunication as a *poena*; see also *RB*, 44.3, 5, 8, and 9, for the abbot's regulation of satisfaction.

[37] *RB*, 24.7, and see the blessing given after due satisfaction in 44.10 and 71.8, signifying pardon. In *RB*, 43.11, the *remissio* perhaps refers to the lifting of the penalty of remaining in last place in choir as much to pardon in the sense of *venia*, forgiveness.

[38] Read *RB*, 23 and 44 together, and note the contumaciousness opposed to satisfaction in 71.9.

A second text is in chapter 45, where mistakes in reading are in question.

> If someone should make a mistake while saying a psalm . . . , unless he should humble [himself] there before all by satisfaction, then let him be subjected to a greater punishment, for indeed he did not want to correct by humility the fault he committed by negligence.
>
> Si quis dum pronuntiat psalmum . . . fallitus fuerit, nisi satisfactione ibi coram omnibus humiliatus fuerit, maiori vindictae subiaceat, quippe qui noluit humilitate corrigere quod neglegentia deliquit.

Here, on the contrary, *satisfactio* appears as a form of *vindictam*, "punishment." But two sorts of *vindicta* are clearly envisaged. There is a greater punishment, a *maior vindicta*, which one is subjected to if one does not want *(noluit)* humbly and actively to perform what we might call a "lesser punishment," a *minor vindicta*, except that the *Rule* calls it *satisfactio*. Thus, *vindicta*, broadly, is any privation of good, some rectifying consequence of fault, whether willingly or unwillingly borne. Its first form is a *maior vindicta*, unwillingly born—for presumably, if one does not willingly undertake the *minor vindicta*, one does not willingly undertake a *maior vindicta*. Rather, one is subjected to it *(subiaceat)*. Its second form is a *minor vindicta*, which is satisfaction willingly performed. The difference in degree by which the forms are designated indicates a kind of material identity between satisfaction and punishment strictly speaking, in that they are both unpleasant, or privations of some good, we might say. But the difference as to from whose will these two *vindictae* proceed indicates exactly the distinction between punishment and satisfaction as in St. Anselm.

A third text is from chapter 71. If a junior angers or disturbs or is corrected by the abbot or a senior, we read:

> [L]et him immediately and without delay throw himself down prostrate before his feet. . . . But if he should think this contemptible and not do it, then let him be subjected to corporal punishment, or, if he should be contumacious, let him be expelled from the monastery.
>
> [M]ox sine mora tamdiu prostratus in terra ante pedes eius iaceat satisfaciens. . . . Quod qui contempserit facere, aut corporali vindictae subiaceat aut, si contumax fuerit, de monasterio expellatur.

Here, we have again a straightforward alternative, where the monk at fault either willingly makes satisfaction or is subjected to punishment (or expelled).

8. Eighth and finally, satisfaction is supererogatory, in the sense that the acts that are satisfactory are not otherwise expected of the monk except when he is at fault. That is, they are not part of his ordinary service under the *Rule*. They are provided for by the *Rule*, but precisely as something extra, additional, by which infractions of the *Rule* may be repaired.

Thus, the first note of Anselm's notion of satisfaction is verified as per (3) and (4), above: Satisfaction takes place in the context of disrupted personal relations. The second note is verified as per (5) and (6), above: Satisfaction is the appropriate means, on the part of the offender, of seeking the forgiveness of the one offended. The third note is verified as per (2) and (7), above: Satisfaction is distinct from punishment as the willing from the unwilling bearing of the consequences of offense. And the fourth note is verified as per (8), above: Satisfaction is supererogatory.

Emendatio *in the* Rule

A fuller discussion of satisfaction in the Rule would require an examination of such associated vocabulary as *paenitere, corrigere, correptio/corripere, admonitio/admonere, castigatio/castigare* (to repent, to correct, reproof/to reprove, warning/to warn, punishment/to punish) as well as a complete examination of *poena* and *vindicta, culpa, delictum, peccatum,* and the like.[39] However, the need for brevity constrains us to add but a few remarks on "amendment" and "to amend" or "to make amends"—*emendatio/emendare.*

In general, it can be said that while satisfaction regards making up for past fault, *emendatio* and *emendare* regard future fault; they mean ceasing to commit now and avoiding the same fault in the future.[40] There are three uses of the noun, however, that warrant special attention for the purposes of this essay.

First, in chapter 29, we read:

> If a brother who has left the monastery by his own fault should wish to come back, let him first promise every amendment for having left, and then let him be received in the lowest rank, so that in this way his humility can be tested.
>
> Frater qui proprio vitio egreditur de monasterio, si reverti voluerit, spondeat prius omnem emendationem pro quo egressus est, et sic in ultimo gradu recipiatur, ut ex hoc eius humilitas comprobetur.

---

[39] In passing, we may note that *correptio* seems always to mean some reproof as punishment, as something inflicted, while *corripere* indicates an oral reproof.

[40] All fifteen uses of the verb require or can receive this meaning. For *emendatio,* cf. *RB,* Prol. 36 and 47, 2.40, and perhaps 43.16.

The *pro quo* can be taken either as *pro eo quod,* "because," or as *pro vitio pro quo,* "for, or in proportion to, the fault for which."[41] If the second, then *emendatio* is even more clearly doing duty for *satisfactio.* The connection with humility perhaps argues this as well.[42] Here, then, satisfaction would consist in taking the last place in seniority in the monastery, so demonstrating humility. The alternative to this satisfaction is not being received back into the monastery, contrary to the monk's request.

Second, in chapter 43, if someone is offered something by a superior, refuses it, and then wants it, then "let him receive absolutely nothing until [he has made] fitting amendment" *(omnino nihil percipiat usque ad emendationem congruam).* Since the whole chapter concerns making satisfaction for tardiness at choir or table, and since in chapter 24 we read of a *satisfactio congrua, emendatio* seems to be doing duty here, too, for *satisfactio.*

If both of the above uses of *emendatio* are correctly to be taken to be equivalent to *satisfactio,* then we have but further evidence of the willingness with which satisfaction is to be performed on the part of the offender.

Third, in chapter 46, the negligent monk is expected of his own accord *(ultro)* to admit his fault and make satisfaction. However, "if it should come to light through another, let him be subjected to a greater amendment" *(dum per alium cognitum fuerit, maiori subiaceat emendationi).* Here, *emendatio* seems clearly to be doing duty for *vindicta,* punishment. This is Dom Adalbert de Vogüé's opinion: Benedict seems to be under the influence of a text of St. Augustine here.[43] Thus, there is here a fourth clear instance of the alternative, *aut satisfactio aut poena,* in the *Rule.*[44]

---

[41] *RB* 1980. *The Rule of St. Benedict in Latin and English with Notes,* ed. Timothy Fry (Collegeville, MN: Liturgical Press, 1981), 226*n.*

[42] See above, section 1 (6).

[43] Adalbert de Vogüé, *La Règle de saint Benoît,* t. V, *Commentaire, Sources Chrétiennes,* 185 (Paris: Éditions du Cerf, 1971), 824–26, who notes also that in the *RB,* of thirteen uses of *subiaceat,* this is the only time it occurs with *emandatio.* Here is the text from Augustine, Epistola 211, 11 (CSEL 57, 365): "Quaecumque autem in tantum progressa fuerit malum, ut occulte ab aliquo litteras vel quaelibet munuscula accipiat, si hoc ultro confitetur, parcatur illi et oretur pro ea; si autem deprehenditur atque convincitur, secundum arbitrium praepositae vel presbyteri vel etiam episcopi gravius emendetur."

[44] Santantoni, "La confessione dei pensieri," 662, reads *RB,* 46.1–4 as if we are to understand that two faults are in question, that of the breakage or loss of some tool, etc., and the fault of hiding this first fault. The additional or more severe punishment spoken of in 46.4 is for this second fault. Thus, spontaneous admission of fault does not mitigate punishment due to the first fault; it obviates the need to punish a second fault, that of subterfuge. This reading is perhaps overly fine. One, and only one, fault is mentioned, and the text explains how this one fault is to be handled.

The Originality of the Rule

We have now to ask after the originality of the *Rule*'s notion of satisfaction in relation to the previous western monastic tradition utilized by St. Benedict, that is, Cassian and the *Regula Magistri*.[45] De Vogüé writes:

> Cassien et le Maître ne connaissent qu'une peine. Celle-ci frappe le coupable dès que le délit est commis et elle cesse avec la satisfaction. Chez Benoît, le système pénal se présente différemment et paraît comporter deux échelons: la première peine consiste à satisfaire immédiatement; la seconde en cas de non-satisfaction immédiate, consiste en un châtiment plus grave.[46]

That Benedict conceives of "two levels" of punishment bears on the most important point in St. Anselm's notion of satisfaction.

Cassian distinguishes two kinds of punishment in Book IV of the *Institutiones*, chapter 16, an *increpatio spiritualis*, "spiritual reproach," which is in fact prostration, and an *emendatio plagis*, "amendment by blows"— that is, we might say, we have either an *increpatio* or a *vindicta corporalis*.[47] But these are not alternatives insofar as the monk at fault does or does not prostrate himself. No, spiritual punishment is meted out to lesser faults; corporal punishment is given for more serious faults. There is no alternative for one and the same fault—*aut satisfactio* (spiritual punishment) *aut poena* (corporal punishment)—insofar as the offender does or does not embrace the first alternative of his own will.

As to the *Rule of the Master*, however, de Vogüé's summary opinion quoted above must be modified. For in chapter 13, "How an excommunicated brother ought to be dealt with," the Master says:

> But if the excommunicated brothers remain so proud that, persevering in pride of heart until the ninth hour of the third day, they do not want to satisfy the abbot, let them be guarded and beaten with the rod even to the point of blood, and should it please the abbot, let them be expelled from the monastery.[48]

---

[45] For the previous extra-monastic use of *satisfactio*, consult the works in note 20, above.

[46] De Vogüé, *Commentaire,* 821–22.

[47] PL 99, 174; compare with the beginning of the chapter, 99, 172, and with chapter 7 of Book III, 99, 136–40.

[48] *La Règle du Maître,* II, text and trans. by Adalbert de Vogüé, *Sources Chrétiennes,* 106 (Paris: Éditions du Cerf, 1964), 46 (verses 68–70): "Excommunicati vero fratres, si ita superbia extiterint, ut in superbia cordis perseverantes in tertia die hora nona satisfacere abbati noluerint, custoditi usque ad necem caedantur virgis, et si placuerit abbati, de monasterio expellantur. "

Here, for the same fault, there is an alternative: either satisfaction willingly performed[49] or corporal punishment undergone. In the *Rule* of Benedict, however, we can safely say that this alternative is much more express and frequent (four times).

De Vogüé points especially to St. Augustine for Benedict's insistence on voluntary avowal of fault.[50] But St. Augustine does not speak of this as, or in conjunction with, *satisfaction*.[51]

Thus, from Cassian, we have the distinction between an *increpatio spiritualis* and an *emendatio plagis*, the first of which can be taken as making satisfaction by prostration.[52] From the *Regula Magistri*, there is the possibility that either one or the other of the above two modes of correction can be applied to an offender for the same fault, in that, if the offender is unwilling to make satisfaction, then he is subjected to the rod. From St. Augustine, there is the emphasis on spontaneous, willing avowal of fault.

St. Anselm's Acquaintance with Monastic Satisfaction

The question now to be addressed is to what extent St. Anselm was familiar with the properly monastic context of *satisfactio* such as can be found in the *Regula Monachorum*. Happily, and supposing there could be serious doubt on this score, this matter can be easily checked from Anselm's Letter 105, written while he was still Abbot of Bec, about the year 1085, thus some thirteen years prior to the completion of the *Cur Deus homo* (1098). Interceding for an apostate monk of St-Pierre-sur-Dives, Anselm prays the abbot, Fulco, to receive him back. The body of the letter is short enough to quote in full.

> Your son, who left your paternity in confusion, repenting and prepared for every satisfaction according to your judgment, humbly returns. He does not so much ask that you remit him the punishment he has merited as that by your mercy you establish him the last among the flock that he left by his fault. Therefore, I pray your holiness that your strictness not so much consider what he did by sinning as that your piety think what he does by humbly repenting. I pray the brothers, also our lords, your sons, that, imploring for him the mercy

---

[49] For grave faults, which incur excommunication from both table and oratory, satisfaction consists in prostrations and the promise of amendment; for lesser faults, which-incur excommunication from table, satisfaction consists in kneeling before the abbot or deans and the promise of amendment.

[50] De Vogüé, *Commentaire,* 824.

[51] Ibid., 824*n*85.

[52] See above, note 47.

of your paternity, they show themselves joyful that their brother "had been dead and has revived, had perished and has been found" [Lk 15:32]. But in what measure you ought to show judgment or mercy to that brother—as it is written: "Lord, I will sing to you mercy and judgment" [Ps 100:1]—belongs to your power and prudence; only, let mercy triumph over judgment [cf. Jas 2:13].[53]

The following remarks are in order.

First, the appropriate chapter of the *Rule*, the twenty-ninth, "Whether brothers who leave the monastery ought to be received again," is quite evidently behind this letter. If by nothing else, this is indicated by the expectation that the apostate will be assigned the last place in the monastery: *"in ultimo gradu recipiatur,"* the *Rule* reads.

Second, therefore, we are encouraged to read "prepared for every satisfaction" *(ad omnem satisfactionem paratus)* as a recollection of the *Rule's* requirement that the monk who has left "should first promise every amendment" *(spondeat prius omnem emendationem).*[54]

Third, Anselm is careful to mention the humility (twice) of the monk who wants to return. This, too, accords with chapter 29 of the *Rule*, for the assignment of the monk to the last place is a test of his *humilitas.*

Fourth, just as the *Rule* assigns to the abbot's judgment the amount of satisfaction to be required for a fault,[55] so for Anselm the satisfaction here in question will be "according to your [the abbot's] judgment" *(secundum vestrum [abbatis] iudicium).*

Fifth, the citation of James 2:13—"let mercy triumph over judgment" *(superexaltet misericordia iudicio)*—also appears in chapter 64 of the *Rule*, where the abbot is encouraged to be merciful. Similarly, this chapter urges

---

53 Schmitt, III, 238: "Filius vester, qui a paternitate vestra inordinate abierat, paenitens et ad omnem satisfactionem secundum vestrum iudicium paratus humiliter redit. Qui non tam postulat, ut illi poenam quam meruit remittatis, quam ut vel ultimum illum intra gregem, quem sua culpa dimiserat, vestra misericordia constituatis. Precor igitur ego sanctitatem vestram, ut non tam consideret districtio vestra quod ille fecit peccando, quam penset pietas vestra quod facit humiliter paenitendo. Precor etiam fratres et dominos nostros alios, filios vestros, ut paternitatis vestrae misericordiam pro eo exorantes gaudium se monstrent habere, quia frater eorum "mortuus fuerat et revixit, perierat et inventus est" [Lk 15: 32]. Qua vero mensura erga eundem fratrem iudicium sive misericordiam vestram ostendere debeatis—sicut scriptum est: "misericordiam et iudicium cantabo tibi, domine" [Ps 100: 1]—: vestrae potestatis est et vestrae prudentiae; tantum ut superexaltet misericordia iudicio [cf. Jas 2: 13]."

A translation of all the letters of St. Anselm can be found in *The Letters of Saint Anselm of Canterbury*, 3 vols., trans. and annotated by Walter Fröhlich (Kalamazoo, MI: Cistercian Publications, 1990).

54 See above, II, section 2.

55 See above, II, section 1 (6).

the abbot to act *prudenter* in correcting faults.[56] Anselm does the same with Fulco.

Thus, the multiple allusions to the *Rule* in this brief letter dealing with a point of monastic discipline indicate St. Anselm's acquaintance with *satisfactio* in the monastic context. And the fact that he so gracefully alludes rather than laboriously cites indicates, perhaps, a quite intimate and living acquaintance with the thought and application of the *Rule* in matters disciplinary.[57]

Satisfactio and St. Anselm's View of Monastic Life

We have now briefly to examine what we know of St. Anselm's view of monastic life, for which the notion of satisfaction is quite important. For him, the whole of the monastic life can be understood as satisfactory. This strengthens the argument for the monastic provenance of the notion of satisfaction as applied to the work of Christ.

It is true that two of the writings now to be appealed to—the *De humanis moribus per similitudines* and the *Dicta Anselmi*—both date from after the composition of the *Cur Deus homo*. The *De moribus*, either an unfinished work of Anselm himself or a recording of his instructions by an anonymous secretary, can be plausibly dated from the years 1106 to 1109.[58] The *Liber Alexandri monachi Cantuariensis ex dictis beati Anselmi*, avowedly not from Anselm's own hand, but considered a trustworthy report of various of his discourses, likely incorporates material from the years 1100 to 1109.[59] However, even if this material, which contains the half of what has come down to us of Anselm's view of monasticism,[60] a view to which the notion of satisfaction is essential, is later than the *Cur Deus homo*, the fact that Anselm so easily finds this central category of his Christological work applicable to monastic life argues just as much for a prior unity as for a progression in his thought. That is, it need not be thought that Anselm first worked out the notion of satisfaction in the *Cur Deus homo* and then and only then discov-

---

[56] *RB,* 64.12, 14. See also the *disciplinae mensura* of *RB,* 24.1.

[57] Letters 140, 141, 142, 143, and 193, which also bear on apostates, can be consulted as well.

[58] Robert W. Southern and F. S. Schmitt, eds., *Memorials of Saint Anselm* (London: Published for the British Academy by Oxford University Press, 1969), 6–8. This volume contains the texts of the *Dicta* and the *De moribus.*

[59] Ibid., 9–24. The *Liber de S. Anselmi similitudinibus* in PL 159 is a conflation of the *Dicta* and the *De moribus.*

[60] The other half might be reckoned to be found in the Letters and in various prayers and meditations; see P. Salmon, "L'ascèse monastique dans les letters de saint Anselme de Canterbury," in *Spicilegium Beccense,* 509–20.

ered its utility for understanding the monastic life. Just as easily, we may suppose that he already understood monastic life in terms of satisfaction.

In what follows, it will be fruitful to report two chapters from the *De moribus* in some detail, to ask after the connection of Anselm's view of monasticism with the *Regula Monachorum*, and finally to close this section with some remarks on what might be called St. Anselm's fondness for finding "limit concepts."

Chapters 82 and 83 of the De Moribus

Chapter 82 of the *De humanis moribus* is a defense of monastic profession against the charge that "it would be better to serve God freely, without profession, than to be forced to serve unwillingly, binding oneself by profession in a monastery." The defense asks us to consider a comparison between two men with the same master. The first one says to him that, though he wants to serve him, he does not want to promise to serve him, lest, should he fail him, he be worthy of a greater punishment *(graviori vindicta dignus)*. The second man, the monk, declares his love for his master and promises him fidelity and submission. Should he fail him, he begs his master not judge him as a stranger, but rather correct him as his own servant *("ut . . . non me iudices ut alienum, sed emendes ut proprium servum")*.

When therefore both men fail, the master does indeed judge as a stranger the one who did not promise fidelity, and requires the whole of the debt from him.[61] And the master says to the one who had promised him fidelity that for that reason he ought to have been more careful. But the one who promised, the monk, replies: "After I repent of my sin, ought I to suffer worse, because I promised you fidelity before I sinned, than he who does not want to promise you this even after he has sinned?" The master sees the point of this reply; he will punish the monk as "his own." And the comparison concludes:

> Now in the same way, God too judges between the professed monk and the one who does not want to profess, if they repent of having sinned against him. But not only does he judge the professed monk more mildly *[mitius]* than the non-professed man, but he also judges him more mildly than any layman still established in the world. For although both may commit the same sin, yet if from his whole heart the monk repents having sinned, and with fervent love keeps the rule *[ordo]* to which he has submitted himself, he will obtain greater mercy *[maiorem misericordiam]* than the layman, however much the layman who is still held back in the world repents. But if the monk

---

[61] *De moribus* 82; *Memorials,* 72, l.13–14: The "last farthing," the *ultimum quadrantem* will be required (cf. Mt 5:26).

should not want to repent, he will be subjected to a greater damnation *[maiori damnationi]* than the layman.[62]

Thus, we may conclude, the monastic life raises the stakes. But also, we may conclude that it is a life of satisfaction. For either one embraces monastic life, or for the same sin, one is subjected to a greater punishment. Either monastic life or punishment: that is, *aut satisfactio aut poena.*[63]

That the category of satisfaction is appropriate for understanding chapter 82 is clear from chapter 83, where Anselm once again compares a sinful monk to a sinful layman. Here, but even more expressly, what distinguishes the monk who promises fidelity to God is his greater love.

> But suppose the other loves his master to such an extent that he prefers to serve as a member of the household, keeping nothing for his own but giving everything to his master.[64]

Thus, should the monk sin, God will take whatever redress he wants as from his own property *("de seipso non de re aliena sed ut de proprio . . . vindictam assumat")*. Now suppose the layman and the monk both sin, and both repent, and wish to amend *(emendare)*:

> But the first [the layman, wishes to make amends] from out of what he has, the whole of which he still does not want to give for the satisfaction of his fault; but the second [the monk, wishes to make amends] from out of himself, the whole of which he had also previously given up to his master.[65]

In these circumstances, Anselm asks, will not the master have greater mercy *[maiorem misericordiam]* and deal more mildly *[milius]* with the monk? Yes, for he sees that the monk has loved him more. The monk can say to his master:

---

[62] Ibid., 72, l.24–31.

[63] For the same idea about monastic life, but without the use of the term *satisfactio*, see Anselm's Letter 121; Schmitt, 3:261.34–43.

[64] *De moribus* 83; *Memorials*, 82.37–83.1: "Alter [monachus] vera dominum adeo diligat ut nil proprium retinere, sed omnibus ei dimissis familiarius malit servire."

[65] Ibid., 73.4–6: "sed ille [laicus] de proprio quod nec adhuc vult dare pro satisfactione culpae illius, iste [monachus] de seipso quem etiam totum domino mancipaverat prius."

Does it seem just that I should have less mercy because I have loved you more? On the contrary, you should have greater mercy for me for this reason that I can make you no greater satisfaction.[66]

Thus, once again, the whole of monastic life is to be described as satisfactory; the monk gains pardon more quickly for having made this satisfaction ("God more swiftly gives the monk pardon"; *Deus celerius indulget monacho*). Thus the old disjunction takes a properly monastic form: either monastic life, which is satisfaction, or greater punishment.[67]

In these chapters, thus, one can easily verify the first three of the four notes of the notion of satisfaction in the *Cur Deus homo*.[68]

Monastic Life as Satisfactory and the Rule of Benedict

Does this general view of monastic life, in which the notion of satisfaction, which originally names a transaction *within* monastic discipline, is taken to describe the *whole* of monastic discipline, find any warrant in the *Rule* of St. Benedict? I think we may very confidently answer "Yes," for in the first place, the monastic life is quite correctly and traditionally, and on the basis of the *Rule*, to be understood as a life with a penitential character.[69]

"The life of a monk ought to be a continual Lent," chapter 49 of the *Rule* reads. Again, in the Prologue, we find this apology for the monastic life:

The Lord waits for us daily to translate into action, as we should, his holy teachings. Therefore our life span has been lengthened by way of a truce, that we amend our misdeeds *[propter emendationem malorum]*.[70]

The conclusion of this reflection is that one ought to become a monk. And proximate to the notion of *emendatio* in the *Rule*, as we have indicated, is the notion of *satisfactio*.

Finally, there is the connection between humility and satisfaction in the *Rule*. Chapter 7, on humility, is ordinarily taken as the great charter of Benedict's spirituality. And satisfaction (often, prostration) is especially and explicitly related to humility twice in the *Rule*.[71] Now, the connection between satisfaction and humility is explicitly drawn in the *Dicta Anselmi*, where the

---

[66] Ibid., 73.4–6: "Iustumne videtur ut, quia te magis dilexi, minorem debeo misericordiam consequi? Immo eo maiorem mihi facere debes misericordiam, quo nullam maiorem tibi facere possum satisfactionem."

[67] See also *De moribus* 84.

[68] And as for satisfaction being supererogatory, see *De moribus* 73.

[69] See G. Anelli, "Vita monastica esistenza teologica," in *San Benedetto agli uomini d'oggi* (Rome: Abazzia de S. Paulo fuori le muri, 1982), 321–23.

[70] *RB,* Prol. 35–38.

[71] *RB,* 27.3, 45.1; cf. 29.1–2.

seven degrees of humility there distinguished are together said to satisfy God for fault.[72] And in chapter 109 of the *De moribus*, we have expressed once again the important alternative: Either one accomplishes the seven degrees of humility Anselm distinguishes, or one can expect more punishment.[73]

Thus, St. Anselm's view of monastic life as satisfactory can be seen to be sufficiently grounded in reflection on the *Rule*. It is an understandable interpretation of the *Rule*.

Satisfaction as an id quo malus cogitari nequit

The integration of St. Anselm's theology as a whole with his monastic theology can be made evident in yet another way. It is well known that the dynamism of Anselm's thought characteristically pivots on the location of something beyond which we cannot think anything greater. So God is *"id quo maius cogitari nequit"* in the *Proslogion*.[74] Toward the end of the *Cur Deus homo*, of God's mercy in the work of redemption we read that it is "so great and so concordant with justice . . . that something more just cannot be thought" *(tam magnam tamque concordem iustitiae . . . ut nec iustior cogitari nequit)*.[75] In his third *Meditatio*, Anselm argues as follows with regard to the satisfaction of Christ.

> For the life of this man [Christ] is more precious than all that is not God, and goes beyond all debt that sinners owe for satisfaction. For if killing him goes beyond the whole multitude and magnitude of sins that can be thought outside of God, then it is clear that his life is more good than all sins that are outside of God are bad.[76]

Christ's satisfaction is thus, we might say, something than which a greater cannot be thought, *ea qua maior cogitari nequit*.[77]

And what of monastic life? We have already seen in chapter 83 of the *De moribus* that the monk can say of his monastic profession that he can effect *nullam maiorem satisfactionem*. And that this thought recorded in

---

72 *Dicta Anselmi,* I; *Memorials,* 113.33–114.3.

73 Ibid., 81.30–82.4.

74 *Proslogion,* 3; Schmitt, 1:102.9–103.2.

75 *CDH,* II, 20; Schmitt, 2:131.28–29.

76 Meditatio, III; Schmitt, 3:87.89–93: "Pretiosior namque est vita hominis illius [Christi] quam omne quod deus non est, et superat omne debitum quod debent peccatores pro satisfactione. Si enim interfectio illius superat omnem multitudinem et magnitudinem peccatorum, quae cogitari possunt extra personam dei: palam est quia vita eius magis est bona quam sint omnia peccata mala, quae extra personam dei sunt."

77 Cf. *CDH,* I, 21 (Schmitt, 2:110.9–10, 111.10–12); II, 6 (2:101.3–4); II, 14 (2:114.22–24).

the *De moribus* reflects a long-standing and typical assessment of monasticism by Anselm appears from his Letter 121, written some twelve years before the completion of the *Cur Deus homo*. Encouraging a certain Henry to embrace monasticism, Anselm writes:

> For he pleases God more, even after grave sin, whose proposal is both before and after his sin that which something greater cannot be had—he pleases him more than the man who neither before nor after a similar sin wants to propose something than which he cannot propose better.[78]

And so we return to the point at which Hans Urs von Balthasar left us. The best analogy for understanding Christ's satisfaction is the monastic vow. Neither are required by God; both are the better thing to do, supposing Christ and the monk will to do them. As the *Cur Deus homo* has it, discussing in what sense Christ ought to have made satisfaction:

> Though the creature has nothing of himself, yet when God grants him the liberty of doing or not doing a thing, he leaves the alternative with him, so that, though one is better than the other, yet neither is positively demanded. And, whichever he does, it may be said that he ought to do it; and if he takes the better choice, he deserves a reward; because he renders freely what is his own. For, though celibacy be better than marriage, yet neither is absolutely enjoined upon man; so that both he who chooses marriage and he who prefers celibacy, may be said to do as they ought.[79]

And why is the monastic vow the better thing to do? It is a pledge of greater love, as we have seen. Thus the heart of Christ's work, too, is correctly to be seen as a work of greater love, an amor *"quo maior cogitari nequit."*

---

[78] Letter 121; Schmitt, 3:261.38–40: "Plus namque placet deo, etiam post grave peccatum, cuius propositum est et ante et post quo maius habere non potest, quam ille qui nec ante nec post simile peccatum vult proponere quo melius non potest." See also *De moribus* 73; *Memorials*, 64.27–29.

[79] *St. Anselm: Basic Writings,* trans. S. N. Deane (LaSalle, IL: Open Court, 1962), 281; see *CDH* II, 18; Schmitt, 2:128.13–20: "Quamvis creatura nihil habeat a se, quando tamen concedit illi deus aliquid licite facere et non facere, dat illi ita suum esse utrumque, ut licet alterum sit melius, neutrum tamen exigatur determinate, sed sive faciat quod melius est, sive alterum, debere facere dicatur quod facit; et si facit quod melius est, praemium habeat, quia sponte dat quod suum est. Nam cum virginitas melior sit coniugio, neutrum tamen ab homine determinate exigitur, sed qui coniugio uti et qui virginitatem servare mavult, quod facit debere facere dicitur."

Conclusion

"Only those theologies became vitally effective in history which bore their spirituality not as an addition but within themselves, which embodied it in their innermost being." Thus Hans Urs von Baltahasar.[80] Thus also the presuppositions of the foregoing essay; first, in every great theologian there is a unity of theology and sanctity, theology and spirituality;[81] second, St. Anselm is a great theologian ("effective in history"), and never more so than in his theology of satisfaction.

It follows that to the extent one can hope to explore the fonts of Anselm's theology of satisfaction, one should explore the fonts of his spirituality insofar as they are available to us. Now, a preeminent font (at least) of Anselm's spirituality is the *Rule* of St. Benedict. And we can in some measure tell what St. Anselm made of this font—or what it made of him—from his letters, the *De moribus*, and the *Liber Alexandri*. Hence the material visited above.

And hence the conclusion to be drawn. Given that St. Anselm really is a great theologian, given the identity of the notions of satisfaction in the *Rule* of Benedict and the *Cur Deus homo*, and given the possibility of expressing the meaning of monastic life in terms of satisfaction, then if one knows the authenticity of Benedictine monasticism, one should conclude to the authenticity of Anselm's theology of satisfaction, and if one knows the power of Anselm's theology of satisfaction, one should conclude to the validity of Benedictine monastic spirituality.

---

[80] Hans Urs von Balthasar, "The Unity of Theology and Spirituality," in *Convergences*, trans. E. A. Nelson (San Francisco: Ignatius Press, 1983), 44.

[81] See also Hans Urs von Balthasar, "Theology and Sanctity," in *Word and Redemption*, trans. A. V. Littledale (New York: Herder & Herder, 1965), and Bernard Lonergan, "Theology and Praxis," in *A Third Collection*, ed. F. E. Crowe (New York: Paulist Press, 1985).

7

Rahner and Balthasar on
the Efficacy of the Cross

TWO OF THE MOST important accounts of the efficacy of the Cross of Christ from contemporary Roman Catholic theologians are doubtless those of Karl Rahner and Hans Urs von Balthasar. Both accounts are highly speculative; both are quite innovative; both are very influential. Unfortunately, both cannot be true, since they contradict one another markedly and at more than one point. Balthasar's account, indeed, is formulated often enough expressly in contrast to Rahner's. Unfortunately again, a comparison of the two in an attempt to adjudicate their differences is made difficult by the circumstance that each account is tightly integrated into the whole of the thought of each thinker. There can be no question, therefore, of any final word in this brief essay. Nonetheless, it will not be useless to compare the two men narrowly on the question of the Cross. While such a comparison cannot lay to rest the larger issues about their differences of methods and basic theological commitments, it can indicate, and from a (the?) central focus of Christian dogmatics, why such a more thoroughgoing assessment is desirable.[1]

In what follows, it will be useful in the first place to draw up a sort of preliminary inventory of the differences between them. Next will follow short expositions of their positions, with more attention to Balthasar's as more probably the less familiar. Last, there is offered some way of coming to terms with their differences, about which it should be said only that the reader can expect no proposal of some "higher viewpoint" or synthesis.

---

[1] One is reminded of the title and claim of P. T. Forsyth's *The Cruciality of the Cross* (London: Independent Press, 1948). That Balthasar would accept the Cross as the central focus of Christian dogmatics seems clear. Whether this is so for Rahner is a more difficult to say.

A Conflict of Accounts

Summing up the criticisms of St. Anselm that Rahner makes in "The One Christ and the Universality of Salvation," we can see what kind of a theory of the efficacy of the Cross he wants.[2]

1. First, he wants a theory in which it is manifest that the salvific will of God is the cause, not the effect, of the Cross; the Cross is the cause of salvation only in a quite restrained sense, after the manner of a sacrament.

2. Second, it will be one that avoids the "inconceivable notion" that Christ is our representative on the Cross or does anything in our stead.[3] He does something for our good, but not in our name. More positively, Rahner wants an account that makes more evident the role of our own subjective and free appropriation of God's forgiveness and grace, that is, an account in which "self-redemption" has a prominent place.[4]

3. Congruently with both of the foregoing, third, it will be a theory in which the anger of God at sin and the sinner becomes a minor or even non-existent theme.[5] For presumably, there is no wrath in God to neutralize (from 1), and if there were, how could it be borne by another in our stead (from 2)?

4. Fourth, evidently, the transaction of the Cross will be primarily a transaction between the God of grace and the sinner himself, and not a transaction between Father and Incarnate Son.

5. Fifth, it will be a theory in which there is no introduction of the "metaphysically impossible idea" of a change in God.[6] This requirement is bound up with the first and third.

Balthasar, on the other hand, can fairly be seen as wanting the exact opposite of what Rahner wants.[7]

---

2 *Theological Investigations* (hereafter *TI*) 16 (London: Darton, Longman and Todd, 1979), 206–8; in German, "Der eine Jesus Christus und die Universalität des Heils," *Schriften zur Theologie* 12 (Einsiedeln: Benziger, 1975), 260–63. I will cite the German in parentheses after the English citation.

3 "The One Christ," 208 ("Der eine Jesus Christus," 262), quoted below in note 11.

4 Ibid., 206–7 (260–61).

5 Ibid., 208 (262).

6 Ibid., 208 (262), quoted below in note 10.

7 For Balthasar's solution, I will refer mostly to his *Mysterium Paschale* (Edinburgh: T&T Clark, 1990), hereafter *MP*, which is the translation of Chapter 9 of *Mysterium Salutis*, hereafter *MS*, ed. J. Feiner and M. Löhrer, vol. III/2, *Das Christusereignis* (Einsiedeln: Benziger Verlag, 1969), and to the *Theo-Drama: Theological Dramatic Theory*, vols. 2, 3, and 4 (San Francisco: Ignatius Press, 1990, 1992, 1994)

1. First, although of course the Cross follows from God's salvific will and love, it is an effective cause of the reconciliation of the world to God in a way beyond and stronger, for Balthasar, than that of a quasi-sacramental cause.

2. Second, Christ is a substitute for sinners, and in their very character as sinners. The Cross is a "bearing of the total sin of the world."[8]

3. Third, the biblical assertion of the wrath of God is to be taken seriously. The wrath of God follows from his (outraged) covenant love and faithfulness; ready to fall on the sinner, in fact it falls on Christ, who identifies himself with the sinner.

4. Fourth, the Cross is thus first of all and foundationally an event within the Trinitarian economy, a transaction between Father and Son, and only in the second place a transaction between the sinner and God, according as the sinner is inserted into the action between Father and Son.

5. Last, then, if the Cross, an event in the economy, is an event between Father and Incarnate Son, the immutability of God is very much an issue for Balthasar.

Rahner's Solution

Within Roman Catholicism, the traditional account of Christ's death as effective of our salvation has been some form of St. Anselm's theory of satisfaction. Once again following the exposition in "One Christ," we learn that Rahner rejects this account principally on two grounds.[9] First, he alleges that it obscures the fact that the principal cause of salvation is in the loving and merciful will of God, in that it rather seems to envisage the sacrifice of Christ as effacing God's anger and so changing him. "Almost of necessity," the traditional theory "introduces the metaphysically impossible idea of a transformation of God."[10] Second, it requires what is for

---

(hereafter *TD* 2, 3, 4), which correspond to *Theo-Dramatik*, vol. II/1, *Die Personen des Spiels: Der Mensch in Gott*; II/2, *Die Personen in Christus*; and vol. III: *Die Handlung* (Einsiedeln: Johannes Verlag, 1976, 1978, 1980). Hereafter, parenthetical references, with roman numerals for volume numbers, are to the German edition.

8 *MP*, 137 (with explicit contrast to Rahner) (*MS* III/2, 224): "Es geht über all dies . . . hinaus um ein völlig einmaliges Tragen der Gesamtschuld der Welt."

9 For a comprehensive examination of Rahner's soteriology, see Anselm Grün, *Erlösung durch das Kreuz. Karl Rahners Beitrag zu einem heutigen Erlösungsverständnis* (Münsterschwarzach: Vier-Türme-Verlag, 1975).

10 "The One Christ," 208 ("Der eine Jesus Christ," 262): "[D]iese Theorie insinuiert doch fast zwangsläufig den Gedanken an eine Umstimmung Gottes, die metaphysisch unmöglich ist."

Rahner the equally problematic notion that "Jesus is man's representative and is opposed to the correct understanding of self-redemption."[11] The "correct understanding" insists on the role of our freedom in our own salvation, which after all consists formally in our acts of faith, hope, and love.[12] Nothing and nobody can substitute for us in this respect.

On the other hand, Rahner says that he wishes to make good the traditional claim that our salvation is truly dependent on Christ, that his Cross is a true cause of our salvation.[13] And he thinks to do this by likening the causality of the Cross to that of a sacrament.

> [T]he cross (together with the resurrection) of Jesus has a primary sacramental causality for the salvation of all men, in so far as it mediates salvation to man by means of salvific grace which is universally operative in the world. It is the sign of this grace and of its victorious and irreversible activity in the world. The effectiveness of the cross is based on the fact that it is the primary sacramental sign of grace.[14]

---

[11] Ibid., 208 (262): "Die Satisfaktionstheorie . . . fördert die Idee einer letztlich undenkbaren Stellvertretung der Menschen durch Jesus und steht dem rechten Verständnis der Selbsterlösung entgegen."

[12] Ibid., 206–7 (260–61). See also "The Christian Understanding of Redemption," *TI* 21 (New York: Crossroad, 1988), 240–42, where the concern is to deny any understanding of the efficacy of the Cross that would imply a synergism between God and man; and in the same volume of the *Investigations*, see "Reconciliation and Vicarious Redemption," 265–66.

In the article "Salvation" in *Sacramentum Mundi* 5 (New York: Herder & Herder, 1968): 430, Rahner repeats as well some of the other standard criticisms of St. Anselm. "Satisfaction" is a category of Germanic law and little suited to describe personal relations; there is no way in which a moral action already due to God can be compensation for offense, and if the death of Christ is regarded as supererogatory, this divorces it from his life and destiny; there is a merely extrinsic connection between Christ's merit and our redemption; and if Christ satisfies for sin, what role is there for the satisfaction of the sinner? These objections are mostly obviated in St. Thomas's deployment of "satisfaction," though that argument cannot be taken up here. As to the provenance of the notion of satisfaction, see G. Mansini, "St. Anselm, *Satisfactio,* and the *Rule* of St. Benedict," in this volume.

[13] "The One Christ," 200, 204 (" Der eine Jesus Christ," 251–52, 257).

[14] Ibid., 212 (267): "Das Kreuz (samt der Auferstehung Jesu) hat insofern eine ursakramentale Ursächlichkeit für das Heil aller Menschen, als es dieses Heil durch die in der Welt überall wirksame Heilsgnade vermittelt; es ist Zeichen dieser Heilsgnade und ihrer siegreichen Irreversibilität in der Welt. Die Wirksamkeit des Kreuzes beruht darauf, daß es ursakramentales Zeichen von Gnade ist."

This is a causality "proper to the sign as such and is not something added to the sign."[15] The sign of grace and the grace signified are not two separate realities, he explains. Rather:

> We should . . . speak of two moments in a process of historical and ontological fulfillment, even if the conditions of each are different. In this sense the sacramental sign is a cause of grace. The sign belongs to the essential actualisation of this grace which thereby finds irreversible historical expression. The sign is in fact brought forth by grace as its "real symbol," so that grace itself achieves fulfillment.[16]

Given the history of human sin and the uncertainty of God's response to it, this "ambivalence" can be taken away, and the outcome of history as a history of salvation "fixed," "if God were to communicate himself to a man in such a unique manner that this man would become the definitive and irreversible self-gift of God to the world."[17] The man to whom God's self-gift is irreversibly given is of course Jesus of Nazareth, who for his part seals the gift in his acceptance of it in death.

> He would also freely accept the divine self-gift in such a manner that this too would be irreversible, i.e. through his death as the definitive culmination of his free actions in history. If salvation history is irreversibly directed in this sense to salvation, and not to damnation, through a concrete event, then this historically tangible occurrence must be a sign of the salvation of the world in the sense of a "real symbol," and so possesses a type of causality where salvation is concerned. To this we wish to apply a well known theological concept and call it "sacramental."[18]

---

15 Ibid., 212 (268), where he speaks of an "Ursächlichkeit . . . die dem Zeichen als solchem zukommt und nicht als etwas anderes zum Zeichen hinzutritt."

16 Ibid., 213 (268): "Vielmehr ist von zwei Momenten eines sich geschichtlich bildenden Wesensvollzugs zu sprechen, auch wenn die gegenläufigen Bedingungen nicht derselben Art sind. In diesem Sinn ist das sakramentale Zeichen Ursache der Gnade. Das Zeichen gehört eben zur Vollendung des Wesens dieser Gnade, die sich gerade darin geschichtich als irreversibel meldet. Das Zeichen wird nämlich gerade von der Gnade als deren Realsymbol hervorgebracht, so daß sie selbst zur Vollendung kommt."

17 Ibid., 213–14 (269): The *Ambivalenz* of the history of human and divine freedom can be determinately fixed and decided *(innergeschichtlich festlegen)* "wenn Gott sich in unüberholbarer Weise einem Menschen so mitteilt, daß dieser zur nicht mehr rücknehmbaren Selbstzusage Gottes an die Welt wird."

18 Ibid., 214 (269): "[E]r selbst in seiner Freiheit solche göttliche Selbstzusage annimmt in einer Weise, die ebenfalls nicht mehr rückgängig zu machen ist, d.h. durch seinen Tod als Ende und Endgültigwerden menschlicher Freiheitsgeschichte überhaupt. Ist nun die Heilsgeschichte in diesem Sinn durch ein konkretes Ereignis

Rahner is here relying on a certain understanding of death as the culmination of human freedom, as well as on his prior work on the nature of symbolic reality and of sacramental causality.[19]

Since in this article he equates saying that the death of Jesus "causes" salvation with saying that it has a "meaning" for us,[20] and since the Cross is supposed to *cause* simply because it *signifies*, he tries to anticipate the objection that his position does nothing more than reduce the Cross to an event of revelation, a sort of demonstration of God's love, and that it would therefore be merely a restatement of the position imputed to Peter Abelard.

> The objection may be raised that a sign, which can only be directed and addressed to men, may possibly be a significant cause of their awareness but cannot be the cause of the reality signified, i.e. the salvation of men. In reply to this it should be pointed out that a notion of "sign" is here being assumed which is a quite inappropriate for a sacramental sign. . . . [I]n a sacramental sign the saving will of God and grace find historical expression. Sign and signified are essentially one . . . so that the reality signified comes to be in and through the sign, and the sign, therefore, in this specific and limited sense, causes the reality signified.[21]

In this way, according to Anselm Grün, Rahner effects a unity of objective and subjective redemption. Objectively, the Cross bespeaks the availability of grace to man; subjectively, it evokes the reception of grace on the part of those whom it addresses. The crucified Jesus is thus the "effective exemplar"

---

auf das Heil und nicht auf das Unheil irreversibel festgelegt, dann muß solch ein geschichtlich greifbares Geschehen Zeichen im Sinn von Realsymbol für das Heil der ganzen Welt sein und jene Ursächlichkeit für dieses Heil haben, die wir unter Gebrauch eines bekannten theologischen Begriffs 'sakramental' nennen möchten."

19 See *On the Theology of Death*, 2nd ed. (New York: Herder & Herder, 1965), 26–31; "The Theology of the Symbol," *TI* 4 (Baltimore: Helicon Press, 1966), 223–31, 241–43; and *The Church and the Sacraments*, in *Inquiries* (New York: Herder & Herder, 1964), 216–22.

20 "The One Christ," 212 ("Der eine Jesus Christus," 267).

21 Ibid., 215 (270–71): "Gegen eine naheliegenden Einwand, daß ein Zeichen, das sich immer nur an den Menschen als Adressaten richten kann, zwar für dessen Erkenntnis möglicherweise ursächlich bedeutsam ist, nicht jedoch für die bezeichnete Sache selbst, das Heil des Menschen nämlich, muß darauf hingewiesen werden, daß hier ein Verständnis von 'Zeichen' vorausgesetzt wird, das gerade beim eigentlich sakramentalen Zeichen unzutreffend ist. . . . im sakramentalen Zeichen setzt sich eben der Heilswille Gottes und die Gnade selber in geschichtlicher Weise. Zeichen und Bezeichnetes sind damit im Gegensatz zur erwähnten Voraussetzung wesentlich eins, so daß sich das Bezeichnete in und durch das Zeichen ereignet und das Zeichen in diesem bestimmten und begrenzten Sinn das Bezeichnete verursacht."

(produktive Vorbild) of the divinizing and forgiving self-communication of God, because he enables and empowers our free reception of salvation.[22] Through the objectivity and historical concreteness of the Cross, the situation of our freedom is so characterized that the subjective appropriation of grace in freedom is truly caused by the historicization of grace that the Cross is.[23]

We might say that, so to speak, the Cross acts as a catalyst between the grace of God, already conditioning human freedom as an existentiale, and this freedom as moving itself (under grace) to accept grace. The causality of the Cross is therefore something of the historical, categorical order ("historical expression"). The grace that moves human freedom, however, is not caused by the Cross; both this grace and the Cross find their single cause in the salvific will of God. The Cross acts, in a historically expressive manner—precisely as a sign, that is—to evoke in those who behold it the acceptance of a grace always already available and conditioning freedom. Or, as Rahner indicates, grace itself causes the sign of grace; the sign is not the prior cause of grace: "[T]he sign is in fact brought forth by grace."[24] As he says in another place, the causality of the Cross is fundamentally in the line of material and formal causality.[25]

Balthasar's Solution

If for Rahner Anselm goes too far in the direction of supposing that the Cross really changes things (for he thinks it implies a change in God), and too far in the direction of supposing that Christ substitutes for or represents us, for Balthasar Anselm does not go far enough in either direction.[26] It is difficult to summarize Balthasar's solution, but for the sake of exposition, it can be construed as one extended argument whose point of departure is the

---

22 Grün, 107; he is citing the German original of Rahner's "Self-Realization and Taking Up One's Cross," for which last see *TI* 9 (New York: Herder & Herder, 1972), 256.

23 Grün, 108–9.

24 "The One Christ," 213 (" Der eine Jesus Christ," 268): "Das Zeichen wird nämlich gerade von der Gnade als deren Realsymbol hervorgebracht." As also in *The Church and Sacraments*, 221.

25 "Christian Understanding," 251. Evidently, the question of the correctness of Rahner's view is intimately tied to the adequacy of the theorem of the supernatural existentiale and the way he conceives the relation between the transcendental and the categorical. For critical remarks on his view of sacramental causality itself, see William van Roo, "The Church and the Sacraments," *Catholic Theological Society of America, Proceedings* 19 (1964): 161–71.

26 An appreciation of Anselm is to be found in Balthasar's *The Glory of the Lord*, vol. 2: *Studies in Theological Style: Clerical Styles* (San Francisco: Ignatius, 1984), 211–59; but for his criticism of Anselm, see *TD* 4:255–61 (III:235–41).

Cross as really effective of the reconciliation of God and the world, which proceeds thence to representation, "wrath," and the Cross as Trinitarian event, and whose conclusion is the assertion of change in God.

The starting point, then, is the Cross as truly effective of a change in the economy. It is no mere "symbolic illustration" of God's grace and mercy, and this is said with explicit reference to Rahner.[27] More trenchantly, it is not just a "visual aid" in demonstration of God's already actual grace and mercy.[28] To the contrary, the Cross is an act, a work.[29] Nothing less really takes the New Testament at its word. The Cross averts the wrath of God from us; it destroys our sin; it frees us from the death of sin.[30] It does not just effect a modification of our situation before God; it changes us, effecting an "ontological shift" in us, and this is prior to any act, even the act of faith, on our part.[31] This seems to mean that what Rahner identifies as the existentiale of grace conditioning human freedom is itself the effect of the Cross, and not something already present under whose influence the signifying power of the Cross provokes human freedom to act.

It follows that, because the Cross works its effect prior to any exercise of our freedom, Christ must be our representative in the strongest possible sense, even our substitute. In virtue of his love for us, he must so identify with us that he takes on our sin. So, there is a "real assumption of universal guilt" by Christ;[32] "the sinner as sinner is hanging on the cross," "and not only in some vague representation."[33] For if sin is destroyed in the destruction of his death, it must be that he has taken it on himself, nor is it enough to say that he takes on the effects of our sin—the punishment justly due sin. No, he takes on the very sin itself.

---

27   *TD* 3:240 (II/2:221): "Wer hinter die grundlegenden Intuitionen Anselms zurückgeht, verfälscht und verkleinert die Sendung Jesu, die dann notgedrungen zu einer bloßen symbolischen *Darstellung* dessen wird, was ohnedies schon *ist*."

28   *TD* 3:117 (II/2:106): "Indem man einseitig den Ton darauf legt, daß in Jesus Gott selber an der Menscheit gehandelt und ihr seine gnädige Gesinnung erwiesen hat, entseht der Anschein, Passion und Aufersthung Jesus seien nichts weiter als ein symbolischer Anschauungsunterricht."

29   *TD* 4:362 (III:337).

30   *TD* 4:242 (III:222), the third aspect of atonement in the New Testament.

31   *TD* 4:389 (III:363): "[J]ene, für deren Schuld gelitten und gesühnt worden ist, in ihrem Sein an eine andere Stelle gerückt worden sind." See also *TD* 4:403 (III:376), and *TD* 3:121 (II/2: 110).

32   *MP,* 01 (*MS* III/2:194): "[V]ielmehr wird man tiefer die hypostatische Union als Bedingung der Möglichkeit eines realen In-sich-Tragens der Gesamtschuld beschreiben müssen."

33   *MP,* 134 (*MS* III/2:221): "[D]er Sünder *als Sünder* am Kreuz Christi hängt, real und nicht nur in einer vagen Repräsentation."

[N]othing would be achieved by men unloading their sin if the one onto whom they load it were incapable of receiving it in its totality, as what it is: it presupposes that he is both willing and able to bear sin.[34]

It is not, of course, that he himself becomes really guilty of sin. So, strictly, he is not punished, where "punishment" means the just infliction of suffering on the guilty. Still, subjectively, Christ experiences what he bears as punishment.[35] He takes on the very experience of sin, the experienced alienation from God that sin is, and there is "an inner appropriation of what is ungodly and hostile to God, an identification with that darkness of alienation from God into which the sinner falls as a result of his No."[36]

From Christ's representative role so starkly conceived, it would seem to follow as a strict corollary—or perhaps as a mere restatement—that the wrath of God, the judgment of God on sin, falls on Christ. That indeed is what Christ undergoes on Good Friday and Holy Saturday according to Balthasar.[37] That this is so is a function of God's mercy, of his covenant love, which cannot remain indifferent to man's refusal, and which finds in Christ the only one capable of so bearing God's repudiation of sin that the grace offered man does not destroy him.[38] Notwithstanding both the origin of wrath in love and the sinlessness of Christ, however, it can and must be said that "God unloaded his wrath upon the Man who wrestled with his destiny on the Mount of Olives."[39] Again:

---

34 *TD* 4:334 (III:311): "[D]as Aufladen ihrer Sünde von seiten der Menschen nichts fruchten würde, wenn der, dem sie aufgeladen wird, unfähig wäre, sie als ganze und als das, was sie in Wahrheit ist, entgegenzunehmen, was sowohl seine Fähigkeit wie seine Willigkeit dazu voraussetzt."

35 *TD* 4:337–38 (III:314).

36 *TD* 4:334–35 (IV:311): "[D]ie Stunde der innerlich eindringenden 'Macht der Finsternis' (Lk 22:53) . . . *er* nimmt sie auf sich, sie wird ihm nicht von außen her aufgezwungen . . . sie eine *innere* Übernahme des Un- und Widergöttlichen fordert, eine Identifikation mit jener gottfernen Finsternis, in die der Sünder durch sein Nein gelangt." Again, he is "solidary with us not only in what is symptomatic of sin, the punishment of sin, but also in co-experiencing sin, in the *peirasmos* of the very essence of that negation, though without 'committing' (Hebrews 4:15) sin himself" (*MP*, 137 [*MS* III/2: 223]: "Gott nicht nur solidarisch mit uns wird in dem, was Symptom der Sünde, Strafe für die Sünde ist, sondern in der Mit-Erfahrung, im Peirasmos des Wesens des Nein selbst, ohne es selbst zu 'begehen' [Hebr 4:15]").

37 *MP*, 120, 138–39 (*MS* III/2:209, 225); see also *MP*, 168–74 (*MS* III/2:243–48), on the "second death" and "the experience of sin as such."

38 *MP*, 20–121 (*MS* III/2:209).

39 *TD* 4:345 (III:322): "Kann man ernstlich von einer Entladung des Zornes Gottes über dem am Ölberg Ringenden, dann Gekreuzigten sprechen? Man muß es."

> In love and obedience [Christ] will not surrender this solidarity [with sinners]; in consequence, he drinks deeply of the darkness of man's God-forsakenness. . . . God's anger strikes him instead of the countless sinners. . . .[40]

In this way Christ experiences not sin, but the "hopelessness" of the sinner's "resistance to God and the graceless No of divine grace" to this same resistance.[41] Only so, apparently, is sin annihilated in the destruction of the Cross.

> The injustice [of sin] is not cleared away by half-measures and compromises, but by drastic measures which make a clean sweep of it, so that all the world's injustice is consumed by the total wrath of God, that the total righteousness of God may be accessible to the sinner.[42]

In still other words that Balthasar also does not fail to use, Christ bears the punishment of the damned and experiences hell and damnation.[43]

Now, since it is God the Father who visits his wrath upon Christ, the incarnate Son,[44] and since it is by this event that sin is destroyed, it is easy to see why the Cross is foundationally a transaction between Father and Son. This is exactly where Balthasar moves things. "The world's darkness" is "taken into the inner light of the Trinity."[45]

> In the end, therefore, [the Son's death] is the human expression of a shared love-death in a supereminently trinitarian sense: the One who forsakes is just as much affected (in his eternal life) as the One who is forsaken, and just as much as the forsaking and forsaken love that is One in the Holy Spirit.[46]

---

[40] *TD* 4:348 (III:324): "Jesu sowohl gehorsamer wie lebender Wille, diese Solidarität nicht preiszugeben, läßt ihn deren gottverlassne Finsternis eben deshalb so tief schmecken. . . . Indem der Zorn Gottes ihn anstelle der Unzähligen trifft."

[41] *TD* 4:349 (III:325): "Deshalb erfährt er in sich—nicht ihre Sünde, sondern das Hoffnungslosse ihres Widerstands gegen Gott und das gnadenlose Nein der göttlichen Gnade gegen diesen Widerstand."

[42] *MP,* 121 (*MS* III/2:209): "Nicht Halbwegs und in Kompromissen das Unrecht wegschafft, sondern durchgreift und vollkommen aufräumt, so daß er seinen ganzen Zorn die ganze Ungerechtigkeit der Welt aufzehren läßt, um Gottes ganze Gerechtigkeit dem Sünder zugänglich zu machen."

[43] *MP,* 167, 172–73 (*MS* III/2:242, 246–47); and see Edward Oakes, *Pattern of Redemption: The Theology of Hans Urs von Balthasar* (New York: Continuum, 1994), 282.

[44] *TD* 4:348 (III:324).

[45] *TD* 4:349 (III:326): "Die Hineinnahme der weltlichen Finsternis in das innertrinitarische Licht besagt ein Wunder der Transfiguration."

[46] *TD* 4:501 (III:466): "Und nichts hindert, diesen Tod des Sohnes . . . als einen Liebestod für den Vater, für die Durchführung seines Willens bis ins Äußerste zu verstehen, und deshalb schließlich als den menschlichen Ausdruck eines gemeinsamen

The Father is no mere spectator of the drama of the Cross; he is in the drama.

The Father seems to remain above the play since he sends the Son and the Spirit; but in fact he could not involve himself more profoundly than by thus sending them.[47]

Moreover, it is because of the distinction of Father and Son that Christ can represent humanity in the first place. The Son's absolute distinction from the Father within the Trinity is the *topos*, Balthasar says, wherein he can take on that other distance from the Father, namely the distance of sin.[48] The eternal and interior drama of the Trinity contains and surpasses all possible dramatic distance, even that of sin, between God and the world; the separation of the Persons in God includes and grounds every other separation.[49]

And from the Cross as a transaction between Father and Son, there follows the last conclusion of what has here been construed as one argument; that is, there follows the questionability of the immutability of God.

It is now time to press some questions. First, how does Christ's Cross really do any good for us? Balthasar himself puts the question that directly.

[W]hy should this be efficacious for all the rest? ... The only help is to be had from the New Testament's idea of the divine love that *out of love* takes upon itself the sins of the world; and this love *must* have a double character, as the love of God the Father, who allows God the Son to go into the absolute obedience of poverty and self-abandonment where he can be nothing else than the total object that receives the divine "wrath," and as the love of God the Son, who identifies himself out of love with us sinners (Heb 2:13), and thereby fulfills the will of the Father in free obedience (Heb 10:7).[50]

Liebestodes in einem überschwenglichen trinitarischen Sinn, in dem der Verlassende (in seinem ewigen Leben) ebenso affiziert wird wie der Verlassene, wie die im Heiligen Geist gemeinsam verlassend-verlassene Liebe."

[47] *TD* 3:514 (II/2:371): "Der Vater, der als der Sender des Sohnes und des Geistes scheinbar oberhalb des Spieles verharrt, könnte sich nicht tiefer engagieren als durch diese Sendungen."

[48] *TD* 4:333–34 (III:310).

[49] *TD* 4:325, 327 (III:302, 304).

[50] *The Glory of the Lord: A Theological Aesthetics*, vol. 7: *Theology: The New Covenant* (San Francisco: Ignatius Press, 1989), 207; in German, *Herrlichkeit: Eine Theologische Ästhetik*, vol. III/2/2: *Theologie: Neuer Bund* (Einsiedeln: Johannes Verlag, 1969), 192: "Doch weshalb soll dies für die übrigen alle wirksam sein? Hier hilft weder eine juridische Imputationslehre ... noch eine physische Solidaritätslehre ... endgültig weiter, sondern einzig der neutestamentliche Gedanke der göttlichen Liebe, die *aus Liebe* die Sünden der Welt auf sich nimmt; und zwar *muß* diese

Rahner too appeals ultimately to love. But where for him the Cross moves us to respond to the already active love of God for us, for Balthasar, the resolution is more exactly Trinitarian: God can love us effectively only in the engagement of the love between Father and Son, which must be enacted in the economy.

Still, how is such engagement effective? Let us try a second question: How are sins really "annihilated"? This is not at all easy to see. What Balthasar consistently offers, however, is something like the following. The distance that is between the sinner and God, which Christ takes on and identifies with is, as it were, simply swallowed up in the still greater "distance" (distinction) between Father and Son. Such a distance is itself, however, always already overcome by their mutual personal love whose seal is the Holy Spirit. We have already adverted to this line in Balthasar. But here it is more fully, in a passage that expresses many of the themes to which attention has already been called.

> [W]e should not say that the Cross is nothing other than the ("quasi-sacramental") manifestation of God's reconciliation with the world, a reconciliation that is constant, homogeneous and always part of the given: rather we should say that God, desiring to reconcile the world to himself (and hence himself to the world), acts dramatically in the Son's Cross and Resurrection. This dramatic aspect does not entangle the immanent Trinity in the world's fate, as occurs in mythology, but it *does* lift the latter's fate to the level of the economic Trinity, which always presupposes the immanent. This is because the Son's eternal, holy distance from the Father, in the Spirit, forms the basis on which the unholy distance of the world's sin can be transposed into it, can be transcended and overcome by it.[51]

Liebe eine doppelte sein: Liebe Gottes des Vaters, der Gott dem Sohn gestattet, in den absoluten Gehorsam der Armut und Überlassung zu gehen, wo er nur noch reine Aufnahme sein kann für den göttlichen 'Zorn,' und Liebe gottes des Sohnes, der sich aus Liebe mit uns Sündern identifiziert (Hb 2:13) und dabei in freiem Gehorsam den Willen des Vaters erfüllt (Hb 10:7)."

51 *TD* 4:362 (III:337): "Man soll also nicht sagen, das Kreuz sei nichts anderes als die ('quasi-sakramentale') Manifestation einer immer gleichen, immer schon erfolgten Versöhntheit Gottes mit der Welt, vielmehr handelt der Gott, der die Versöhnung der Welt mit ihm (und darin auch seine Versöhnung mit der Welt) herbeiführen will, dramatisch in Kreuz und Auferstehung des Sohnes. Diese Dramatik verstrickt die immanente Trinität nicht mythologisch in das Weltschicksal, wohl aber hebt sie dieses Schicksal in die ökonomische Trinität hinein, deren Voraussetzung die immanente bleibt, sofern die ewige heilige Distanz des Sohnes vom Vater im Geist der Grund dafür ist, daß die unheilige Distanz der Weltsünde in sie hineingestellt, von ihr überholt und durch sie überwunden werden kann." See as well *TD* 3:530 (II/2:484); and Gerard F. O'Hanlon, *The Immutability of God in the Theology of Hans Urs von Balthasar* (Cambridge: Cambridge University Press, 1990), 27, 38, 119.

On the basis of the two passages quoted immediately above, we have, first, the assertion that the love between Father and Son, once the Son has identified himself with sinners, is strong enough to deal with sin, and second, what appears to be no more than a metaphor. A smaller distance can be contained in a larger; sin is a smaller "distance" from God than is that of Son from Father; therefore . . . and so on. But if sin is not really a distance, and if the distinction of Son and Father is not really a distance, then we are returned once again to love.

A last question: In view of the Cross, is or is not God immutable for Balthasar? Two approaches that Balthasar takes to this question can be distinguished. First, there is the line such as one finds in *Mysterium Paschale*, according to which sin is destroyed by the transaction between Father and Son in the event of the Cross in virtue of a sort of prior agreement of God, in perfect freedom, to be himself conditioned by it. Christ is the "Lamb slain before the foundation of the world" (Rev 13:8).[52] What this means is that, already, in the decision to create, and foreseeing and permitting human sin, Father and Son in their eternal love freely decide that their love will be capable of being so stretched by the Son's identification with sinful man that it will not break the bond of their own love. No change is worked on God because of his neediness, or from outside him and independently of his will. It is a matter of God from eternity having determined to integrate the economy into his own Trinitarian relations of love. He freely wills himself to be conditioned, to be really other than he would have been, because of the created order, and especially, because of the redemption of created freedom that he foreordains in the Cross.[53]

So, on the basis of this prior eternal decision, the transaction of the Cross is spoken of as effecting something in God; one can speak of an "event" in God.[54] Something new must be thought to happen to God. As he says:

---

52 *MP,* 34 (*MS* III/2:152).
53 *MP,* 35 (*MS* III/2:152–53); see O'Hanlon, *The Immutability of God,* 17–19. As well, according to O'Hanlon, 124–25, it is a matter of seeing the love between Father and Son within the Trinity as requiring a "more," a growth, that escapes the strictures of classical ontology.
54 *MP,* 24 (*MS* III/2:144): "[W]ill man das (vielleicht ursprünglich 'mythologische Schema' [of Phil 2:5–11]) christlich verstehen, und ist man deshalb gezwungen, es im Horizont der Christologie und damit der Trinitätslehre auszulegen, so muß man ein 'Geschehen' im überweltlichen und 'unveränderlichen' Gott annehmen, und dieses Geschehen, das mit den Worten 'Entleerung' (Vernichtung) und 'Herabniedrigung' beschreiben wird, ist ein 'Fahrenlassen' der 'Gottgleichheit,' . . . was den kostbaren Besitz der 'Glorie' angeht." And see *MP,* 27, 34–35, 125 (*MS* III/2:146, 152–53, 212–13), the remarks on abandonment.

> The event of the Incarnation [the kenosis of which culminates in the Cross] of the Second Person does not leave the inter-relationships of the Persons unaffected.[55]

And the following passage is also helpful.

> For such obedience [as Christ's], a divine decision must truly be required, a decision that as such implies the "surrender" of the *forma Dei*, and therefore we must at least attempt to consider how such a surrender can be possible for the God of whom we cannot postulate any alteration as this is found in creatures, nor any suffering and obeying in the manner proper to creatures. . . . [I]t will be necessary to posit an incomprehensible freedom in God that allows him to do more, and to be other, than the creature would suppose of him on the ground of his concepts of "God."[56]

So, there is a change, but not a change such as we know anything of. Such an affirmation is difficult, for it is not an instance of an ordinary deployment of analogy, according to which we say of God that such things as love or wisdom are verified in him (though not, of course, in any *manner* of which we have acquaintance) and which takes account of the difference between "pure" and "impure" perfections.

But there is also a second kind of approach in Balthasar. Here, there is the more tractable assertion that within the Trinitarian relations, there is no suffering, but there is the ground of whatever separation and suffering occur in the economy.

> The action whereby the Father utters and bestows his whole God-head, an action he both "does" and "is," generates the Son. This Son is infinitely Other, but he is also the infinitely Other *of the Father.* Thus he both grounds and surpasses all we mean by separation, pain and alienation in the world and all we can envisage in terms of loving

---

55 *MP,* 30 (*MS* III/2:149): "Nimmt man das Gesagte ernst, dann läßt das Ereignis der Fleischwerdung der zweiten Person Gottes die Beziehung der göttlichen Personen nicht unaffiziert." See further *MP,* 33 (*MS* III/2:151), quoting Paul Althaus approvingly.

56 *The Glory of the Lord,* 7:213 (*Herrlichkeit,* III/2/2:197): "Demgegenüber muß wirklich ein göttlicher Entschluß gefordert werden, der als solcher die Preisgabe der 'forma Dei' besagt, und dafür muß wenigstens der Denkversuch gemacht werden, wie eine solche Preisgabe für den Gott möglich sei, dem wir keine kreatürliche Veränderung und kein kreatürliches Leiden und Gehorchen zuschreiben können. Schon um diesen Denkversuch überhaupt zu unternehmen, wird es nötig sein, eine unfaßliche Freiheit in Gott anzusetzen, die es ihm erlaubt, mehr zu tun und anders zu sein, als die Kreatur ihm (aufgrund ihrer Gottesbegriffe) zumuten würde."

self-giving, interpersonal relationship and blessedness. He is not the direct identity of the two, but their presupposition, sovereignly surpassing them.[57]

In this line, the only thing to change because of the Incarnation and Cross is not God but our "perspective" on God, and we realize the divine being is richer and grounds more modalities of its (economic) appearance than we thought, while at the same time "we can see how unnecessary it is to speak of a 'change' in God."[58] In this line, we have a position like that of Herbert McCabe, where the history, death, and Resurrection of Jesus is the display in the created and sinful order of the eternal and unchanging relation of Father and Son within the Trinity.[59]

But even having said this, which seems to mean that there is no modification of God or the Trinitarian relations either by a created reality or by a divine decision in view of created reality, Balthasar still speaks of Father and Son being "affected" by the Cross,[60] and man's refusal causes God to suffer.[61] So at the end of the third volume of the *Theo-Drama*, explaining how the economic form of the Trinity is "suspended" and "absorbed" into the immanent at the Resurrection, he says both things in the same breath:

> This prevents the Son's Incarnation from implying a "mythological" change in God. It is not that God, in himself, changes but that the unchangeable God enters into a relationship with creaturely reality,

---

57 *TD* 4:324–25 (III:302): "Die Gebärde, mit der der Vater die Ganze Gottheit ausspricht und dahingibt (eine Gebärde, die er nicht nur 'tut,' sondern 'ist'), kann, sofern sie den Sohn als das unendlich Andere seiner selbst zeugt, nur gleichzeitig die ewige Voraussetzung und Überholung all dessen sein, was Trennung, Schmerz, Entfremdung in der Welt, und was Liebeshingabe, Ermöglichung von Begegnung, Seligkeit in ihr sein wird. Nicht unmittelbare Identität von beidem, sondern überlegene und überholende Voraussetzung für beides." See also *TD* 4:327–28 (III:304–5).

58 *TD* 2:284 (II/1:258): "Damit sind (die Perspektiven der Menschwerdung des Wortes vorwegnehmend) der Plan, die Bestimmtheit und die Begleitungsrichtung der Vorsehung gemäß der einzigen Weltidee Gottes formal umrissen. Man erkennt hier nochmals, wie unnötig es ist, bei der Universalität der göttlichen Idee von einer 'Veränderung' Gottes zu reden: das unerschöpfliche Eine kann sich innerweltlich 'epochal' je neu darbieten, ohne sich zu verändern. Nur die Perspektive an das Eine heran hat sich gewandelt." On the other hand, there are more equivocal statements within this same chapter, at 2:278–79, and 280 (II/1:253–54, 255).

59 See his "The Involvement of God," in *God Matters* (London: Geoffrey Chapman, 1987), 39–51.

60 *TD* 4:501 (III:466), quoted above, note 46.

61 *TD* 4:328 (III:305): "[I]n Gott ist der Ansatzpunkt für das, was Leiden werden kann, wenn die Vorsichtslosigkeit, mit der der Vater sich (und *alles* Seinige) weggibt . . . auf eine Freiheit stößt, die diese Vorsichtslosigkeit nicht beantwortet."

and this relationship imparts a new look to his internal relations. This is not something purely external, as if this relationship ad extra did not really affect him: rather, the new relationship to worldly nature, which is hypostatically united to the Son, highlights one of the infinite possibilities that lie in God's eternal life.[62]

So, (1) there is no change in God—at least, no "mythological" change; still, (2) he is "affected" "not purely externally";[63] and (3) this is to assert merely that one of his "possibilities" has been "highlighted." Gerard O'Hanlon thinks that in such passages Balthasar achieves a "higher viewpoint" that sublates classical theism with the concerns that process theology as well as a kind of "pain of God" theology justly but inadequately try to deal with. On the other hand, it is arguable that Balthasar retains "immutability" only as a cipher for God's transcendence, while evacuating it of content. If so, Balthasar's account of the Cross will be vulnerable when measured against Rahner's.[64]

Just as when he speaks of how the Cross annihilates sins, so when addressing the annexed question of immutability, Balthasar often achieves a stunning and wholly religious poetic impact in his marshaling of biblical themes and his insistence that we take the biblical affirmations seriously. Whether, for the task of understanding the Cross, and beyond a sort of virtuoso repetition of the New Testament, he achieves any insight not already available in the New Testament and in just the way the New Testament offers it, is another question.[65]

Picking Up the Pieces

How shall we compare these two accounts of the Cross? It is worth repeating here that in what follows, there can be no question of an adequate treatment

---

62 *TD* 3:523 (II/2:479): "Daß dem so ist, verhindert, daß die Menschwerdung des Sohnes eine 'mythische' Veränderung in Gott besagt. Nicht Gott in sich verändert sich, sondern der unveränderliche Gott geht eine Beziehung zur Geschöpflichkeit ein, die seinen innern Relationen ein neues Aussehen gibt; freilich nicht rein äußerlich, als beträfe diese Beziehung nach außen ihn nicht wirklich, sondern so, daß die neue Beziehung zu der weltlichen Natur, die dem Sohn hypostatisch geeint wird, eine der unendlichen Möglichkeiten, die in Gottes ewigem Leben liegen, ins Licht setzt."

63 See also *TD* 4:324 (III:302), where an "intramundane suffering" is excluded, but still "something happens" to God.

64 Note Rahner's observation, as quoted in Oakes, *Pattern of Redemption,* 281n11: "it does not help me to escape from my mess and mix-up and despair if God is in the same predicament."

65 For an assessment of this kind, see Aidan Nichols, "Balthasar and His Christology," *New Blackfriars* 66 (1985): 322.

of these two formidable positions in modern Catholic theology. Still, there is perhaps some utility in asking what we would be left with if we let what is apparently strong in each position knock out what is weak in the other.

It is hard to quarrel with Rahner's starting point, which is that the salvific and merciful and forgiving will of God is the first cause of our redemption, the cause of the Cross itself, which therefore cannot be thought of as changing him from an angry to a placated God. In his own way, Balthasar recognizes this, but he gives greater place to the "wrath of God" because of the way he conceives Christ's representative role. And he does this, it has been argued, because he wishes to take seriously the straightforward assertions of the New Testament to the effect that something happens, that something is effected by the Cross, namely reconciliation between the world and God. Against this standard, Rahner can be seen to fall short and not really make good the "event" character of the Cross. He assimilates the deed of the Cross to a word of revelation. Although it is an effective word, it effects not the availability of grace as such, but the historical appropriation of grace by the individual. If this be thought inadequate, then one recognizes the justness of Balthasar's starting point.

If both starting points are correct, one at least has gone astray. It might be argued that Rahner does not do justice to the New Testament foundations of the notion of representation.[66] His motive for jettisoning this notion, he says, is to ensure the recognition of the role of our own freedom in the process of redemption. The idea that Christ represents us, or substitutes for us, however, never meant to deny this. It meant rather to indicate that the offer of the grace of conversion was, in fact and as determined by God, costly. It was costly to God's incarnate Son. But the offer remained an offer, and did not elide the necessity of a cooperative response. It is hard not to suspect that the real reason he excises the notion is to avoid the implication of change in God. He takes it, perhaps, that Christ's representation of us, and prior to our freedom, makes one thing with the view that the only change that the Cross can effect is a change in God. But it is a mistake to suppose that if the Cross does not change God, it changes nothing. To the contrary, it can work an economic change without that implying a change in God. This point will be taken up briefly further on.

Before proceeding further, however, we must consider whether Rahner really and truly is opposed to Balthasar on the issue of immutability. For in an important article on the theology of the Incarnation, he himself seems to qualify the immutability of God very substantially.[67] Explaining what it

---

[66] See Balthasar's criticism of Rahner on this point, *TD* 4:274–75, 278–80 (III:253–54, 257–59).

[67] "On the Theology of the Incarnation," *TI* 4 (London: Darton, Longman and Todd, 1966), 105–20; in German, "Zur Theologie der Menschwerdung," *Schriften zur*

means to say that God becomes man, he informs us that, if we take this with due seriousness, we will see that the immutability of God, while to be affirmed, is to be affirmed only in dialectical tension with the statement of the becoming of God in the Incarnation. If God is immutable "in himself," it is nonetheless true that he can change "in another." And this means neither to deny immutability nor to assert that all the change is really only in the other of the humanity of Jesus.[68]

Two remarks are in order here. If we are to take this position as controlling for Rahner, then there does indeed seem to be a possibility for a radical rapprochement of the two positions, as Balthasar himself seems to indicate.[69] Of course, the question as to the coherence of Rahner at this point would then be raised, just as it is raised for Balthasar.[70] But second, why does not Rahner himself remember at this point of his soteriology that the immutability of God is but a "dialectical truth," to be kept in tension with the truth that God becomes? Evidently, it is because, while God can be said to become man, he cannot be said to become willing to communicate himself in divinizing and forgiving grace in virtue of the Incarnation and death of the Son. On the contrary, the Incarnation proceeds from the same prior loving and forgiving will of God as does the supernatural existentiale. So at this point, and whatever he wishes to say about the Incarnation, here the immutability of God controls the dialectic of mutability-immutability.

If at this juncture we side with Rahner against Balthasar on the issue of immutability in the theology of the Cross, we are doubtless on familiar enough traditional ground, the ground Rahner indicates, presumably, by speaking in "The One Christ" of the idea of change in God as "metaphysically impossible." Infinite perfection cannot change; and if God really is eternal, there are no temporal parts in his duration for talk of change to make sense, since the notion of change absolutely requires *time*. If it is

Theologie 4 (Einsiedeln: Benziger, 1960), 137–55. This article is substantially reproduced in *Foundations of Christian Faith* (New York: Seabury Press, 1978), 213–28.

68 "Theology of the Incarnation," 113–14*n*2 (" Zur Theologie der Menschwerdung," 147*n*3), where Rahner says, of the Incarnation: "Wenn wir dies eine Veränderung nennen, dann müssen wir (weil Gott an sich unveränderlich ist) sagen, daß der in sich selbst unveränderlich Gott am andern sich ändern könne (eben Mensche werden könne), und man darf dieses 'sich am andern ändern' weder als Widerspruch zur Unveränderlichkeit Gottes in sich betrachten noch es einfach zurückfallen lassen in die Aussage einer 'Veränderung *des* andern.' "

69 *TD* 4:277–78 (III:256–57).

70 Dom Illtyd Trethowan thinks Rahner incoherent; see "A Changing God," *Downside Review* 84 (1966): 247–61. For a quite different reading of Rahner, see Thomas G. Weinandy, *Does God Change?* (Still River, MA: St. Bede's Publications, 1985), 163–74, who thinks that Rahner is simply upholding the truth of the communication of idioms.

right on such grounds to dismiss any talk of change in God as nonsense, then it must be that Balthasar has somewhere gone astray.

If Balthasar moves from Christ's representation of us in bearing sin and the experienced alienation of the sinner from God, to Christ's bearing the wrath of God, to the Cross as inner-Trinitarian event, to the mutability of God, and if this conclusion is to be rejected, where is he to be stopped? If the movement of Balthasar's thought really is tight, then we must stop him at the point where representation includes bearing the experience of sin and the sinner's experienced alienation from God. If it is not, then perhaps we can stop him at the penultimate station, the inner-Trinitarian event. If we stop him too soon, we face the serious danger of failing to recognize something essential to our appreciation of the passion, if Christ has indeed experienced the pangs of hell. On the other hand, if we do not stop him somewhere, we end up imputing a change to God that either destroys the divine transcendence, and thence the doctrine of creation itself, or threatens theological discourse with incoherence.

If we try to save as much of Balthasar as possible, then we try the last option as to where to stop things. Let us say, then, that Christ bears the "wrath of God," that is, the consequence of violated covenant love. Does this mean that the Father, personally, does something to the Son, personally, in the economy (a "doing" or action that is, doubtlessly, already pre-contained in some way in the immanent Trinitarian relation)? Such an answer, oddly enough, would seem to confuse the divine and human natures. It is the Incarnate Son who bears the pangs of hell. The predication goes all the way really and truly to the supposit, in that the Son, one of the Trinity, suffers the pangs of hell. But he does this in virtue of the assumed human nature. It is his experience of alienation, indeed. The nature of this experience, however, is human, for the Son has a human consciousness, feeling, knowledge, response to whatever it is he is conscious of, feels, knows, responds to. That he can have this experience truly reveals his character as Son; it is an economic manifestation of whatever there is of "mission" and "obedience" that are to be verified supereminently in the eternal procession.[71] As an economic manifestation, however, it remains a created reality. As *created*, it is the common work of the Three *ad extra*. It is not then, correctly described as a new "event" or "happening" within the Trinity.

To say otherwise is to confuse the natures. And this, I think, Balthasar does. Writing on the mission of Christ, he says that the obedience of the Son reveals not only the Person, but the divine nature.[72] On the contrary,

---

[71] See, for example, *TD* 3:157–59, 227, 516–18 (II/2:143–45, 208, 473–75).
[72] *The Christian State of Life* (San Francisco: Ignatius Press, 1983), 78; see also *TD* 3:157–59 (II/2:143–45).

the union is hypostatic, in and according to the Person; it is not a union in and according to the natures. The Incarnation reveals the Trinity to us; it does not tell us what God is.[73]

What Balthasar ends up contributing that is new and that is acceptable, therefore, is a more simple and profound reading of the cry of abandonment on the Cross. This contribution is a lot, and cannot adequately be appreciated here. But that is all; the rest of his construction must be abandoned.

Where does this leave us? What is true in Rahner is that something in the economy can only manifest, and not change, what is immanent in God and the Trinity. Thus, the Cross is the revelation of the mercy and grace of God; it is not some sort of condition of it—as, for Balthasar, it seems to be the eternally known condition of salvation such that also it implies that God, eternally, is different than he would have been had he not willed the Cross.

On the other hand, what is true in Balthasar is that the Cross is an event, that it changes things. So, it is not merely the manifestation of the antecedent salvific will of God (Rahner), but is also a change—but only in the economy.

What is the change? It is the positing of something in the economy that is a greater good and that God loves more than the created good (human nature as ordered to God) that sin destroys. It is something that God loves more than he hates sin, and so is "satisfactory."[74] More, the eternal and unchanging God wills our redemption really and truly to depend on the satisfactory death of Christ, a created expression of the incarnate Son's love and obedience, a greater created good than that destroyed by sin. And this is fitting, for since it is also a greater created good than that of the preservation of the order of justice by the device of punishment, satisfaction can be preferred to punishment. Precisely because it is the greater created good than that destroyed by sin, it merits not only the abrogation of punishment, but the renewal of grace. So loving the Son in his final obedience and love, God fittingly offers the grace of conversion

---

[73] See Herbert McCabe, "Freedom," in *God Matters*, 18–19. If the Person is one with the nature, how is the incarnation not a revelation of the nature as well? Although there is no real distinction between them, there is a distinction of reason between the nature and the Person. If this distinction is understood in the wisdom of St. Thomas, it is understood as well by the divine Wisdom. But what the divine Wisdom can conceive, it can effect, since there is no distinction between the divine Wisdom and the divine Power. So, the divine Wisdom understands, and the divine Will makes it be, that the union is hypostatic and not of the natures. See Bernard Lonergan, *De constitutione ontologica et psychologica Christi* (Rome: Gregorian University, 1961), no. 69.

[74] *Summa theologiae* III, q. 48, a 3, c and ad 2.

for those for whom that Son died. So, objectively, God wills our reconciliation to depend on the satisfaction of Christ and, subjectively, to be a participation in the satisfaction of Christ—a participation in our redemption than which no greater can be conceived.

In other words, where we are left after we use Rahner to criticize Balthasar, and Balthasar to criticize Rahner, is with the prior tradition, the tradition of St. Anselm and St. Thomas on "satisfaction."

Ecclesiology and Sacramental Theology

CHAPTER **8**

On the Relation of Particular
to Universal Church

The Ecclesiology of Communion

AN ECCLESIOLOGY of communion understands the Church as a communion of Churches. Dioceses, and not national conferences, are the "Churches" in question. And Churches are "in communion" when they share a common faith, a common life, and a common worship. Worship is perfectly shared when the Churches recognize and are welcome at one another's Eucharist. Shared Eucharist requires a perfectly common ecclesial life, where Churches recognize the apostolicity of each other's pastors, the bishops. Full recognition occurs only when all the pastors preach the same gospel and so elicit the same faith in the same creed and the same obedience to the same commandments.

Such an ecclesiology finds its model of communion in the Trinity. The Holy Spirit is the subsistent Fellowship, Communion, *Koinonia* between Father and Son. Furthermore, it is this same Holy Spirit, operative in each Church, who is the uncreated and personal principle of their communion.

Such an ecclesiology finds the sacrament of communion in the Eucharist. The common sacrifice makes all who partake in it members of Christ and the Body of Christ. Sharing in the table is even now to share in the wedding feast of the Lamb; such sharing is therefore a realization of ecclesial reality as Bride of Christ. Most especially for thinking of communion, Eucharistic sharing is both the effect and so the sign of the unity of the Churches, and as well, it is the cause of the unity of the Churches. It is the effect of unity, because the apostolic ministry required for presidency of the Eucharist is guaranteed through its installation and continued recognition by the apostolic ministers of other Churches. Eucharistic sharing is also the cause of unity, since the *res* of the sacrament is charity.

Because of these irrefrangible bonds of union, the Spirit of Christ and the Sacrament of Christ, the Churches easily recognize one another as Churches across the differences of cultures that mark the expression of their common faith. They see themselves in one another even in the different ways in which they engage the political economies in which they are embedded. Such differences will arise and necessarily so from the common mission of all the Churches, since each society bears its own wounds of inhumanity and injustice that the Churches bind up, and each displays its own glories of humanity and human achievement that the Churches strengthen. Moreover, because the Spirit of Christ is the Spirit of charity and the Sacrament of Christ is the sacrament of charity, the Churches are moved to help one another in their common mission across the divides of geography, culture, and history.

A Question in the Ecclesiology of Communion

Beyond the relation of one Church to another, however, there is the relation of each of the many Churches to the one Church. It is the understanding of this relation that has generated some controversy. The controversy arises, in part anyway, because of its consequences for the relation of the particular Churches to Rome—more exactly, to the successor of Peter. These consequences are in part determined, moreover, not just by the abstract question of the relation of local to universal Church, but by many issues of pastoral concern and practical organization. These issues cannot be dealt with here; it will be enough to determine just one part of the "abstract" question.

That part, the lightening rod for much of the more recent discussion, has to do with the sense of the Congregation for the Doctrine of the Faith's 1992 *Letter to the Bishops of the Catholic Church on Some Aspects of the Church Understood as Communion.* In its ninth paragraph, the *Letter* states that the universal Church is prior to the particular Churches both ontologically and temporally.[1]

The Priority of the Church to the Rest of Creation

The interpretation of this statement is complicated by two factors. First, the *Letter* says the universal Church is ontologically prior even to creation itself. Second, the statement shifts from speaking of the Church's priority to particular Churches (for instance, giving "birth to the particular Churches as her daughters") to speaking of the universal Church's priority to *local*

---

[1] For a summary and review of the exchange between Cardinals Joseph Ratzinger and Walter Kasper, see Kilian McDonnell, "The Ratzinger/Kasper Debate: The Universal Church and Local Churches," *Theological Studies* 63 (2002): 227–50.

Churches (said to be "particular expressions of the one unique Church of Jesus Christ" and likewise said to "arise out of" the universal Church).

If the universal Church, "the Church that is one and unique, precedes creation," and this is so "ontologically," and if particular Churches are created, then it certainly follows that the universal Church is prior to them. The trouble is that this will suggest to many that the universal Church is some unimaginable eternal and so uncreated fourth hypostasis in addition to the persons of the Trinity. What does the Congregation mean here? It purports at this juncture to be representing nothing but the teaching of the Fathers, and cites as authorities for this statement *The Shepherd of Hermas* and Clement of Rome's Second Letter to the Corinthians.

The Shepherd of Hermas, Vision II, Chapter IV, reads as follows.

> Now a revelation was given to me, my brethren, while I slept, by a young man of comely appearance, who said to me, "Who do you think that old woman is from whom you received the book?" And I said, "The Sibyl." "You are mistaken," he said; "it is not the Sibyl." "Who is it then?" I say. And he said, "It is the Church." And I said to him, "Why then is she an old woman?" "Because," he said, "she was created first of all. On this account is she old. And for her sake was the world made."

And then there is the Second Letter to the Corinthians, attributed to Clement, at 14,2.

> I do not suppose you are unaware that the living "Church is the body of Christ"; for the Scripture says, "God created man male and female." The male is Christ, the female is the Church. Moreover, the books and the apostles declare that the Church belongs not to the present, but existed from the beginning. For she was spiritual, as was also our Jesus, but was made manifest in the last days that she might save us.

Evidently, the Congregation is not endorsing the view that the Church is a sort of hypostasis distinct from God that exists before or independently of creation. Rather, what the *Shepherd* gives us to believe is that the Church is first in the divine intention, and that it is for the sake of the Church, in which the mystery of our salvation is realized, that all things else are created. The created order finds its point, its *telos*, in the Church. Final causes, too, are matters of "ontology." For its part, the Second Letter teaches us that, in the same sense in which Christ exists from the beginning, so does his body and bride, the Church. But just as little does this mean that the humanity of Christ existed before it was assumed from

Mary the Virgin, so little does it mean that there is a Church before the Church, a Church before the foundation of the world, except in the mind and intention of God.

We must read the *Letter to the Bishops* in this way, since in addition, although the Congregation holds that the universal Church is not composed of the particular Churches *as a federation*, it does hold that the universal Church is composed of particular Churches—"they are 'part of the one Church of Christ'" (no. 9, quoting John Paul II). So, the Archdiocese of Indianapolis is a part of the universal Church. If we then say that the universal Church exists before creation, we would have also to say that the Archdiocese of Indianapolis exists before the foundation of the world. To the contrary, *The Official Catholic Directory* says that it was not erected till 1834. Therefore, we must think of the existence of the Church "before creation" as existence in the mind and intention of God.

Things being so, as Cardinal Walter Kasper has pointed out, this kind of ontological priority of Church to creation does not go very far in showing the priority of universal Church to particular Church. For the particular Church of, say, Louisville, is just as much in the eternal mind of God, and so prior to creation, as the whole Church.

The patristic citations therefore seem to some not to advance but rather to obscure the Congregation's case, unless we take existence in the mind and intention of God to connote at the same time the standards of purity and charity and faithfulness that the Churches must all strive to live up to. Even so, the Congregation's case would still not be very clear. The ontological priority of the universal Church perhaps means nothing more than the priority of the divine to the human element in the mystery of the Church.[2] But if so, the claim of priority is not very interesting. Clarity and interest both will come if we take up the second complicating factor, and think about "local Church" and "particular Church."

Particular and Local and Universal Church

At first sight, the seeming equivalence of "local Church" and "particular Church" serves to complete the argument for the contemporaneity of universal Church and particular Churches. For if the universal Church is not some supratemporal hypostasis, then it has its feet in time and on the ground—that is, in a location—just as much as any particular Church. A Church that is not in a place, a Church that is not *located*, a local Church, is not an existent Church. Therefore, must not the relation rather be that particular and local Churches are not posterior to, but rather coeval with, the universal Church?

---

[2] See *Lumen Gentium* 8. This is perhaps part of what Ratzinger has in mind; see McDonnell, "Ratzinger/Kasper," 235, 237.

It must be granted that the *Letter* certainly seems not to distinguish "particular Church" and "local Church." It is also to be granted that for many, and perhaps, most purposes there would be no reason to distinguish. There is one point, however, at which we really should distinguish, and if we do, we can make the *Letter*'s claim about priority plain as day.

This point is the temporal beginning of ecclesial reality, the beginning where all endowments have been given Christ's Bride because the Pascal Mystery has been completed in the Bridegroom and, taken up on high, "he gives gifts to men." Old Israel has passed through another sea and crossed over another Jordan; the time of preparation is over and the time of perfection has come. This moment of fulfillment is the day of Resurrection in John, and the day of Pentecost in Luke. In either case, the Church has now been shown the entire gospel she is to herald; she has been given all the instruments of sanctification with which to bring forth and nourish her children; she has been furnished with all the ligaments and joints needed for the motions of a common life. It is just as Acts 2:42 has it, where the Church is fitted out with a common teaching, a common way of life, a common Eucharist.

Evidently, this Church is a local Church, since it is in Jerusalem. But it not a particular Church; it is rather the whole Church, all the Church there is, the universal Church.[3]

The particular Churches come later and indeed as daughters of the original, Jerusalem Church. They come according as the apostles go out from the great Church, and depart from the one place in which they first were gathered as witnesses of the accomplishment of the mission of Jesus, and found other communities. And when the apostles go out, and make other Churches, then the Jerusalem Church herself is no longer the whole Church, but just a particular Church.

The Church from the Churches and the Churches from the Church

Why is this? Part of the wholeness of the universal Church is her authority to teach with the authority of Christ, binding both minds and consciences. The subject of this plenary ecclesial authority is the college of apostles, and the head of that college. In Jerusalem, at the beginnings, there are Peter and the rest of the twelve, and therefore we behold there in the Pentecostal Church the Church in the fullness of its authority both to witness to the truth of the gospel and to arrange its life in accord with that truth.

It then follows that as soon as the apostles leave to execute the mission of the Church, and to found the Churches, that that wholeness is divided

---

[3] Kasper's contention that the Church of Pentecost must itself be understood to be composed of smaller, local Churches seems, well, contentious, and is just that kind of evisceration of theology in the name of the "empirical" that Ratzinger fears.

into parts, the particular Churches. Once these particular Churches are founded, then it will be true to say that the one Church exists in and from the many particular Churches (*Lumen Gentium* 23, quoted in the *Letter*, no. 9), but not before. Compared to the original whole, any single Church will be less ecclesially full, dense, weighty—"ontologically" posterior to the whole. Compared to the now existing whole, of course, no part, no local Church, is adequately distinct from the whole.

On the day of Pentecost, then, there was only one local Church, and perforce that one Church was the universal Church. It was not a part of anything greater—it was not a particular Church; it was the whole, the *catholica*. It was a local Church because it was in a place, and indeed one place, and there was no other place where the Church could be said to be. Now, today, any local Church is a particular Church. Today, it is true, the universal Church is a communion of particular Churches. But on the day of Pentecost, the universal Church was not a communion of Churches. We see at Pentecost that future communion signified in the gift of tongues. But in itself, at Pentecost, the Church was just the one local Church, which in its singularity and uniqueness was all the Church there was.

Therefore, the whole Church that was the Jerusalem Church was prior both in time and in the density and fullness of its ecclesial reality to all subsequent local Churches, including the Jerusalem Church itself once the college no longer resided there. Similarly, the communion of all the Churches at whatever time we take it, which is to say the whole at whatever time we take it, which is to say the one Church once again understood with its entire apostolic ministry and so in the completeness of its authority both to teach and to govern itself, is prior both in time and in ecclesial density to any local Church now newly founded in addition to it. Local Churches, which are always particular Churches, can be said to be formed out of her. This, too, the *Letter* says, quoting the Holy Father just after recalling *Lumen Gentium* 23.

So, summarily, we can say, "the Church from the Churches; the Churches from the Church." The first part of the diptych makes of the Church a collective whole. That is, the Church is a whole composed of parts, whose good is increased or diminished according as a new part should be added or an old part be taken away. In this way, the Church is composed of dioceses the way that Indiana is composed of ninety-two counties. We cannot be thinking of the universal Church if we exclude the Archdiocese of Indianapolis, just as we cannot be thinking of the State of Indiana if we exclude Spencer County. Even so, as the Letter says, still in no. 9, the great Church is not composed of the Churches "as a federation." The pieces of a federation are prior to the federation, the way the thirteen colonies preceded the United States. But as we have seen, every particular Church is posterior to and formed from the universal Church. The particular Churches are really parts, but not federational parts, not antecedent parts.

The Church in the Churches and
the Churches in the Church

Another way to get at the relation of particular and universal Church is to say, as the *Letter* does, that there is a "mutual interiority" of local Church and universal Church (no. 9). This is to say that the particular Church is in the great Church, and that the universal Church is in the particular Church. And the second part of that relation would not hold if the Church were a federation of Churches. It does not hold of the Church considered as a collective whole.

The particular Church is "in" the universal Church as a part of a whole. This is perhaps easier to imagine that the other half of the statement. It is easy to think of the Church as a collective whole, which, in some measure it is. So, the diocese is in the Church the way Spencer County is in Indiana. Moreover, we think to see the pieces as pieces, of the whole and in the whole, when we see gatherings of bishops, the heads of the Churches, assemble and bring parts into conjunction with other parts, as it were. On the other hand, the second part of the phrase is more difficult. Where do we see the "interiority" of the great Church in the particular, local Churches of today? This relation of interiority, moreover, does not hold for a collective whole, for the State of Indiana is not in Spencer County the way the great Church is in the Archdiocese of Indianapolis.

The presence of the great Church in the particular Church makes of the Church more a distributive than a collective whole.[4] That is, the universal Church has the nature of "Church," and so does every particular Church. The predicate "Church" is truly predicated of the whole, and of each particular Church. If some kind of Platonism were true, we might think there were some sort of universal man of which it would be true to predicate "man." Be that as it may, as to the particular Churches, "Church" is predicated of each diocese just the way "man" is truly predicated of each individual man. In this way, Indiana is certainly not a distributive whole. "State of Indiana" is not truly predicated of Spencer or Perry or any county. Spencer County, we must say, is just part of Indiana.

A sign that the Church is a distributive whole is the fact that membership in Indianapolis means membership in the great Church, in such a way that this membership demands membership in any other local Church if the member moves. Baptism introduces one into the great Church, not

---

[4] For this terminology of collective and distributive wholes, see Thomas Gilby, *Between Community and Society: A Philosophy and Theology of the State* (London: Longmans, Green, 1953), 107ff.

mediately, the *Letter* says, but immediately, and consequently "whoever belongs to one particular Church belongs to all the Churches" (no. 10).

This fact of membership, however, is not what makes the Church a distributive whole. What makes the Church a distributive whole is the presence in each particular Church of the principles that make the Church the Church. The *Letter* points to two of these principles, the Eucharist and the episcopacy.

Wherever the Eucharist is validly celebrated, there the whole treasure of the Church, Christ, is made present. This good of the ecclesial whole, Christ, is not present in the great Church any more than it is present in a particular Church, nor in one particular Church more than another. Because it is Christ who makes the Church be the Church, because he is the new Adam from whose side the Bride is drawn, the *Letter* can say in no. 17: "in every valid celebration of the Eucharist the one, holy, catholic and apostolic Church becomes present." That is, the great Church is in the little Church. And just so also, the *Letter* says, "From the eucharistic center arises the necessary openness of every celebrating community, of every particular Church; by allowing itself to be drawn into the open arms of the Lord, it achieves insertion into his one and undivided Body" (no. 11).

The priority of universal Church to particular Church means that it is the communion of all Churches that sets the criteria for admission to communion. These criteria are especially criteria of faith, and criteria of obedience to the commandments of love. The whole sets them. No part does. This is a question of Church governance. In a way, all issues of Church governance come down to the question as to who is and who is not to be given communion at the Eucharist. Concretely, it is a question for the episcopacy.

In the second place, then, the great Church is in the Churches not only because of the Eucharist, but because of the episcopacy. There is the fact of the presence at Indianapolis, for instance, of a successor of the apostles, a member of the episcopal college that rules the whole. As long as he remains in communion with college and pope, then he is a part of the college by which every particular Church and the whole Church is governed, and that supreme authority is by his communion made present in his particular Church (no. 13).

The Church in the Churches, the Church as a distributive whole, the priority of the universal Church—this means that criteria of membership are not a matter of the particular Church to set in independence of the whole. It means that the fullness of apostolic authority such as can infallibly interpret the gospel exists in the whole communion of Churches, not in any one local Church such as Indianapolis. It means that the Eucharist celebrated in Indianapolis is recognized by the great Church because received from her. Evidently, this arrangement of things is good, and very good. For if a particular Church could do any of these things, there would no longer be any sense in speaking of a communion of Churches, or of a whole. And then the Bridegroom would have to be imagined as unchastely having many brides, and the Head as monstrously having many bodies. And so he would be no real Bridegroom or real Head, no Christ of God or Son of the Father.

An appeal could also be made to the Holy Spirit as a principle making the Church present in each particular Church. The Spirit makes the parts into the whole, and is wholly in each part, just as according to St. Thomas the soul, which is the unity and intelligibility of the organic body, is wholly present in each part of the body.[5] The *Letter* of course mentions the role of the Holy Spirit in producing communion (no. 4). But the *Letter* does not make much appeal to the Holy Spirit for understanding the relation of particular Church to great Church. Perhaps this is so for the reason that it is concerned especially with the visibility of communion, the visibility of the relations of Church to Church and Church to great Church (cf. no. 6). And in this vein, there is one more visible link of which to speak.

The Church of Rome and its Bishop

The last piece of the puzzle of the relation of particular Church to universal Church is Peter.

Just as the promises made to the college of apostles were made also to Peter alone, so we think the subject of plenary ecclesial authority is the college of bishops, and as well the head of the college, the pope. Now the pope is the bishop of Rome, and the Church of Rome is a particular Church. If Indianapolis deals with the diocese of Rome, is it therefore dealing with the universal Church? By no means. If Indianapolis deals with the bishop of Rome, is it therefore dealing with the whole Church? Yes, in a way. This is not because of something special about Rome, and so it is not because he is the bishop of Rome, but because he is the successor of the head of the apostolic college and so himself head of the episcopal college. This bishop, because head, has the distinction of being able to speak for the whole. That means that the relation of the local, particular Church to Rome is both like and unlike the relation of the particular Church to the universal Church. To deal with Rome, meaning the diocese of Rome, is not to deal with the universal Church. But to deal with the bishop of Rome is to deal with one who can speak for, and speak to, and bind, the universal Church.

While no diocese is adequately distinct from the universal Church—to recall something noted above—no bishop is the bishop of Rome except the bishop of Rome. Every other bishop, not adequately distinct from the

---

[5] *Summa theologiae* I, q. 76, a. 8. Cf. *Lumen Gentium* 7.

college (since each bishop is a part of it), is adequately distinct from the Holy Father.

In other words, there is a way to locate the fullness of authority of and for the whole without gathering the whole in a council of its pastors. The fullness of authority can be located by locating the bishop of Rome. The *Letter* points to this also in no. 13, where the ministry of Peter is said to be "interior" to each particular Church. This is the *Letter's* formulation of the teaching of the First Vatican Council that the pope's universal episcopal authority is immediate. This leads to the following, concluding formulation of things.

This communion, as the whole that it is with the unity Christ wants for it, and with all the means of salvation, is prior in reality and was prior in time to the Churches of Indianapolis, Owensboro, Toledo. "Was prior in time"—because now, insofar as particular Churches are true and genuine parts, the universal Church is not its whole self without including each extant local and particular Church. Even so, even now, the universal Church "*is* prior in reality" to any particular Church. Why not also "was prior in reality"? For after all, it remains the case as just pointed out that the universal Church is not now the whole she is without Toledo, without Owensboro, without Indianapolis. And that is true enough, and we should speak so, if the subject of plenary authority is taken to be the college as a college and only that. But also, the subject of plenary authority is the pope. Which means that the fullness of authority can be identified in a subject extrinsic to and really distinct from any individual bishop and particular Church. The universal Church comes to expression in every particular Church; also, it comes to another kind of expression in Peter and his successors. Therefore, because of the Petrine office, the universal Church exists now, in a way, prior to any particular Church. That is, its plenary authority exists in such a way that it can be identified independently of this, that, or the other individual bishop of a particular Church. In this fashion, there is an abiding priority of the universal Church in the one who has care for the whole as whole and in its unity.

Concluding Remarks

However much we must deny that the universal Church is to be identified with the Church of Rome, or with the pope, and however much the simultaneity of local Church and universal Church is to be affirmed, and however much we insist upon the mutual interiority of local and universal Church, the truth of the primacy also remains. The underlying reality of this truth remains, which is expressed in saying the universal Church is ontologically prior to the particular Church. Moreover, the adjective describing the priority, "ontological," is nicely chosen. Let us imagine some other alternatives.

Would it not, on the showing of this essay, be simpler to speak of the juridical priority of the universal Church over the local, and the juridical priority of the Roman See, if what is at stake is the papal primacy? Simpler, but by no means adequate. Ludwig Hertling insisted that the ecclesial communion of the ancient Church was juridical, but not just juridical. He styled it a sacramental-juridical reality.[6] So also the place of the bishop of Rome in that communion is not just juridical. The place of the bishop of Rome, too, is rooted in and not separable from sacramental reality. "Ontological" more nearly reflects that deeper level, that denser reality, than saying "juridical" all by itself would.

Would it not be sufficient to speak more simply of "the inner priority of unity" relative to the ecclesial reality than of the ontological priority of universal Church to particular Church?[7] No, because that does not address the issue of the kind of unity in question. The particular Churches might be unified in a way that "college" said of the collection of bishops meant that all were exactly of the same quality and all of the same rights and privileges. In this way, however, there would be no permanent manifestation of that collegial unity just as such. Collegial unity would appear as such only when the reality being exercised as in a council. But there would be no abiding and always easily found touchstone of it. There would be no sacrament of it. To the contrary, because there is a sacrament of it, the universal Church is ontologically prior to the particular Church—always.

So, yes, there is an alternative to describing the priority as "ontological." We could say, with just as great propriety and adequacy, that the universal Church is sacramentally prior to the particular Church, and meaning here that this sign and instrument are located in the bishop of Rome.[8] For let us think what "sacrament" means. To paraphrase a recent formulation, to say someone is a sacrament would mean that he speaks the words that are not his, words indicative and even in some manner effective of a reality he does not make.[9] He is sign and custodian of a reality that can only be

---

6 See Ludwig Hertling, S.J., *Communio: Church and Papacy in Early Christianity,* trans. Jared Wicks, S.J. (Chicago: Loyola University Press, 1972), 47–48.

7 See McDonnell, "Ratzinger/Kasper," 243, 245, 248–49.

8 Because the pope's is an episcopal function relative to the whole Church such as each bishop plays relative to his particular Church, there is no eighth sacrament or fourth part of orders for the papacy.

9 Joseph Ratzinger, *Called to Communion: Understanding the Church Today* (San Francisco: Ignatius Press, 1991), 115: "Sacrament means: I give what I myself cannot give; I do something that is not my work; I am on a mission and have become the bearer of that which another has committed to my charge."

gift, because not made by human hands. If the pope is that kind of "sacrament" relative to the universal Church, it is a good no less than what we might expect from the One who gives us so many and countless blessings through his Son and in the Holy Spirit.

CHAPTER 9

On Affirming a Dominical Intention of a Male Priesthood

M UCH OF THE examination of the Church's exclusion of women from presbyteral orders has focused in large part on the theological intelligibility of the exclusion. Granted the fact of the "constant and universal tradition of the Church," theologians have sought to explain its theological significance, and, in fact, have located it precisely in the order of "significance": A male priest more fittingly communicates the agency, both historical and present, of Christ in the constitution of the sacrament of the Eucharist. Furthermore, the maleness of Christ, as well as male-gendered designations of God, are bound up with the signification of the transcendence of God to the created order.[1]

"Granted the fact"—largely, the fact of the constant tradition has been granted, notwithstanding skirmishes over such matters as Junias in Romans 16 and the status and function of deaconesses.[2] The demand of the argument has therefore been as follows. Even supposing the "constant and universal tradition of the Church" in this matter, we cannot tell whether this tradition is properly *theological* or not unless we can discern why the tradition of exclusion is a "good thing," as opposed to an accident of human history having nothing to do with revealed truth and the communication of grace. So, it is not enough simply to appeal to the material fact of the

---

[1] I will mention here only Benedict Ashley's "Gender and the Priesthood of Christ: A Theological Reflection," *The Thomist* 57 (1993): 343–79, which is especially comprehensive as to the entire gamut of questions involved.

[2] So, for instance, the Draft Study Paper of the CTSA, "Tradition and Woman's Ordination: A Question of Criteria," *Origins* 26, no. 6 (June 27, 1996): 90–95, raises no questions about the fact of the constant exclusion of women from presbyteral orders.

tradition of the exclusion of women. It is but a dead fact unless we can discern in it some soul of theological intelligibility.

When such intelligibility is provided, however, the argument promptly returns to the question of the tradition and, specifically, its foundation. Grant the intelligibility of the exclusion delimited in the "iconic" argument and in such appeals to presbyteral action *in persona Christi* as we have seen over the years. Still, it can be alleged, there is no reason to maintain the tradition, intelligible as it may be, unless we know that this tradition is willed by Christ. There can be lots of intelligent arrangements of things in the Church that, for all that, are not functions of the divine or dominical will. The bare example of Christ (i.e., "he didn't, in fact, call women to be of the Twelve") is a brute fact. Why take it, as does *Ordinatio sacerdotalis*, as indicating the Lord's will and intention? Is it, too, rendered "non-brute" by the theological intelligibility delimited just above? If it is applied to the example of the Lord from outside of it, so to speak, as something stuck on, then we are no closer to a discernment of dominical intention. And apart from that, it may be urged, the tradition, intelligible as it may be, is not normative.[3]

The relation of the intention of Christ to the theological intelligibility of the exclusion of women from presbyteral orders, then, is the same as that of the fact of the constant tradition. They are necessary, but not sufficient, conditions for asserting that the exclusion is intended by Christ. If Christ willed the exclusion, then it will follow both (a) that there is a constant tradition of not ordaining women and (b) that there is some theological intelligibility to the exclusion. For first, if he willed the exclusion, it must be that the Church has remained faithful to his intention concerning her substance. Second, the Lord could have no purely arbitrary intentions touching the substance of the Church. If there is no theological point to the exclusion, therefore, he could not have intended it. Still, to assert the intention of Christ on the grounds of (a) and (b), either alone or together, is the fallacy of affirming the consequent.

It seems that nothing will satisfy except some more direct argument manifesting the intention of Christ. It is my intention to here to show how such an argument might be made. Two difficulties stand in the way. First, since this manifestation can hardly be expected to appeal to an express intention of the Lord, some sense has to be given to an appeal to an "implicit"

---

[3] There is also a question raised about the constancy in the tradition of the expression of the intelligibility that the exclusion is alleged to have; so the CTSA's "Tradition and Women's Ordination," 91–92. But supposing that some past explanations, or the earliest explanations, of the exclusion appeal to an inferiority of women to men that cannot be sustained, it is hard to see that this implies anything against either the correctness of current explanations that make no such appeal or the possibility of dominical intention.

intention.[4] Second, such an argument evidently assumes, generally, that the Lord intended both an apostolic ministry in the Church, and indeed, the Church. It supposes that he instituted the Church and her ministry.

It is perhaps with this second matter that we locate the concealed but real sticking point for many who have difficulty with the Church's teaching and practice excluding women from orders. They find it preposterous to impute any intention on this matter to the Lord because they have been taught by a skeptical fundamental theology that it is preposterous to impute any intention to the Lord concerning the Church at all, and this notwithstanding the straightforward teaching of the Church that, together with her ministry in its current and lived form, she has indeed been instituted and willed by Christ.[5]

All that F. S. Fiorenza, for instance, feels himself able to defend is that the Church is in dynamic continuity with Jesus of Nazareth, not that she is instituted by him. That is, the Church does the things and says the things that Jesus did and said. There is a continuity of teaching and praxis. That is all that can be critically historically asserted, and so that is all that Fiorenza feels himself able to assert theologically.[6] Francis A. Sullivan, to take another instance, tries to elide the question. He downplays the importance of any "mere act of institution" by Jesus of Nazareth, and prefers to concentrate on the Church as the "fruit" (effect) of the Paschal Mystery.[7] And relative to the ecclesial form of the apostolic ministry, Sullivan defends the divine, but not the dominical, institution of the monarchical episcopate.[8]

My own position will become clear in what follows, but it will perhaps be helpful for me to state some matters of principle at the outset. First, the statement that Jesus of Nazareth founded or instituted the Church is a statement that, while in principle falsifiable by history, is not such as to be wholly accessible except to faith. History can falsify or support, but not establish, it. Supposing it true, however, that all that critical historical studies can

---

4 I mean to bracket here Manfred Hauke's controverted reading of 1 Cor 14:37 in his *Women in the Priesthood?* (San Francisco: Ignatius Press, 1986), 363–90.

5 See, for instance, *Lumen Gentium*, 18ff., and the *Catechism of the Catholic Church*, nos. 763–66, 874.

6 *Foundational Theology: Jesus and the Church* (New York: Crossroad, 1984), 168: "Something is divinely instituted to the degree that it mirrors the relations between Jesus and the Church as normatively described in the New Testament." But the New Testament is not interested in the relation of "foundation" (131); the only normative relations are those of continuity of praxis and preaching. See especially his reading of Mt 16, pp. 141–46.

For the notion of "dynamic continuity," see A. Cody, "The Foundation of the Church: Biblical Criticism and Ecumenical Discussion," *Theological Studies* 34 (1973): 3–18.

7 F. A. Sullivan, *The Church We Believe In* (New York: Paulist Press, 1988), 9, 21, 69–70.

8 Ibid., 182–84.

establish is "dynamic continuity" between Christ and the Church, there is no reason to take that as a limit, as Fiorenza does, to what in faith we confess the historical Jesus did and intended.[9] On the contrary, the critical establishment of probable continuity provides just what is needed from historical science, no more, no less, to assert, in faith, that Jesus of Nazareth founded the Church. Stated differently, critically established "dynamic continuity" provides rational warrant for seeing such things as the celebration of the Last Supper and the election of the Twelve as acts of foundation.[10]

The exclusion of women from priestly orders has the same sort of status, it seems to me, as does the statement that Christ founded the Church.

Second, I do not think it is possible in the end to maintain a divine but not dominical institution of our Church, her ministry, her structure, her sacraments, and so on. But this Christological matter will best emerge only later.

Since we can hardly speak of an intention to exclude women from presbyteral orders unless we can defend in some way that these orders themselves are intended by Christ, I offer a general reconstruction of the constitution of the Church's ministry relative to the "intention" of Christ. This is largely coincident, evidently, with the relation of the monarchical episcopate to the intention of Christ. This section will have the advantage, I hope, of indicating the way to allay skepticism as to the foundation of the Church generally, as well as showing us how the argument is to be constructed as bearing on the exclusion of women. Second, the argument as bearing on women is picked out in detail. Third, I anticipate some objections to the idea of "implicit intention."

The Institution of the Church's Ministry

If such things as the monarchical episcopate and the exclusion of women from orders cannot be tied to an express dominical word, either before or after the Resurrection, how can we speak of Christ's intending these things

---

[9] It is true that Fiorenza says as much (82–83), but I think he in fact decides that the absence of a historical demonstration of foundation means we cannot assert it even theologically.

[10] This is different, evidently, from holding that historical reason all by itself establishes foundation on the basis of such things as the institution of the Eucharist and the election of the Twelve.

On the "criterion of dissimilarity," see Ben F. Meyer, *The Aims of Jesus* (London: SCM Press, 1973), chapter 4, and on the relation between faith and history, chapter 5. See also the third proposition of the International Theological Commission's "The Consciousness of Christ Concerning Himself and His Mission," *International Theological Commission: Texts and Documents, 1969–1985* (San Francisco: Ignatius, 1989), 311–13, and note the appeal to "ecclesiastical-dogmatic" exegesis (306).

at all? How can the Church teach that "he willed that their [the apostles'] successors, the bishops namely, should be the shepherds in his Church"?[11]

The Church can do so according to some such story as the following, in which the priestly ministry of the Church is seen to be constituted in the concatenation of the following temporally discrete moments.

1. The Lord Jesus before his passion, death, and glorious Resurrection chose twelve apostles whose function is: (a) to signify the fullness of the eschatological gathering of Israel set afoot by the Lord; (b) in the future Kingdom, to judge the twelve tribes of Israel (Mt 19:28); (c) even before the Paschal Event, to help effect the gathering of Israel by preaching the same message as that of the Lord, namely the nearness of the Kingdom (see the missioning in Mt 10 and Mk 6, for example); and (d) after the Paschal event, but signified prior to it, to bind and loose on earth in a way effective for heaven (Mt 18:18; cf. Mt 16:19).

   The third function derives from the first. The Twelve are truly signs because they help bring about what they signify. And the fourth derives from the second, for it is according as one recognizes Jesus now that he is recognized by the Lord in the eschaton (Lk 12:8), and so it is according as one conforms to the witness of the Twelve that he is saved, and therefore also, the witness and preaching of the Twelve must even now be authoritative and normative. If one thinks that the sayings that indicate (2) are plausibly historical, then it seems that the sayings indicating (4) are so also, for there is no great leap from one to the other: Eschatological fate depends on present faith, just as in Luke 12:8.

2. On the night before he died, the Lord further charged the Twelve (e) to celebrate the Supper as a memorial of him and his mission.

3. The Risen Lord showed himself to the corporation of the Twelve and so gave them the further function (f) of witnessing to the inauguration of the Kingdom as already effected by his redeeming passion and Resurrection, and by the outpouring of the Holy Spirit; and (g) of baptizing (Mt 20); and (h) of forgiving sins (Jn 20). If one wants, one can say that (g) and (h) are contained in (f): Witnessing to the forgiveness of sins effected by Christ and to the gift of the Spirit is not some abstract announcement, but is consummated in the communication of forgiveness and the Spirit in baptism.

   As confirmed and consolidated by the Resurrection and their function of witnessing to the Resurrection (f), (c), itself a consequence of

---

[11] *Lumen Gentium,* 18 (Flannery edition).

(a), founds the post-Resurrection preaching function of the apostolate; (d), itself a consequence of (b), and in conjunction with (g) and (h), founds their ruling or shepherding function in respect to that visible gathering of those destined to the Kingdom, namely the Church; and (e), again in conjunction with (g) and (h), founds their responsibility for the Christian cult.

4. The late first-century Church (as the Gospel of John witnesses) discerns in the complex of (1), (2), and (3) an intention of the Lord that those whom the Lord sends as in (c) are themselves sent with the power to send, even as was he (Jn 17:18; 20:21). For the gospel as we have it envisages a time when the Twelve will die (Jn 21:21ff.). Furthermore, the Third Letter of John, written by an "elder," is addressed to a Gaius, who is a leader of some sort, and speaks of Diotrephes, another leader, probably a proto-bishop. There is also witness to the same intention in the First Letter of Clement (44). It is, furthermore, implausible to suppose that the Lord thought that eleven disciples would be sufficient to make disciples of all nations (Mt 28:19). These indications do not necessarily mean, however, that we have to impute to the pre- or even post-Pascal Lord a signifying of this intention that is more than implicit. We should, however, be quite clear about the fact that the late-first-century Church was in a better position to discern the intentions of the Lord than we are.

5. In the Holy Spirit, the late first-century Church also determines that the commissioning or sending by the apostles or their collaborators of further witnesses is by the laying on of hands, as evidenced by the Pastorals. This is nothing except to find a cultic and sacramental way of signifying access to a sacramental ministry that has responsibility for the Christian cult.[12] Such congruence suggests the unfolding of what is implicated, implicit, in the original establishment of the apostolic ministry.

6. The monarchical episcopate emerges in the late first and early second century as an institutional response to docetism and gnosticism, and so is to be ascribed to the work of the Holy Spirit of Christ. This emergence is a determination of the reality of apostolic office as already con-

---

[12] "Sacramental ministry" is meant here in the sense picked out by Cardinal Ratzinger on the basis of such texts as Mt 10:40 and Jn 15:5: "[A] ministry . . . in which the human being on the basis of divine communication acts and gives what can never be given or done on the basis of human resources is in the church's tradition called a *sacrament*"; see his "Biblical Foundations of Priesthood," *Origins* 20, no. 19 (October 18, 1990): 312.

stituted by the Lord, both pre- and post-Paschal (1, 2, 3) as already understood by the Church (4) and regulated by the Church (5). It is a way of structuring apostolic ministry within the local Church. Can we say that it, too, is implicitly intended by Christ? In the Letters of St. Ignatius of Antioch, the monarchical episcopate appears as a sort of (non-demonstrative) deduction from an appreciation of the reality and requirements of the unity of a local Church: the unity of faith and love; the unity of worship around "one altar"; the unity of local presbytery and Church as imitating the unity of the apostles under Christ and of all things under God the Father. If such unity can be ascribed to the intention of the Lord (Jn 17:21), then so can the means to achieve it. The formation of the monarchical episcopate, as well, then, can be understood to be implicitly intended by the Lord.

7. Also in the second century, when the question arose of ordaining or not ordaining women, the Church consciously and of set purpose did not do so, and on the basis of an appeal to the intention of the Lord. Therefore, he intended the exclusion of women from orders. But of this last more later.

The Intention to Exclude Women from Orders

Sections 4 through 7, above, appeal to the notion of an "implicit" intention. The nature of this appeal has now to be clarified; the condition of rightly appealing to it has now to be stated.

The notion itself was introduced by the 1993 "Clarifications" of the second Anglican-Roman Catholic International Commission.[13]

> [T]he sacramental ministry is something positively intended by God and derives from the will and institution of Jesus Christ. This does not necessarily imply a direct and explicit action by Jesus in the course of his earthly life. A distinction needs to be drawn between what Jesus is recorded as saying and doing, and his implicit intentions, which may not have received explicit formulation till after the resurrection, either in words of the risen Lord himself or through his Holy Spirit instructing the primitive community.

There are explicit, formulated intentions, and unformulated but still real intentions implicit in what is explicitly formulated and actually done. Granted this distinction, part—but only part—of the argument in Section 6, for instance, runs as follows. Whatever can be imputed to the Church's

---

[13] *Origins* 24, no. 17 (October 6, 1994): 303.

determination in the Holy Spirit of apostolic office, and as required for its existence, can be imputed to the Lord's intention, express or implicit; however, a monarchical episcopate can be so imputed; therefore, it can be imputed to the Lord's intention. But since there is no direct or explicit word or action of Jesus so signifying, it must be ascribed to an implicit intention. The key idea is that whatever is required for the existence of an institution is a means to the end of the existence of the institution, and that he who wills the end wills (and intends) the means. In willing the existence of apostolic office, the Lord willed what is required for its existence.

It may be objected that this argument simply identifies without warrant what the Church in fact decided with a decision in the Holy Spirit and an intention of the Lord. This, however, is not so, and the above formulation captures but part of the argument. There must be some word or action in which the implicit can be seen to be contained. And that is a condition of responsibly appealing to an implicit intention. So, with regard to the monarchical episcopate, the alleged warrant consists in the sort of things St. Ignatius evokes, such as the presidency of the Lord over against the apostles, or more simply the implied concern that a teacher— the Teacher—has for his students to remain in his teaching and so be of *one* mind. In other words, the Lord has so to indicate the shape of the end that the means settled on by the Church really do suggest themselves as the requisite means. For here, after all, the "means" are not extrinsic to the "end," but rather more simply specifications of it, or internal articulations within it. It is more like figuring out how an artist intended to complete a portrait than it is like figuring out what road to take to the county seat.

Is there anything like that, however, when it comes to the exclusion of women from orders? Yes, there is. It consists in the convergence of two things. First, there must be an appreciation of apostolic ministry as rightly described as ministry *in persona Christi*, as "representing" the Lord, on the basis of such texts as Matthew 10:40, "He who receives you receives me."[14] Second, there must be an appreciation of the dominical adoption of the sexual symbolism of the Old Covenant in such sayings as Matthew 9:15 ("Can the wedding guests mourn as long as the bridegroom is with them?") and the story of the wise and foolish virgins (Mt 25).[15] As Louis Ligier observes, in virtue of the Incarnation, the nuptial symbolism of the Old Testament passes from the order of figures to that of reality, and

---

[14] See Ratzinger, "Biblical Foundations," 312, on the mission of the apostles as a continuation of the mission of Christ, such that "someone becomes Christ's voice and hands in the world."

[15] See the further reflections of this symbolism in Jn 3:29 ("he who has the bride is the bridegroom"); the miracle of Cana in Jn 2 as an allegory of the marriage of Christ and his Church; and Rev 19:7; 21:2,9; 22:17; 2 Cor 11:2; Eph 5:23.

acquires a sacramental sense.[16] But the point I emphasize here is that this symbolism is applied by the Lord to himself. The convergence of these two things—apostolic mission as an extension of the mission of Christ and Christ's understanding of his mission in terms of the nuptial symbolism of the Old Covenant—permit us to see his example of electing only men to the Twelve as instinct with an "intention." These are the "explicit" things in which the Church can discern an "implicit" intention.

It will be observed that the "implication"—either for the monarchical episcopate or for the exclusion of women—is pretty loose. From what the Lord is taken to have done and said, there is no strict demonstration of either of these things. This should not surprise us. For presumably, we have learned that the development of doctrine is not really conformable to any of the various theories of the "theological conclusion." Development, just as it is not antihistorical, is not antilogical. But neither is logic its adequate instrument. Development of doctrine is theological, and therefore, when it is said that the Church determines things "in the Holy Spirit," the addition is not superfluous or idle.[17]

"Implicit Intention"

I will skip the host of objections of a purely historical and exegetical nature that can be put to the foregoing story; for instance, such questions as to whether the missionary commissioning of the Twelve in Matthew 10 is a retrojection of post-Paschal practice, or as to the relation of the "Twelve" to the "apostles," or as to the antihierarchical character of John, or as to the presidency of the Eucharist, and so on. This ground has been fought over for a long time. I suppose everyone knows the issues and knows his or her own mind on them.

I turn rather to objections to the form of the argument and, especially, the notion of an implicit intention.

The utility of the distinction between an express and an implicit intention is that it lets one take with all seriousness the relative probabilities, as determined by a consideration of texts, times, and cultures, of someone being able to ask questions about office in the Church. The relevant questions cannot be formulated prior to the practical situations that generate them. Prior to the situations that call for discernment and decision, it is neither prudent,

---

[16] Louis Ligier, "Women and the Ministerial Priesthood," *Origins*, 7, (44; April 20, 1978): 698.

[17] For the distinction of logical and theological accounts of development, see Jan H. Walgrave's magisterial *Unfolding Revelation: The Nature of Doctrinal Development* (London: Hutchinson, 1972).

possible, nor necessary for the Lord to give direction. It is not prudent, for one does not effectively teach in the absence of real questions. It is not possible, for one cannot formulate answers to unaskable questions. It is not necessary, for it is enough for the Lord: (1) to establish the reality of office; and (2) to send his Spirit onto the Church.

The point of the distinction might be put as follows. If the historian says, "There is no evidence of an express intention of Jesus of Nazareth relative to such things as the episcopate, the laying on of hands, and the exclusion of women," that is fine. On the other hand, if it is thence to be concluded that Jesus of Nazareth did not intend these things at all, and that therefore they are human inventions, and that consequently they may be revised, that is something else. But it is the ascription of these things to an implicit intention that takes account of the absence of evidence for an express intention.

At this juncture, it is to be emphasized that an implicit intention is being taken to be an unexpressed, but actual, intention. One may, for instance, express his will of an end but not express his will of the means.

"I want to go to the store."

"Are you taking the Ford or the Chevy?"

"The Chevy; the Ford doesn't have any brakes, remember?"

We may say that in the expression of an intention to go to the store, the intention to take the Chevy was already implicitly present. Again, in expressing one's will of some reality under a general description, one may implicitly intend a specification of that reality, which specification would come to light under appropriate questioning.

There is, however, another way one might want to analyze an implicit intention.

"I want to go to the store."

"You better take the Chevy, since the Ford is unreliable."

"Thanks, I didn't know that; I'll take the Chevy."

We might say here, too, that there was an intention to take the Chevy already present in the intention to go to the store. Evidently, however, the cognitive situations of the one intending at the time he first speaks are quite different in the two cases. In the second, there is a real ignorance, and the settled intention to take the Chevy is present only potentially or virtually. And it is nice, in this way, to keep "implicit intention" for the first case, and say "virtual intention" for the second.

Now, it might be objected that, for such matters of Church order as are in question here, there is no reason to impute more than a virtual intention to the Lord. What warrants imputing an actual, implicit intention to him? Are we not rather going beyond what historical considerations can deliver? Doesn't taking it in this way in fact mean that one is not taking the relative probabilities of someone being able to ask and answer questions about office seriously? And, in any case, why would we want to take it as an actual, implicit intention?[18]

To answer the last question: There is in the first place a very simple dogmatic reason. When the Church teaches that the Lord instituted the Church and her ministry, then, without proof to the contrary, this teaching should be understood to mean that he knew whereof he intended. For the appeal to a virtual intention does not in fact preserve the meaning of "intention." What it really does is to assert a counterfactual: If he had known such and such, then he would have intended and willed thus and so. But in fact, he didn't know such and such, and so, really and truly, he had no intention thus and so. I think it would be very difficult to sustain such an understanding of the Church's teaching about dominical institution over the last nineteen hundred years.

But there is also a Christological reason for taking his intention to be implicit, actual, and not just virtual, namely, the traditional imputation to the Lord of an immediate vision of the divine essence. Such a vision entails an actual knowledge of the entire economy of salvation as known by the divine mind and willed by the divine goodness. The grounds upon which one asserts an actual intention of the Lord for a monarchical episcopate or the exclusion of women from orders, therefore, turn out at this juncture to be the grounds upon which one asserts the theorem of his human mind's immediate vision of the divine essence. These grounds are such things as his communication, and so knowledge, of his own divine identity and his knowledge of the nearness of the kingdom of God. Arguably, such things cannot be known by a human mind without "seeing God."[19]

For some, however, such considerations will seem to imply that theology is either dictating to historical science or at least on holiday from it. This is not, I believe, the case. But seeing that it is not depends on distinguishing very carefully between the kind of knowledge possessed by historical persons such as historical science can impute to them, and the kind of knowledge asserted in the theorem of the immediate vision of God. Such knowledge is "a-thematic," "non-conceptual," "ineffable."[20] The knowledge that is the object of historical science, on the other hand, is quite thematic, conceptual, expressible, and indeed, expressed. The attempt to understand faith in the divine identity of Jesus and his communication of it

---

[18] See, for instance, St. Thomas's notion of implicit faith in *Summa theologiae* I–II, q. 2, a. 5.

[19] For the argument, see Guy Mansini, "Understanding St. Thomas on Christ's Immediate Knowledge of God," in this volume.

[20] See especially B. Lonergan, *De Verbo Incarnato* (Rome: Gregorian University, 1964), Thesis 12.

deals in the first kind of knowledge. The historian is left to reach his own judgments about the second kind of knowledge.

The argument in the foregoing has not been that Jesus of Nazareth possessed an immediate knowledge of the divine essence in which the economy of salvation, including matters of the ecclesial and sacramental order, were known; therefore, he knew that the episcopate was to be monarchically determined and that women were to be excluded from orders. It has rather been argued that what the Church determined as to the structure and requirements of apostolic office, thinking to follow the mind of the Lord, depended centrally on what the Lord communicated—expressly, conceptually—but in which communication there can be seen to be folded other things not expressed. In other words, there can be no appeal to an intention of the Lord apart from the sort of evidence that would enable one to assert at least a virtual intention. That is, on the basis of what the Lord did say and do, one concludes to what he would say and do if he were in other circumstances. But once this is achieved, and granted the reasons for imputing an immediate knowledge of the divine essence to Christ's human mind, then one passes from the assertion of a virtual intention to the assertion of an actual, though implicit, intention.

Of course, the simple illustration of an implicit intention as given above is not wholly analogous to the case of our Lord. For the illustration remains wholly within the realm of the "conceptual." But a conceptually possessed intention has not been imputed to the Lord. So, if one wants, there is indeed an element of virtuality in the Lord's intention of the episcopate or in his intention to exclude women from orders. To render his actual intention actually expressible would require not a simple evocation of the concepts and categories involved in the question about orders and Church order, but the acquisition of the concepts and categories involved in being able to ask the question. Nonetheless, such acquisition of concepts and categories would serve to render expressible what is already known and intended in virtue of his (human) participation in the divine knowledge of the economy. It would be like finding a language to say what one knows, and not just using a language one already has to say what one knows.

In the introduction, I made critical mention of any position that asserts a divine, but not a dominical, institution of the Church, orders, and the like. It should now be clear why. It should be clear, as well, why there has been little attention in the foregoing to whether we speak of the pre- or post-Paschal Jesus. For, to begin with the last, the immediate knowledge of God's essence, including centrally the plan of salvation and the disposition of the Church, is the same in our Lord before and after the Resurrection. Whatever the Lord knew of the divine plan and intended in its fulfillment after the Resurrection, he knew and intended before. Further, the content of the divine plan and the disposition of the economy is a content of knowledge common to the Three Persons. Whatever the Holy Spirit inspires with regard to the economy or the disposition of the Church is also known by the Word. And whatever the Word knows relative to this economy and disposition is also known by him through the human mind of the assumed nature.

Indeed, it is usual in the tradition to speak of the Church deciding or discerning what to do and how to act "in the Holy Spirit." This does not mean the Holy Spirit inspired things of which the Lord knew not. It is rather an indication of the fact that the Church's discernment of what is implicit in what the Lord explicitly said and did cannot be rendered in a syllogism that demonstrates what we used to call a "theological conclusion." The Church's discernment of the mind of the Lord is rather a properly theological act moved by the Holy Spirit. Understanding that such discernment is not strictly measured by human reason goes for reason in its Scholastic, as well as in its historical, guise.

It has been my intention here to show how one can assert that the Lord intended the exclusion of women from orders. I have done nothing, I hope, but assemble theological elements and analyses known to every theologian. If there is any merit to the assemblage, it is in the reminder of the relevance of the theorem of the Lord's immediate knowledge of the divine essence, and perhaps, also, of the nature of doctrinal development.[21]

---

[21] I would like to thank Prof. Lawrence J. Welch of Kenrick Seminary for help with this paper.

CHAPTER **10**

Representation and Agency
in the Eucharist

I N SEVERAL ARTICLES on how to understand the presbyteral *min-isterium* within the Eucharist, Dennis Ferrara proposes to return us to a core doctrinal commitment of Catholic Eucharistic theology that he thinks was compromised by bad arguments both for and against the ordination of women.[1] This core commitment is that the realization of the sacramental presence of the true body and blood of the Lord is first of all and principally the work of the Lord himself. Whatever we want to say about whatever it is the ordained priest does or effects in the celebration of the Eucharist, therefore, is to be governed by this principle, which makes of the priest a strictly instrumental agent of the realization of the true body and blood. Ferrara finds, however, that the standard symbolic or "iconic" argument against the ordination of women (as well as some rejoinders to it) in fact obscures the primacy of the agency of Christ.

In sorting out questions of agency and representation, agency and its signification, Ferrara furthermore proposes that we be guided by a strict attention to the visible rite of the Eucharist. Whatever is said about the priest's representative function within the Eucharist, about whose agency is signified, and about how and in what manner it is signified, must be supported by the rite as actually celebrated.

---

[1] I will deal principally with his "Representation or Self-Effacement? The Axiom *In Persona Christi* in St. Thomas and the Magisterium," *Theological Studies* 55 (1994): 195–224 (hereafter RSE), and "*In Persona Christi*: Towards a Second Naïveté," *Theological Studies* 57 (1996): 65–88 (hereafter SN). But see also his "Reply to Sara Butler," *Theological Studies* 56 (1995): 81–91, and "*In Persona Christi*: Representation of Christ or Servant of Christ's Presence?" *CTSA Proceedings* 50 (1995): 138–45.

In all of this, moreover, Ferrara thinks that he is recovering St. Thomas's understanding of what it means—and what it does not mean—to say that the priest consecrates the elements at Mass *in persona Christi.*

It is of course difficult to take exception to a concern for the primacy of Christ's agency and the priority of the rite as evidence for what we say about sacramental signification. And it is almost as difficult to resist an appeal to St. Thomas. Unfortunately, Ferrara's development of his position, especially in "Second Naïveté," compromises the very things he wants to make good about Christ's agency and the priority of the rite. Moreover, his reading of St. Thomas cannot be sustained.

In what follows, I first present Ferrara's position. Second, I argue that, when pressed, his position paradoxically leads him where he does not want to go. It obscures the agency of both the principal and the instrumental agents, Christ and the priest, and offers a construction little consonant with the immediate signification of the visible rite. Third, I raise the question of his reading of St. Thomas.[2]

Ferrara's Position

In his first article, "Representation or Self-Effacement," Ferrara says he is going to propose a wholly non-representational view of the priest.[3] The priest is indeed an instrument of Christ, and rendered such by the reception of the character that ordination imparts; however, instruments do not have to be representations of the principal agent using them.

Formal to Ferrara's argument is an appeal to St. Thomas, according to which there need be no likeness between instrumental and principal agent.[4] On the contrary, the minister's own "form" is indifferent to his instrumentality. The instrumental power of the priest, moreover, is something invisible, residing in the soul of the priest.[5] It therefore follows that whatever is visible and sensible about the priest is indifferent to the ministerial instrumentality effected by orders.[6] Even more, since the form of the instrument is immaterial

---

2 See also the criticism of Sara Butler, "A Response to Dennis M. Ferrara," *Theological Studies* 56 (1995): 61–80, and *"In Persona Christi,"* CTSA *Proceedings* 50 (1995): 146–55. Her rebuttal of Ferrara's charge that the symbolic argument against the ordination of women remains covertly an appeal to the natural subordination of women is important. As to the differences between Ferrara and Butler on the argument from tradition, Ferrara's remarks on the texts in question, though arguably just, are also beside the point that Butler is making.

3 RSE, 196.

4 Ibid., 201. See especially *Summa theologiae* [hereafter *ST*] III, q. 64, a. 5, c, and Suppl. q. 19, a.4, ad 1.

5 RSE, 204, and SN, 68–69.

6 RSE, 213–14.

to its functioning as instrument, St. Thomas's position "excludes in principle any representation of Christ in the sacramental minister."[7]

Nor does the assertion that the priest acts *in persona Christi* argue the contrary, according to Ferrara. In its "technical sense," the phrase has an "apophatic" sense relative to the minister and means that Christ alone is signified as speaking or acting.[8] Further, since this signification is accomplished by word alone, by pronouncing the *forma sacramenti* of the Eucharist, it requires nothing more in the priest (given his having been made an instrument by ordination) than the ability to quote.[9] To act in the person of Christ means not the representation of Christ, therefore, but on the contrary the priest's self-effacement.[10] If to act *in persona Christi* means to act in such a way that only the word and act of Christ is signified, and since this happens through the quotation of the word alone, the priest's maleness is evidently irrelevant.

In a footnote, Ferrara distances himself not only from the view that women can be priests because they can image and represent Christ but as well from the view that a woman can be a priest because the priest's representation of Christ is grounded on a prior representation of the Church—he acts *in persona Christi* because he first acts *in persona Ecclesiae*.[11] On the contrary, for Ferrara the priest is not a representation of anything at all, of either Christ or the Church.

But if the priest is not a representation, this does not mean he is not a representative.[12] He is an ambassador, a representative speaking the word of Christ. The distinction Ferrara is drawing is plain enough. To say *X* is representative of *Y* may mean *X* is a good example of *Y*: This oak is a good example of the oaks you will find in this forest; the particular oak will look a lot like the other oaks; it will share many properties with them. But if *X* is *a* representative of *Y*, we will fill the blanks with persons: George is a representative of Bill because George is charged to speak or act for Bill. Of course, George might also be representative of members of his family, and so, looking at George, you will see some of the same features you would if you looked at Bill, his brother (all the brothers are tall). Here, in some measure, George is a representation of Bill. And whether he is a representative or a representation of Bill, we will say that he "represents" Bill. But as a representative, George rather *makes* a representation for or on behalf of Bill, and is not himself a representation of Bill. He makes a representation on Bill's

---

[7] Ibid., 202.

[8] Ibid., 212; see also 206.

[9] Ibid., 211.

[10] Ibid., 212.

[11] Ibid., 196*n*3.

[12] Ibid., 215.

behalf by speaking Bill's mind or conveying his intention, or pleading for him. Now, the priest, Ferrara wants to say, makes a representation for Christ, and is his representative, but is by no means his representation. The representation he makes is to speak the words of Christ that he quotes within the institution narrative.

In the article, "Second Naïveté," Ferrara speaks of the priest as also a representative of the Church, and grounds his being a representative of Christ on that fact. But again, the priest is not a representation of the Church. No, he is a representative of the Church as speaking her word of faith, because sacramental acts are first of all acts of the believing Church.[13]

Why this development of the second article? Ferrara says he wishes to allay the impression that the priest is "hanging in midair between Christ and the Church."[14] We might say that the priest, even as the pure and non-representational instrument the first article has made of him, is not distinct from the Church as standing over against her in the celebration of the Eucharist.[15] The only thing standing over against the Church is Christ. The second article, therefore, undertakes to insert the priest firmly within the Church, not just in the sense that the priest is himself of course a believer, but in his ministerial signifying function, even as speaking the words of institution. And indeed this seems to be required by the non-representational line Ferrara embraces in the first article, for if the priest were between Christ and the Church, then to that extent it would be possible to think of him as representing Christ precisely in Christ's own distinctness from the Church.

The second article accomplishes this by observing that the sacraments are first of all acts of the Church.[16] Further, they are acts of the Church in that the Holy Spirit, the principle of the union between Head and members, is the agent of the sacramental action.[17] However, because the Spirit is the Spirit of Christ and as such the basis of the union of Christ and the Church,[18] the Eucharistic word is a word not only of the Church but also becomes a word of Christ, spoken *in persona Christi*, spoken by the priest as representative of Christ. This occurs in that the Spirit transforms the priestly word of the Church into the word of Christ. This bears quoting at length.

---

[13] SN, 71.

[14] Ibid., 70.

[15] I mean here to recall *Pastores Dabo Vobis* 16: "Quatenus repraesentat Christum Caput, Pastorem et Sponsum Ecclesiae, sacerdos non tantum in Ecclesia, sed etiam erga Ecclesiam ponitur." The priest occupies a place *coram Ecclesia* through his *ministerium*, "quod non nisi signum et continuatio sacramentalis et visibilis est Ipsius Christi, qui coram Ecclesia et mundo unus auctor et origo est Salutis."

[16] SN, 70–72.

[17] Ibid., 77–79.

[18] Ibid., 76.

[I]n the midst of the ecclesial proclamation [of the Eucharistic Prayer], that which is recalled out of the past becomes actual in the present: the living word of Christ supervenes upon the priestly anamnesis to change the elements into his body and blood. This Christ does by the agency of his sovereign Spirit, the fire from heaven that transforms the gifts, as Eastern theology insists, an agency exercised by the Spirit not "from below," as *anima Ecclesiae*, but "from above," as sent by the heavenly Christ from the Father of Lights, for, like the creation of the world, it is a strictly divine act. And in this supervening word of Christ, this descending fire of the Spirit, lies the true meaning and the true mysteriousness of *in persona Christi*, for in virtue of this divine fire, the priestly word of the Church is transformed and sacramentally identified with the word of Christ.[19]

Evidently, speaking anamnestically ("On the night before he died . . ."), the priest speaks in the person of the Church, with the faith of the Church. Because of this anamnestic frame, the words of consecration remain a word of the Church.[20] While this seems to mean that the priest acts *in persona Christi* because he acts *in persona Ecclesiae*, Ferrara wishes to avoid this implication for the Eucharistic word. He seems to grant the implication for the sacraments generally,[21] but wishes to deny it for the Eucharist. He maintains that, in the Eucharist, to speak in the one person is complementary with, and not opposed to, speaking in the other,[22] and he affirms the magisterial teaching that the priest celebrates the Eucharist in the person of the Church because he first celebrates it in the person of Christ.[23] It is the activity of the Spirit of Christ that ensures this priority.

Finally, as to the texts of St. Thomas that seem unmistakably "representational," and that seem to make of the priest a representation of Christ as Head and Spouse of the Church, Ferrara undertakes already in the first article to deny them any symbolic significance for the Eucharist.[24] In the

---

[19] Ibid., 86.

[20] Ibid., 83: "That the priest consecrates *in persona Christi* pertains solely to his recital of the words of Christ. It does not pertain to the anamnestic form in which Christ's words are recited. But it is precisely this anamnestic form which makes of the eucharistic recital the act of the Church's faith."

[21] Ibid., 79, 82.

[22] Ibid., 81.

[23] Ibid., 82: "[T]he priest, as the magisterial texts . . . state, does celebrate the Eucharist as representative of the Church *(in persona Ecclesiae)* only because he first celebrates it as representative and minister of Christ *(in persona Christi)*."

[24] *ST* III, q. 8, a. 6 (prelates and as well those who take Christ's place by preaching and by binding or loosing are called heads); III, q. 65, a. 1 (orders generally are said to be for ruling); IV *Sent.* d. 8, q. 2, a. 3, ad 9 (the priest, in express distinction from the Eucharistic word, is said to play the role of Christ); IV *Sent.* d. 24, q. 3, a. 2, qu. 1,

first place, it is to be noted that nuptial imagery does not enter expressly into the form of the Eucharist, or into the *sacramentum tantum*;[25] there is therefore no need in the Eucharist of such a symbolic resonance as provided by a male priest. Second, the hierarchical and pastoral function of the priest, apropos of which some of these texts appear, is subordinate to his sacramental function, and not vice versa.[26] Fitness for pastoral ministry, in the sense of acts bearing on the *corpus Christi mysticum*, should be determined solely by the requirements for discharging sacramental acts bearing on the *corpus Christi verum*, and not the other way round. Since males are not required for the latter, neither are they for the former.

Words and Speakers, Actions and Agents

While he intends to maintain and indeed bring to the fore the agency of Christ in the Eucharist, Ferrara in fact obscures it because of a confusion about the consecratory word and who speaks it. This is of course highly paradoxical in view of his emphasis in the first article on the fact that the priest does nothing except quote Christ. However, in order to avoid the possibility that the priest may be taken to represent Christ precisely in his distinction from the Church, Ferrara is led to attribute this word to the Church as well. But it is this very attribution, in which the consecratory word is also said to be spoken *in persona Ecclesiae*, that is both refractory to the plain sense of the quotational form of the consecration that Ferrara himself emphasizes and it obscures the agency of both Christ and the priest.

The way Ferrara attributes the consecratory word to the Church in "Second Naïveté" presents a number of contradictions. We start off unexceptionally enough. Christ and the Church are "other" but "inseparable";[27] the Bride is always united to her Spouse and the Spirit is the bond of their union;[28] the Head works through the Body.[29] Beyond this, we are warned of the danger of a "formally 'ecclesial' view" that "threatens the uniqueness of the Eucharist" as differing not only in degree but also in kind from the other sacraments.[30] How then can one say that the consecratory word is

---

ad 3 (every minister is in some way a type of Christ, and the bishop especially is said to be *sponsus Ecclesiae*); *In I ad Tim.*, cap. 3, lect. 1, n. 96: Presbyters and bishops (see n. 87) are to be the husband of one wife "propter repraesentationem sacramenti, quia sponsus ecclesiae est Christus."

[25] RSE, 214; SN, 69–70.

[26] RSE, 219, appealing to the well-known texts on binding and loosing as the secondary act of the priest.

[27] SN, 76.

[28] Ibid., 77.

[29] Ibid., 79.

[30] Ibid., 80.

spoken *in persona Ecclesiae*? "In the foundational act of consecration . . . the priest does not speak 'in the person of the Church' . . . as an active subject distinct from Christ, but in the very person of Christ."[31] The priest is rather a passive subject, indistinct from Christ as at that moment is also the Church, in whose person he continues to speak, though, like the Church, not actively, and not as distinct from Christ. Will this not preserve the uniqueness of the Eucharist? Again, "the consecrating word of Christ is uttered through and in the Church"; it belongs to the Church; it "is also the word *of* the Church, indeed its supreme word."[32] To say that it was a priestly but not an ecclesial word would deny that the priesthood is the Church's priesthood.[33] After all, the consecration is framed by the anamnesis of the Eucharistic Prayer, spoken for and by the Church, in the faith of the Church.[34] Further, if we say that the priest "utters the consecratory words" not only *in persona Christi* but also *in persona Ecclesiae*, these must be taken as "complementary rather than opposed assertions."[35] And all of this, mark, to avoid the consequence of agreeing with John Paul II in *Pastores Dabo Vobis*, for did we not affirm that the consecratory word is spoken *in persona Ecclesiae*, there is the danger we would so identify the priest with Christ "that he faces the Church as Christ does, as Head of the Body."[36] And that would mean the priest is a representation of Christ, and *that* might mean we cannot ordain women.

We will examine more closely the three solutions Ferrara has just offered: the invocation of complementarity ("complementary assertions"); the idea of a speaking subject, the Church, that is at once indistinct from another subject, Christ, and passive; last, the appeal to instrumentality (Christ speaks the word through the Church).

First, complementarity. Truly, it is not contradictory to assert that "the Church says *X*" and then again to assert that "Christ says *X*," and this is so whatever *X* is. But it may be that the Church and Christ contradict one another, and this depends very much on what they are saying. So, Christ and the Church might be said to speak the same word, as for instance in the Mass both Christ and the Church (especially the present congregation), the whole Christ, offers itself, the whole Christ, to the Father. However, this is not how the *consecratory* word can be understood. The consecratory word is "This is my body." But the people do not say, "This is my body," for the very good reason that the bread does not become their body, but Christ's

---

[31] Ibid., 82.

[32] Ibid.

[33] Ibid., 82–83.

[34] Ibid., 83.

[35] Ibid., 81.

[36] Ibid., 80; see note 15, above.

(and it is rather that they become the Body, sacramentally, at communion). It cannot be that it is "complementary" to say the consecratory word is spoken in both persons. It is simply false.

Next, there is the idea of a passive speaker or subject indistinct from another speaker or subject. As for the indistinction, as already said, two speakers can speak the same thing, depending on what they are saying. Once again, however, the deictic "my" in the consecratory word prevents this here. What is new at this point is the idea of passivity, the idea of a passive speaking, that is, the idea of a passive acting. This, if not straightforwardly contradictory, leads to the idea of instrumentality.

Therefore, what Ferrara envisages is a situation of one word, two speakers, where the speakers are related as principal and instrumental speaker. Even where Christ and the Church are offering the sacrifice, moreover, we might think that this is a better way to describe things. So, Christ speaks through the Church, and the word of consecration is the speaking of both, just as in the action of making a table, there is one action of both carpenter and saw, not in the way two men pull on the same rope, but in that the saw is moved by the carpenter.

But this will not do either, for, while speaking may be an action, words are not. The consecratory word is not the word of the Church, once again for the simple reason that the Church does not say that "this" is *her* body. That is the point, one would think, of drawing attention to the fact that the priest is quoting. The one who quotes, though he may agree with the statement quoted (part of the point of saying that the priest quotes *significative* and not just *recitative*),[37] indicates that it is not the word of the one who quotes, but that of another, the quoted person. Nor is the speaker's *word* the instrument of the one quoted. The speaker is the instrument—his voice, the speaker intending to quote and signifying that he is quoting. But it is not the speaker's word that is the instrument. My word might be said to be an instrument of another when I explain another's word. So, a commentary on a text, a commentarial word, might be called an instrument of the word of the author of the text. But the consecratory word is nothing like that. It is not the priest's word, nor the Church's word; it is Christ's word. That it is not the priest's word, which Ferrara seems to want to say in his first article, means that it is not the Church's word, either, though that is what he does want to say in the second article. And this is true because of the order of signification, for the priest's quotation signifies that it is the word only of the one he is quoting, Christ.[38] The attribution to the Church, moreover, is an easy enough, though mis-

---

[37] *ST* III, q. 78, a.5.

[38] This, moreover, is the "technical sense" of speaking *in persona Christi* in the Eucharistic context picked out by Bernard Dominique Marliangeas, *Clés pour une*

taken, slide from the attribution of a quotation to the Church to the attribution of what is quoted to the Church.

Now, to make it the Church's word is to make problematic the agencies involved. So that the priest cannot appear as signifying Christ in distinction from the Church, the consecratory word is held to be "also" the word of the Church. In fact, the *persona* of the Church would seem to be first in the field as a speaker, from the beginning of the Eucharistic Prayer. Ferrara thus finds himself in the position of having to explain how the word of the Church becomes the word of Christ. To this newly invented problem, the solution is a new and unwonted invocation of an agency bearing on the word of the Church. Just so, "the priestly word of the Church" (the words of consecration) are "transformed" by the fire of the Holy Spirit to become the word of Christ.[39] There is first a word and so an action of the Church speaking through her representative, the priest. Second, Christ sends the Holy Spirit onto this word of the Church to make it his word. Third, this word of Christ effects the transformation of the elements.

How are we to think that Christ through the Holy Spirit makes a word that is not his own into his own? One person can make the word of another his own by repeating ("Yes, I think that X is Y too") or otherwise signifying that he adopts the word as his own. But there is nothing like that in the Mass. The word is already signified as Christ's; it is a quoted word. What agency is signified bears on the elements, not on the words. The Holy Spirit is invoked indeed—but to transform the elements, not the words of the priest. Ferrara seems to have entered into a kind of theologizing that he otherwise condemns for building a theological structure, which departs from what is given in the rite.

On the contrary, St. Thomas's point in saying that the priest speaks *in persona Christi* is that since it is the real body and blood of Christ, Christ himself, that is made present on the altar, the principal agent of this making present is Christ; and for this reason, the instrument, the priest, speaks purely as Christ's representative, and not in his own person.[40] Speaking purely as a representative, he also perforce represents Christ precisely in distinction from the Church. Here, indeed, the word is the word of Christ in a simple and straightforward manner, for the priest is quoting Christ. And since it is Christ's word, and not the Church's word, the priest speaks in the person of Christ, and not in that of the Church.

As the agency of Christ, so that of the priest is obfuscated by Ferrara. This agency is by way of a word, by way of quoting, but it is more than

---

théologie du ministère: In persona Christi, In persona Ecclesiae (Paris: Beauchesne, 1978), 98–99.

[39] SN, 86.

[40] *ST* III, q. 78, aa. 1 and 4.

the proffering of an ordinary declarative word, for it effects something. It is not just a matter of the ability to speak, of the ability to manifest the real, or even to quote. Anybody can quote; but only the priest can quote and (instrumentally) effect now at the celebration what first was effected at the Last Supper.[41] Two things follow from Ferrara's position. First, he cannot really make good why the character of orders is required to speak the confecting words. For St. Thomas, priestly character is required—it is known to exist in the first place—because the priest *does* something not every baptized person can do, namely, confect the Eucharist. But for Ferrara, all the priest does is produce a sort of word-material that it is the part of the Holy Spirit to consecrate and so make effective. The priestly doing is collapsed into a mere speaking. Furthermore, if the word of the priest is also and necessarily a word of the Church, it should follow that the Church can revoke a priest's sacramental power, just as she can withdraw his mandate to preach in her name. But she cannot. The distinction between *potestas ordinis* and *potestas jurisdictionis*, maligned or misused as it may be, recovers here its point.[42]

Ferrara's Reading of St. Thomas

Ferrara's appeal to St. Thomas is in two steps. First, there is an argument about instrumentality, and second, an argument from the form of the Eucharist.

The argument bearing on instrumentality proceeds as follows. Generally, agents act so as to produce a likeness of themselves. But we must distinguish principal and instrumental causes. In *Summa theologiae* III, q. 64, a. 5, c, St. Thomas tells us that an instrument does not act in accordance with its own form, but by the power of the principal agent. Therefore, as the reply to the first objection has it, a sacrament likens its recipient not to the instrument, but to Christ, the principal agent. Congruently with this, the Sentences commentary, whose material reappears in the Supplement of the *Summa theologiae* at q. 19, a. 4, ad 1, tells us that just as there is no requirement of similarity of form between an instrument and its effect, so there is no such requirement as between the instrument and the principal agent. Whence Ferrara concludes that St. Thomas excludes similarity between the priest, an instrumental cause, and Christ, the principal agent of the Eucharist. So, the priest cannot be a representation of Christ. This

---

[41] *ST* III, q. 82, a. 1 and ad 1. This is the other part of the point of saying that the priest says the words not just *recitative* but also *significative*; see here Sara Butler, "Response to Ferrara," 70–73.

[42] See *ST* III, q. 82, a. 7, ad 3, and a. 8, ad 2. Ferrara does see this implication and denies it (SN, 87), but his denial does not refute the logic of his position.

conclusion is stronger than warranted; strictly, one can conclude only that there need not be any similarity of form, not that there cannot be. The modesty of this conclusion is important.

In a second step, Ferrara observes from *Summa theologiae* III, q. 78, a. 1, c, that St. Thomas says that the only thing the priest does in the confection of the Eucharist is to quote the words of Christ. That being the only thing he does, there is nothing else that the priest does or may do that is relevant to the confection of the Eucharist and upon which some argument for representation (in addition to being a representative) might be built.

Moreover, according to Ferrara it is in the Eucharist that we find St. Thomas's "technical" and "theoretical" sense of the instrument-minister's action *in persona Christi*.[43] Those texts in a Eucharistic context that relate acting in the person of Christ to being a representation of Christ are non-theoretical remnants of an earlier and uncritical style of symbolic theology (e.g., St. Bonaventure). Moreover, when texts that speak of pastoral power make the same connection, it is to be remembered that the theology of orders finds its formal essence in its relation to the *corpus verum*, not to the *corpus mysticum*. Therefore, neither are those texts relevant.

Ferrara's reading requires certain unwarranted moves. First, he claims that St. Thomas uses the locution *in persona Christi* in technical and non-technical senses back to back, as it were. In *Summa theologiae* III, q. 82, a. 1, c, St. Thomas refers back to q. 78, a. 1, c, and argues from this "technical" sense of the phrase. But in the reply to the fourth objection, in the same article, where the bishop is said to exercise pastoral power in the Person of Christ, we have a sense of the phrase that we are to dismiss as non-technical.

Second, he ignores the limited context for which St. Thomas invokes the principle that an instrument need have no similarity of form with the principal agent. The issue of *Summa theologiae* III, q. 64, a. 5, is whether wicked ministers can confer the sacraments, and the "form" in question, the likeness at stake between instrument and effect therefore, is that of habitual grace (see also Suppl. q. 19, a. 5). Just so, in Suppl. q. 19, a. 4, the issue is whether the personal sanctification of the instrument-minister is formal to the use of the keys, and the answer is that it is not. It is quite a stretch to argue from the non-necessity of this kind of likeness to the irrelevance of any likeness whatsoever in all cases between instrument and effect.

In fact and to the contrary, St. Thomas's "technical" consideration of sacramental agency calls for just such a likeness in the visible, properly sacramental order. The argument is quite simple. In *Summa theologiae* III, q. 62, a. 1, St. Thomas asks the foundational question whether sacraments are causes of grace. The first objection argues that, since the sacrament is a sign of grace, it cannot also be a cause of grace. The reply is as follows.

---

43 RSE, 212; see Marliangeas, *Clés pour une théologie*, 97, 98–99.

> A principal cause cannot properly be called a sign of an effect, though hidden, even if this cause itself be sensible and manifest. But an instrumental cause, if it be manifest, can be said to be a sign of a hidden effect, for the reason that it is not only a cause, but in some way also an effect, insofar as it is moved by the principal agent. And according to this reasoning, the sacraments of the new law are causes and signs.

Thus, for instance, baptismal washing, an instrumental cause of the cleansing of the soul, is also a sign of that cleansing, insofar as it is moved by God.[44] If it were true, as Ferrara thinks, that instruments cannot represent or signify the effect they are ordered to producing, then evidently St. Thomas's sacramental theology would be at odds with itself at a quite fundamental level. For that is precisely what a sacrament is: an instrument that is a sign of its effect; a sign that is an instrument.

Ferrara is well aware, of course, of such texts that assert a likeness between the sacrament and the effect of the sacrament.[45] He does not gainsay the similitude of sacrament to sacramental effect, he circumscribes it quite carefully. The likeness is absolutely not any likeness to the mysteries of Christ. Rather, appealing to *Summa theologiae* III, q. 65, a. 1, where the number of the sacraments is made intelligible by an argument *ex convenientia* from human life both individual and in community, we read that, as natural signs, the sacraments "represent the basic structure and dynamism of human existence." This is true enough, as far as it goes. But the exclusion of the relation of the natural symbolism to the mysteries of Christ is very false. Speaking of the matter of baptism in III, q. 66, a. 3, St. Thomas argues its suitability both as signifying the effect of the sacrament, as spiritual cleansing, and as signifying the mystery of Christ's death and burial, by which we are saved. For Ferrara these two things must be really distinct, and the second being a holdover of precritical, pretheoretic, mystical, and symbolic theology. Of course, it is nothing of the sort. Spiritual cleansing *is* conformation to the death of Christ, and dying with Christ in baptism *is* the dying to sin that is spiritual cleansing,[46] and the faith required for the sacrament of faith is faith in the saving passion and death of Christ.[47] To drive a wedge between the effect of the sacrament and its signification of conformity to Christ's death would mean that St. Thomas is taking his

---

[44] See *ST* III, q. 66, a. 10.

[45] See his "Reply to Sara Butler," 86.

[46] See *ST* III, q. 66, a. 12: "Passio Christi operatur quidem in baptismo aquae per quandam figuralem repraesentationem"; q. 69, a. 1, c; and the *Lectura* on Romans, c. 6, lect. 2, nos. 473–74.

[47] *ST* III, q. 61, a. 4.

leave not only from the entire patristic tradition but from St. Paul himself.[48] But why the wedge? Why such a huge effort to separate St. Thomas not only from his tradition but from his own text? Only so that there can be no argument contrary to the ordination of women on the basis of a relation of natural resemblance between the ministerial priest and the unique High Priest.

If it is kept in mind that sacramental instruments are likenesses of their effect, St. Thomas's next premise is easily anticipated: The priest is an instrumental cause of consecration. He is rendered an instrument in virtue of the character, the instrumental power, imparted at ordination, as we discover in III, q. 63, a. 1, q. 64, a. 1, c. And the priest's instrumentality in the consecration of the Eucharist is explicitly affirmed at III, q. 82, a. 1, ad 1. The instrumental cause that the priest is, however, is a manifest and visible one. Therefore, he can also be a sign of the hidden effect, which in the case of the Eucharist is the true body and blood, that is, Christ, insofar as he is moved by the principal agent. Lastly, it is to be noted that the "effect" of this exercise of agency is not distinct from the principal agent, Christ. Therefore, in the Eucharist, the priest can be a sign—a representation—of Christ.

The foregoing argument concludes with a possibility; it induces an expectation that St. Thomas will affirm the symbolic, iconic, representational function of the priest in the Eucharist. The expectation is realized in *Summa theologiae* III, q. 83, a. 1, ad 3:

> The priest bears the image of Christ in whose person and power he pronounces the words to consecrate, as is evident from what was said above. And so in a certain way the priest and the victim are the same.[49]

That is, the minister is the same as the victim of the sacrifice, Christ, in that he is a representation of Christ. The reference to what has already been said above is to III, q. 83, a. 1 (and a. 3), which itself refers us back to III, q. 78, a. 1, on the form of the Eucharist, where Ferrara finds the "technical sense" displayed. In other words, there is no gap, not the slightest crevice, between the representational and the representative senses of *in persona Christi.*

The above text from *Summa theologiae* III, q. 83, moreover, is not the only one where it is either stated or implied that the priest is a representation

---

[48] I am grateful to Professor Lawrence Welch for this point.

[49] "Sacerdos gerit imaginem Christi, in cuius persona et virtute verba pronuntiat ad consecrandum, ut ex supra dictis patet. Et ita quodammodo idem est sacerdos et hostia." This is even stronger in IV *Sent.* d. 8, q. 2, a. 3, ad 9, where there is a comparison of the word and the priest as instruments: "quia sacerdos est similior principali agenti quam verbum, quia gerit eius figuram, ideo, simpliciter loquendo, sua virtus instrumentalis est maior et dignior, unde etiam permanet."

of Christ. In the *Lectura* on 1 Timothy, commenting on the requirement that an *episcopus* be the husband of one wife (3:2), we read:[50]

> But what is the reason of this institution? . . . I answer that it must be said that the reason is not because of incontinence alone, but on account of the representation of the sacrament [*propter repraesentationem sacramenti;* cf. the *magnum sacramentum of Eph 5:32*], because the spouse of the Church is Christ, and the Church is one, as it says in the fifth chapter of the Song of Songs, "my dove is only one."

Furthermore, St. Thomas explains earlier that "presbyters are to be understood with bishops" here, since the names, though not the realities, are interchangeable.[51] It is hard not to see in this text a recognition of an "iconic" value to priests and bishops that includes more than the quite narrow representative function, manifested in quotation alone, that Ferrara recognizes. There are more "Bonaventuran" patches in St. Thomas, it would seem, than III, q. 83, a. 1.[52]

Is not this witness from the *Lectura* on 1 Timothy a "hierarchical-regitive" text, however? Indeed it is. But then it is to be observed, first, that however one wishes to relate the *munera* of sanctifying-sacramental ministry and hierarchical pastoral rule, whether giving primacy to the first or to the second, there is no difference between them as to the matter of representation. For St. Thomas, sacramental action *in persona Christi* not only does not exclude, but rather calls for, the priest as a representation of Christ, and so there is no warrant for dismissing the same implication of the hierarchical-regitive texts because they do so as well.

Second, and more importantly, Ferrara evidences a sort of suspicion of hierarchy that seems theologically inappropriate. So he asks rhetorically in the first article: "Is the priest first and foremost the hierarch, among whose ruling powers the sacramental power is included? Or is the priest first of all and formally Christ's servant and instrument whose hierarchical authority is grounded in and normed by this Christ-derived and Christ-directed service?"[53] Let the priest be first and foremost the instrument of Christ in the Eucharist; but it is hard to understand the fateful consequence Ferrara seems

---

[50] C. 3, lect. 1, no. 96.

[51] C. 3, lect. 1, no. 87. The same holds good for deacons too; they are to be husbands of one wife on account of the *signification sacramenti* (c. 3, lect. 3, no. 120).

[52] And on the basis of this text from the *Lectura* on 1 Tim, one easily erects the same argument against the ordination of women as St. Bonaventure offers, IV *Sent.* d. 25, a. 2, q. 2. For a contemporary presentation of the argument, see Sara Butler, "The Priest as Sacrament of Christ the Bridegroom," *Worship* 66 (1992), 498–517.

[53] RSE, 219.

so evidently to feel—unless "ruler" and "hierarch" are being taken in some extra-ecclesial sense according to which they are synonyms for "oppressor" and "tyrant."

Of course, when all is said and done perhaps while St. Thomas affirms a representationalist view of the priest in the Eucharist, Ferrara is right about the devastating and harmful consequences of such a view. Ferrara thinks assigning such a role to the priest is "out of place" in the Eucharist, "since, both symbolically and functionally, it interposes the priest between Christ and that Church which is, after all, Christ's and not the clergy's bride."[54] But then, it must be added that St. Thomas does not himself think that these deleterious consequences follow. He does not think representations function the way Ferrara thinks they do. In *Summa theologiae* III, q. 25, a. 3, taking up the question of whether images are to be adored latreutically, he writes:

> [T]here is a twofold motion of the soul to an image: one to the image itself according as it is a certain thing; in another way, to the image insofar as it is the image of another. . . . [T]he second motion, which is unto the image insofar as it is an image is one and the same with the motion which is unto the thing [of which it is the image].[55]

Reverencing the image of Christ as an image of Christ is "one and the same" with reverencing Christ.[56] This holds for icons, pictures, and crosses and crucifixes (see a. 4). It is hard to see why it does not hold for the priest when, moved by the Principal Agent, he bears the image of Christ *(gerit imaginem Christi)* in the Eucharist, unless one takes "representation" in a typically Cartesian and modern sense, one that has nothing to do with the ancient and medieval context.[57]

Conclusion

Ferrara pretends to show us a rigorous but hitherto unnoticed implication of St. Thomas's sacramental theology, according to which there can be no

---

[54] SN, 81.

[55] "Duplex est motus animae in imaginem: unus quidem in imaginem ipsam secundum quod est res quaedam; alio modo, in imaginem inquantum est imago alterius. Et inter hos motus est haec differentia, quia primus motus, quo quis movetur in imaginem prout est res quaedam, est alius a motu qui est in rem: secundus autem motus, qui est in imaginem inquantum est imago, est unus et idem cum illo qui est in rem."

[56] Here it is useful to consult Robert Sokolowski, "Picturing," in *Pictures, Quotations, and Distinctions* (Notre Dame, IN: University of Notre Dame Press, 1992), 3–26.

[57] See Robert Sokolowski, *Eucharistic Presence* (Washington, DC: Catholic University of America Press, 1994), 179–86, 198–200.

representational function of the priest relative to Christ, and therefore no argument for the exclusion of women from orders on that basis. Contrary to Ferrara, instrumental causes can be representations of their effect, and indeed must be if a sacrament is to be a sacrament. Contrary to Ferrara, sacraments do signify the mysteries of Christ. Contrary to Ferrara, representations or icons or symbols or signs of Christ are presences of Christ, not blocks to the faithful and adoring Christian mind.[58]

---

[58] I would like to thank D. Ferrara for a lengthy review of an earlier draft of this essay and am grateful for his careful attention.

11

Episcopal *Munera* and the Character of Episcopal Orders

DESPITE THE FACT of the universal recognition of the sacramentality of the episcopate since the Second Vatican Council, together with the council's related assertion that episcopal consecration imparts the *munera* of teaching and ruling as well as the *munus* of sanctifying, there has been no great attention paid to what these two assertions mean for the character that, according to the council, episcopal consecration imparts.[1] *Lumen Gentium* 21 asserts that episcopal consecration is the fullness of orders, confers the functions of teaching and ruling and sanctifying, and gives as well the Holy Spirit and a sacred character such that the bishop does these things in the person of Christ. About the relation of these things one to another the council is not wholly forthcoming.

Broadly speaking, if before the council the tendency was to conceive the character exclusively as *potestas ordinis*, not worrying about its relation to other episcopal functions and about what else episcopal ordination might confer in their regard, now the tendency is to think of it (if one thinks of it at all) simply and inclusively as the threefold power itself. Neither of these lines is acceptable. The first, by speaking of the effects of the sacrament of orders as sacramental power and grace, does not take full account of what the liturgy of orders declares is going on. The second, which tries to do this, thinks of orders as giving the power to rule and teach in the same way as it does the power to sanctify. But this does not respect the difference between teaching and ruling, on the one hand, and sanctifying, on the other, and so

---

[1] The need for such consideration was, however, pointed out immediately; see John Donahue, "Sacramental Character: the State of the Question," *The Thomist* 31 (1967): 461–62.

does not respect the difference between the kind of capacities whence these activities spring.[2]

In fact, however, one notices that not much attention is paid to the notion of the character of orders. Herbert Vorgrimler largely ignores it.[3] Gisbert Greshake treats it briefly in his section on the spiritual life of the priest.[4] In part, perhaps, such inattention is explained by the fact that the whole theology of sacramental character has been attacked and the notion sidelined as much as possible.[5] In part, perhaps, it is because attention shifted first to a theology of ministry, where ministry was to be undertaken by all the baptized, and next to the question of women and orders.

There is, however, a need to think out what we should say about the character of episcopal orders relative to the three *munera*. First, the council by no means sorted this out.[6] Second, it needs to be worked out, if (1) the

2 Perhaps the best representative of the first, preconciliar line, is Charles Journet, *The Church of the Word Incarnate* (New York: Sheed and Ward), 1:21–25, 121–26; for the second, see Seamus Ryan, "Episcopal Consecration: The Fullness of the Sacrament of Order," *Irish Theological Quarterly* 32 (1965): 319–21; Raymond Vaillancourt, "Le sacerdoce et les trois pouvoirs messianiques," *Laval Théologique et Philosophique* 22 (1966): 300; Stephen Patrick McHenry's 1983 dissertation, *Three Significant Moments in the Theological Development of the Sacramental Character of Orders* (Ann Arbor, MI: University Microfilms, 1983), 188, 282–83; Jean Galot, *Theology of the Priesthood* (San Francisco: Ignatius Press, 1984), 209; Patrick Dunn, *Priesthood: A Re-Examination of the Roman Catholic Theology of the Presbyterate* (New York: Alba House, 1990), 148–49 (following Galot); Peter Drilling, *The Trinity and Ministry* (Minneapolis: Fortress Press, 1991), 76; Avery Dulles, *The Priestly Office: A Theological Reflection* (New York: Paulist Press, 1997), 73–74; Dermot Power, *A Spiritual Theology of the Priesthood* (Washington, DC: Catholic University of America Press, 1998), 82 (following Galot). At the time of the council, in 1963, Wilhelm Bertrams spoke of the *munus* of ruling as "inhering" in episcopal character; see *The Papacy, The Episcopacy, and Collegiality* (Westminster, MD: Newman Press, 1965), 56–86.

3 Herbert Vorgrimler, *Sacramental Theology* (Collegeville, MN: Liturgical Press, 1992).

4 Gisbert Greshake, *The Meaning of Christian Priesthood* (Westminster, MD: Christian Classics, 1989), 108–11.

5 See Edward Schillebeeckx, *Ministry. A Case For Change* (London: SCM Press, 1981), 60–65, 72; but already much earlier, he had reduced the character to a relation to the community in *Christ the Sacrament of the Encounter with God* (New York: Sheed and Ward, 1963), 157–58; Joseph Moingt, "Nature du sacerdoce ministériel," *Recherches de Sciences Religieuses* 58 (1970): 257–58; Vorgrimler, *Sacramental Theology*, 267. See Galot's summary of Schoonenberg, Schillebeeckx, et al. in *A Theology of the Priesthood*, 195–96.

6 Joseph Lécuyer, "L'Episcopato come Sacramento," in *La Chiesa del Vaticano II*, ed. G. Baraúna (Florence: Vallecchi Editore, 1965), 729–30, says that beyond asserting the existence of the character, "il Concilio non precisa altro, lasciando ai teologi la cura di dillucidare la natura di questa grazia episcopale e di questo carattere, come

assertion that orders imparts a character is true; (2) the character is not reduced to a Catholic version of Congregationalist designation of ministers; (3) teaching and ruling, if rightly united with, are importantly different from, sanctifying; and (4) we want a theology whose tradition is a matter of continuity as well as of innovation.

This essay pursues a theology in continuity with what St. Thomas taught about the character of orders. Granted his understanding of the character as a power, an instrumental power relative to Christ, the principal agent of sacramental action, how shall we think about it in relation to all the *munera*? If there are still good reasons for thinking it a power, and not a habit or relation, then it will be hard to identify it with all the *munera*. Again, how shall we think about it today when, because of the liturgical and other data, we make the episcopate the primary instance of orders, episcopal consecration the primary instance of ordination, episcopal function the primary instance of sacerdotal function, and the episcopal character the primary instance of the character imparted by orders?

In what follows, the first section is an assembly of necessary materials from the liturgy, sacramental theory, and ecclesiastical practice. The second section sorts out what ordination does and does not give for the discharge of episcopal teaching and ruling. The study concludes, first, that if character be the permanent effect of ordination, it consists exclusively in sacramental power. Second, however, the power to ordain can itself be counted as part of the capacity to rule. Third, the sacrament gives grace to teach and rule, such as can be thought of after the pattern of the gifts of the Holy Spirit. And like the gifts of the Holy Spirit, the gifts for teaching and ruling are lost with the loss of charity.

Assembling the Elements: Ministries, Powers, Character, *Munera*

The following is an assembly of materials needed for a construction of the notion of episcopal character. We begin with the witness of the ancient liturgy to what a bishop is and what the rite of ordination does before proceeding to the sacramental theology of the twelfth century and beyond.

The Effect of Episcopal Ordination According to the Liturgy

1. The Second Vatican Council styles the episcopacy the fullness of the sacrament of orders (*Lumen Gentium* 21). The earliest language about

---

pure i rapporti fra l'uno e l'altro." Giuseppi Rambaldi, "Note sul sacerdozio e sul sacramento dell'Ordine nella Cost. *Lumen Gentium*," *Gregorianum* 47 (1966): 527–38, makes the same observation. Galot, on the other hand, *Theology of Priesthood*, 208–9, speaks as if the council did indeed understand the character as the foundation of all three *munera*.

Church offices, as well as the first records of the liturgy, supports the teaching that episcopal consecration is the primary instance of orders, that episcopal orders are logically prior to presbyteral orders.

First, the New Testament uses *episkopos* and *presbyteros* seemingly interchangeably. This is a sign of the non-distinction of such ministries within the New Testament and argues for a later, ecclesiastical institution of the distinction.

Then, too, the facts of the postapostolic but still ancient nomenclature are important. In the first centuries, a *sacerdos* simply and unqualifiedly speaking was a bishop; a priest-presbyter was a "priest of the second rank." This indicates at the least that the primary instance of priesthood is to be found in bishops. That is, we see its full nature there, and so see its nature there more easily than by looking at priests.[7]

Third, and most especially, the liturgical evidence is overwhelming: Bishops are ordained to be priests; presbyters are ordained to be helpers to the bishop; they are the elders of Numbers 11 relative to the bishop that the ancient liturgies saw figured in Moses.[8] Whatever priest-presbyters do, therefore, is auxiliary to what bishops do, a sort of lesser version of what bishops do.[9]

2. To say that the episcopacy is the fullness of orders is, among other things, to say immediately that it installs a man in an *ordo*; it aggregates a man to the episcopal order. This can be read off from the very surface of the rite, whereby from the ancient practice of the Church, it is prescribed that there be at least three ordaining bishops. Episcopal consecration is signified as a collegiate act, and just so, it makes someone a member of the college of bishops.[10]

3. Not for nothing does *Lumen Gentium* speak of apostles before it speaks of bishops. The point of the rite can be expressed more fully by saying, first, that it is the act whereby the college that succeeds to the apostolic college is maintained. The rite is an instrument of apostolic succession in the Church, guaranteeing that there will be exercised in the Church those apostolic functions without which the Church cannot be the Church as it was founded by Christ. The most ancient witnesses to the Church's liturgy refer the episcopacy to apostolic power or function.[11]

7 Ryan, "Episcopal Consecration," 315–16.

8 Antonio Santantoni, *L'Ordinazione Episcopale,* Analecta Liturgica 2 (Rome: Editrice Anselmiana, 1976), 214–15.

9 Ryan, "Episcopal Consecration," 309–12.

10 Ibid., 306. Cf. Moingt, "Nature du sacerdoce ministériel," 257–58.

11 Canons Regular of Mondaye, "L'évêque d'après les prières d'ordination," in *L'Épiscopat et l'Église universelle,* ed. Yves Congar and B.-D. Dupuy (Paris: Cerf, 1962), 749–52.

Apostolic functions, however, are in the first place the functions of
Christ, and so we can say, second, that the rite constitutes a man as a
representative of Christ, an image of Christ, a sacrament of Christ as
Priest, Prophet, and King, as someone through whom Christ can continue to sanctify, instruct, and guide the People of God.[12]

4. According to the ancient prayers of consecration, the rite—the imposition of hands—confers the Holy Spirit, gifts of the Spirit, power, grace,
   authority, holiness, episcopal virtues, the episcopacy.[13] There is no
   point here in doing once again what has been done many times in the
   past decades, and undertaking a comprehensive review of the liturgical
   data.[14] It will be enough to note material from the *Apostolic Tradition
   (AT)*, the *Canons of Hipolytus (CH)*, the *Apostolic Constitutions (AC)*,
   the *Testamentum Domini (TD)*, and the *Sacramentary of Sarapion
   (SS)*.[15] Ordination gives the power of the "princely spirit" for rule *(AT,
   AC, TD)*, so that the bishop may be shepherd *(AT, CH, AC, TD, SS)*.
   It gives the spirit of high-priesthood *(AT)*, the fellowship of the Spirit
   (AC), which means the power to forgive sins *(AT, CH, AC)*, to ordain
   (AT, AC), to loose the bonds of Satan, and to cure *(AT, CH, AC, TD)*.
   It gives Christ's Spirit so that the man may keep sound doctrine *(TD)*,
   as well as understanding and wisdom *(TD)*. It gives holiness *(CH)* and
   the virtues of humility, discipline, maturity, understanding, and more
   (TD). It confers the wherewithal to do the things the bishop is
   ordained to do: sanctify, teach, rule.[16]

   Of course, one text emphasizes one thing and another text another.
   The Apostolic Tradition focuses on ruling (shepherding) and priestly
   functions. The *Testamentum Domini* brings teaching to the fore. Nor
   are distinctions made between these various gifts as to their kind or

---

[12] See here Othmar Perler, "L'Évêque, représentant du Christ selon les documents des
premiers siècles," in *L'Épiscopat et l'Église universelle*, 31–66, for a review of the
patristic and liturgical evidence.

[13] Also, ordinations to the episcopate *per saltum* attest to the sacramentality of episcopal ordination; see Ryan, "Episcopal Consecration," 313, or J. Lécuyer, "Orientations présentes sur la théologie de l'épiscopat," in *L'Épiscopat et l'Église
universelle*, 786.

[14] See notes 6 and 11; also, Joseph Lécuyer, *Le sacrement de l'ordination: Recherche
historique et théologique* (Paris: Beauchesne, 1983); Paul Bradshaw, *Ordination Rites
of the Ancient Churches of East and West* (New York: Pueblo, 1990); and very suc-
cinctly, Ryan, "Episcopal Consecration."

[15] All are conveniently assembled in Bradshaw, *Ordination Rites*.

[16] Santantoni, *L'Ordinazione*, 216. See also Lécuyer, *Le sacrement de l'ordination*,
211–24, for testimony both liturgical and patristic that the rite confers the Holy
Spirit, the gifts of the Spirit, grace.

quality or nature. All the things make part of "episcopacy," of the "high-priesthood."

A Permanent Effect

In the first centuries, moreover, this charism, grace, gift, broadly understood to include whatever the bishop needs from God to be bishop, is also supposed in some way or fashion to be permanent, in spite of infidelity or sin, irregular ordination, deposition, or incapacity to function.[17]

The abiding charism of orders is recognized by St. Augustine. In the twelfth century, within a synoptic consideration of the rites of the Church, the permanent effect of orders comes to be called a "character."[18] The word St. Augustine had already used for the "abiding sacrament" of baptism is now used for the abiding sacrament of orders.[19] Furthermore, when the distinctions worked out for the sacrament of the Eucharist are applied generally to all the sacraments, the character is identified as the *res et sacramentum* of orders.[20] So, the character is a disposition to grace.[21] Further, it is a configuration to Christ the priest.[22] St. Thomas brings a certain closure to the developing theology of priestly character by conceiving it as a power. First, however, there must be a word about jurisdiction and orders.

Potestas Jurisdictionis, Potestas Ordinis

Also from the twelfth century, it has been customary to distinguish *potestas ordinis* from jurisdiction. In Gratian, there appears the distinction of the right to ordain from the power to ordain, as well as the distinction between the exercise of a power and the bare possession of a power.[23] It is the growing prevalence of "absolute ordinations" that fosters the awareness of a difference between sacramental power and ruling power.[24] Originally, a man was ordained bishop or priest only to a determinate office, the discharge of

---

17 Lécuyer, *Le sacrement*, 235–47.

18 This was done by Sicard of Cremona; see Jean Galot, *La nature du caractère sacramentel: Étude de théologie médiéval* (Brussels: Desclée de Brouwer, 1957), 45, no. 2.

19 For this felicitous terminology, see Colman E. O'Neill, *Sacramental Realism: A General Theory of the Sacraments* (Chicago: Midwest Theological Forum, 1998), 128–38.

20 This was done by Hugh of St. Cher; see Galot, *La nature du caractère sacramentel*, 86–92.

21 William of Auxerre takes it to be a material disposition for grace; see Galot, *La nature du caractère sacramentel*, 74–75. St. Thomas (*Summa theologiae* [hereafter *ST*] III, q. 69, a. 10) makes it a formal disposition.

22 This the view of Philip the Chancellor, who will be followed by St. Albert, St. Bonaventure, and St. Thomas; see Galot, *La nature*, 115–20, 147–48, 159–61.

23 Lécuyer, *Le sacrement*, 248, 252

24 Bertrams, *The Papacy, the Episcopacy, and Collegiality*, 49–54; for other factors, see the more complete history in Eugenio Corecco, "L'origine del potere di giurisdizione

which meant that the man was ruler over and judge for some part of the Church. The ordination functioned also as the man's very installation in the office. When men were ordained without being destined for a determinate office (so, "absolutely"), however, such installation was arranged by juridical act and only so did the man possess "jurisdiction," the right to rule and judge. Once this arrangement was in place, the question could be asked: What does ordination all by itself do, what all by itself does it give, prior to installation in an office? The answer to the question was *"potestas ordinis."* Raymond of Penyafort (+1271) completes the conceptual work by collecting in the power of orders all the acts that depend on the power given with the sacrament and conceiving all other hierarchical acts whatsoever as acts of "jurisdiction."[25]

This analysis can be found substantially unchanged for the next seven centuries. *Potestas ordinis* is given by sacrament, is for sacramental action, makes a man an instrument of Christ in such sacramental action, is stable and cannot be lost. Jurisdiction involves the simple assignment (assignment of one's subjects) as by the instrument of the *missio canonica*; it is for ruling; it makes a man a vicar of Christ in teaching and ruling; it is not stable in the same way *potestas ordinis* is and can be lost.[26]

The subsequent separation of the powers both conceptually and in practice has been often lamented, but the fact of separation indicates a real distinction, not only of functions, but of what enables the functions to take place. Even if, with Klaus Mörsdorf, one wants spiritual power to be something fundamentally one and only subsequently divided, the division is such that the powers can be separated.[27]

St. Thomas

St. Thomas makes use both of the previous theology of character and of the distinction of orders and jurisdiction in thinking about ecclesiastical order.

---

episcopale. Aspetti storico-giuridici e metadologico-sistematici della questione," *La Scuola Cattolica* 96 (1968): 3–42, 107–41, esp. 6–10.

[25] Corecco, "L'origine," 10.

[26] See the contrast in Journet, *Church of the Word Incarnate,* 1:23–24. The coordination of episcopal activity evidently requires regularization of jurisdiction. The coordination ensured in the early Church on a provincial level by the metropolitan, a coordination provided for from the beginning by the very form of the ordination as effected by three ordaining bishops, is now formally and expressly arranged by the primate of the episcopal college. According to Bertrams, *The Papacy,* 77–78, this coordination was always a primatial right (for apart from this right, the pope's universal and ordinary episcopal jurisdiction cannot be asserted); now it is formally exercised as such.

[27] See Klaus Mörsdorf, "Ecclesiastical Authority," in *Sacramentum Mundi* (New York: Herder, 1968), 2:135–37.

For St. Thomas, the character is the objective deputation of a man to the Christian cult; baptismal character enables reception of the sacraments, and sacerdotal character enables confection of the sacraments.[28] Like grace, the character is given by the rite independently of the worthiness of the minister, and it is what enables the minister, even unworthy, to be used by Christ, who sanctifies through the sacraments the minister confects. Sacerdotal character is thus an active, though instrumental, power, what is called *potestas ordinis*. Moreover, it is the primary instance of character in comparison to the character of baptism, for if both are powers, the power of baptism is more passive than the power of orders.[29] Again, character is configuration to Christ, to Christ the priest.[30] Having it, a man is a ministerial priest, fitted to be an instrument of Christ the Priest and to act in the person of Christ.[31] Last, character is a disposition for grace.[32]

The character is a configuration to Christ, as mentioned, and this already bespeaks its quality as a sign. It is thus easy to understand that St. Thomas keeps the idea that the character is the *res et sacramentum* of the sacraments that imprint it, and so a sign of the grace that ordination gives the ordained.[33] Such grace is fittingly given so that a man may perform with subjective holiness the worship to which he is deputed by the sacrament.[34]

When in the *Commentary on the Sentences* St. Thomas discusses episcopal consecration, he denies that it imprints a character.[35] He does this, however, not because it does not have a permanent effect, but because the effect it has does not, he says, mean a new relation to the Eucharist, and "characters" are numbered and distinguished by just such a relation.[36] What is the effect of episcopal consecration in addition to that of presbyteral ordination? It is, he says, a relation to, a power with respect to, the Church. It is under-

---

28 *ST* III, q. 63, aa. 2 and 3. In addition to Galot, *La nature,* 171–97, see especially Colman O'Neill, "The Instrumentality of the Sacramental Character," *Irish Theological Quarterly* 25 (1958): 262–68.

29 Galot, *La nature,* 179–81; see *ST* III, q. 63, a. 2.

30 *ST* III, q. 63, a. 3. It could be said, perhaps, that the configuration of the ministerial priest is, as such, a greater participation in the priesthood of Christ insofar as priesthood bespeaks action on behalf of others.

31 For consecration of the Eucharist in the person of Christ, in common with simple priests, see *ST* III, q. 82, aa. 1 and 5. For power relative to the Church exercised by the bishop in the person of Christ and in virtue of the effect of his consecration (what we would call episcopal "character" even though St. Thomas does not), see *ST* III, q. 82, a. 1, ad 4.

32 *ST* III, q. 63, a. 4, ad 1.

33 *ST* III, q. 63, a. 3, ad 2.

34 *ST* III, q. 63, a. 4, ad 1.

35 IV *Sent.,* d. 24, q. 3, a. 2, sol. 2, ad 2 (= *ST* suppl. q. 40, a. 5, ad 2).

36 For discussion of this point, see H. Bouëssé, "Le caractère épiscopal," in *L'Évêque dans l'Église du Christ,* ed. H. Bouëssé (Brussels: Desclée de Brouwer, 1963), 363–65.

standable in view of later terminology that some have identified this power with jurisdiction. The Roman Catechism of 1566 identifies jurisdiction with power relative to the mystical body of Christ, the Church.[37] The power St. Thomas is speaking of, however, is or at least includes the power to ordain. Jurisdiction, furthermore, is given *simplice injunctione* and is revocable;[38] the power over the Church St. Thomas is speaking of is given by the sacrament of orders and cannot be lost.[39] Moreover, it is by possession of this power that the bishop rules *in persona Christi.*[40]

One readily sees the point, however, of calling the power to ordain a power over the Church. To ordain is to make ministers; ministers are for the service of churches; one would not suitably ordain unless there were reason to ordain, therefore, and ordinarily, such reason would be the supply of suitable ministers to a determinate service, a determinate portion of a bishop's flock. This means that the one ordaining should ordinarily be expected to have administrative power over the church in question. Episcopal ordination gives this expectation; if it does not give jurisdiction according to St. Thomas, the sacramental power it does give can be thought of as itself a basic power of ruling. What is given, to be sure, as it were calls for jurisdiction and makes it suitable that one so ordained have jurisdiction. As Eugenio Corecco says:

> This power, however, is not identified with that of jurisdiction, because jurisdiction can be taken away, while the power of the bishop to confer the priesthood and confirmation is never lost. It is a power of ruling that has as its duties those specific to the head of a society of Christians, for example that of conferring tasks and offices, of pasturing the People of God, of defending the People from errors. This kind of power is not something more or less than what priests also have; it is a power of a different kind that can be communicated to priests through delegation.[41]

---

[37] *Roman Catechism,* Part II, chapter 7, q. 6.

[38] *ST* II–II, q. 39, a. 3.

[39] IV *Sent.*, d. 25, q. 1, a. 2, sol. and ad 2 (= *ST* suppl. q. 38, a. 2, c and ad 2). See for this important point Joseph Lécuyer, "Les étapes de l'enseignement thomiste sur l'épiscopat," *Revue thomiste* 57 (1957): 33, 51.

[40] *ST* III, q. 82, a. 1, ad 4. This is the broader usage of that notion in St. Thomas, which does not require quoting the very words of Jesus, as in the consecration at Mass (III, q. 78, a. 1). See Bernard Dominique Marliangeas, *Clés pour une théologie du ministère: In persona Christi, in persona ecclesiae,* Théologie historique, 51 (Paris: Beauchesne, 1978).

[41] Corecco, "L'origine," 12, no. 43: "Questo potere però non si identifica con quello di giurisdizione, perché quest'ultimo può essere tolto, mentre il potere del vescovo di conferire il sacerdozio e la cresima non va mai perso. E un potere di reggenza che ha come compiti quelli specifici del capo di una società di fedeli, per esempio quello di

According to Joseph Lécuyer, for St. Thomas bishops are ordered in the first place to govern the people of God; for this reason, moreover, their chief task is to teach.[42] Their consecration by the imposition of hands gives them the wherewithal, not just to ordain in the narrowest sacramental sense (which it certainly does also do, and as a stable power that simple priests do not possess), but to rule. It is as if the power to ordain just is or is part of the power to rule.[43]

So interpreted, it is to be noted that St. Thomas's position is perfectly congruent with the liturgical evidence cited above, according to which episcopal ordination enables the discharge of all episcopal functions. It might also seem that this view of St. Thomas's position supports such authorities as Jean Galot, who wish to see in the character all the *munera*. We will see in the last part of this essay, however, that things must be more complicated.

Some Post-Thomist Positions and Complications

Not every position claiming the authority of St. Thomas can be said to be congruent with the liturgical evidence. The unity of the Church requires a coordinated and therefore unified jurisdiction, and the papal primacy entails the location of supreme jurisdiction in the Roman pontiff. The pope's primacy, moreover, could find no stronger foundation than the supposition that he is the source of all ruling authority, of all jurisdiction in the Church. That means that episcopal consecration can give no jurisdiction. Further, if there is no *potestas ordinis* that consecration gives since, after all, it imprints no character, and if there is no power of ruling not to be identified with the power of jurisdiction, then the difference between bishop and priest reduces to the jurisdiction granted to the former, and the very institution of the episcopacy, as distinct from a simple priesthood, becomes an ecclesiastical, human institution. Such, roughly, is the position of John of Torquemada in the fifteenth century, Thomas de Vio Cardinal Cajetan in the sixteenth, and Diego Laynez, the minister general of the Jesuits, at the Council of Trent.[44]

---

conferire incariche e uffici, di pascere il Popolo di Dio, di difenderlo dagli errori. Questo tipo di potere non è un piu or un meno di quello che hanno anchi i sacerdoti; è un potere di natura diversa che può essere communicato ai preti per delegazione."

[42] Lécuyer, "Les étapes de l'enseignement thomiste sur l'épiscopat," 51.

[43] Thomas Marsh, "The Sacramental Character," in *Sacraments: Papers of the Maynooth Union Summer School 1963*, ed. Denis O'Callaghan (Dublin: Gill and Son, 1964), 126, thinks that according to the *Commentary on the Sentences* "the sacramental character confers an instrumental power to perform sacramental acts and also other sacred actions which pertain to the faithful," ones of the regal and prophetic order, and in this differs from the *Summa*, which restricts character to founding sacramental acts. It seems better to follow Lécuyer and Corecco and take the power to rule in question as not really distinguished from sacramental power.

[44] Corecco, "L'origine," 16–24. Torquemada, for his part, nevertheless holds to the divine institution of the episcopate, *Summa de Ecclesia* (Venice, 1561), I, c. 79. It is

This position seems to be reinforced by the papal concession to ordain granted to certain abbots in the fifteenth century. Innocent VIII (1489) granted to certain Cistercian abbots the faculty to ordain subdeacons and deacons. Even more strikingly, Boniface IX (1400) granted to the abbot of St. Osyth in Essex the faculty to ordain priests.[45] St. Thomas did not think such a thing possible.[46] Evidently, Pope Boniface and Pope Innocent did. Such ordinations seemed to make the bishop's sacramental difference from priests, his difference in *potestas ordinis*, hang by the very slender thread that no one except bishops could ordain bishops. But if a bishop really is nothing but a priest with a diocesan jurisdiction, why could a priest not in principle ordain one destined for such an office?

If at first these concessions of the faculty to ordain meant that bishops were seen as priests with the addition of jurisdiction over a diocese, they can just as easily mean that priests are diminished bishops. And this is how Yves Congar interpreted the upshot of the data. The distinction between bishops and priests is not of divine, but only of ecclesiastical, institution.[47] What is divinely instituted, dominically instituted, is the episcopacy—an office of apostolic ministry succeeding the apostles. It is this ministry, therefore, this ministry in its fullness, that we should think to be contemplating when we read the New Testament and consider the mystery of the Church. We must first make sense of the bishop before we make sense of the priest. It was precisely this kind of thinking, already in the 1930s, that helped lead to the council's assertion of the sacramentality of the episcopacy, and of the episcopacy as the fullness of orders, and so, by implication, the primary analogate, as it were, of ministerial priesthood. In order to understand priesthood, we should look at episcopacy. This means we have to start thinking of priests as diminished bishops, and not of bishops as priests with something extra added on.[48]

---

still possible to find authors who impute the position that bishops differ from priests only by jurisdiction to St. Thomas; Seamus Ryan suggests this in "Episcopal Consecration," 324. See to the contrary Lécuyer, "Les étapes de l'enseignement thomiste sur l'épiscopat."

[45] For discussion of these concessions and their import, see Yves Congar, "Faits, problèmes et réflexions à propos du pouvoir d'ordre et des rapports entre le presbytérat et l'épiscopat," in *Sainte Église: Études et approaches ecclésiologiques* (Paris: Cerf, 1963), 275–302.

[46] IV *Sent.*, d. 25, q. 1, a. 1, ad 3 (*ST* suppl. q. 38, a. 1, ad 3).

[47] Congar, "Faits, problèmes et réflexions," 294.

[48] For the maintenance of the old position in a new context, see George Tavard, *A Theology for Ministry* (Wilmington, DE: Michael Glazier, 1983), 88, 132, who takes the implication the other way: priesthood is primary; bishops are inessential to the Church; presbyteral ordination is not ordination to a share in the bishop's power.

We are, therefore, almost at the point where all the elements constituent in the council's challenge have been marshaled. There is but one more.

Munera

From the nineteenth century, it has been customary to distinguish three *munera*, sanctifying and teaching and ruling. These functions are verified first in Christ, Priest and Prophet and King (Shepherd); they are shared in some way by the Church as such and by everyone in the Church; they were devolved authoritatively and "officially" first to the apostles and thence to the bishops.[49]

Conformably to the liturgical evidence, we will say that ordination gives all three *munera*. It gives not only *potestas ordinis*, but the radical capacity to teach and rule as well. This is what *Lumen Gentium* and the "Nota praevia explicativa" to *Lumen Gentium* both say. However, by its nature, as the "Nota" also indicates, the discharge of these *munera* involves one's relations with the rest of the college and so with the primate of the college. Therefore, if ordination confers the radical capacity to rule, then there can be no *exercise* of this power prior to the reception of the canonical mission.[50]

Remembering the liturgical evidence, and given the teaching of the council, therefore, ought we not say that the character of episcopal orders just in itself includes all three *munera*? That is, as we used to identify it with *potestas ordinis*, shall we say now that it also comprises a power of ruling and a power of teaching distinct from *potestas ordinis*? This is what Galot does, and he thinks the council mandates it.[51] However, it is clear from the key sentences of *Lumen Gentium* and the "Nota praevia explica-

---

[49] For the history of the introduction of this division into Catholic theology, see Yves Congar's translation of the first chapter of Josef Fuch's dissertation, "Origines d'une trilogie ecclésiologique à l'époque rationaliste de la théologie," *Recherches de sciences religieuses* 53 (1969): 186–211; see also Peter J. Drilling, "The Priest, Prophet and King Trilogy: Elements of its Meaning in *Lumen Gentium* and for Today," *Église et Théologie* 19 (1988): 179–206, and Raymond Vaillancourt, "Le sacerdoce et les tres pouvoirs."

[50] See Bertrams, *The Papacy,* 62, for whom ordination gives the "substance" of the power to govern, which power is jurisdiction and which power is inefficacious apart from the "requisite external structure" given by the mission, and Mörsdorf, "Ecclesiastical Authority," 38–139, for whom ordination gives a "kernel" of sacred power as the basis of the bishop's power to govern, which kernel, or *Grundbestand*, is not strictly speaking jurisdiction. This position should be linked up with that of G. V. Bolgeni in the eighteenth century, for which episcopal consecration gives a sort of general and universal jurisdiction in virtue of which each bishop rightfully has active voice in a general council. See Lécuyer, "Orientations présentes," 809–10; and Corecco, "L'origine," 29–32.

[51] Galot, *Theology of Priesthood*, 208–9.

tiva" that no such conclusion follows. All paragraph 21 says is that from the liturgy and use of the Church it is evident that by ordination "gratiam Spiritus Sancti ita conferri et sacrum characterem ita imprimi, ut Episcopi . . . ipsius Christi Magistri, Pastoris et Pontificis partes sustineant et in Eius persona agant." Thus, becoming fit to rule, teach, and sanctify in Christ's name is a function of both grace and the character, and not the character exclusively. Moreover, the "ontological share" in the *munera* given by episcopal ordination that the second paragraph of the "Nota" speaks of is not identified by that text as "character." Grace, too, is something "ontological."[52]

How then should *munus* be translated? We can say "task, function, office." Can we say "power"? The "Nota" explains that *munus* is used in place of *potestas* only in order to avoid the implication that we are speaking of powers *ad actum expedita*—powers proximate to act, needing nothing more to be exercised. So, the *munus regendi* is a power; but as conferred by ordination, without the canonical mission, there is no exercise of it. Further, if one wants to say that jurisdiction just means a power *ad actum expedita*, then ordination does not give it, and the *munus regendi*, which is given by ordination, is not jurisdiction. If one wants, with Wilhelm Bertrams, to distinguish jurisdiction as to its substance and its exercise, one can say that ordination gives the first but not the second. To speak in the first way lets us keep the analysis of jurisdiction according as it does not exist without a relation to subordinates.[53]

So, *Lumen Gentium* indicates that ordination confers the three *munera*. It associates them with the character at paragraph 21. Strictly, however, there is no identification of the *munera* of teaching and ruling with the character. The "Nota praevia explicativa" speaks of an ontological share in the *munera*. Neither does this of itself require identification of all three *munera* with the character.

Episcopal Character and Episcopal *Munera*

Supposing therefore that episcopal ordination gives an "ontological participation" in the three *munera,* and supposing at the same time that the permanent effect analogous to "character" imparted by episcopal ordination is what St. Thomas said it was—hereafter simply "character"—and supposing as well that the character configures to Christ, as both St. Thomas and the

---

52 Nor does the *Catechism of the Catholic Church*, nos. 1581–82, draw the relation of priestly character to the three *munera* any more tightly.

53 See Torquemada, *Summa de Ecclesia,* II, c. 56, ratio 8. Cf. Mörsdorf, "Ecclesiastical Authority," 139: "To suppose that the power of jurisdiction is substantially conferred by ordination but still requires an essential element from outside [as with Bertrams], only postpones the problem."

council say, how should we think about what ordination effects relative to the *munera*?

The argument that on St. Thomas's position episcopal ordination ought to be understood to give all three *munera*, all three powers, and that all of them are ineradicable in the same sense as the character as traditionally conceived, and that therefore for all intents and purposes the character includes them, could be made as follows.

In several places, St. Thomas gives us to understand that episcopal power for ruling, the bishop's power over the *corpus Christi mysticum*, is simply his power to confirm and ordain, what we would identify as belonging to the bishop's *potestas ordinis*.[54] Further, St. Thomas says we may speak of orders as a sacrament (and so as related to the Eucharist) or as directed to hierarchical actions.[55] But just as the action of confecting the Eucharist depends on a power that cannot be lost, so the hierarchical actions of confirming and ordaining depend on a power that cannot be lost,[56] and therefore also we may conclude that the power whence the hierarchical actions of ruling proceed also abides. The actions relative to either way of speaking of orders equally derive from a capacity bestowed by consecration. Among hierarchical actions belonging to the bishop, moreover, is the action of teaching.[57]

This argument slides from the actions of confirming and ordaining to other hierarchical actions of ruling, for which jurisdiction is required. This, however, is not the main problem. For we ought indeed to say that ordination gives the bishop the ontological basis of all his ministry, on the ground above explained that the power to ordain already and of itself is ordered to ruling a church.[58] Even so, a foundation is not a house, and there are several reasons why the *munera* of teaching and ruling ought not be identified with the character *tout court*.

Three Arguments for the Non-identity of Character and the Munera

1. First, recall that St. Thomas styles the character a power and not a habit because it can be used either well or badly, while a habit, if good, can be

---

54 IV *Sent.*, d. 25, q. 1, a. 1, sol. (= *ST* suppl. q. 38, a. 1); d. 24, q. 3, a. 2, sol. 1 and ad 3 (= *ST* suppl. q. 40, a. 4, c. and ad 3); *ST* III, q. 82, a. 1, ad 4; and *De perfectione vitae* 24.

55 IV *Sent.*, d. 24, q. 3, a. 2, sol. 2 (= *ST* suppl. q. 40, a. 5).

56 IV *Sent.*, d. 25, q. 1, a. 2, sol. and ad 2 (= *ST* suppl. q. 38, a. 2, c. and ad 2).

57 IV *Sent.*, d. 24, q. 2, a. 1, sol. 2 (= *ST* suppl. q. 37, a. 2); cf. *ST* III, q. 67, a. 2, ad 1.

58 This is the understanding of St. Thomas that Lécuyer and Corecco give. This is the understanding as to the reality that Mörsdorf gives, "Ecclesiastical Authority," 138: "I consider this kernel [of sacred power given by ordination] to be his personal episcopal character and above all the inalienable power which a bishop always has to confer valid holy orders."

used only well.[59] The reason for saying this is very simple, a point to be read off from the experience of the Church. A bishop may ordain for either a good or bad end, a wise or foolish purpose, but in either case, he ordains, and insofar as we consider the effect of ordination just in itself, he does not ordain one man better or more perfectly than he does another. Strictly, we should say: Christ, through the bishop, does not ordain one man better or more perfectly than another. On the other hand, the bishop teaches more or less effectively, and rules more or less prudently according as the relevant virtues—habits—are weakly or strongly present. These activities, therefore, teaching and ruling, seem to spring immediately from habits and remotely from powers, while the act of ordaining just in itself and abstracting from the conditions of the act springs immediately from a power.

If the character that St. Thomas speaks of were a habit, then it would be easier to include the other *munera* in it.[60] But if it is not, then they cannot be simply tacked on, so to speak, to what he was intending when he spoke of the character imparted by orders. Again, if the character were purely relational, it would be no problem to include some other relations in the group, as it were.[61]

2. Another but not unrelated reason for denying the identity is that it seems wise to conceive Christ's relation to episcopal function variously and not univocally. This is not to gainsay the fact that the liturgical and patristic evidence Lécuyer gathers enables us to say that Christ rules and teaches and sanctifies through the bishop, and that the bishop acts in Christ's person in all these ways.[62] But if we say he preaches and sanctifies and rules through the bishop, this "through" contains several relationships, concealing their differences, for the relation of Christ to episcopal sanctifying is not the same as his relation to episcopal teaching and ruling.

Christ is the principal agent of the sacraments. The action of ordination is his action. The action of confecting the Eucharist is his action. The action of ordaining is his action. However, while the content of the bishop's preaching is Christ and is received from Christ, and

---

59 *ST* III, q. 63, a. 2, sc.

60 Dulles, *Priestly Office,* 73–74, makes the character a habit, and therefore includes the other *munera* in it without conceptual problem.

61 This is what we find in Schillebeeckx, *Christ,* 170; and Moingt, "Nature du sacerdoce ministeriel," 265, 268.

62 Lécuyer, "L'Épiscopato," 714, 731; Drilling, "Priest, Prophet and King Trilogy," 187, reports that the 1963 schema of the Constitution on the Church spoke of Christ as the "principal agent" in all three episcopal functions; and *Lumen Gentium* 21 speaks of the bishop acting in the person of Christ in all three functions without distinction.

so we can say we hear Christ in the bishop, the very action of preaching is not Christ's, but rather the bishop's. The bishop acts at the behest of and as representing Christ; he is acting vicarially; he is acting in the place of Christ. But in the sacraments, he is not in the place of Christ. Christ's place cannot really be taken in the same way in the sacraments as in preaching.[63]

A sign that preaching is the bishop's action, and not Christ's, is that the bishop can be mistaken as to what is to be said, and so obscure the reality to be displayed. There are no mistakes in that way in the sacramental action, however, and the reason is that the action is principally Christ's, and only instrumentally the minister's. Just so and in the extreme, a bishop can become a heretic, and yet retain the power to ordain.[64]

So also, the end to which the ruling of the bishop is directed is Christ, and he undertakes so to direct the flock at the behest of and in the place of Christ. But the action of ruling (legislating, judging, administering) remains the bishop's in the same way as does the action of preaching.

3. As noted above in the assembly of elements where St. Thomas was treated, there is a point to saying that the power to ordain is, or calls for, the power to rule. Insofar as the power to ordain is that power, then of course ordination will be said to confer the power to rule, and this is just the understanding of St. Thomas given by Lécuyer and Corecco, above, and the understanding of the reality offered by Mörsdorf. There is reason to say, however, that while the power to rule may include or depend on the power to ordain, it is not simply to be identified with the power to ordain.

For one thing, ruling springs from habits and dispositions that depend on acquired knowledge, the knowledge of faith, prudence acquired and infused, and, as we shall see, the gifts of the Holy Spirit. Preaching, also, is more complexly founded than the instrumental power that makes a man an instrument of Christ in the sacraments.

Further, St. Thomas was perfectly aware of this complexity. As mentioned, ruling and teaching both require knowledge. So, according to *Summa theologiae* II–II, q. 185, a. 3, only one who is already able to instruct and govern others is to be ordained bishop. Again, while not

---

63 Journet, *Church of the Word Incarnate,* 1:124–26, reaches here for the distinction of instrument and secondary principal cause, as does also Jerome Hamer, *The Church Is a Communion* (London: Geoffrey Chapman, 1964), 120. The appeal is to John of St. Thomas.

64 IV *Sent.,* d. 25, q. 1, a. 2, sol. (= *ST* suppl. q. 38, a. 2).

much knowledge is required to say Mass, those who are placed over others, both in respect of hearing confessions and as episcopal rulers, are to have the requisite knowledge before ordination.[65] Earlier, St. Thomas had noted that ordination does not drive out ignorance in the one ordained, but is ordered to driving out ignorance in those the ordained minister to.[66]

And again, such knowledge, as it is installed before and independently of ordination, can be corrupted and lost after ordination, as the heresy of prelates shows. But the character, *potestas ordinis* narrowly understood, is given only with ordination and is indelible.

The Root of the Difference: Doing and Displaying

The three matters just discussed point to a fundamental difference between orders on the one hand and teaching and ruling on the other whence all the others follow. It is the difference between *doing* something and *displaying* something by way of saying how something is. With Mörsdorf, we are founding the distinction of jurisdiction or ruling and the power of orders in the prior distinction of word and sacrament. However, these are not just two forms of "communication," or "revelation," though they are also that. The word, and notwithstanding the biblical and "Hebrew" concept of the effective divine word, is first of all simply a matter of displaying reality. This is true even in the word of command; when God commands, he displays something as a "to be done," a "to be chosen as good."[67] Sacraments, on the other hand, while they change things by displaying something, really do change things in a way displaying reality does not. In the sacrament, God acts to forgive sins, give the Holy Spirit, give created grace, give a character, change bread and wine into the body of Christ, and so on. He does this, however, through an instrument, namely the minister of the sacrament, who is able to be a minister because he has an instrumental efficient power given him in order to make him the fit instrument of such action that in itself only God himself is competent for.[68]

On the other hand, teaching and ruling, while they are not entirely the same, are nonetheless both displays. They both show how things are. Authoritative teaching addresses the speculative intellect of one's subjects, and the exercise of jurisdiction in the sense of ruling addresses the practical intellect of one's subjects.[69] Teaching, simply speaking, displays something as what it is, as such and such, as distinct from another thing, and so

---

[65] IV *Sent.*, d. 24, q. 1, a. 3, sol. 2, and ad 1 (= *ST* suppl. q. 36, a. 2, c. and ad 1).

[66] IV *Sent.*, d. 24, q. 1, a. 2, qla.,1, ad 1 (= *ST* suppl. q. 35, a. 1, ad 1).

[67] To command is an act of reason in *ST* I–II, q. 17, a. 1.

[68] *ST* III, q. 82, a. 1.

[69] Journet, *Church of the Word Incarnate*, 1:122, 338.

on. Ruling, giving a command, is also a function of intellect, displaying something as "to be done."

Because the main agent, the main doer, in the sacrament is the Lord, sacramental power escapes complete juridical control. Displaying, saying how things are, on the other hand, is always simply to be measured by faithful contemplation of the Paschal Mystery, of the already given and revealed word. When the words of one prelate disagree with the words of the Church, this will be noted, and can itself be displayed so that no one be led astray.

Words can be repeated on the sole condition that they are understood, and so there is no necessary enabling of the messenger by way of giving him an instrumental efficient power to speak and repeat the word of God. A man understands the word of the Gospel so as to be able to teach given the real assent of faith and the "charism of truth."[70] The only other thing that is necessary for him to speak the word authoritatively, it seems, is that he be recognized as possessing that charism. This recognition constitutes him an authoritative messenger of the word, and is a matter of simple designation, of commissioning by way of the *missio*.

Something is not a fit instrument of efficient causality, however, unless the "matter" of the instrument is fashioned in the right way. Fashioning the instrument changes what is fashioned. The change remains unless the one who makes the change erases it, undoes it. Here, the one making the change is the Lord, not the Church. Constitution of authoritative messengers, on the one hand, and fashioning of fit instruments, on the other, thus differ in their effects. The first is revocable; the second is not. One may choose not to use the instrument once fashioned, but it remains the instrument it has been fashioned to be.

Further, since it is the Lord who uses the man in the sacraments, the bishop always ordains or makes the Eucharist successfully. Since his teaching and ruling depend on his knowledge, his faith, his constant receptivity to the inspiration of grace, his teaching and ruling are sometimes more and sometimes less successful.

Of course, it is fitting that all three *munera* are discharged by the same man, since they call for one another: for the word of God authoritatively addressed to us is to repent, to seek baptism, to approach the table of the Lord, and so on, as well as to believe in the Gospel and follow the commandments of love. One who authoritatively charges the faithful to live according to the commandments of love has the competence effectively to order, that is govern, the community so constituted by this love.

---

70 See Louis Ligier, "Le *Charisma veritatis certum* des évêques: ses attaches liturgiques, patristiques et bibliques," *L'Homme devant Dieu: Mélanges offerts au Père Henri de Lubac* (Paris: Aubier, 1973), 1:247–68.

What Ordination Gives for Teaching and Ruling

We are now prepared to close on our question: What can ordination be thought to give relative to teaching and ruling?

First, it gives the *call* to teach and rule. That is, the charge to sanctify, the duty to sanctify, brings in its train the duty to teach those whom one is obliged to sanctify, and to provide for the good order of the community in which one does so. In other words, as William van Roo says, the character, understood as *potestas ordinis*, is a sort of deputation to ruling and teaching, even if such deputation is indeterminate (made determinate for a bishop by his integration into the college of bishops).

This answer, however, does not seem to give real force to the idea that ordination gives an "ontological share" in the three functions. Therefore, second, there is the "grace" of the sacrament. As van Roo says:

> The sacramental grace of orders perfects the one ordained who is suitably disposed unto the end of his whole function: sanctifying, ruling, teaching. Priestly holiness and a proper sacerdotal spirituality belong to his state and vocation, and is proportioned to his whole sacerdotal or episcopal function.[71]

This sacramental grace can be understood especially as the gratuitous grace of the "word of wisdom and knowledge." It is this grace that is ordered to the public teaching of prelates.[72] This grace, moreover, is really identical with the gifts of wisdom and knowledge, gifts of the Holy Spirit, and differs from them only according as it bespeaks an especial fullness of the gifts.[73] So much for teaching. As to ruling, the gift of counsel also can be a gratuitous grace.[74] It is the gift associated with practical wisdom,[75] with prudence,[76] and so with governing. The gifts of the Holy Spirit, recall, render a man especially receptive to actual grace, to the promptings of the Holy Spirit[77]— here, the inspirations relative to teaching and instructing and being practically wise. Such gifts are better understood as habits rather than as powers,[78]

---

71 William van Roo, *De Sacramentis in Genere* (Rome: Gregorian University Press, 1960), 262: "Gratia sacramentalis ordinis perficit ordinatum apte dispositum ad finem totius muneris sui: sanctificandi, regendi, docendi. Sanctitas sacerdotalis, et spiritualitas sacerdotalis propria est statui et vocationi ejus, et proportionata est integro muneri ejus sacerdotali vel episcopali."

72 *ST* II–II, q. 177, a. 2.

73 *ST* I–II, q. 68, a. 5, ad 1; I–II, q. 111, a. 4, ad 4; II–II, q. 45, a. 5, c. and ad 2.

74 *ST* II–II, q. 52, a. 1, ad 2.

75 *ST* I–II, q. 68, a. 4.

76 *ST* II–II, q. 52, a. 2.

77 *ST* I–II, q. 68, a. 1.

78 *ST* I–II, q. 68, a. 3.

and this in contrast to the character imprinted by orders.[79] Last, the gifts of the Holy Spirit can be lost, and are lost with the loss of charity.[80]

This understanding seems to include everything we need. First, ordination gives the capacity to teach and rule in that it gives an especial and certainly fitting abundance of the relevant gifts of the Holy Spirit. Second, where we are not interested in strictly distinguishing habits from powers, we can call this capacity a power in the broad sense. Third, since the gifts are habits and bound up with charity, they can be lost; they are not as stable as is the character, where that is identified with *potestas ordinis*. Fourth, the knowledge and wisdom in question do not supply for the knowledge and wisdom acquired through study.

Note, then, what ordination supplies for ruling and teaching, and how it supplies it. For ruling, there is the power to ordain—character!—and the gift of counsel, part of the grace of the sacrament. To rule one also requires, doubtless, acquired knowledge and prudence, and the relevant infused virtues. For teaching, there are the gifts of knowledge and wisdom, which also do not obviate the need for acquired knowledge and the relevant infused virtues.

The above can be summarized apropos of an especially important text of St. Thomas. In *Summa theologiae* III, q. 63, a. 3, ad 2, we read:

> The sacramental character is a *res* [thing] as regards the exterior sacrament [the *sacramentum tantum*], and a *sacramentum* in regard to the ultimate effect [grace, the *res tantum*]. Consequently, something can be attributed to a character in two ways. First, if the character be considered as a sacrament: and thus it is a sign of the invisible grace which is conferred in the sacrament. Secondly, if it be considered as a character. And thus it is a sign conferring on a man a likeness to some principal person in whom is vested the authority over that to which he is assigned. . . . And in this way those who are deputed to the Christian worship, of which Christ is the author, receive a character by which they are likened to Christ.

Still, the character is one reality, so we can say that the likeness to Christ is at the same time what is a sign of grace. If we begin with the idea that the character is an instrumental power, then things fall out as follows.

First, instrumentalization implies configuration to Christ, likeness to Christ. As the wood is conformed to the shape of the hand and becomes a handle, so being rendered the instrument of Christ who ordains, who blesses the bread, who forgives—this renders the man like Christ the

---

[79] *ST* III, q. 63, a. 2.
[80] *ST* I–II, q. 68, a. 5.

priest. The priest's being fitted out as an instrument is what his likeness to Christ consists in.[81] It is permanent.

Second, the bishop's capacity to sanctify—his priesthood, his possession of *potestas ordinis*, and especially as this includes the power to ordain—just is a sort of competence to rule, and this means that he ought to teach those whom he rules and sanctifies. Therefore, objectively, it calls for jurisdiction, for a canonical mission.

In the third place, it also calls for grace. For if the bishop is to sanctify worthily, he must do so with the correct interior disposition that does not exist apart from grace. So also, if the bishop is to teach and rule worthily, he must do so with the correct interior disposition that does not exist apart from sanctifying grace. Also, however, if the bishop is to teach and rule not only worthily but effectively, he must have the sure charism of truth, the relevant gifts of the Holy Spirit as detailed above. These gifts are habits; they are relatively stable, can be increased, and make a man more patient to actual grace. If sanctifying grace and charity are lost, however, then they are lost.

Is there a practical consequence of this attempt to link up the liturgy, the council, and St. Thomas? Yes. A bishop does not need to be a prayerful person in order to ordain. He needs to pray in order to ordain worthily. On the other hand, in order to rule and to teach, he needs to pray—to be open to and call for the inspiration of the Spirit to which the gifts of the Holy Spirit dispose him. He needs to pray, and to be prayed for, not just to teach and to rule worthily, but to teach and to rule at all.

---

[81] Lécuyer, *Sacrement de l'ordination,* 267–68.

12

Sacerdotal Character at the Second Vatican Council

THE TEACHING of the Second Vatican Council on the sacramentality of the episcopate, together with its insistence that all three *munera* of teaching, sanctifying, and ruling are imparted by episcopal ordination, seems to lead naturally to the idea that the character imparted by the sacrament is the locus of the *munera* of teaching and ruling in the same way as it has always been thought to be the seat of the power of sanctifying. Moreover, certain conciliar passages seem practically to suggest this. So, *Lumen Gentium* 21b, just after stating that all three *munera* are conferred by consecration, adds the following:

> [I]t is very clear that by the imposition of hands and the words of consecration the grace of the Holy Spirit is conferred in such a way and a sacred character is imprinted in such a way, that in an outstanding and visible way, bishops discharge the functions of Christ himself as Teacher, Pastor and Priest, and act in his person *[perspicuum est manuum impositione et verbis consecrationis gratiam Spiritus Sancti ita conferri et sacrum characterem ita imprimi, ut Episcopi eminenti ac adspectabili modo, ipsius Christi Magistri, Pastoris et Pontificis partes sustineant et in Eius persona agant].*[1]

Presbyterorum Ordinis 2c also says:

> [T]he priesthood of presbyters is conferred by that special sacrament in which presbyters, by the anointing of the Holy Spirit, are signed with a special character and thus configured to Christ the Priest, in such a

---

[1] See also the *Nota praevia explicativa* 2: "in consecratione [episcopali] datur ontologica participatio sacrorum munerum"; all three *munera* are meant.

way that they can act in the person of Christ the Head *[Sacerdotium Presbyterorum . . . peculiari . . . illo Sacramento confertur, quo Presbyteri, unctione Spiritus Sancti, speciali charactere signantur et sic Christo Sacerdoti configurantur, ita ut in persona Christi Capitis agere valeant].*

Acting in the person of Christ the Head, moreover, is a matter of instructing, sanctifying, and ruling the Church his body—all three—as is clear from the first part of *Presbyterorum Ordinis* 2c.

It is not surprising, therefore, to find certain scholars, among them the most able, asserting that the character is, or is the locus of, all three *munera*, and without making any distinctions. Thus Jean Galot, commenting on the passage from *Presbyterorum Ordinis*: "The character provides the foundation for the empowerment to speak in the name of Christ, to proclaim the Word of God, and to expound with authority the gospel message. . . . Note that the power conferred by the character is not just cultic and sacramental." If the character has in the past been understood to be limited in that way, that is a mistake that we need not repeat, according to Galot.[2] For Ghislain Lafont, the council "expands the meaning of the [character]: it cannot be reduced to an instrumental power over the Eucharist." The character makes the bishop pastor, and "confirms and consecrates a Christian's charism of presiding over a particular Church." It "habituates" him generally and across the board "to act responsibly in the name and with the authority of Christ . . . in the acts of his ministry."[3] And Sara Butler has this to say apropos of *Lumen Gentium* 21:

> According to the council . . . the sacrament itself confers a new share in Christ's threefold office of priest, prophet (or teacher), and pastor. The character imposed by episcopal ordination is explicitly linked to the sacramental role of bishops, who "take the part of Christ himself, teacher, shepherd and priest, and act as his representatives" or *"in eius persona."*[4]

The first statement is unassailable; it is the second I wish to contest. For thinkers such as Butler and Galot, presumably, just as the character has been understood (especially by Thomists) to be or at least to include the

---

[2] Jean Galot, S.J., *Theology of the Priesthood* (San Francisco: Ignatius, 1984), 208–9.

[3] Ghislain Lafont, *Imagining the Catholic Church,* trans. John Burkhard (Collegeville, MN: Liturgical Press, 2000), 159. However, Lafont continues, we need not think of a power that is " 'physically' permanent," but only of a permanent "configuration to Christ the Pastor" (ibid., 160).

[4] Sara Butler, "Official Teaching on the Ministerial Priesthood," unpublished paper of October 12, 1995, 8; but for the same idea see her "Priestly Identity: 'Sacrament' of Christ the Head," *Worship* 70 (1996): 303.

stable and inamissible power of sanctifying, so also it is or at least includes similarly indelible powers of teaching and ruling.

Lumen Gentium 21b conduces to this view, however, only if it is read in such a way that the character alone enables the bishop to act in the person of Christ the teacher, pastor, and priest. But this is certainly contrary to the literal sense of the text, which mentions grace in addition to the character. Both grace and the character enable the bishop to function in the said way. The English translation in the Flannery edition indeed reads: "[T]he grace of the Holy Spirit is given, and a sacred character is impressed in such wise that bishops . . . take the place of Christ himself, teacher, shepherd and priest." Here, grace and the character are separated by a comma, and no comma separates the character from episcopal action in the person of Christ. This suggests founding all three *munera* in the character. But the Latin text joins grace and the character in one breath, and separates off acting in the person of Christ from both with a comma, more easily supporting the reading that both grace and the character conspire to produce that effect.[5] Moreover, the English omits the first *ita*, the one that says "grace is conferred *in such a way*," and keeps only the second, "a character is imprinted *in such wise*." But the double use of the Latin *ita* makes it perfectly plain that the result clause *(ut Episcopi . . . sustineant et . . . agant)* is a function of both grace and the character.

Neither the commentary of Gérard Philips on *Lumen Gentium* as a whole nor that of Joseph Lécuyer on paragraph 21 supports viewing the character as the locus of the *munera*; neither of them announces any such thing as an intended development concerning the nature of the character in the theology of orders.[6] On the contrary, Lécuyer notes that the council leaves to theologians the task of elucidating the nature of the grace and character conferred by the sacrament, and the relation between them.[7] Lécuyer knows; he served on the subcommittee of the doctrinal commission charged with assembling *De Ecclesia*.[8]

Presbyterorum Ordinis 2c seems more favorable to the view of Galot and Butler. The character itself is presented as a function of the outpouring

---

[5] Nor does the "ontological participation" in the *munera* of the *Nota praevia* further the problematic reading, since grace is as much a reality as is the character.

[6] G. Philips, *L'Église et son mystère au deuxième concile du Vatican: Histoire, text et commentaire de la constitution* Lumen Gentium (Paris: Desclée, 1967), 1:246–76.

[7] J. Lécuyer, "L'Episcopato come Sacramento," in *La Chiesa del Vaticano II*, ed. Guilherme Baraúna (Florence: Vallecchi Editore, 1965), 729–30. Further, it is in virtue of both grace and character that the bishop is said to discharge the three *munera* in the place of Christ.

[8] J. Komonchak, "The Struggle for the Council During the Preparation of Vatican II (1960–1962)" in *History of Vatican II*, ed. Giuseppe Alberigo and Joseph A. Komonchak, vol. 1 (Maryknoll, NY: Orbis, 1995), 286.

of the Holy Spirit, and without break, it is the character alone of which we read that it is imprinted that "thus" *(sic)* they are configured to Christ "in such a way" *(ita)* that they are able to act in the person of Christ the head. Configuration to Christ has long been associated with the theology of the character.[9] The last clause seems to draw from the fact of configuration the ability to represent Christ. This text, then, looks like it makes the character itself the factor in virtue of which the priest acts in the person of Christ the teacher, the pastor, and the priest.

The trouble with such a view can be briefly stated. While it is certainly part of the received tradition of the Church that sacramental acts of validly consecrated bishops are themselves valid, and so have the effect intended, it is by no means part of the tradition of the Church that the magisterial and gubernatorial acts of validly ordained prelates are similarly never other than successful. That is, bishops can teach heresy; also, bishops can so govern as to tear down and not build up the Church. The teaching and ruling functions of bishops and priests can misfire in a way their sanctifying function cannot.[10]

This essay examines whether the council in fact commits us to the view that the character is a power for teaching and ruling in the same way it has been thought to be the power of sanctifying, that is, *potestas ordinis.* Did the council fathers intend to teach that the character imparted by episcopal ordination is substantially the same as the powers or *munera* of teaching and ruling? The *Acta Synodalia* will answer this question directly and in fairly short order. The answer is no, and this is perfectly clear from the *relationes* accompanying the final versions of the documents.

It will be necessary, however, to canvass all the speeches and observations of the fathers to see whether and to what extent and with what approval they entertained the view of Galot and Butler. The meager results of this canvass show the council was hardly aware of the possibility of reading things as do Galot and Butler. But the speeches and observations of the fathers also contain some resources for thinking about the *munera* in their difference and distinction. A concluding section will suggest a more comprehensive view of the matter on the basis of these resources.

The *Acta Synodalia* for *Lumen Gentium* 21

A survey of the *Acta* reveals that there is nothing to support reading number 21 as conducing to the problematic view.[11] Neither Philips nor Lécuyer

---

9 From Philip the Chancellor, followed in this by Albert, Bonaventure, and Thomas.

10 Saving that teaching function of the Holy Father or of the college as a whole when they teach definitively.

11 For much of what follows, one can consult Francisco Gil Hellín, *Lumen Gentium: Constitutio Dogmatica de Ecclesia Concilii Vaticani II Synopsis in ordinem redigens*

alerts us to any development concerning the idea of the sacramental character of bishops because there is nothing to alert us to.

We can begin with the *relatio* of Cardinal König (September 21, 1964) presenting the next-to-final version of *Lumen Gentium (LG)* 18–21. This version of *LG* 21, König explains, rearranges the paragraphs so as to start with the priesthood of Christ.[12] The text prefers to speak of the episcopacy as the fullness rather than as the highest grade of orders, so as to indicate a whole in which priests participate. More nearly touching our concern, it states positively and unambiguously that consecration confers all three episcopal *munera*.[13] Very nearly touching our concern, it states the sacramentality of the episcopate more positively than the previous text. Instead of saying that a bishop cannot be returned to the state of a layman or simple priest, it speaks rather of his acting in the person of Christ. Since it was on the basis of the character that it was said that a bishop could not become again a simple priest or layman, is it on the same basis that a bishop acts in the person of Christ in discharging all three *munera*? This would be a reasonable inference. It sets up the view of Galot and Butler. It is also, as we shall see, what one prominent father thinks the text implies. Directly touching our question, however, König explains that in affirming that consecration imparts a character, "the words were chosen in such a way as to abstract from disputed questions: namely, whether it be a new character or only a broadening of presbyteral character, and so on."[14] Evidently, there is no innovation or development intended as to the understanding of the character of orders. König notes that the text intends also to avoid the question—*obscura quaestio*—of presbyteral ordinations (i.e., ordinations to the priesthood and deaconate by priests), and says merely that, through the sacrament of orders, only bishops assume new members into the episcopal body.[15]

In the *relatio* with which the final text was presented (November 17, 1964), the Doctrinal Commission declares that consecration imparts not just an aptitude or disposition for the *munera* of ruling and teaching, but the *munera* themselves.[16] For the commission's understanding of *"munus,"* we can appeal to the *Nota praevia explicativa* 2, which says that "the word *munus* is used, and not power *[potestas]*, because that could be understood as a power

---

schemata cum relationibus necnon patrum orationes atque animadversiones (Vatican City: Libreria Editrice Vaticana, 1995).

[12] *Acta Synodalia Sacrosancti Concilii Vaticani II* (Rome: Typis Polyglottis Vaticanis, 1970–), III/2:202. Hereafter, *AS,* and indicating volume/part:page.

[13] *AS* III/2:203.

[14] *AS* III/2:204.

[15] *AS* III/2:204. For the question of presbyteral ordinations, see, for example, *DS* 1145, 1435.

[16] *AS* III/8:62; modus 39.

ad actum expedita." However, to the request that the text say that the powers of ruling and teaching derive from the power of sanctifying, the Commission thinks it good that the text do no more than state the fact of the conferral of the powers, "and not enter into the question of their connection with one another."[17] To the request to add text stating explicitly that the council intends to settle no disputed questions as to the origin of jurisdiction and the power of teaching or any question concerning character, it is answered not that the council is here settling such questions, but that the theological qualification of the text has already been sufficiently declared.[18] Finally, to the request that the character imparted by orders be described as dispositive, once again the Commission thinks it good not to enter into disputed questions.[19]

These two *relationes* make it impossible to see *Lumen Gentium* 21 as positively teaching and intending to teach that the character consists of the three powers together. On the other hand, there was evidently some sentiment for expressing things differently, or more fully, relative to the character. In turning to the speeches and written comments of the fathers, I canvass widely for remarks on or relative to episcopal character.

Speeches and Comments, First Session, on the First Schema De Ecclesia

The schema *De Ecclesia* was distributed to the council fathers on November 23, 1962.[20] The composition of chapter 3, on the sacramentality of the episcopate, had been left to Joseph Lécuyer. Number 11 of this chapter states (1) that episcopal consecration confers the power of sanctifying, (2) that the powers of teaching and governing, instituted by Christ, are closely united *(arcto vinculo coniungeretur)* with the power of sanctifying, (3) that consecration confers grace, and so (4) the episcopacy is the highest grade of the sacrament of orders. Further, (5) a consecrated bishop also receives a sacramental character, such that (6) he can never become a simple priest or a layman again, nor (7) lose the power of validly confirming and of validly ordaining ministers.[21]

---

17 *AS* III/8:61; modus 38.

18 *AS* III/8:63; modus 45, which refers to p. 56, modus 10, where the Doctrinal Commission's declaration of March 6, 1964 is repeated to the effect that no definition should be understood to be made except where such is openly declared as being made.

19 *AS* III/8: 63–64; modus 49.

20 For the history of this schema, see J. Komonchak, "The Struggle for the Council During the Preparation of Vatican II (1960–1962)" in Alberigo and Komonchak, eds., *History of Vatican II*, 1:285–300, 311–13.

21 *Acta et documenta Concilio oecumenico Vaticano II apparando; Series secunda (praeparatoria)* (Rome: Typis Polyglottis Vaticanis, 1969), II/3:1038 (hereafter, *ADP*, and volume/part:page). Or *AS* I/4:23.

The fourth chapter of the schema, on residential bishops, was entrusted to H. Schauf. It tackled the difficult question of jurisdiction at number 14, and took the line that jurisdiction is not conferred by ordination, but results, directly or indirectly, from papal mission.[22] This did not survive the consideration of the Central Preparatory Commission, however, and the text was altered to read that ordination confers together with the munus of sanctifying the *munera* of teaching and ruling as well. The exercise of jurisdiction, nevertheless, is said to be received not from ordination but from the pope.[23]

Discussion of the schema lasted seven days, beginning on December 1, 1962.[24] There was considerable focus on the origin of jurisdiction, but no discussion of character. The written observations are more interesting for our topic. There are many observations to the effect that consecration imparts all three *munera*, with due care taken often enough to distinguish this from particular jurisdiction or its exercise. Bishop Charue will say that "the power to teach exists ontologically in every consecrated bishop."[25] There is also considerable concern that episcopal power be said to be radically collegial, so that the *munera* are exercised in virtue of consecration *and* location in the college. In all this, the focus is on the simple affirmation that consecration imparts a responsibility for the whole Church, exercised by the college of bishops as such. A few observations contain some more thoughtful view of the *munera*.

Cardinal Richaud wants to say that the basic or radical power of a bishop, including titular bishops, for ruling the whole Church in association with the other members of the college, comes from consecration, not from a share in papal jurisdiction, although consecration does not of course of itself give particular jurisdiction for a diocese. Richaud makes episcopal jurisdiction for the whole Church depend on the principle of St. Thomas that distinction of orders depends on relation to the Eucharist: "[T]he power of jurisdiction in regard to the Mystical Body belongs to bishops from its connection with the fuller and more complete power which they enjoy for the Eucharistic Body, the permanence of which bishops alone can guarantee through the ordination of priests."[26] In this way a principle that

---

[22] *ADP* II/3:1040. See J. Komonchak, ed., "The Struggle for the Council During the Preparation of Vatican II (1960–1962)" *History of Vatican II*, 1:294.

[23] Cardinals Frings, Richaud, König, Döpfner, and Bea, and Patriarch Saigh all spoke in some way for some such change; *ADP* II/3:1048, 1051–53, 1054, 1056, 1058, 1062–65.

[24] See Giuseppe Ruggieri, "Beyond an Ecclesiology of Polemics: The Debate on the Church," in *History of Vatican II*, eds. Giuseppe Alberigo and Joseph A. Komonchak, vol. 2 (Maryknoll, NY: Orbis, 1997), 2:328–40.

[25] *AS* I/4:437. The focus is rather on consecration as giving responsibility for the whole Church.

[26] *AS* I/4:409.

previously had been used to deny the sacramentality of episcopal orders—since bishops and priests were said to be the same in that they had equal power to consecrate the Eucharist—is made to ground their distinction.[27] Here, the capacities to teach and rule might be said to flow from the power of sanctifying, and all three *munera* would be rooted in the character.

There are two interventions on the nature of teaching that nicely balance each other. First, Bishop Bergonzini holds that as when a minister sanctifies, Christ sanctifies, so when a bishop teaches, Christ teaches (recalling Augustine: "It is Christ who preaches Christ" *[Christus est qui Christum praedicat"]*).[28] This puts the exercises of the *munera*, and perhaps the munera themselves, all on the same footing. If the power to sanctify is identified with the character, then so also might be the power to teach. On the other hand, Bishop Darmancier criticizes the schema where it says (chapter 7, *De ecclesiae magisterio*): "whoever hears this magisterium hears, not men, but Christ himself teaching" *(hoc magisterium qui audit, non homines sed Christum docentem audit)*." He agrees that "he who hears you hears me" but not that "he who hears you does not hear you." For men who preach the gospel are free, and have minds already much informed. "A human instrument must mix something of himself with the teaching of Christ, since in all instrumental operations, the nature and quality of the instrument cannot be changed without the effect being changed. The same writer using two different typewriters will produce two different pages; and the more living and conscious the instrument, the more he will impress his own character on the work."[29] And this, in turn, argues for a difference in the standing of the two *munera*.

The three hundred pages of the second series of written observations submitted between the first and second periods rarely touch on the relation of the *munera* to one another or to character.[30] I report three observations of more interest.

Archbishop Joseph Lefèbvre quotes Lécuyer to the effect that by ordination bishops enjoy the power of ruling, and are strengthened with the grace and charisms for their pastoral mission.[31] This is important since it puts more in play than simply "power" and "grace."

Bishop Elchinger wants to say that episcopal consecration inserts a man into the college of bishops; as well, he wants an affirmation of charac-

---

[27] See *Summa theologiae* [hereafter *ST*] suppl., q. 37, a. 2, and q. 40, a. 5. See Joseph Lécuyer, "Les étapes de l'enseignement thomiste sur l'épiscopat," *Revue Thomiste* 57 (1957): 33, 51.

[28] *AS* I/4:423.

[29] *AS* I/4:452.

[30] The Polish Episcopate criticizes the text for not indicating the exact connection between ordination and the powers to rule and teach (*AS* II/1:599).

[31] *AS* II/1:469.

ter. Indeed, a man is modified by the sacrament in his being, in his position relative to God and men. He becomes the voice of God and the hand of God, and Elchinger speaks of these two things seemingly as both functions of the character.[32] This is reminiscent of Bergonzini.

Father Prou, superior general of the French Benedictine Congregation, takes a Trinitarian line. The *missio* of Christ confers authority, jurisdiction, on those sent; the *missio* of the Holy Spirit confers the instrumental power of orders and as well the gifts *(dotes)* for assistance in teaching in order that the *missio* from Christ be fulfilled. As the mission of the Son is the mission of the Son breathing the Spirit, and as the Spirit is not from the Father alone, so the mission from the Son cannot be fruitfully fulfilled without the *virtus* of the Spirit, nor can the *virtus* of the Spirit be legitimately exercised except by an inheritor of the mission of Christ.[33] Accordingly, one is constituted a member of the college by consecration and *missio* together. Consecration gives instrumental power to sanctify and the assistance of the Holy Spirit for teaching; the canonical mission is a continuation of the mission of the Son, and is a *potestas auctoritativa* (St. Albert).[34] Again, there is an awareness that there is more in question than sanctifying grace and character understood as inamissible power. Also, there is a distinction between a power or capacity to do something and the proximate authority to do it.

The New Draft Schema: The Text of G. Philips

As has been many times told, the mass of the criticism the first schema *De Ecclesia* encountered in the opening session of the council urged its abandonment. In place of that text (the production of A. Ottaviani, S. Tromp, and R. Gagnebet) the Doctrinal Commission's subcommission on the Church adopted a text prepared by G. Philips.[35]

The Philips text is a step backward in that it repeats the first schema's number 11 in saying only that the powers of teaching and ruling are aptly united with the power of orders. The statement of the first schema at number 14, that consecration gives these powers, is dropped. The new schema also drops the idea that a bishop can never lose the power to confirm and ordain, and so elides the question of the distinction of bishop and priest at this point. On the other hand, it keeps the idea that the bishop cannot be reduced to the state of a simple priest or layman, and

---

[32] *AS* II/1:505.

[33] *AS* II/1:555.

[34] *AS* II/1:557–58.

[35] For the genesis and adoption of the Philips text, see Jan Grootaers, "The Drama Continues between the Acts: The 'Second Preparation' and Its Opponents," in Alberigo and Komonchak, eds., *History of Vatican II*, 2:400ff.

this as a function of the character. The chief focus of the council's considerations of the episcopate, however, was collegiality. This topic the Philips
text brings forward as it makes the college of bishops, the successor of the
college of apostles, the subject of supreme teaching and governing power
in the Church. From this strategic move, all else will follow.

First Comments on the Philips Text

The Philips text was sent to the fathers on April 22 and July 19, 1963.
Extensive written observations were submitted during the intersession
between the second and third periods of the council. Again, there are calls
for a statement of the sacramental origin of the threefold *munera*. Practically equivalently, there are assertions that consecration inserts a man into
the college of bishops. Bishop Carli wants a declaration that consecration
imparts a proper character to the bishop. He does not say but probably
understands that it is the *potestas ordinis* in virtue of which a bishop cannot lose the power to confirm or ordain, since he wants that phrase
restored.[36] Bishop Elchinger observes that all three *munera* are exercised in
the celebration of the Eucharist.[37] Prior General Healy, O. Carm., notes
that while *potestas ordinis* inheres perpetually, the assistance of the Holy
Spirit that confers indefectibility is capable of more or less and is not inhering.[38] Elchinger's view conduces to identifying the character with the three
powers; Healy's does not, since the assistance of the Holy Spirit enabling
teaching at the highest level is not a stable power. Evidently, however, these
are not necessary implications.

Speeches and Written Observation on the Philips Text

Bishop Cirarda Lachiondo's speech indicates there was no common mind
of the fathers on our topic. He wants to say nothing about the character
except that it exists since there is no agreement on its nature or distinction
from presbyteral character.[39] As to the substance of the issue, Bishop
Höffner, speaking for many German-speaking bishops, distinguishes the
three *munera* and two *potestates*. The former are offices or ministries in
which power is to be concretized.[40]

---

36 *AS* II/1:635. Carli was a member of the theological commission of the Italian
   Bishops' Conference and member of the Conciliar Commission on Bishops
   (Andrea Riccaud, "The Tumultuous Opening Days of the Council," in Alberigo
   and Komonchak, eds. *History of Vatican II*, 2:17, 23). He resolutely opposed the
   understanding of collegiality finally adopted (Gerald P. Fogarty, "The Council
   Gets Underway," in Alberigo and Komonchak, eds., *History of Vatican II*, 2:105).

37 *AS* II/1:661.

38 *AS* II/1:670.

39 *AS* II/2:458; in the same vein, Bishop Enciso Viana, *AS* II/2:593

40 *AS* II/2:522.

Material from the written observations can be put into four batches. First, there is more expression of the view that consecration gives all three *munera* and locates a man in the *collegium*. Second, there is the question of the distinction of bishop and priest.

Third, there are a considerable number of observations that distinguish and relate the *munera*. In line with Höffner, for whom *potestas sanctificandi* is given with consecration but the other two functions only as *munera* not yet proximate to act, Archbishop Calabria takes the text correctly to mean that the three *munera* are given indeed by ordination, as are the graces to discharge them, but only one power, *potestas ordinis*.[41] This sort of remark indicates an apprehension that the *munera* do not all have the same footing, but is more concerned for preserving order in the Church that anything else. Some think of the *munus* of teaching in such a way that the sacrament can be seen to give more than fits in with the ordinary categories of power and grace. So, Bishop Lamont distinguishes the *virtus sacramentalis* given by consecration, the same for all bishops, and the charism of divine assistance for, for example, teaching infallibly.[42] Again, Bishop Cantero Cuadrado and three others say that bishops have the capacity so to teach "from the constant power and help of the Holy Spirit who was promised and given by the Lord" *(ex virtute et adiutorio perenni divini Spiritus a Dominus promisso ac dato)*."[43] Bishop Topel for his part orders the *munera* and has it that the *munera* of teaching and ruling are *praeambula* to the *munus sanctificandi*.[44] Similarly, Archbishop Olaechae Loizaga thinks the ministry of word and rule is founded in the sacrificial ministry of making the Eucharist, and not in a simple canonical mission.[45] This could be developed in such a way as to locate all three powers in the character. For his part, Bishop Graziano thinks the text already ascribes all episcopal power to character, and wrongly, to the detriment of the monarchical nature of the Church.[46] Last, Bishop d'Almeida Trindade importantly distinguishes the function of sanctifying from the other two in relation to Christ, who is not present in the same way in the three functions: as priest, the bishop is an instrument of Christ; but he is not an instrument of Christ in teaching and ruling, strictly speaking. Rather, he teaches and rules in his own name or in the name of the Church.[47]

Fourth, there is the observation of Bishop Paul Yoshigoro Taguchi, which deserves a place by itself for the interest it has and the speculative

---

[41] *AS* II/2:689–90.
[42] *AS* II/2:794.
[43] *AS* II/2:694.
[44] *AS* II/2:890.
[45] *AS* II/2:833.
[46] *AS* II/2:762: "potestas episcopalis characteri sacramentali fere exclusive ascribitur."
[47] *AS* II/2:714.

satisfaction it gives.⁴⁸ Commenting on number 19 (the bishop as teacher), he notes that the *munus docendi*, the episcopal capacity to teach, is a gift of the intellectual order, like the light of faith or the light of glory. It is not a mere right to teach—which belongs to the *potestas regiminis*—but an internal power, leading to infallibility, an *augmentum intellectuale*, bespeaking the assistance of the Holy Spirit. The capacity to teach is a gift for declaring the *magnalia Dei* with power to convert men, or, he has it, it is an illumination for writing, or the power of a two-edged sword for debating and rendering testimony before tribunals, or spiritual unction for writing in the saints and doctors of the Church. Again, it is the assistance of the Spirit for infallible definition, a gift in the way of prophecy. And the *munus regendi—a ius*—includes but is not exhausted by the other two. This is part of the solution. The *munera* of teaching and ruling are rights, although not merely rights. The distinction between a *right* to teach and rule (given at least fundamentally to whoever has the episcopal power to sanctify and given by that act that gives the power to sanctify) and a *capacity* to teach and rule is to be remembered.

Closing on the Final Text

An amended text was distributed to fathers in the third session of the council on September 15, 1964. In this version, chapter 2 is devoted to the People of God and chapter 3 to the hierarchy. This is the next-to-last draft before the final version of *Lumen Gentium*. It is where we started our review of the *Acta*.

The teaching on the episcopacy as a sacrament, as we have seen, now comprises the following assertions. (1) Episcopal consecration transmits the same spiritual gift as the apostles gave to their helpers by the imposition of hands. (2) This consecration is the fullness of the sacrament of orders (and no longer the "highest grade"). (3) With the *munus* of sanctifying, consecration confers the *munera* of teaching and ruling, which "of their nature" cannot be exercised except in communion with the episcopal college and its head. This is a return to the original schema of *De Ecclesia*, number 14. (4) Imposition of hands and the words of consecration so impart grace and so impart a sacred character that bishops take the part of Christ the Teacher, Shepherd, and Priest, and act in his name. This evocation of the bishop as acting in the person of Christ according to all three *munera* is new. (5) Wherefore, only bishops can assume new members into the episcopal body through the sacrament of orders. The Philips text had dropped the statement that from the character, bishops have an inamissible power to confirm and ordain; the new text drops as well the statement that, because of the character, a bishop cannot be reduced to a simple priest or layman again.⁴⁹

---

⁴⁸ *AS* II/2:897–98.
⁴⁹ *AS* III/1:214–15.

The accompanying *relatio* for number 21 anticipates what Cardinal König will say on September 21. It adverts to the desire to conceive presbyters as participating in the powers of the bishop, hence the change from "highest grade" to "fullness" of orders. It explains that it wishes to avoid the question of whether priests can ordain priests; hence the simple assertion that bishops can be made only by bishops. It explains also that the inability of a bishop to become a layman again is dropped and that the dignity of the bishop is expressed more positively. This more positive expression is the statement that bishops act in the person of Christ. "Bishops are said to act in the person of Christ, and not only as Priest, but also as Teacher and Pastor: for the whole *munus* of bishops ought to find expression."[50]

It is here, it will be recalled, that the text opens up to the reading of Butler and Galot. Since it was on the basis of the character that it was said a bishop could not become again a simple priest or a layman, it seems reasonable to infer that is it on the same basis that a bishop acts in the person of Christ in all three *munera*. In fact, as we observed at the very beginning of this essay, the text does not exactly say that, and as to the nature of the character itself, the *relatio* says only that "the words prescind from the disputed questions which some of the fathers touched on."[51]

Written observations on this emended text, as touching our question, were brief. There is continued minority resistance to the sacrament as conferring all three *munera*, sometimes on the ground that the positions remain disputed questions. On the other hand, Bishop Groblicki wants the text to go further than it does, and to state that priests and deacons do not have the power to ordain; because of the power to ordain, the *munus dirigendi pascendique gregis* belongs to bishops connaturally, as it does not to priests.[52] There is here the idea of consecration conferring some sort of basic right to rule and teach.

Relative to conferral of *munera* of teaching and ruling, Cardinal Browne says that "if the word *munera* is taken for the gifts of grace *(dona gratiae)* by which the one consecrated is rendered apt to exercise the office of teaching and ruling, the text, as is evident, can be admitted." If it is taken to mean that consecration confers the very *potestas* of teaching and ruling *ex auctoritate*, however, it is not to be admitted.[53] Here, we might say, ordination gives a capacity in the form of gifts and graces, but it does not give power *ad actum expedita*, as the *Nota praevia explicativa* will have it.

Cardinal J. Lefèbvre speaks for many when he distinguishes the *munus regendi* and jurisdiction, the first a sacred power given by God with

---

[50] *Relatio, AS* III/1:241.
[51] *AS* III/1:241.
[52] *AS* III/1:581–82.
[53] *AS* III/1:630.

consecration, the second a *temperatio* of the power, received by law; the question of the origin of jurisdiction remains open.[54]

Bishop Carli's remarks bear more explicitly on our question. He stands with those for whom the distinction between the substance and exercise of jurisdiction, its immediate derivation from God, and episcopal character as a new impression are all disputed questions.[55] Nor for him does the liturgy settle the issue of jurisdiction.[56] Especially important for us, he wants to drop the statement that bishops act *in persona Christi magistri et pastoris*, for, he explains, the character configures the bishop to Christ the priest, and not necessarily to Christ as teacher and shepherd.[57] Notice, then, that he understands the text to affirm the interpretation of Butler and Galot.

Conclusions

Four conclusions can be drawn from a survey of conciliar material. First, although the question of the identity of the *munera* with the character is quite beyond the intention of the text of *Lumen Gentium*, it seems to be suggested if not strictly entailed by some views of some fathers. Second, Elchinger and perhaps Richaud seem close to conceiving this very idea of the identity of the *munera* with the character, and seem to favor it. Third, it is only Carli and Graziano of whom we can say with certainty that they clearly and expressly entertain the idea of the identity, only to disapprove of it. Fourth, there are some fathers who are concerned, variously, to trace the differences of the *munera*, or to conceive of an effect of the sacrament in addition to grace and power, or to make a distinction between a power and a right.

The *Acta Synodalia* for *Presbyterorum Ordinis* 2c

We noted that the relevant text from *Presbyterorum Ordinis* seemed to support the problematic view that, in the same way that the character is the power of sanctifying it is also the power of teaching and ruling. Once again, we can begin with the last *relationes* and then review the constitution of the text from the beginning.[58]

The final text was distributed December 2, 1965. The accompanying *relatio* reports a change from saying presbyters are given a character (*spe-*

---

54 *AS* III/1:631; he appeals to Lécuyer on St. Thomas for same view (635).

55 *AS* III/1:655.

56 *AS* III/1:660.

57 *AS* III/1:661–62.

58 See for much of what follows Francisco Gil Hellín, *Presbyterorum Ordinis: Decretum de Presbyterorum Ministerio et Vita Concilii Vaticani II Synopsis in ordinem redigens schemata cum relationibus necnon patrum orationes atque animadversiones* (Vatican City: Libreria Editrice Vaticana, 1996).

ciali charactere donantur) to saying they are marked with a character *(speciali charactere signantur)*. But to the suggestion that the *sic* of *sic Christo Sacerdoti configurantur* should be suppressed, lest one conclude that it is in virtue only of the character alone and by itself that the priest is configured to Christ the priest, the commission observed that although the text indeed says by what reason the priest is configured to Christ, namely, the character, "it is by no means suggested that the character is the only thing by which priests are configured to Christ."[59] Nor therefore can it be concluded that it is in virtue only of the character that the priest acts in the person of Christ for the triplex *munera*.

Substantially, this answers the question about what the council intends to teach with these lines, but as with *Lumen Gentium*, so here we will canvass the background of this text to see what thought was given to this matter by the fathers.

De Clericis, Schema Propositionum de Sacerdotibus, De Vita et Ministerio Sacerdotali

Jean Frisque very justly remarks that "l'histoire de ce Décret est aussi longue que celle du Concile lui-même."[60] We begin with the *De Clericis*, distributed 21 April 1963, the *Schema Propositionum de Sacerdotibus* (May 1964), and the *Schema Propositionum de Vita et Ministerio Sacerdotali* (October 1964).[61] The prehistory of the text of *Presbyterorum Ordinis* that concerns us, however, does not start until paragraph 2 of the schema of November 20, 1965. There are only a few things of note to report before that from a discussion that rarely bears on the character as an important theme.

De Clericis 2 speaks of the priest as made an instrument of Christ by the sacrament of orders and the character it imparts; by this consecration, moreover, priests represent the priesthood of Christ and act in his name. For his part, Archbishop Ménager called for precision on the notion of an instrument. The priest is an instrument of Christ in the strict sense—only in things like consecrating the elements at Mass; he is not an instrument, but only a minister, in non-sacramental acts, for "he acts from himself (for instance, in speaking and preaching) even if he is expounding the teaching of Christ and preaching in the name of Christ and the Church."[62] This kind of observation is important in thinking about the difference of the *munera*.

---

[59] *AS* IV/7:121; response to modus 24.

[60] Jean Frisque, "Le décret *Presbyterorum Ordinis*. Histoire et commentaire," in *Les Prêtres: Décrets* Presbyterorum Ordinis *et* Optatam totius, ed. Jean Frisque et Yves Congar (Paris: Éditions du Cerf, 1968), 133.

[61] For comment on this material, see R. Wasselynck, *Les Prêtres. Élaboration du Décret de Vatican II. Histoire et Genèse des textes conciliaires. Commentaire* (Paris: Desclée, 1968).

[62] *AS* III/4:907.

Second, a very high theology of priesthood finds expression at this moment of the council. So, Bishop Théas laments the loss in the *De Vita et Ministerio* of a statement that the priest acts *in persona Christi*. The priest's whole ministry is so to be characterized, and therefore the priest is rightly styled an *alter Christus*.[63] Again, Bishop Flores Martin speaks of the priest as "Christ himself mystically incarnate."[64]

Third, there is an important speech of Archbishop Sartre, also on the *De Vita et Ministerio*. For him, the point of departure of the council's statement on priests should be the mission of the whole Church, the apostolic mission as received from the Father, through the Son, in the Spirit, so that men may share in the Paschal Mystery. Within this comprehensive ecclesial mission, the priest's mission has its origin in that of Christ himself. What is distinctive of the priest's cooperation in the apostolic mission, moreover, is that it is essentially sacramental, in both origin and end, while the cooperation of the laymen is purely spiritual.[65]

Many of the written observations on the *De Vita* bear on the very issue of priestly mission raised by Sartre. "Mission" might be taken in a more juridical or a more theological sense, and that is the source of some disagreement. This means there is some replay of the discussion building to chapter 3 of *Lumen Gentium* about jurisdiction. It also begins a line of development that suggests the position of Galot and Butler.

Resuming the concerns around chapter 3 of *Lumen Gentium*, Bishop Bereciartua y Balerdi and seven fathers do not think it can be said that a priest's mission is given with ordination; ordination gives only *potestas ordinis*.[66] And for Archbishop McQuaid, mission is joined to the sacrament, rather than coming from it.[67] On the other hand, in the line that will invite identifying the character with the *munera*, Bishop Ferrari understands mission more theologically. By consecration, there is established a relation to the Trinity: to the Father, in the acquisition of a supernatural personality; to the Son, in being configured to Christ the Priest, Teacher, and King and so sharing in the action of these offices; and to the Spirit, as sharing the mission of Christ.[68]

Last, for Archbishop Shehan, the foundation of the priest's call to holiness is not only that by the sacrament and the character he is made an

---

[63] *AS* III/4:247. Cardinal De Barros Câmara agrees (*AS* III/4:403).

[64] *AS* III/4:476.

[65] *AS* III/4:471–472. See Wasselynck, *Les Prêtres*, 43–45.

[66] *AS* III/4:547.

[67] *AS* III/4:611. See also Bishop Philippe (*AS* III/4:624) and Bishop Parker (IV/4:945).

[68] *AS* III/4:577. The canonical mission determines the mode and scope of the mission received in consecration (III/4:578). And see the Bishops of Oceania (*AS* III/4:663).

instrument of Christ and can act in his person, but also that by the sacrament and character he is configured to Christ and given a special role in his priesthood, his mediatorship.[69] By sacrament and the character—but what if one just says "character," and makes that the basis of acting in the person of Christ for all three *munera*? Again, for Bishop Philippe, it is by force of the character that the priest is *alter Christus*: "since it is by force of the character of orders that he is the minister and instrument by which Christ continues his saving work, especially in the Eucharistic sacrifice" *(cum sit vi characteris Ordinis eius minister ac instrumentum quo operam suam salvificam Christus continuat, praesertim in Sacrificio eucharistico)*."[70] "Especially" *(praesertim)*, but not exclusively.

To this point, the character is not connected in any explicit way to the teaching and shepherding functions of the priest. There are, however, suggestions of this connection. First, configuration to Christ is traditionally imputed to character, and Ferrari speaks of configuration to Christ in the threefold office. Second, character is associated with acting in the person of Christ, and "acting in the person of Christ" is expanding its range.

To Presbyterorum Ordinis

The schema *De clericis* and its subsequent transfigurations could not easily support the heavy demands of the fathers. There was the desire to speak of the priest in his relation to the laity, to bishops, to other priests, and to Christ. There was the desire to relate the priest's holiness more closely to his ministry. There was the need to balance the priest as one consecrated with the priest and as one sent. A new point of departure in a new draft was ready by November 20, 1964.[71]

Text of November 20, 1964 (First Draft of Presbyterorum Ordinis*)*

Following the *prooemium*, this text addresses the nature of the priesthood in its first paragraph. The point of departure is the mission of the Church, in which all the faithful exercise a royal priesthood, offering spiritual sacrifices to God through Christ. Everyone has a part in the mission of the Church, but only some are consecrated to represent the priesthood of Christ the Head and act in his person. It is through these priests that the Church offers a visible sacrifice, the sacrifice Christ offered of himself on the cross. These priests share in the authority by which Christ instructs, sanctifies, and rules his body, and it is by a special sacrament that they are incorporated into the mission of the bishops, which insertion is a share in

---

[69] *AS* III/4:639.

[70] *AS* III/4:624.

[71] Wasselynck, *Les Prêtres*, 23, 37–38; the old material was not abandoned but recontextualized.

the priesthood of Christ. Just as bishops are configured to the person of Christ the Head by force of their consecration, in the same way, although subordinately, priests are consecrated to Christ the Head.[72]

In all this, there is no mention of priestly character at all. The concern is not to knit up any loose threads of the customary theology of orders and its appreciation of the effects of orders, but firmly to reinsert the entire theology of orders within an ecclesiological framework hammered out in the production of *Lumen Gentium.*

Written comments on this text prior to the next conciliar session were extensive, but not much concerned with the theology of the character.[73] Archbishop Philippe understands that it is character that configures to Christ, which configuration to Christ grounds the priest's share in the bishop's mission.[74] Does this mission the priest shares by his character include teaching and ruling?

For Cardinal Döpfner, this would seem so. He wants the character to be mentioned at number 1 in the following wise: "[A]dorned with the sacerdotal character, priests are able to exercise the special power of Christ the Head in his body which is the Church" *(charactere sacerdotali ornati [sacerdotes] peculiarem potestatem Christi Capitis in corpus suum quod est Ecclesia exercere valent)."*[75] This suggests a conception of character that includes more than *potestas ordinis,* power in regard to the Real Body of Christ, just as did his comments leading to *Lumen Gentium.* Döpfner maintains that the priest represents the priesthood of Christ "especially" in offering Mass, but that he acts in the person of Christ in exercising all three *munera.* His explanation of that proposed text, however, does not declare his mind on this.

Bishop Elchinger's observations are characteristically noteworthy. He wants the priest to be seen in the context of the mission of Christ, of the Church, of the bishop. He wants the priest's spirituality to be seen as rooted in discharge of a threefold *munus,* as with St. Thomas, for whom the priest must live in the acts of his ministry. Further, "priestly ordination does not in the first place confer the power to celebrate the Eucharist or to preach the Word of God. By the presbyterate, the bishop sacramentally gathers helpers to himself who, even if they are dispersed in order to accomplish their ministry, must exercise it at the interior of a collective pastorate that is referred to the Episcopal College."[76] This suggests that the character is to be the locus of all three *munera.*

---

72   *AS* IV/4:834–35.
73   See Wasselynck's analyis in *Les Prêtres,* 30–31: Concern with the "nature" of the presbyterate finishes dead last, much after such things as celibacy or the priest's relation to the bishop.
74   *AS* IV/4:948.
75   *AS* IV/4:874.
76   *AS* IV/4:924.

Revised Schema sent June 12, 1965
(Text of the Debate of October 1965)

The changes can be briefly summarized. The priest is defined no longer first in relation to the baptized—his priesthood in relation to the priesthood of faithful—but in relation to the apostles and bishops. *Lumen Gentium* 28 is repeated, according to which, through the apostles, Christ made their successors, the bishops, share in his own consecration and mission. Bishops in turn pass on their ministry in a subordinate mode to priests. The priest is fashioned after the image of Christ the High Priest to discharge the threefold *munera* and shares in the authority of Christ the Head to do so. By ordination he is configured in a special way to Christ the Priest, and so, sharing in the mission of the bishop, he can act in the person of Christ the Head, Teacher, Priest, and Rector. Rather than being incorporated into the mission of the bishop, he is now said to share in it; and both together share in the priesthood of Christ.[77]

This is the text debated in October 1965, and there is still no mention of character at number 2. There will be calls for its insertion into the text, but the center of the debate is rather over how fundamentally to think of the priest. Should he be seen first of all as one consecrated to God or as one sent?[78] Archbishop Marty called attention to just this fact in his *relatio* of October 16, 1965. There are, he said, two conceptions of the priest in the requests of the fathers, and both find a place in the new schema. First, there is an emphasis on consecration, by the sacrament, and on personal union with Christ, the source of holiness; second, there is a focus on mission, received in the sacrament from Christ, and by which the priest becomes a member of the presbyterium and so becomes a helper of the bishops and acts in the person of Christ.[79]

The forces brought to bear shaping the final text are very evident in the speeches of October. There is much support for a statement of the "ontological" consecration of the priest, his "ontological" participation in the priesthood of Christ. This is quite traditionally allied with a call to mention the character imparted by the sacrament of orders. There is also great support for describing the priest as one sent, one sharing in the mission of Christ, and so exercising all three *munera* of sanctifying, teaching, and ruling. And then there is the mediating position, the position that identifies the ontological consecration of the priest with his being given a share in the mission of Christ. At that point, one is close to seeing the character, traditionally understood as the very ground of the ontological consecration, as giving also the *munera*, the powers, to teach and to rule,

---

[77] *AS* IV/4:337; Wasselynck, *Les Prêtres*, 47.

[78] Wasselynck, *Les Prêtres*, 48.

[79] *AS* IV/5:70–71.

and not only to sanctify. Some fathers—Döpfner, Henriquez Jimenez—
come very close to saying this very thing, and Weber will say it in fact. The
text will not say it, although that is its drift. By a sort of accident of composition, as we shall see, that is the drift—not the intention—of the text.

Cardinal Richaud speaks strongly for the priest as one consecrated. He
wants a statement that is less exclusively oriented to the activity (ministry)
of the priest, and one that takes in the life of the priest as founded in his
consecration, beginning with the priest's donation of himself in love to
God. Moreover, "the excellence of the sacramental character is not to be
forgotten, because it seals in the intimate heart of presbyters the bond of
love between God and the priest and effects a true and special consecration in the soul of the priest, just as in baptism and in confirmation the
sacramental character places in the depths of the Christian soul something
sacred, under the action of the Holy Spirit."[80] Others speak in the same
vein for a greater stress on the ontological condition of the priest, but
without always mentioning character.[81] These bishops speak of mission,
but it is subordinate to consecration. The priest shares in the mission of
the bishop because he shares in the priesthood of Christ, and not vice
versa as in the text.[82]

We turn to the other line of thought. Bishop de Roo and 133 others
take the mission of the Church to the world as the controlling point of
departure. Within this mission, the hierarchy is a "sacrament of Christ,
Shepherd and Head," and the priest is one "in whom Christ the Shepherd
prosecutes his call sacramentally." The priest is therefore leader of the
flock. "By priestly ordination, God gives the priest the mandate and the
specific grace for this task *[munus]* and sends him." And de Roo speaks of
"varia munera," both traditional and newly come to light, that are united
in the priest's ministry.[83] By force of the sacrament and in all three of the
standard *munera,* "priests become a sacrament of Christ, a visible and
effective sign of his mission in the Church" *(sacramentum fiunt Christi,
signum visibile et efficax eius in Ecclesia missionis)."*[84]

It is just the emphasis on ordination as effecting a share in the apostolic mission that swings us into the comprehensive, mediating position.
Cardinal Rugambwa has it that the priest's mission is from ordination.
Broadly, he seems to be thinking of the mission in threefold terms. He
does not mention character, but conveys the idea. The priest is "incorpo-

---

80 *AS* IV/4:732.

81 For example, Bishop Charue (*AS* IV/4:808). And see Bishop Soares de Resende,
    for whom sacerdotal character is a reality analogous to the Incarnation of Christ
    (IV/5:65).

82 Cardinal Shehan (*AS* IV/5:28). And this is fixed in the next draft.

83 *AS* IV/5:163–64.

84 *AS* IV/5:165, and reading just after line 30, p. 12, of the schema.

rated with Christ in an ineffable and indelible way" *(ineffabili et indelebili modo Christo concorporatus)*."[85]

Consider the view of Bishop Henriquez Jimenez. He wants the point of departure in number 1 to be in the priest's "ontological configuration to Christ the priest, as well as in his real participation in Christ's unique and eternal priesthood" *(ontologica configuratione Christo Sacerdoti necnon in sui ipsius unici et aeterni sacertotii reali participatione)*." Priests are signed by the character of Christ's priesthood and so offer the unbloody sacrifice; and their participation in his priesthood is not a mere "external deputation," but is an ontological consecration, a real configuration to Christ the priest, a true and indelible and permanent power "by which the power of the priesthood of Christ is rendered visibly present in the Church and the world" *(qua virtus sacerdotii Christi in Ecclesia et mundo visibiliter presens redditur)*."[86] It is only from this point that we should proceed to existential questions. Therefore, the character should be mentioned in number 1: "[T]he teaching about character should be brought to light," and "sacerdotal being placed once again in the ontological configuration to Christ the priest, and in a real, though ministerial, participation in His priesthood." Further, this ontological share in the priesthood of Christ is also a share in his mission.[87] It is a true sharing in the ministry and *munera* of bishops, and ordination confers the *munera* of sanctifying, teaching, and ruling in a mode subordinate to that of the bishops (and not to be exercised apart from hierarchical communion). Therefore, number 1 is to be emended: By ordination priests are "in a new way ontologically configured to Christ the Priest" *(novo modo Christo sacerdoti ontologice configurantur)*."[88] For all this, the bishop does not identify all the *munera* with character and seems rather to take the character as for *potestas ordinis* ordinarily understood.[89] The implication of saying that the character is an ontological share in the mission of Christ as a whole is not seen.

Last in this development, let us consider Cardinal Döpfner, speaking for another 65 German-language bishops. They think it good that the schema takes in the threefold *munera*.[90] Arguing that we should not speak of participation in the mission of the bishop, but rather in the mission of Christ, they say: "The reason why the priest can act in the person of Christ consists in his participation (sacramental) in the mission of Christ."[91] There is a "sacramental" share in Christ's mission; it is threefold, and we are just next

---

[85] *AS* IV/5:15.
[86] *AS* IV/4:747.
[87] *AS* IV/4:749.
[88] *AS* IV/4:749–50.
[89] *AS* IV/4:747.
[90] *AS* IV/4:464.
[91] *AS* IV/4:468.

door to thinking that character, which used more narrowly to be understood as a sacramental share in priesthood of Christ, founds all three *munera*.

The same things can be noted in the written observations. First, there is again expression for the view in which the priest's ontological consecration is fundamental.[92] There are also many expressions in line with seeing the priest as one sent.[93] And there are observations that keep both emphases. Archbishop Morcillo González says that presbyters were immediately instituted by the apostles or their successors, and that this priesthood is a configuration to the priesthood of Christ and a participation of the priesthood of Christ; priests are subordinate to bishops, but their *munera* and ministry are given by ordination itself.[94] And there is Bishop Weber: "By the imposition of our hands an inamissible grace is given to them which they call up daily. . . . This grace consists in the special sacramental character of orders, whence there flows a share in the *munera* of the priesthood of Christ himself." This seems to include *munera* with respect to the body of Christ that is the Church. It seems to be the position of Galot and Butler.[95]

Text Distributed November 12, 1965

This is the next-to-final text, approved paragraph by paragraph, 12–13 November. In this text, the mission of the priest, the work of evangelization, is styled, after St. Paul, as itself a cultic act and one that ends in the celebration of the Eucharist. The glory of God that is the end of priestly ministry consists in the free and conscious acceptance of the work of God in Christ. So has been balanced the missionary and cultic-consecratory lines of thought.[96] This text is the first to mention that ordination gives the priest a character; however, there is no observation on or explanation of this in the *relatio*.[97] As for *Lumen Gentium*, the concern was not the intricacies of the ontology of the effect of orders. The focus was on the priest's relation to the mission of the Church, to the faithful and their priesthood, to the bishops, and on holiness, life, and ministry.

The same conclusions can be drawn from this survey of material as were drawn for the material surrounding *Lumen Gentium*. First, although the question of the identity of the *munera* with the character is quite

---

92 For example, Bishop Cecchi (*AS* IV/5:265) and Bishop Muldoon (*AS* IV/5:415).

93 See, for example, Bishop Hervás y Benet (*AS* IV/5:353). Bishop Plourde (*AS* IV/5: 443–44) appeals to *ST* I–II, Q. 102, a. 4, ad 3: If in the Old Testament the ministries of priest and prophet were divided, they are not divided in Christ; temple and synagogue come together in a Church whose sacrifice is spiritual.

94 *AS* IV/5:412–13. He does not mention character.

95 *AS* IV/5:514.

96 Frisque, "Le décret," 140–43.

97 *AS* IV/6:347, 390.

beyond the intention of the text of *Presbyterorum Ordinis*, it is suggested if not strictly entailed by some views of some fathers. Second, Döpfner, Elchinger, Henriquez Jimenez, and perhaps Philippe seem close to conceiving this very idea of the identity of the *munera* with the character, and seem to favor it. Weber does conceive it. Third, there are some few fathers who are concerned to trace the differences of the *munera* and their exercise.

Concluding Synthetic Proposal

What is to be salvaged from the mountain of conciliar material touching on, or at least coming close to, the idea of sacerdotal and episcopal character? Not very much. Still, there are some hints, some few thoughtful distinctions that emerge from the vast ocean of words of the *orationes* and *animadversiones* so faithfully preserved in the *Acta*. If we put them together, we cannot say that we have the teaching of the council; on the point at issue, the council is silent, as the final *relationes* accompanying the texts make plain. But we may be able to outline some more satisfying view of the nature of the effect of episcopal and priestly ordination than Galot and Butler give us.

There are three steps. First, we need to say something about the differences of the *munera*. Second, we need to think in a more capacious way about the effects of the sacrament, and find some effect of the sacrament in addition to a sort of generally conceived "grace" and an indelible "power." Third, we need to distinguish the *munera* as rights and as powers.

Differences of the Munera

The differences of the *munera* are to be told from the differences of their exercises.[98] We need first simply to think about sanctifying, teaching, and ruling as actions. That is the *priora quoad nos*, after all. Whatever we say about what enables these things must have its point of departure in the things enabled. For this we have to look at the experience of Christians and to the judgment of the Church as to when and under what circumstances teaching, ruling, and sanctifying are successful and when not. Looked at this way, there are very great and important differences between sanctifying, on the one hand, and ruling and teaching, on the other.

Our experience as Catholic Christians, and the judgment of the Church, is that a validly ordained priest's sacramental actions are themselves always valid, as long as the priest (or bishop) "intends to do what the Church intends." The priest or bishop may be foolish, may be badly instructed, or may even be wicked. But if the priest intends to consecrate

---

[98] In what follows, I try to develop my previous "Episcopal *Munera* and the Character of Episcopal Orders," in this volume.

the elements at Mass, the elements are consecrated, the action successful. And if the bishop intends to ordain a man, the man is ordained, the action of ordination successful.

Why does the success of the action demand (as a minimum, not as an ideal) so little on the priest's or bishop's part? The answer is that the only indispensable thing he contributes is the constitution of the sign of the sacrament. For this he must have enough of his wits about him to mean the sign. But he need not believe the sign truly signifies what it does, much less truly effects what it does. In the first place, the sign is presented to the recipient's faith, not to the priest's faith. In the second place, the priest is not the principal agent of the sacramental action, the sanctifying action. He is a tool to provide a tool, namely the sign, to the one who is the principal agent, namely Christ.

Why then, it will be asked, cannot anyone with enough wit to make the sign be the instrument of the sacramental action? Once again, the answer is that the minister is an instrument. To be such, however, he must be made to be such. That is, the priest or bishop must be rendered apt to be the instrument he is. Not all consecrate or ordain in the Church. If this is not a brute, but an intelligible, fact, then we shall say as well that not all can consecrate or ordain. In the "can" is contained the idea of capacity or power. Nor is the power merely an ecclesially juridically constituted power. For Christian experience and Church judgment recognize that even outside and against the law, validly ordained priests validly consecrate, and validly ordained bishops validly ordain.

Why this is a good and saving arrangement of the economy of sign and rite in which the power of the Lord's Cross is extended to touch the believing Christian gathered into the assembly of the Church, we cannot go into here. But this arrangement is the arrangement recognized by the Church as fact.

For all that the essential action of the minister of sacrament is to provide a sign, we must not mistake the sacraments as teachings merely. They teach and instruct, surely; but first of all they are doings. The sacraments change things. If one wants to say in reply that a teaching can change things, too, we must observe that it does so first by changing the mind. That is, the display of reality a teaching is serves in the first place merely to show something to someone who may choose to exercise his agency on the basis of that display, but who is first of all simply a beholder of the display. Teaching addresses the mind, and if it changes things, it does so through the agency of the one who beholds the display. But sanctifying touches the heart. Indeed, it does so through the display of the sacramental sign apprehended in faith. This sign, however, is in the last place the instrument, not of the minister, but of the one who by his word makes all things, and by this sacramental word makes the Christian heart different than it is. True, the sign "works" through its apprehension in faith on the part of the recipient. But there is no subsequent choice on his part to act; apprehending and believing what the sign says, he is rather acted upon.

The action of priestly sanctifying is therefore something inserted into Christ's sanctifying; it is just an instrumental piece of the Lord's activity of baptizing or forgiving sins. All that is required is that one has to be made a suitable instrument, and one must intend to do what the Church does.

If sanctifying is a doing, the Lord's doing using the action of the priest, teaching and ruling are by contrast both displays. Teaching shows us what is. Ruling is a teaching that shows us what is to be done. It is the display of some action as a good action, and therefore to be embraced by the one ruled. In neither of them is the priest an instrument in the way he is in sanctifying.

Let us speak first of teaching. We can say that sanctifying and teaching both are ministerial, but unlike sanctifying, teaching is not itself a piece of the Lord's preaching. We could perhaps rather say that teaching is a repetition of the Lord's preaching. The Lord's preaching, his very own discourse, is of course like the minister's a display and not a doing. It so displays the world that it evokes a doing, an action, on the part of the hearers. But first, it is an articulation of how things are: "[T]he kingdom of God is at hand." Second, it evokes response—"Repent!"—but it is not itself the response—it is not an action.

Now, because it is a display, it is quotable. When I quote someone, we can say, if we want and as Bergonzini and Elchinger said at the council, that the one quoted speaks.[99] Certainly, what was first made present in his speech is made present in the speech of another. Although it accomplishes the very display of what first was displayed by the original speaker, however, quotation is nonetheless not the very speaking of the original speaker. This is the point of Ménager.[100] If speaking were a doing, and changed some piece of the world, we should say rather that it is imitable rather than quotable. For in a doing, the very particularity of what is acted on prevents it from being transportable in the way speech is. Just because display does not change, but lights up, it is movable in a way it could not otherwise be. Crossing the Rubicon as Caesar did, in his time and place, could happen but once. Just because it is not a doing, but a displaying, however, saying "Caesar crossed the Rubicon" is infinitely reproducible. The display that it is of what Caesar did but once can be rearticulated again and again. Because things once displayed can be redisplayed across space and time, the message of the Lord can be made present in many places and times. And that is sufficient description of the teaching of the

---

[99] See above, notes 28 and 32.
[100] See above, note 62.

Church, the teaching of priest or hierarch. We need not say as well that the Lord is the very one speaking as we must for baptism say that he is the very one baptizing. The baptizing of this one is not repeatable. It is a doing. Telling of this baptism, or of baptism as such, is repeatable. Teaching is display; baptizing or consecrating is a doing.[101]

What the apostle or bishop or priest does subsequently to the teaching of the Lord, therefore, is to repeat the news he first delivered, redisplay his original display of how God's eschaton is now available in time. Better, in Robert Sokolowski's sense, the preaching of apostle or priest is a quotation of it.[102] This is the difference. In quoting, I display something *as displayed* by a previous speaker. In repeating, I let slip away the display as previously displayed; I say the words and make the articulation, as it were, on my own. Evidently, the preacher is to quote believingly, but it is altogether formal to the discharge of his function that he "quote"—that is, that he not let slip the fact that the news in question is not delivered on his authority, but on another's. Moreover, in ordinary quotation, the one who quotes can in principle check things out for himself. "Mary said the car was out of gas." But I can myself verify this, and then I no longer need to take Mary's word for it. But if I take it as true that the kingdom is at hand, on the ground that the Lord said so, I am not in a position to check this out on my own. If I pass on this message, I must therefore not give the impression that I say it on my own authority. I must always quote. I must always display the presence of the kingdom as first displayed by Christ.

Now, in this way, there is an important difference between the ways in which sanctifying and preaching or teaching can fail. Sanctifying fails if I do not intend to do what the Church does in the sacrament. The essential thing I contribute is the constitution of a sign—the pouring of the water and the words of baptism, for instance. I can constitute this sign even if I do not believe that baptism cleanses consciences, even if I do not believe there is a God. What I "intend" is not the action of cleansing consciences; if I do not believe baptism does that, there is no such action for me to approve or "intend." Even if I do believe, my priestly intention is not that consciences be cleansed, for the very good reason that I do not think myself the principal agent who is so cleansing consciences. What I am intending is the liturgical action, the bare *sacramentum tantum*, the sign of the sacrament, which, if I have faith, I am confident the principal agent uses to cleanse consciences. Failing that—failing the making of the sign—moreover, the principal agent has no instrument to use to cleanse consciences sacramentally, and there is no sacramental cleansing.

---

101 See Darmancier above, note 29, who is trying to articulate this distinction.

102 See his "Quotation," in *Pictures, Quotations, and Distinctions: Fourteen Essays in Phenomenology* (Notre Dame, IN: Notre Dame Press, 1992), 27–51.

Evidently, for the teaching of the priest and bishop to be successful, it must at least accurately repeat the teaching of the Lord. It has the most audacious because most humble aim—audacious as reporting the words of the Lord of hosts; humble as a mere messenger who presents himself always only as such. Because teaching is a repetition of a display originally not the speaker's own, however, the priest or bishop can get it wrong, even when he intends to get it right. He can forget parts; he can add on parts that were not originally there but that he thinks are restatement or statement of implication. When he does this, he fails in his audacious/humble task of being a messenger. Christian experience and the judgment of the Church are quite certain of the fact that priest and bishop sometimes teach as the gospel what is not the gospel. For all that they are validly ordained, their teaching is not a universally and unfailingly successful as their sanctifying activity. This several of the fathers pointed out.[103] That means that if ordination gives the power to teach, it does not give a power like the power to consecrate or ordain. The power to teach is quite fully "delible."

In fact, preaching and teaching can fail far more easily than sanctifying. Especially, a lack of faith will seriously erode successful teaching. Let us recall Gadamer's discussion of teaching in *Truth and Method*. Teaching, preaching, is an act of interpretation. All interpretation depends on the foreunderstanding with which one approaches the text. The relevant foreunderstanding with which to approach and understand the Scriptures is faith.[104] So, if there is no faith, there is no understanding of the message, and therefore no successful quotation of the message.

Of course, there can be literal quotation in the very words of the Gospels—reading the text—just as there can be literal quotation (and there had better be) of the liturgical texts for the sacraments. But if teaching the text is interpreting the text, then interpreting the text is also applying the text.[105] This usually takes more than only saying once again the very words. So, apart from faith, teaching the gospel, whether evangelically, catechetically, or theologically, really cannot go forward.

The same is true for ruling. Let us think of the ruling in question as the application of a kind of law. This law is not simply a collection of administrative rules ensuring administrative efficiency and valid for any bureaucracy. Such is part of ecclesiastical governance, but it is not the most important part. The most important part is ordering the life of the community according to the law of the gospel. This is the law of the Cross, as when Paul urges us to have the mind of Christ, who although he was divine, emptied himself. It is the law whereby he who was rich became

---

[103] Healy, above at note 38; d'Almeida Trindade, at note 47.
[104] Hans-Georg Gadamer, *Truth and Method* (New York: Seabury Press, 1975), 295–96.
[105] Ibid., 275.

poor for our sake. It is the double law of love, love of God with our whole heart, love of neighbor as ourselves. The intelligibility of these laws, the fact that they really do conduce to the common good of the community, is not obvious. It, too, is beheld in faith, or not at all. Therefore, one's ability to rule by these laws is strictly dependent on faith.

Preaching in the first place aims to say what is; ruling aims as well to say what should be. Arguably, it is more difficult, and is more easily corrupted. It requires an exercise of prudence, of political prudence, as teaching does not, or not to the same extent. This prudence will be the marshalling of means unto the common good, where the common good of the Church is an order not just of justice but of charity. So, it will not happen without charity. Ruling seems more dependent, requires more. If teaching depends especially on faith, ruling depends on both faith and charity. Ruling can therefore fail in more ways than teaching. The priest can fail to remember the gospel law, change it, add to it. Also, priest or bishop can fail in charity and so render himself incapable of applying the law of charity.

Now, ordination is not the basic grant of faith to a Christian, just as it is not the basic grant of charity. But the things that it does give for the discharge of teaching and ruling are parasitic on faith and charity and can be lost if they are lost, the way the power to sanctify cannot be so lost. What are these things?

The Effects of the Sacrament

The things given in ordination are the things prayed for in the ordination prayers. Some of these things, once received, are more stable than others— a fact that is generally recognized.[106] Most stable, as implied by Christian sacramental experience and the Church's judgment of the validity of sacramental acts, is the power to sanctify in celebrating the sacraments. It is this power that St. Thomas identifies with a character that cannot be lost.

What of other endowments? Lefèbvre spoke of charisms, Prou of *dotes*, for teaching and the fulfillment of a bishop's mission.[107] For teaching infallibly, there are *dona* (Browne), or the charism of divine assistance (Lamont), or the *virtus et auxilium* of the Spirit (Cantero Cuadrado).[108] Taguchi speaks variously of an illumination or an *augmentum intellectuale* or of something like the gift of prophecy for teaching.[109]

For infallible teaching, supposing more is wanted than an *assistentia per se negativa*, we could very well imagine a transitory assistance like that which

---

[106] For example, Yves Congar, "Le sacerdoce du Nouveau Testament: Mission et culte," in Frisque and Congar, *Les Prêtres*, 246.

[107] See above, notes 31 and 33.

[108] See above, notes 53, 42, and 43, and Calabria at 41.

[109] See above, note 48.

St. Thomas supposes for prophecy.[110] But on the supposition that the endowment in question is something for the teaching of the bishop in general, something therefore more stable, we shall have to reach for the category of habit—a relatively permanent but by no means indelible determination of a power.[111] So, St. Thomas knows of a gratuitous grace, "the word of wisdom and knowledge," a grace that is ordered to the public teaching of prelates.[112] This grace, moreover, is really identical with the gifts of wisdom and knowledge, gifts of the Holy Spirit, and differs from them only according as it bespeaks an especial fullness of the gifts.[113] As to ruling, the gift of counsel also can be a gratuitous grace.[114] It is the gift associated with practical wisdom, with prudence, and so with governing.[115] The gifts of the Holy Spirit, we recall, render a man especially receptive to actual grace, to the promptings of the Holy Spirit[116]—here, the inspirations relative to teaching and instructing and being practically wise, the very things a bishop needs every day. Such gifts are better understood as habits rather than as powers, and this in contrast to the character imprinted by orders.[117] These gifts, moreover, can be lost, and are lost with the loss of charity.[118]

The **Munera** *as Rights and as Powers*

As a final step, we need to distinguish between the right to teach and rule on the one hand and a capacity to teach and rule (to discern the true, to behold what is to be done) on the other. If by the first we mean a legally constituted and recognized right, then the second is more a "natural right" so to teach and rule.

So, in giving a certain fullness of the gifts of the Holy Spirit, we can say that ordination gives the capacity to teach and rule, the capacity to interpret Scripture for these people now and the capacity to see how the law of Christ is to be fulfilled here and now. Is this also the right to teach and rule? Taguchi had it that what is given for teaching by the sacrament, an *augmentum intellectuale*, is not a "mere right" to teach. It is not a merely juridical reality, because it is a real capacity.[119] It is, we might say, a natural right to teach, in the sense that any such capacity bespeaks a sort of native rightness

---

[110] *ST* II–II, q. 171, a. 2, c.

[111] It would be no less "ontological" for being a habit but not a power; see above, Charue, note 25.

[112] *ST* II–II, q. 177, a. 2, c.

[113] *ST* I–II, q. 68, a. 5, ad 1; I–II, q. 111, a. 4, ad 4; II–II, q. 45, a. 5, c, and ad 2.

[114] *ST* II–II, q. 52, a. 1, ad 2.

[115] With wisdom, *ST* I–II, q. 68, a. 4, c; with prudence, II–II, q. 52, a. 2, c.

[116] *ST* I–II, q. 68, a. 1, c.

[117] Gifts as habits, *ST* I–II, q. 68, a. 3, c; character as power, III, q. 63, a. 2, c.

[118] *ST* I–II, q. 68, a. 5, c.

[119] See above, note 48.

of its exercise. Moreover, the right to teach is included in the bishop's *potestas regiminis*, a right to rule that includes the right to exercise the *munus* of sanctifying, too. We might, then, line things up as follows.

First, it should be mentioned that just in giving the power to sanctify, ordination gives a call, an aptitude for the other *munera*, in the sense that it is fitting that the one who sanctifies teach and rule. Groblicki seemed to have a sense of this: who has the power to ordain connaturally rules and teaches.[120]

Second, as the Doctrinal Commission insisted, ordination is not a mere deputation to rule and teach; it gives real capacities so to do.[121] If we think of these capacities as a kind of abundance of the relevant gifts of the Holy Spirit, then we can recognize them as by nature giving title to be exercised. The capacity just is a sort of natural right to be used. But if the capacities can be lost, then this kind of right can be lost too.

Third, there is juridical right, as granted with the canonical mission and exercised only in hierarchical communion. This may be given to and not withdrawn from one who has not the real capacities to rule and teach as grounded in the gifts. It may be given to one who once had but lost the capacities. Also, given by law, it is revocable by law, and is revoked when someone shows himself manifestly incompetent to teach and rule.[122]

Conclusion

In this way, we recover the older and entirely sane sense of the relatively less stable capacities, in comparison to the power to sanctify, possessed by prelates and priests. Not recovering this sense conduces to bad consequences. First, we may be tempted to inflate episcopal (and, in their order, presbyteral) acts of teaching and ruling. Second, when such inflation becomes unbearable because of heresy or malfeasance, we will be tempted to reject the whole idea of a sacred hierarchy. We must distinguish. What is true is that we are given a sacred hierarchy permanently sacred in its sanctifying function, sacred in its teaching function when discharged by men of faith, and sacred in is ruling function when discharged by men of charity.

The idea that the powers of ruling and teaching are as stable as that of sanctifying and for the same reason is suggested by the wording of the texts, and Galot, Lafont, and Butler cannot be faulted for seeing it there. It is suggested because the council associates the three *munera* with the

---

120 See above, note 52; and Olaechae Loizaga, for whom the ministry of word and rule are rooted in the sacrificial ministry (above, note 45); Elchinger, for whom the bishop exercises all three *munera* in the celebration of the Eucharist, above, note 37); and Plourde (above, note 93).

121 See above, at note 16.

122 Cf. Browne (above, note 53): Consecration does not give the power to teach and rule with authority; and Prou (above, note 34): The mission given by consecration is not *potestas auctoritativa*.

ideas of configuration to Christ and acting in the person of Christ, and these ideas themselves once upon a time were more narrowly associated with the power of sanctifying, itself identified with the character. But the idea that the powers of ruling and teaching are as stable as that of sanctifying and for the same reason is not stated by the texts. To the few, very few, persons who saw this possible implication of the texts, the final *relationes* replied that it is not a legitimate inference from the texts. Indeed, it is evident from the *Acta* that there is really not much concern at all with the nature of the character, presbyteral or episcopal. The association of themes that leads to the idea of founding all the *munera* in the character is, in fact, quite accidental. For the text of *Presbyterorum Ordinis* is imitating the text of *Lumen Gentium,* and the crucial wording of the text of *Lumen Gentium* is an accident of wanting to state positively what had been stated negatively in a previous draft, namely the dignity of episcopal office, and expressing it with respect to all the *munera* in words formerly restricted to expressing it with respect to just one.

13

The Durable Synthesis of *Presbyterorum Ordinis**

Co-authored with Lawrence J. Welch

OUR INTEREST in the *Decree on the Ministry and Life of Priests* of the Second Vatican Council is primarily doctrinal, and therefore we focus especially on *Presbyterorum Ordinis* 2. We begin our commentary by recalling some of the history of the composition of that key paragraph and interpret it against the background of prior Catholic tradition. Although the *Decree* is novel in conception and expression relative to much modern theology of the priesthood, this originality functions to assert more important continuities with the greater breadth of Scripture, the ancient liturgy, and the fathers. We then look forward from the council to the challenges the theology of priestly identity and function has faced in the last forty years, and show how the *Decree* forearmed the Church in meeting these challenges.

Presbyterorum Ordinis on the Nature of the Priesthood

The history of the *Decree on the Ministry and Life of Priests, Presbyterorum Ordinis,* is as long as the Second Vatican Council itself and therefore hard to summarize.[1] From envisioning a purely disciplinary decree dealing with

---

* A portion of this essay previously appeared as Guy Mansini, O.S.B., and Lawrence J. Welch, "The Decree on the Ministry and Life of Priests, *Presbyterorum Ordinis*," in *Vatican II: Renewal within Tradition*, ed. Matthew L. Lamb and Matthew Levering (New York: Oxford University Press, 2008), 205–27.

[1] See Jean Frisque, "Le Décret 'Presbyterorum Ordinis.' Histoire et commentaire," in *Les Prêtres: Décrets "Presbyterorum Ordinis" et "Optatam totius,"* ed. J. Frisque and Y. Congar, Unam Sanctam 38 (Paris: Cerf, 1968), 123–89; Joseph Lécuyer, "History of the Decree," in *Commentary on the Documents of Vatican II*, vol. 4, ed. Herbert

practical matters of ministry and spiritual life, the fathers gradually came to realize the necessity of saying something about priests comparable in dignity and fundamentality with what the council said of bishops and laity. In other words, the *Decree* would in some measure have to address doctrine.[2] This realization, however, was tardy, as witness the late date of the rejection of the draft schema *De Vita et Ministerio Sacerdotali* that followed from it— October 19, 1964.[3] Only one more session of the council remained.

Remarkably, in little over one month, the Commission for the Discipline of the Clergy and the Christian People, charged with drafting a new text, was able to distribute a draft of a new schema to the council fathers on November 20, 1964. One of the important differences from previous drafts was the title, *De Ministerio et Vita Presbyterorum,* which signaled that the subject was not the priesthood in general *(sacerdotium),* inclusive of the bishops, but the presbyterate *(presbyteratus),* priests of the second order. Moreover, the reversal in the order of "life" and "ministry" reflects the fact that ministry will be treated first (part two) and as determinative of what priestly life should be like (part three).[4] At this pass, it was natural for the Commission to take guidance from previous conciliar work, and look back to the *Dogmatic Constitution on the Church, Lumen Gentium* 41, for a word about priestly spirituality, and to *Lumen Gentium* 28 for the all-important first, doctrinal word. It was over the content of this doctrinal word that the council fathers divided. After the fathers sent in their written comments to the Commission in January of 1965, the schema was revised. The modified text was transmitted to the fathers on May 28, 1965, but was not publicly debated until the 148th General Congregation on October 14, 1965. After several days of discussion, the fathers voted overwhelmingly (1507 to 12) on October 16 to accept it as the *textus recognitus,* that is, the basis for the final version. Still, important work remained.

Vorgrimler (New York: Herder & Herder, 1967), 183–209; René Wasselynck, "Histoire du Décret," in *Les Prêtres. Élaboration du Décret de Vatican II. Commentaire* (Paris: Desclée, 1968), 15–34; Paul Cordes, *Sendung zum Dienst: exegetische-historische und systematische Studien zum Konzilsdekret Vom Dienst und Leben der Priester* (Frankfurt am Main: J. Knecht, 1972). Lécuyer played a principal role in the production of the *Decree;* Frisque, too, collaborated.

[2] Lécuyer, "History of the Decree," 193–94.

[3] Frisque, "Histoire," 125, 128–29. Norman Tanner summarizes the speeches of October 13–15, 1964, critical of the schema in "The Church in the Word *(Ecclesia ad extra),*" *History of Vatican II,* vol. 4, ed. Giuseppe Alberigo, English version ed. Joseph A. Komonchak (Maryknoll, NY: Orbis, 2003), 347–53.

[4] Lécuyer, "History of the Decree," 195.

Paragraph 2 and the "Two Conceptions" of the Priesthood at the Council

Because of its indebtedness to *Lumen Gentium*, the very first draft of *Presbyterorum Ordinis* inserts the priest into the theology of mission, proceeding from Christ to the apostles, and from the apostles to the bishops, and it did so at the express request of 124 fathers.[5] This did not, however, satisfy those with an allegiance to other ways of understanding the priesthood, especially that cultivated by the French School. At the distribution of the first emendation of the first draft text of *Presbyterorum Ordinis*, just after acceptance of this emended text as the *textus recognitus*, Archbishop François Marty famously summarized the divergence of views.

> As to the specific nature of the ministry and life of presbyters. On this matter, there have been expressed two conceptions which seem to differ at first glance. For one of them insists more on the consecration of the presbyter worked by the sacrament of Orders, and on the personal union of the presbyter with Christ, who is the font of holiness and spiritual efficaciousness. The other conception, however, insists on the mission of the presbyter, which mission he receives from Christ through the sacrament: that is, the presbyter, since he becomes a member of the Order of presbyters, by that fact becomes a helper of the Order of bishops, so that he acts in the person of Christ unto the building up of the Church.
>
> In fact, each of these two conceptions puts in light an aspect of great importance in the ministry and life of presbyters. Therefore, our commission will take care to show how these two conceptions combine with one another harmoniously and indeed complete each other, so that they go together in the unity of presbyteral ministry.[6]

It is easy to illustrate Marty's summary. So, on the one hand, responding to the first draft, Archbishop Darmajuwana thought the text should emphasize

---

[5] *Acta Synodalia Sacrosancti Concilii Vaticani II* (Rome: Typis Polyglottis Vaticanis, 1970–), IV/4:863. Hereafter, *AS*, and indicating volume/part:page. Or see Francisco Gil Hellín, *Decretum de Presbyterorum Ministerio et Vita, Prsbyterorum Ordinis: Concilii Vaticani II Synopsis in ordinem redigens schemata cum relationibus necnon patrum orationes atque animadversiones* (Vatican City: Libreria Editrice Vaticana, 1996), 10, note to the first draft. Hellín's synopsis comprises the last four drafts of the Decree. The same synopsis, but without Hellín's references to the interventions of the fathers and the explanatory reports of the responsible Commission, appears in René Wasselynck, *Les Prêtres: Élaboration du Décret Presbyterorum Ordinis de Vatican II, Synopse* (Paris: Desclée, 1968).

[6] Concluding *Relatio* of F. Marty, Archbishop of Rheims, October 16, 1965, presenting the *"textus recognitus;" AS* IV/5:70–71.

more the priest's service to men, and Archbishop Garrone wanted a text more concordant with *Lumen Gentium*, where episcopal priesthood has its origin in the mission given by Christ and a scope that is the entire world.[7] Bishop Gufflet criticized the first draft for maintaining a conception of priesthood that is "purely cultic" and in contradiction to St. Paul; with Archbishop de Provenchères, he wanted more emphasis on the ministry of the word.[8] On the other hand, Bishop de Langavant wanted a more theo-centric text, expressing the priest's service to God; furthermore, "the sacrifice of the cross, and therefore also the sacrifice of the Mass, has for its first end the glory of God. This is also the most excellent function of the priest. As Christ became incarnate and was immolated on the cross 'on account of the glory of God,' the priest is consecrated in the first place to render glory to God in offering the sacrifice of the Mass, and also in interceding, in praying, in adoring in the name of all humanity."[9]

So also in the speeches of October 13–15, 1965, to which Marty espe-cially refers, we find Cardinal Döpfner praising the emended text for not viewing the presbyterate solely under its "cultic aspect," according to which it is ordered to offering sacrifice and administering the sacraments, but extending it to the threefold *munera* of Christ.[10] For Cardinal Richaud, on the other hand, it was not sufficient to think of priesthood solely under the heading of a mission to humanity; "the first response to priestly vocation lies in a greater love for Christ." This found expression in the text, he noted, but should have been more prominent. Further, "the primordial function of presbyters, which lends value and inspiration to their zeal and ministry, rests in the consecration of the priest to the exte-rior and interior worship of God."[11] In the same vein, Bishop Henriquez Jimenez located the "essential reality" of the priesthood "wholly in the ontological configuration to Christ the Priest as well as in the real partici-pation in his own unique and eternal priesthood."[12]

These two positions came in large part to coalesce around the ques-tion whether the ministry of sanctification, especially in saying Mass, or the ministry of the word and evangelization should be emphasized in the document. The three *munera* were in fact prominent in the text from the first draft at the express request of 116 fathers.[13]

---

[7] *AS* IV/4;916 (Darmajuwana); *AS* Appendix, 660 (Garrone).

[8] *AS* IV/4:929 (Gufflet); *AS* IV/4:918 (de Provenchères).

[9] *AS* Appendix, 653–54; but from this worship, it is to be noted, will come the priest's "zeal for the apostolate" (654).

[10] *AS* IV/4:764.

[11] *AS* IV/4:732.

[12] *AS* IV/4:747; it is therefore too little to say that the priest shares in the mission of the bishop (748).

[13] *AS* IV/4:864.

The Commission therefore set itself the task of combining two lines of understanding the priesthood: the priest as conformed to Christ and consecrated unto the service of God and the priest as sharing in the apostolic mission of the bishops, itself a share in the mission of Christ, for the salvation of men. This task can be understood also as a call to insert the Tridentine view of the priest as the one who offers the Eucharistic sacrifice within the larger framework of an earlier and more ecclesiologically oriented understanding of priesthood, where the functions of preaching and ruling are brought to the same level of articulation as that of sanctifying.[14]

At this distance, it may be wondered what the great difficulty was. Marty himself says carefully, and we think accurately, of the positions only that they "seem to differ," and even that only "at first glance." It might be said that it was a difficulty more of temperament or spirituality than of doctrinal synthesis. As Yves Congar remarked long before the council, defining the priesthood in terms of consecration to God is not so much a theological definition as a spirituality.[15] But it is a spirituality that has had powerful and very practical effect. It is the spirituality, for instance, whose working out could be seen in the monasteries and convents of male religious of the 1950s and '60s with many priests, where ten or twelve altars might be packed into one oratory, so that each priest, assisted by one server, might discharge the duty of offering daily sacrifice to God.

Doctrinally, on the other hand and to repeat, the synthesis is not difficult. Congar notes resources within the French School itself, citing St. Vincent de Paul, who gives due attention to mission, functionality, and ministerial finality at one stroke: "The priest is a man called by God to share in the priesthood of Jesus Christ in order to extend the redemptive mission of Jesus Christ in doing what Jesus Christ did, in the way in which he did it."[16] Congar observes as well that if St. Thomas's definition of priesthood ties it to the Eucharist, his enumeration of the acts of the priest firmly characterizes the priesthood as a prolongation of apostolic mission.[17]

Congar for his own part and commenting on the text of *Presbyterorum Ordinis* finds a solution in the Christian cult. His remarks, moreover, are the more weighty as he helped produce the text he comments on.[18] The

---

[14] For the relation of *Presbyterorum Ordinis* to Trent, see the comprehensive study by Henri Denis, "La théologie du presbytérat de Trente à Vatican II," in *Les Prêtres*, 193–232.

[15] Yves Congar, *Lay People in the Church,* rev. ed., trans. Donald Attwater (Westminster, MD: Newman Press, 1967), 154.

[16] Yves Congar, "Le sacerdoce du Nouveau Testament: Mission et culte," in *Les Prêtres*, 233–56, at 237.

[17] Ibid., 234–35.

[18] See Ricardo Burigana and Giovanni Turbanti in *History of Vatican II*, 4:566–67; and see Yves Congar, *Mon Journal du Concile*, présenté et annoté par Éric Mahieu,

Christian's worship of God, Congar tells us, is in the first place the person's interior sacrifice of himself to God, a sacrifice that finds achievement in fraternal charity and care of the poor, and a sacrifice that depends on and is expressed by the Eucharistic sacrifice.[19] Both sacrifices, however, the personal and liturgical, absolutely presuppose the word of the gospel accepted in faith, and so they presuppose the call to and articulation of faith that is preaching. Therefore, the apostolic, evangelical aspect of priestly ministry can never be forgotten, and is a presupposition of the other aspects.[20]

After the council, synthesis of the two views took the form of picking one or another of the three *munera* of the priest and making it architectonic or deriving the other two from it, and there were many essays in this vein.[21] Joseph Ratzinger, for example, notes that the scope and intention of the word of the gospel includes sanctifying and ruling.[22] Therefore, baptism and Eucharist cannot be thought to be alien to the word of the gospel; word and Eucharist cannot be opposed to one another.[23] Rather, the Eucharist is the fulfillment of the word, where the word wants to lead us, and even what it wants to become. It is not just that sanctifying and ruling presuppose faith and so preaching, as Congar points out, but that the word of the Gospel of its nature passes over to the sacrament of the Word made flesh.[24] Karl Rahner similarly privileged the priest as pro-

---

avant-propos de Dominique Congar, Préface de Bernard Dupuy, O.P. (Paris: Les Éditions du Cerf, 2002), 2:202 (October 15, 1964). In pointing to the importance of Congar's commentary, we do not mean it is weighty as an author's comment is weighty. In the first place, the council is the author of the final text. Congar's role was rather that of a gifted secretary helping his master find his own voice. Second, Congar was very aware of this, that the text belonged to the council fathers, not to the *periti*; see, for example, *Journal*, 2:255 (November 11, 1964); 2:447 (October 22, 1965); 2:451 (October 25, 1965).

[19] "Le sacerdoce," 254–55. Note the dependence, 254 (our translation): "Before being latreutic, and in order to be latreutic, the Christian sacramental cult is theurgic and soteriological: it does not consist at first in offering, in making something rise up from us to God, but in receiving the effective gift of God."

[20] Ibid., 256. So also Cardinal Alfrink, Hellín, 625.

[21] See Avery Dulles, S.J., *The Priestly Office: A Theological Reflection* (New York: Paulist, 1997), who canvasses some of the more important of these essays, 20–22, 47–51.

[22] Joseph Ratzinger, "Priestly Ministry: A Search for Meaning," *Emmanuel* 76 (1970): 442–53 and 490–505, at 495–96, 498.

[23] In the same vein, see the International Theological Commission, "The Priestly Ministry," in *International Theological Commission: Text and Documents, 1969–1985*, ed. Michael Sharkey (San Francisco: Ignatius, 1989), 3–87, at 61–62. This text was published in 1970.

[24] In addition to Ratzinger's "Priestly Ministry," see his "Life and Ministry of Priests." This paper was delivered on October 24, 1995, for the symposium on the priesthood, *Priesthood: A Greater Love,* for the thirtieth anniversary of the *Decree Presbyterorum*

claimer of the word, the supreme degree of which makes present what it proclaims in sacrament and for a rightly ordered community.[25] Walter Kasper proposed to unify the conception of priestly ministry in the notion of leadership in teaching, worship, and community relations, and this seems, in fact, to privilege the *munus regendi*.[26]

While the relation of the *munera* to one another is doubtless important, it is only one part of the synthesis of *Presbyterorum Ordinis*, our own view of which we present shortly.

Juxtaposition or Synthesis?

After the acceptance of the *textus recognitus*, there were three substantive changes to the paragraph on the nature of the priesthood. First, there is a return to the first draft's introduction, which speaks of the entire people of God as sharing in the mission of Christ and in his threefold *munus*. Second, there is the addition of 2.d, on the spiritual and existential sacrifice of the faithful, which is treated as finding sacramental consummation through the ordained priesthood. Third, there is the addition of 2.e, on the ultimate purpose of the priesthood, specified as the salvation of men and the glory of God. With various other emendations of the text, these important additions were approved by the council on December 2.[27] This reworking of what was to become number 2 of the final text was principally the work of Congar.[28] On December 7, 1965, the *Decree* was overwhelmingly approved in public session, 2,390 to 4.

Did *Presbyterorum Ordinis* succeed in producing an organic doctrinal statement, bringing together the two views, that of the priest as consecrated by the sacrament of orders for the worship of God, and this preeminently in offering the sacrifice of the Mass, and that of the priest as

---

Ordinis sponsored by the Congregation for Clergy, www.vatican.va/roman_curia/congregations/ccclergy (accessed October 21, 2003).

25 Karl Rahner, "The Point of Departure in Theology for Determining the Nature of the Priestly Office," *Theological Investigations,* vol. 12, trans. David Bourke (New York: Seabury, 1974), 31–38.

26 Walter Kasper, "A New Dogmatic Outlook on the Priestly Ministry," in *The Identity of the Priest (Concilium,* vol. 43) (New York: Paulist, 1969), 20–33.

27 Changes included the revised word order of the title, *latinitatis causa,* to *De Presbyterorum Ministerio et Vita.*

28 Congar, *Journal,* 2:443 (October 20, 1965); 2:511 (December 7, 1965). Congar rewrote nos. 1–3, wrote the first redaction of nos. 4–6, revised nos. 7–9, 12–14, and part of the conclusion. He said the text was three parts the work of Joseph Lécuyer, Willy Onclin, and himself. Lécuyer oversaw the crucial paragraph on celibacy. On the acceptance of Congar's draft of paragraph 2 by the Commission, see *Journal,* 2:457 (October 29, 1965): "Ils épluchent le texte sur quelques expressions, ils ne s'attachent guère au fond. De sorte que le texte passé sans coup férir. C'est inouï! C'était inespéré."

sharing in apostolic mission, the fullness of hierarchical participation in which belongs to the bishop?

It is sometimes said that the missionary perspective ended up encompassing the cultic one, which was absorbed into it. In this way, the missionary view would be the view of the council and *Presbyterorum Ordinis* simply speaking, within which a place is found for the other but now relativized view. So Friedrich Wulf in the Herder commentary on the *Decree*: "The one-sided cultic character of the Catholic priesthood has been absorbed into the wider apostolic ministry, which has found expression above all in the doctrine of the three offices of Christ."[29] On the other hand he laments the characterization of the priest in number 2 as facing the Church, representing Christ the Head, as "one-sided"—he wants the priest to represent the priestly Church, too—and recognizes that the "sacerdotal-cultic idea" of the priest, the concept of the priest as determined by the power of orders, "predominates" in the second and third sections of number 2. He finds better the fourth section of number 2, which "brings into the foreground the missionary aspect, the commission to preach and to sanctify addressed to the New Testament ministry."[30]

Basically, therefore, Wulf treats the text as if its unity were that of a bag containing two cats, sometimes one "predominates," but at other points the text is "one-sided." In this way, the text would illustrate the "juxtaposition" of views, old and new, that Hermann Pottmeyer finds in the production of the council. For him, synthesis on such matters as the relation of pope and episcopal college, the unity of revelation, and the theological relation of the Catholic Church to other churches was not reached but is the part of theologians to achieve.[31] Even so, Pottmeyer expressly forbears accusing the production of incoherence. With regard to *Presbyterorum Ordinis*, this is left to Christian Duquoc.[32] He can say that "a rather classic theology of the priesthood" is "meshed with a quite untraditional presentation of ministerial activity."[33] He thinks the *Decree* suffers from "indecisive-

---

29 Friedrich Wulf, "Commentary on the Decree," in *Commentary on the Documents of Vatican II*, 4:224. Wulf worked on the *Decree* as a *peritus* toward the end, especially on no. 16; see Congar, *Journal,* 2:442–43 (October 20, 1965).

30 "Commentary," 222.

31 Hermann J. Pottmeyer, "A New Phase in the Reception of Vatican II: Twenty Years of Interpretation of the Council," in *The Reception of Vatican II*, ed. Giuseppe Alberigo, Jean-Pierre Jossua, and Joseph A. Komonchak (Washington, DC: Catholic University of America Press, 1987), 27–43, at 37.

32 Christian Duquoc, "Clerical Reform," in *The Reception of Vatican II*, 297–308. Duquoc seems to assume that the reform of the theology of the priesthood at which the council aimed at was also a general "reform" of the manners, ministry, and life of priests.

33 Ibid., 298.

ness" and that there is a "latent opposition" between the old and the new views.[34] The theology of sacrifice found in number 5 can be read as either subsumed into the theology of mission or at odds with it, and therefore, according to Duquoc, as an obstacle to the democratic reformulation of office that the new view of priesthood, which is present but not everywhere controlling in the text, aimed at.[35] Daniel Donovan, too, thinks the council "had to sacrifice consistency" in order to meet the demands of both views; sometimes the mission view predominates, but at other times "priesthood," *sacerdotium,* reabsorbs all the presbyteral *munera* into itself.[36]

For our part, we think the *Decree* is not fairly criticized as incoherent, nor as achieving nothing more than a juxtaposition of views. Nor, finally, is the nature of the synthesis we think to see there a simple matter of picking one of the *munera* and declaring it architectonic. Evidently, moreover, if there is such a synthesis of such a part of the deposit of faith, it will be discerned only against the background of prior theological and dogmatic tradition.

Mission, Munera, Mediation

It is true that the function of sanctifying, which culminates in the presidency of the Eucharist, is said to be but one of three functions or *munera* for which the priest or apostolic minister is sent.[37] In this way, formally, the accent is on mission, and cultic priestly activity is but one thing within a greater whole, as a part of it, in addition to the other two offices or functions.

The text, however, does not leave the three *munera* with identical roles in our understanding of the priesthood, as if they contributed to it in the same way and on the same footing. Paragraph 5, which Duquoc finds ambiguous, is decisive. First, the priest's ministry as a whole, his *opera apostolatus* as such, is said to be ordered to the Eucharist (5.b). This is new with respect to the *textus recognitus.* It is repeated substantially in number 13, where priests "fulfill their highest office"—*munus suum praecipuum adimplent*—in the Eucharist (13.d), which phrase also is new relative to the *textus recognitus.*[38] Second, in a striking phrase, the *munus* of preaching has its

---

[34] Ibid., 299.

[35] Ibid., 300, 303–5.

[36] Daniel Donovan, *What Are they Saying about the Ministerial Priesthood?* (New York: Paulist, 1992), 11; see also 19.

[37] For the priest as sent, sharing in apostolic ministry, see *Presbyterorum Ordinis* 2.b, 2.d; for a share in the *triplex munera,* see 1.b; 4; 5; 6; 7.a, 13.

[38] The interpretation of this text that F. Wulf gives, *Commentary on the Documents of Vatican II,* 4:271, that the Eucharist is preeminent relative only to other sanctifying functions, but not to the other *munera,* is contrary to the text, as well as to the sense of the council to be discerned in the Response to Modus 26 to no. 13, (*AS* IV/7, 198), as well as to *Presbyterorum Ordinis* 5, as well as to *Lumen Gentium* 28. We note

origin in and finds its summit in the Eucharist, *fons et culmen totius evangelizationis* (5.b). This, too, is new with respect to the *textus recognitus*, and must likewise be understood to be responding expressly to the desire to synthesize the two views. Paragraph 5 is at this point doing nothing but paraphrasing number 2.d, the whole of which is an addition where the Eucharistic sacrifice, to which the spiritual sacrifice of Christians is joined, is the goal to which priestly ministry "tends" and that in which it is "consummated." Here, too, the ministry of the priests "begins from the proclamation of the gospel," but "draws its force and strength from the sacrifice of Christ." As to the particular discussion of the ministry of the word in number 4, it makes Congar's point that, since the sacraments are sacraments of faith, the ministry of the word is presupposed to the sacramental ministry, and is even intrinsic to it, as the text states explicitly with regard to the Mass (4.c). Of priestly rule, finally, the fathers teach in number 6 that "no Christian community can be built without having its root and foundation in the celebration of the most holy Eucharist" (6.e). The Eucharist leads to works of charity (6.e), and the law of the community is said to be the law of charity (6.c), which order and union in charity is, of course, nothing but the *res* of the sacrament of the Eucharist. If the *archê* is the end, then we may well say that this last function, ruling in and for charity, rules the other two *munera*. On the other hand, since the sacraments of the New Law—and especially and preeminently the Eucharist—contain what they signify, they cannot be thought of as indicators of something utterly distinct from them, or as instruments extrinsic to what they accomplish. Therefore, it is reasonable to conclude that, if formally the mission view is primary, as introducing and framing the presentation, substantively, the cultic, Eucharistic view is primary.

In this, the text is faithful to the New Testament, for apostolic mission originates with Christ. And Christ is made present in the Eucharist, and makes himself present precisely as enacting the Paschal Mystery. But it is from the fullness of the Paschal Mystery whence the mission arises (Jn 21). Therefore, whatever participation in apostolic mission there may be can and ought to be said to find its origin in the Eucharist, which is the sacramental availability of the Paschal Mystery.[39]

Further, the priestly mission is to bring the laity, those who consecrate their lives to Christ in consecrating the world to him, to a share in Christ's own consecration of himself to the Father.[40] The Eucharist is therefore also

---

here that translations of *Presbyterorum Ordinis* (as of any of the conciliar *acta*) are our own, though we have of course consulted the Tanner and Flannery translations.

[39] For the Eucharist as the origin of mission, see Joseph Ratzinger, "Eucharist and Mission," *Irish Theological Quarterly* 65 (2000): 245–64, at 247, 262.

[40] See *Lumen Gentium* 33, and *Apostolicam Actuositatem* 2.

the terminus of the mission in this world. If the word of the gospel does not pass over to sacramental reality, moreover, and if our action in the world does not join up with the action of Christ, then it is to be wondered whether Christian life is more than just one of many other social constructions of reality.[41] Rather, Eucharist means that Christianity, our union with Christ, is not just a matter of saying and doing, a moral reality, but lands us in a reality deeper than our own by a saying and a doing that is more than our own.[42] So, yes, in the order of generation, so to speak, preaching must be first, and the council explicitly says so (4.a); but in the order of perfection, as containing the reality preaching is about, sanctification is first.[43] This is, in fact, the synthesis paragraph 2.d presents to us.

Consideration of the mediations at stake in the *munera* shows how the "two conceptions" are mutually inclusive. If sanctification is taken quite narrowly to mean performance of and presidency over the cult, then the missionary mandate of the New Testament minister includes that as but one activity to be taken with two others. On the other hand, saying that the New Testament minister is one who is sent adverts to only one side of a double mediation, the side that goes from God to men. In the same way, "preaching" and "ruling" are also similarly one-sided, and move from God man-ward. Priesthood, on the other hand, classically signifies both sides of the mediation, from God to man and from man to God.[44] The downward mediation is first, bringing both the word of divine instruction and interior grace.[45] But the other side, where by sacrifice man arrives in the heavenly sanctuary, this side too is signified by "priest," as it is not by "apostle." The question, then, is what is meant by the Christian cult.[46] If we mean very narrowly the service of the altar in the sanctuary, then saying that sanctifying is but one of three functions of the one sent breaks open priestly activity to include preaching and ruling. But if the cult of Christians is

---

[41] See here John Paul II, *Veritatis Splendor* 19–21.

[42] See Ratzinger, "Eucharist and Mission," 241, 262.

[43] For the same in St. Thomas, see Benoît-Dominique de La Soujeole, "Les *tria munera Christi*: Contribution de saint Thomas à la recherche contemporaine," *Revue Thomiste* 99 (1999): 59–74, at 71–72; the ordering is the same as that for faith (preaching), hope (ruling), and charity (sanctification).

[44] For example, see *Summa theologiae* [hereafter *ST*] III, q. 22, a. 1; and Raymond Brown, *Priest and Bishop: Biblical Reflections* (New York: Paulist Press, 1970), 10–13.

[45] Congar, "Le sacerdoce du Nouveau Testament," 254 (our translation): "Before being latreutic, and in order to be latreutic, the Christian sacramental cult is theurgic and soteriological: it does not consist at first in offering, in making something rise up from us to God, but in receiving the effective gift of God." See also Gisbert Greshake, *The Meaning of Christian Priesthood,* trans. Paeder MacSeumais (Westminster, MD: Christian Classics, 1989), 82–83.

[46] Ibid., 251–56.

"existential,"[47] if the altar of sacrifice is cosmic,[48] then "priest" once again regains its capacity to be the comprehensive appellation of Christian ministry, which gathers a community by preaching, orders it in charity, and consummates its spiritual sacrifice in the sacrament of the sacrifice of Christ.

Moreover, if we consider the *munera* in their original and paradigmatic deployment by Christ, then the office of Christ's priesthood must be said to be preeminent.[49] For it conveys more fully the mediation of Christ, downward and upward, both Son of God and Son of man, than either kingship or prophecy of themselves can do. So, the name Christ receives according to Hebrews 1–2, summing up his divine dignity as Son, King, Lord, and Creator (1:5–14) and his solidarity with us as Son of man, the pioneer of salvation, and brother (2:1–16) is "high priest" (2:17).[50] Priestly concept and reality have also died and been raised in the triumph of the Cross, with the same continuity and discontinuity of the buried and glorified body, of the Old Testament and the New. Downward, priestly mediation consists in the teaching of a new law and its infusion into the heart, and of the forgiveness of sins; upward, it is the offering of a sacrifice that achieves salvation because it places the offerer himself in the heavenly sanctuary really by death or now, and also really sacramentally, in hope. On the contrary, to make of Christian ministry a ministry only of the word, or so to emphasize it when conceiving Christian ministry as a share in apostolic mission as to fail to see any antecedent foreshadowing in the priesthood of the Old Testament, is to confine the Church to the Synagogue, to refuse to enter into the Body that is the Temple.[51]

---

[47] Ibid., 254–55.

[48] Ratzinger, "Eucharist and Mission," 261–62.

[49] According to St. Thomas, Christ as Head has the perfection of all graces that, in the body, are distributed one to a priest, another to a king, and still another to a giver of the law, as was Moses; see *ST* III, q. 22, a. 1, ad 3; *In Rom.* I,1; no. 20. Since the grace of Christ's headship is one with his personal grace, moreover, it is in virtue of the same reality that Christ is Prophet, Priest, and King; see *ST* III, q. 8, a. 5. This is not to say that teaching means sanctifying and sanctifying means ruling, else the question of which is preeminent could not arise. It is, however, to say that his kingship is his priesthood and his priesthood is his messiahship. So also in the doctrine of God, we say that the divine justice is the divine mercy, though justice and mercy do not mean the same thing, and thus there remains the question of which attribute is preeminent.

[50] Albert Vanhoye, *Old Testament Priests and the New Priest according to the New Testament,* trans. J. Bernard Orchard (Petersham, MA: St. Bede's Publications, 1986), 85–87.

[51] See on this Joseph Ratzinger, who correctly resists the tendency to dismiss the Old Testament as having anything to say about Christian priesthood and ministry; see his "Life and Ministry of Priests."

The Synthesis of Paragraph 2

It is important to see that the synthesis of paragraph 2 occurs within the context of the great themes of the council's ecclesiology, for it is made possible by the council's faithfulness to these themes. This faithfulness is declared from the outset, in number 1, where the treatment of the priesthood is related to these themes in a single sentence that forms as it were an ecclesiological preface to the *Decree*. "For, by the sacred ordination and mission they receive from bishops, priests are promoted to the service of Christ the teacher, priest and king whose ministry they share, by which the Church is unceasingly built up here on earth into the people of God, the body of Christ and the temple of the holy Spirit."[52] First, the mission of priests evokes that of Christ and the Church, more expressly developed immediately after in number 2. Second, this mission is ordered to building up the Church as the communion of the people of God, whose Christological and pneumatological dimensions are immediately brought forward, since communion in the Church is communion with the persons of the Trinity. Third, this mission of Christ and the Church that priests share in is given the same threefold articulation as in *Lumen Gentium*. Fourth, the ministry of priests, already situated between Christ who sends them and the people to whom they are sent is tied to that of the bishops, to which it has been a principal goal of the council to give adequate treatment.[53]

The reconciliation and synthesis of the two views occurs at three places, especially: in the attention at 2.a and 2.d to the spiritual sacrifices of the faithful, at 2.b, and at 2.e. Paragraph 2.a affirms that all the faithful are a royal priesthood, offering spiritual sacrifices to God.[54] This looks forward to 2.d, where the synthesis occurs in terms of the relation of priesthoods: The ministerial priest is sent to enable the exercise of the baptismal

---

[52] This sentence is substantially that of the draft of November 20, 1964.

[53] For more on this ecclesiological context of the *Decree*, see Archbishop Julian Herranz Casado, "The Image of the Priest in the Decree *Presbyterorum Ordinis*: Continuity and Projection toward the Third Millenium." This paper was delivered in 1995 for the symposium on the priesthood, *Priesthood: A Greater Love,* for the thirtieth anniversary of the *Decree*, sponsored by the Congregation for Clergy, www.vatican.va/roman_curia/congregations/ccclergy (accessed October 12, 2003). With Alvaro del Portillo, Herranz formed the secretariat of Commission *De Disciplina Cleri et Populi Christiani* responsible for the *Decree*.

[54] It is to be noted that neither *Lumen Gentium* nor *Presbyterorum Ordinis* characterizes the priesthood of the faithful as metaphorical, as did Pope Pius XII, *Magnificate Dominum, AAS* 46 (1954): 669. When the Commission responsible for *Presbyterorum Ordinis* was reproved for treating the "metaphorical" priesthood of the faithful before the ministerial priesthood, it merely noted that *Lumen Gentium* did not so characterize the priesthood of the faithful, and that the finality of the ministerial priesthood terminates in the universal priesthood (*AS* IV/7:118, Response to Modus 15).

priesthood of the faithful.[55] The Christian's sacrifice, which is the whole-offering of all one's life and of every human action to the Father, is rendered possible through the apostolic ministry of priests, which by preaching calls the faithful to this sacrifice, and is consummated in being sacramentally united to the sacrifice of Christ in the Eucharist. Paragraph 2 as a whole shows, as it were, how the spiritual sacrifice of the whole body is to be enabled and sacramentally accomplished in the Eucharistic sacrifice of the Head through the ministry of priests. "To this is ordered and in this is consummated the ministry of presbyters." Moreover, their ministry "which begins from the proclamation of the gospel, draws its force and strength from the sacrifice of Christ."[56]

Before this, 2.b repeats the doctrine of Trent that within the body of Christ there are ministers who in virtue of their sacred power offer sacrifice and forgive sins. These ministers, however, are to be understood in the line of the great sending: Christ to the apostles, the apostles to the bishops. As the bishops are appointed "to share in his [Christ's] own consecration and mission," first mentioned at the beginning of 2.a, so by implication do priests, who are delegated to collaborate with the bishops "to rightly carry out the apostolic mission." Consecration and mission are united in that consecration is unto mission.[57]

The last subparagraph, 2.e, also reconciles the two views. It shows the unity of the theocentric, "consecratory" view with that of the "anthropocentric," apostolic view. Underneath the text there is the recollection of St. Irenaeus's dictum that the glory of God is the life of man, and that the life of man is the knowledge of God.[58] So, as the text has it, priests are certainly devoted to the glory of God, but "that glory consists in this, that human beings consciously, freely and thankfully receive the work of God that was brought to perfection in Christ, and manifest it in their whole lives." The entire life and activity of priests, including preaching, sanctifying, and ruling, and including also most notably the very prayer and adoration of the priest, therefore "contribute both to increasing the glory of God and to advancing men in the divine life." The theocentric and latreutic intent of priesthood is consummated in the sanctification of man.

---

[55] Spiritual sacrifice is the reason for exterior sacrifice; see *ST* II–II, q. 85, aa. 1 and 2; *In Hebr.* II,3; no. 157. More originally, see St. Augustine, *The City of God*, Book 10, c. 5.

[56] In this way, it can be said that the text moves from mission (2.a and 2.b) to cult, in which cult the existential sacrifice of the faithful is joined to the Eucharistic sacrifice of Christ; see Frisque, "Histoire," 140–41.

[57] See Congar's remark on Marty's "two conceptions of the priesthood," *Journal,* 2: 443 (October 20, 1965): "Deux conceptions du sacerdoce: comme consécration (union personnelle au Christ), comme envoyé! Précisément, le concile a redécouvert l'unité de consecration et mission!"

[58] *Adversus Haereses* 4.20.8.

This leaves us with 2.c, the middle section of the paragraph, where the originality of the council comes to light as it presents its summary and controlling dogmatic view of the priest. The text articulates how the priest discharges his apostolic mission by recalling the threefold *munera,* and it explains the nature of the consecration for mission in terms of the sacrament of orders. Presbyteral office is conferred by a distinct sacrament whereby priests are "configured to the priesthood of Christ *[Christo sacerdoti configurantur],* in such a way that they may be able to act in the person of Christ as head of the body *[ita ut in persona Christi Capitis agere valeant]."*[59] Here let us quote Henri Denis apropos of that last phrase:

> It seems to us that it is on this little phrase that the specificity of the hierarchical minister in general and that of the presbyteral minister in particular rests. Indeed, if one looks for what is *original* in the task of the priest in relation to that of the Christian, one is referred to this sign which is essential to the Church: the sign of Christ the Head for his Body. In other words, there is a ministry in the Church in order that the work of Christ in the work of the Church may be signified.[60]

We report the story of the composition of this text shortly. For now, we wish to make some observation on another sense in which paragraph 2 is synthetic. The allusion to St. Irenaeus in 2.e reminds us how deeply rooted the entire paragraph is in the tradition. The text is synthetic, not just conceptually, relative to the "two views," but relative to Scripture and Tradition, too.

At the outset, in 2.a, the text joins consecration and mission in the citation of John 10:36, which speaks of Christ "consecrated and sent into the world." It is right to recall here, too, the Letter to the Hebrews, where Christ is in one breath both the apostle and high priest of our faith (3:1), in that his priestly work includes his authoritative declaration of the content of our profession of faith,[61] while his consecration as priest consists in his

---

[59] Tanner translates the last clause as a purpose clause ("so that,") but it is rather a result clause (signaled by the *ita ut*) and should read "such that" (or "in such a way that"— Flannery edition) they can act in the person of Christ the head." It is a question of stating the certain effect—the result—of the sacrament of orders, not a hope that may be impeded.

[60] Denis, "La théologie du presbytérat de Trente à Vatican II," 215–16 (our translation): "Il nous semble que cette petite phrase est en fait celle sur laquelle repose *la spécificité* du ministère hiérarchique en général et du ministère presbytéral en particulier. Si l'on cherche, en effet, en quoi la tâche du prêtre est *originale* par rapport à celle du chrétien, on est renvoyé à ce signe essentiel à l'Église."

[61] Vanhoye, *Old Testament Priests,* 97–98. And for ruling, see 230.

obedient death,[62] which Christians make actual in their own obedient sacrifice of daily life and charity (13:1–6) and memorialize in the Eucharist,
and indeed, proclaim until he comes again.[63] The linkage of consecration
and mission therefore picks up the original connection of these things in
the Christology of the New Testament, which itself builds on the commissioning narratives of the Old. "Before I formed you in the womb I knew
you, and before you were born I consecrated you; I appointed you a
prophet to the nations" (Jer 1:5). "The Spirit of the Lord is upon me,
because he has anointed me [consecrated me] to preach good news to the
poor; he has sent me to proclaim release to the captives . . ." (Lk 4:18, citing Is 61:1–2).[64] Returning to John's gospel, finally, we recall that Christ's
priestly invocation in chapter 17 declares not just his own consecration,
which is at the same time the achievement of his mission, but that of those
who in chapter 20 are sent as he was sent (20:21).

The threefold character of the mission of Christ collects the anointings
of prophet, priest, and king in the Old Testament, and bespeaks the unity
of the workings of Word and Spirit, of history and grace, and so the inseparability of Christology and pneumatology, in the Incarnation itself. For
the fathers, the trilogy does not move beyond Christology, the explanation
of the name "Christ." It is the liturgy of initiation, the post-baptismal
anointing, that makes the Christian as well as Christ, prophet, priest, and
king.[65] The ancient liturgies of ordination, collectively, attest that ordination enables a man to teach, sanctify, and rule, and although they do not
pick out the three functions as three, Congar thinks they come "bien
proche de notre trilogie."[66] In St. Thomas, the *munera* are invoked for both
Christ and his ministers.[67]

---

[62] Ibid., 73, 83, 132–33, 137, 157.

[63] Ibid., 223–24, 228–29.

[64] See here especially Congar, "Le sacerdoce du Nouveau Testament," 242–46, for a
short discussion of this linkage.

[65] Yves Congar, "Sur la trilogie: prophète, roi, prêtre," *Revue des sciences philosophiques
et théologiques* 67 (1983): 97–115, at 100. Congar makes more of the patristic witness to the trilogy than does J. Fuchs, "Origines d'une trilogie ecclésiologique a
l'époque rationaliste de la théologie," *Revue des sciences philosophiques et théologiques*
53 (1969): 185–211, at 194–97.

[66] Congar, "Sur la trilogie," 100. The consecration of the holy oil in the Apostolic
Tradition invokes the three as three (99–100). See also Bernard Botte, "Holy
Orders in the Ordination Prayers," in *The Sacrament of Holy Orders* (London:
Aquin Press, 1962), 5–23, at 21.

[67] De La Soujeole, "Les *tria munera* Christi," 61–66. It should be noted that to say
with St. Thomas that preaching is "secondary" is not to say that it is accidental; rather,
flowing from the principal function of sanctifying, it is included in what is essential to priestly ministry (ibid., 71). Bishop Carli made much the same point at the
council, *AS* III/4:551. For the subsequent history, see the articles by Congar and

The nature of the ministerial priest as representative of Christ is patristic, though one has to look to the citations of *Lumen Gentium* 21 for a witness to this tradition in the texts of the council. The assertion of the sacramentality of orders repeats Trent, of course, but Trent itself, in repeating the common theology of the thirteenth century on orders and the character imparted by orders does nothing but bring forward the twelfth century's ordering and labeling of the patristic and especially Augustinian inheritance. Best of all, all the foregoing is poured into understanding the priest's place between the sacrifice of the faithful and the sacrifice of Christ, just where St. Paul places his own ministry, the apostle who knew nothing for the Corinthians except Christ crucified (1 Cor 2:2) so that they might be God's temple (3:9, 16) and present their bodies as a living sacrifice to God (Rom 12:1).[68]

The Christological view of priesthood to which the text orients us in 2.c, where priests are "configured to the priesthood of Christ, in such a way that they may be able to act in the person of Christ, the head of the body," exactly reflects our epistemic situation. It is not just that Christ is mediator in his actions and of grace; but also, in the order of our very thinking about him, he is mediator of a new idea of mediation and priesthood. His priesthood, a "better priesthood," is exercised in his death, in the Paschal Mystery; the priesthood of the faithful, for its part, is achieved in the transformation of life in the power of and as uniting themselves existentially to Christ; ordained priests render the mediation of Christ present, especially in the Eucharist, which makes the Paschal Mystery present and unites the spiritual sacrifice of the faithful to that of Christ. Albert Vanhoye says: "If . . . we consider the texts of the New Testament which describe the characteristics of the apostolic or pastoral Christian ministry, we observe that these texts present the ministers of the Church as the living instruments of Christ the mediator and not as the delegates of the priestly people."[69] And again, the specific function of the priest is "the manifestation of the active presence of Christ the mediator . . . , of Christ the priest, in the life of believers in order

---

Fuchs. In English, one may consult Peter J. Drilling, "The Priest, Prophet and King Trilogy: Elements of its Meaning in *Lumen Gentium* and for Today," *Église et Théologie* 19 (1988): 179–206. For further background on this subject in the *Decree*, see Cordes, the section entitled "Die Darlegung der Presbyteraufgaben mit hilfe des Schemas vom dreifachen Amt Christi," in *Sendung zum Dienst*, 117–60.

68 For St. Thomas on the spiritual sacrifice of Christians, see M. Morard, "Sacerdoce du Christ et sacerdoce des chrétiens dans le *Commentaire des Psaumes* de saint Thomas d'Aquin," *Revue Thomiste* 99 (1999): 119–42, and Gilles Emery, "Le sacerdoce spiritual des fidèles chez saint Thomas d'Aquin," *Revue Thomiste* 99 (1999): 211–43, at 222.

69 Vanhoye, *Old Testament Priests,* 316.

that they may explicitly welcome this mediation and by its means transform their whole existence."[70]

Presbyterorum Ordinis 2 is synthetic not in the way of some theological encyclopedia but in the way a magisterial text as at Trent or the First Vatican Council is synthetic. *Pres. Ord.* 2 would have us think of the foundational realities necessary to understand priesthood: the plan of God, revealed in Christ, set in motion by Christ's mission, a mission continued in apostolic and episcopal ministry, and directed toward the consummation of all things at Christ's return. Within this, the true "frame" offered by the council, there is the sacramental priesthood of priests of the second rank, a priesthood deriving from and representing Christ's by the consecration of orders, a priesthood that enables the Eucharistic consummation of the existential priesthood of Christians, that presupposes faith and so evangelization, and that flowers in a community ordered by charity awaiting the Lord's return. That, by any fair stretch of the word, is a "synthetic" view.

Doubtless, not everything is said in one paragraph of the *Decree*. The subsequent unfolding of the text, however, is organically related to this second paragraph. In the second part of the *Decree*, the ministry of priests, paragraphs 4 to 6 take up the *munera* of preaching, sanctifying, and shepherding mentioned in 2.c, and keeping the order of the *munera* among one another worked out in 2.d. Paragraphs 7, 8, and 9 develop the priest's relations to bishop, other priests, and faithful, spelling out the ecclesial references of 2.b.

The third part of the *Decree*, the life of priests, takes as its point of departure the consecration of priests, first mentioned in 2.b; according to number 13, moreover, the holiness of priests is a holiness learned and lived within the discharge of the *munera* mentioned in 2.c. The unity and harmony of the life of priests, number 14, finds adumbration in the last lines of 2.e. In number 15, the priest finds example of the virtues of humility and obedience in the Christ he represents, which harks back to 2.c. Last, in number 16, celibacy shows the priest as friend of the bridegroom, betrothing the faithful to Christ, just as in 2.d the ministry of priests is to lead the faithful to the banquet of the Lamb, which we can also characterize as the *wedding* banquet of the Lamb.

Vetera in Novis: The Doctrinal Novelty of Paragraph 2

The text of paragraph 2 is novel relative to previous magisterial teaching by its combination of a theology of mission and consecration, of word and sacrament, by the very comprehensiveness of the framework in which it

---

[70] Ibid., 317.

inserts priesthood, and in the detail with which it lists the priest's relations to others. Still, none of this touches its most important novelty, a novelty that was not seen at the time for what it was and that, if we think it good, must be attributed solely to the accidents of the composition of the text, which is to say, solely to the providence of God and the guidance of the Holy Spirit, which, as we believe, governed the proceedings of the council.

Taking up *Lumen Gentium* 28 for the text of the second paragraph of *Presbyterorum Ordinis* meant also, indirectly but more basically, taking up *Lumen Gentium* 21. For *Lumen Gentium* understands priests in the first instance as helpers of the bishops such that priests are of the same kind of minister as are bishops, but of lesser degree. If, however, priests are to be understood ecclesiologically in relation to bishops, then the definition of the priesthood and of priestly ministry follows from that of episcopal office and ministry.[71]

In the formation of *Lumen Gentium* 21, which asserts the sacramentality of episcopal ordination, there is repeated the teaching of Trent that ordination imparts a character.[72] And in accord with the standard understanding of the effect of orders and the permanence of the character, the preliminary draft asserted that a bishop could not be reduced to the lay state nor become again a simple priest. The fathers, however, desired a positive expression of the effect of the sacrament. Responding to this wish, the Doctrinal Commission offered in the place of the negative characterization of the effect of ordination to say that, in virtue of ordination, grace was given, and a character imparted in such wise that bishops take the place of Christ himself, and represent him or act *in eius persona* as teacher, shepherd, and priest.

The text means to connect ordination with all three *munera* or offices—teaching, ruling, sanctifying. Ordination equips a bishop, as the ancient ordinals witness, for all three *ministeria*, for the whole and every part of his properly episcopal ministry. In this way, the text implies the unity of the three powers. Ordination gives the radical wherewithal for all, for each is essential to episcopal functioning and is a non-alienable part of episcopacy.

The authors of the text have therefore invoked a quite traditional phrase, *in persona Christi*, by which to express the effect of orders for all three functions. In doing so, however, they extend the range of this phrase and modify its prior usage. If they are not saying something new, they are saying the old in a new and quite succinct and powerful form. For St. Thomas, for

---

[71] For commentary on *Lumen Gentium* 28, see Jean Giblet, "I presbiteri collaboratori dell'ordine episcopale," in *La Chiesa del Vaticano II*, ed. Guilherme Baraúna (Florence: Vallecchi, 1965), 872–95.

[72] For what follows see Guy Mansini, "Sacerdotal Character at Vatican II," in this volume.

example, the priest or bishop acts *in persona Christi* only when consecrating the Eucharistic elements.[73] *Mediator Dei,* less than twenty years before the council, respected this usage.

Lumen Gentium 28 itself, the text immediately in the background to *Presbyterorum Ordinis* 2, can seem to have fallen back to this older usage. Expressly, it speaks of the priest acting *in persona Christi* only in the sacrifice of the Mass, and its reference to *Mediator Dei* likewise takes us back to the old usage. Implicitly, however, *Lumen Gentium* 28 expands the sense of representing Christ to all three *munera.* This is clear from outside the text from the *relatio* of Henriquez Jimenez.[74] But also, the text itself implies it in several ways. First, by the power of the sacrament of orders, priests are consecrated "in the image of Christ *(ad imaginem Christi),* the high and eternal priest . . . to preach the Gospel and pasture the faithful and celebrate divine worship." But doing something to or in or after the image of Christ is representing him in doing it, and representing Christ is acting in his person. Second, sharing "in the *munus* of Christ the one mediator" for evangelizing and exercising "the *munus* of Christ the shepherd and head" in pastoral care are functionally equivalent in the text to "acting in the person of Christ" as in the Eucharistic cult.[75] The text could as well have said for the last that the priest shares in the *munus* of Christ the Priest, and for the former that he acts in the person of Christ the Mediator and Shepherd.

Presbyterorum Ordinis, therefore, follows *Lumen Gentium* 28 in giving *in persona Christi* a broader sense for priests, as *Lumen Gentium* 21 does for bishops, and it did so from the first draft, with very general approval of the fathers. It follows number 28 also in saying expressly, as number 21 did not, that the representation is of Christ as *Head* of the Church, an uncontested and unremarked precision the importance of which emerged only later.[76]

At *Presbyterorum Ordinis* 2, it is true, where it is a matter of the priest acting *in persona Christi* for all his presbyteral functioning, the council appeals to *Lumen Gentium* 10, which asserts the priest so acts only in the Eucharist. And at number 6, speaking of the pastoral or ruling function of the priest, the council harks back to *Lumen Gentium* 28, which has the phrase again in a Eucharistic context, and which itself appeals to *Mediator*

---

73 *ST* III, q. 78, a. 1, c.

74 *AS* III/2:213: "Munus quo sacerdos in persona Christi agit *speciatim* [italics added] in cultu Eucharistico exhibetur verbis Tridentini et Encyclicae *Mediator Dei* confirmatur; sed etiam participatio muneris sacerdotalis Christi in praedicatione verbi, in administratione sacramentorum, necnon in oratione et exemplo et, in gernere, in pascendo grege apparet." The participation in the other two *munera,* it seems, could also be expressed by saying the priest acts in the person of Christ.

75 *Presbyterorum Ordinis* 6, on the shepherding role of the priest, practically quotes this line of *Lumen Gentium* 28 verbatim.

76 See *Mediator Dei* 40, 84.

Dei, correctly and narrowly, for this point. But it is quite certain that *Presbyterorum Ordinis* means to assert that the priest acts in the person of Christ, and indeed in the person of Christ the Head, in discharging all three functions. This is clear from the context, for 2.c speaks of building up (i.e., gathering by teaching), sanctifying, and ruling the body of Christ. It is also clear from the *Acta.* The second draft has it in number 2 that the priest acts *in persona Christi* expressly for all three *munera.* To a *modus* after the third draft, which drops the express listing of all three, requesting the restoration of the earlier text, the answer is that the text evidently enough supposes that all three are in question. The Commission answers that "presbyters are always said to share in the *munera* of the Bishops, which indeed are the ones mentioned."[77] So we are to understand that they share them as to exercise them all, as do the bishops, in the person of Christ.

Furthermore, as *Mediator Dei* spoke of the priest acting in the person of Christ the *Head* in sanctifying, in offering the sacrifice of the Mass, so the council at *Presbyterorum Ordinis* 2 means that for all three functions, the priest acts in the person of Christ the Head.[78] The representation, in each function, is of Christ precisely in his distinction from the Church his body, "facing" the Church, as we might put it.[79] Where the *munera* are named, the representation of Christ in distinction from the Church goes without saying. The teacher is not one of the taught; the shepherd is not one of the sheep; and the high priest enters into the sanctuary alone. Paragraph 2 does not at this point name the *munera*, however, and so the specification of Christ as Head is suitable. While *Presbyterorum Ordinis* does not reprove the denial of this nor insist that this representation is true exclusively of the priest, in keeping with the positive and irenic tone of the entire production of the council, *Mediator Dei* does.[80]

It should be noted that spokesmen for both of the "two views" of Marty's *relatio* strongly approved speaking of the priest acting in the person of Christ for all three *munera.*[81] For partisans of the theology of mission, this way of

---

[77] *AS* IV/7:121.

[78] See also no. 6 and no. 12 of the *Decree.*

[79] Which is how *Pastores Dabo Vobis* puts it; see below.

[80] See no. 84: "[W]e deem it necessary to recall that the priest acts for the people only because he represents Jesus Christ insofar as *[quatenus]* He is Head of all His members. . . . The people, on the other hand, since they in no sense *[nulla ratione]* represent the divine Redeemer and are not mediator between themselves and God can in no way possess the sacerdotal power."

[81] Cardinal Döpfner, *AS* IV/4:874; Bishop de Cambourg, App 657; Cardinal Suenens, 787, 788; and from the other side, Bishop Ndongmo, *AS* IV/5:67–68; Archbishop Perini, *AS* App., 671; commenting on no. 14, the unity of priestly life, Perini writes: "[A]ll things become one if the Presbyter, illumined and led by a *supernatural vision of things, acts always in the Person of Christ*: namely, if thinking,

speaking seems to break the hold of the cult on the priesthood, to break open its hitherto exclusive connection to the Eucharist and sanctification. The others, too, liked this high view of priesthood. It extends the way of expressing the priest's role in the cult to expressing his functioning in whatever he does, and with the same weighty accent; it ties whatever the priest does, and not just in "saying Mass," to the presence, the action—the person—of Christ himself. Both sides came together on the high ground—that is, on a high view of the priesthood. Both sides came together, and this is a sign and reminder that in the council, the mind of the whole Church comes to expression.[82] On the other hand, it is to be denied that it is a new view relative to the tradition as a whole. "Petrus baptizat, hic [Christus] est qui baptizat," St. Augustine says; and again, "Nos Christum praedicamus . . . Christus autem Christum praedicat, quia seipsum praedicat."[83]

What is new in the synthesis of number 2, then, is the enlargement of the reference of acting in the person of Christ the Head as compared with prior, especially Thomist, usage. Now, not just in quoting the words of institution (as for St. Thomas, *Mediator Dei, Lumen Gentium* 28, and *Presbyterorum Ordinis* 5), but for all three *munera*, the priest represents Christ. This makes the entire ministry of the priest something that before was by the customary language said usually only of his activity in the sanctuary. It heightens the worth—or our appreciation of the worth—of the other functions. Is this part of the mission view or cultic view of the priest? It transcends both, and seems to be a happy accident of the production of the text. It takes what once was used to express the priest's agency in the Eucharist and makes it express his whole ministry and activity. This occurs in number 12 even more strongly, perhaps, where priests, acting in the person of Christ, are said also to be "the living instruments of Christ the eternal priest" and to take the place of Christ.

---

if preaching, if administering Holy Things, if visiting the sick, if comforting the afflicted and poor, if praying, if celebrating Mass: he feels in himself, as in the living instrument of Christ, Christ thinking, preaching, exercising charity, praying, offering sacrifice to the Father." See also the bishops of Argentina and France, *AS* IV/5:528, who suggest saying the priest acts "in the name of Christ," since acting "in the person of Christ" is more connected with the Eucharist; and Archbishop de Provenchères, IV/5:308, who says that priests are to preserve the "immediate and constant sacramental presence of Christ, Head and Shepherd, for all the faithful."

82 See Benoît-Dominique de La Soujeole, "En toute chose voir l'unité," in *Ordo Sapientiae et Amoris: Hommage au Professeur Jean-Pierre Torrell*, ed. Carlos-Josaphat Pinto De Oliveira (Fribourg: Éditions Universitaires Fribourg Suisse, 1993), 435–67, at 438.

83 *In Ioannem*, 6.7; 47.3. See the citations at note 22 of *Lumen Gentium* 21, and see Walter Kasper, "Priestly Office," in *Leadership in the Church*, trans. Brian McNeil (New York: Herder, 2003), 45–75, and the manifestation of the necessarily representative character of apostolic office in Scripture, 49–55.

Because the priest represents Christ in his entire ministerial activity, the objective call to a complete holiness of life that priesthood makes becomes obvious, as in number 12, and the prosecution of this holiness within the discharge of the *munera* also becomes evident, as with number 13, and yet the unity of priestly life and holiness in Christ, since his duties have all of them to do with the actions and representation of Christ, also follows naturally in the text at number 14.

It is wonderful that an expression of such power and such unexpected consequence for the future should be produced as it were almost by accident, and yet, at the time, find universal approval. As to unforeseen consequence, yes, the synthesis of paragraph 2, and especially this happy twist of fate in the production of the text whereby the priest represents Christ generally in his ministry and not just at the altar—this synthesis, newly expressed, of ancient tradition, medieval and Tridentine doctrinal precision, and Baroque piety provided the wherewithal to meet postconciliar challenges to the Church's understanding and practice.

This should not surprise us. As Jean Frisque remarks, "[C]arried along as it was by the dynamism of the council, a document like our *Decree* in some measure escapes from its redactors; it no longer belongs to them."[84] Because the council expresses the mind of the whole Church, and does so under the inspiration of the Holy Spirit, we can speak with Benoît-Dominique de La Soujeole of a certain "openness" of the conciliar teaching, by which he means the doctrinal richness "contained in the documents could not have been clearly—at least explicitly—present to the mind of the fathers and could not appear but much later."[85] This we hope to show in Part II of this essay.

Meeting Postconciliar Challenges

Hardly was the council concluded than the contestation of the Catholic priesthood began.[86] To many, the council itself seemed to give impetus to this movement.[87] Did it not recognize the positive elements of truth and

---

[84] Frisque, "Histoire," 133.
[85] De La Soujeole, "En toute chose voir l'unité," 443; he finds an example of this is the conciliar teaching on the sacramentality of the Church.
[86] See already in 1971 the list of troubles in the "Description of the Situation" in the statement of the Synod of Bishops on the ministerial priesthood, *Ultimis Temporibus*. This can be found in *Vatican Council II: More Postconciliar Documents*, ed. Austin Flannery (Collegeville, MN: Liturgical Press, 1982), 672–94. The date given there, 1967, is incorrect.
[87] Kasper, "Priestly Office," 46: "one cause of the present difficulties [about priests and priesthood] results from theological confusions and distortions. More precisely, it is

holiness in the Protestant churches, and positively express a desire for Church unity? But then, what did this say about the possibilities of Church order? And the council seemed to privilege the local, particular Church in a way hitherto unknown in modern magisterial teaching, both by the renewal of the theology of the episcopate (*Lumen Gentium* 20ff.) and by a first step into the ecclesiology of communion (*Lumen Gentium* 26). What did this say about the local Church's capacity to restructure Church order? Furthermore, the theology of the laity expounded by the council seemed to many a sort of invitation to obscure the distinction between the priesthoods of laity and orders, priesthoods that elsewhere the council declared distinct in kind. How could an egalitarian Church of the People of God be at the same time a hierarchical Church? And in the desire of the council to make Scripture a more immediately animating principle of theology, some read an invitation to read the Scriptures as read by liberal Protestantism, that is, in the absence of the Rule of Faith, independently of the patristic tradition of Church order and liturgy, and to read each book extra-canonically, independently of the others. In this way, the council, or at least its upshot, seemed to countenance every criticism of the priesthood made by the Reformers.[88] Moreover, where one hermeneutical norm, the Rule of Faith, is taken away, another will replace it. Postconciliar readings both of Scripture and of the council tended more and more to be postmodern readings, which meant that they brought with them the suspicion that all distinction and all discriminations are nothing but concealments of the will to power. In some treatments of the Catholic priesthood after the council, one discerns the influence of Nietzsche more than of any reformer or historian.[89]

After the council, the two conceptions noted by Marty became the opposition of Protestant and Catholic readings for the New Testament on ministry. Many who championed the ministry of the word and a theology

---

rooted in a superficial and one-sided reception of the ecclesiology of the Second Vatican Council."

[88] See the Congregation for the Doctrine of the Faith, "Notifikation bezüglich einiger Veröffentlichungen von Professor Dr. Reinhard Meßner" (Notification on some publications of Professor Dr. Reinhard Meßner), November 30, 2000, on Meßner's reconstruction of the Church order of "early Catholicism": "Neu ist allenfalls, daß diese klassische Vision protestantischer Dogmengeschichtsschreibung hier als katholische Theologie vorgetragen . . . wird" ("what is new is the fact that this classical vision of Protestant history of dogma is presented here as Catholic theology"). For Ratzinger, the Protestant interpretation of Christian ministry and worship returns the Church to the synagogue; see "Life and Ministry of Priests."

[89] This was especially true in some of the more shrill accusations formulated apropos the ordination of women and celibacy. See, for example, the essays in *The Non-Ordination of Women and the Politics of Power* (*Concilium*, 1999/3), ed. Elisabeth Schüssler Fiorenza and Hermann Häring (London: SCM Press, 1999).

of mission opted for an increasingly Protestant, even Congregationalist, view of ecclesial office, and the conciliar text was characterized as including undigested—by which it was meant still unfortunately unrepudiated—cultic and sacral elements in its view.[90] Where was the legacy of the council with regard to priesthood to be found?

We will take up three issues. First, there is the complex question of apostolicity, Eucharistic presidency, and the relation of the priest to the community. Second, there is the question of the priest's representation of Christ. Third, there is celibacy.[91]

Apostolicity and History, Eucharist and Presidency, Relation to Community

The issues here can be put narrowly or broadly. Narrowly, the questions are whether succession of officers is necessarily included in the apostolicity of the Church, and whether presbyteral ordination is a necessary condition of Eucharistic presidency. Broadly, the issue is whether and how the priest's relation to the community is built into the very understanding of the nature of priesthood.

The issue of what is comprised in the reality of apostolic succession emerged very quickly after the council. A historical-critical reading of the New Testament where tradition was bracketed produced a sort of dehistoricized version of apostolic ministry. And this in turn set the stage for reconceiving and refashioning Roman Catholic Church order. By a dehistoricized view, we mean a view according to which apostolicity is first and fundamentally predicated of the Church as a whole, but within which there is no structure guaranteeing apostolicity that the Church herself, independently of and subsequently to Christ, is not responsible for. There is no question, in other words, of a dominical institution of and historical succession in office. This view was propounded by Hans Küng, who entertained the possibility

---

90 See the already cited article of Christian Duquoc, and in the same vein, the concluding remarks of Eugene C. Bianchi and Rosemary Radford Ruether in *A Democratic Catholic Church: The Reconstruction of Roman Catholicism*, ed. Bianchi and Ruether (New York: Crossroad, 1993), 247–60. More recently, see Peter Hünermann, "A Half-Hearted Reform: The Decree on the Ministry and Life of Priests," in *The History of Vatican II*, vol. 5, ed. Giuseppe Alberigo and Joseph Komonchak, trans. Matthew J. O'Connell (Leuven: Peeters, 2006) 457–65. Hünermann believes that the *Decree*'s presentation of the essence of priesthood does not correspond to that of *Lumen Gentium*.

91 Even so we do not address all things; for instance, proposals that in practice divorce pastoral and sacramental ministry, or proposals for part-time and temporary priests after the council. For these last, see Hans Küng, *Why Priests? A Proposal for a New Church Ministry* (New York: Doubleday, 1972), 75–82. The proposal Küng makes in the book as a whole is to abolish the priesthood.

even now of a so-called charismatic Church order without benefit of the imposition of hands, and for whom pastoral ministry is just one "charism" among others.[92] It was the view also of Edward Schillebeeckx.[93] For Schillebeeckx, doctrine, not structures, were received from the apostles, and the manner of appointment to office is therefore not determinative of apostolicity. Whatever powers inhere in ecclesial office inhere first in the Church itself, and it is therefore always possible in extraordinary circumstances for the assembly of the people of God as such to erect offices and appoint the holders thereof, without prior approbation or sacramental consecration by previous office holders. Therefore, while doctrine must remain, structures are labile; as they were once upon a time the invention and arrangement of the Church, they remain to be refashioned and rearranged as pastoral necessity dictates. Thus, in spite of *Lumen Gentium* 18, we find a more or less Congregationalist attempt to reduce the principle of apostolic succession to identity of doctrine, to the Church's possession of the apostolic faith.

Closely connected with apostolicity is the question of the necessity of an ordained priest for the Eucharist, which Schillebeeckx raised under the title of the community's "right" to the Eucharist. If the community or local Church or congregation has such a right, it seems to follow that it therefore has also the competence to arrange for the exercise of that right. That means, in turn, that ministerial office is radically the construction of the Church, even the local Church. If the ministerial structure of the Church is the construction of the Church, of the assembly, then no minister has any capacity to act as a minister that does not inhere originally in the assembly. Therefore every assembly has the wherewithal to make the Eucharist of itself and to make those presidents of the Eucharistic assembly it needs.

The response to the questions of these first two issues appears in the Letter of the Congregation for the Doctrine of the Faith, *Sacerdotium Ministeriale* of 1983.[94] It is an answer in the strength of council, not just by appeal to the "power" of sacerdotal character, that is, not just by appeal to Trent. Rather, succession is apprehended as the Christological and so historical moment of mission and therefore also of the Eucharist and the continuing and visible Christological headship of the Church. Section 2.b, on

[92] Hans Küng, "What is the Essence of Apostolic Succession?" in *Apostolic Succession: Rethinking a Barrier to Unity*, ed. Hans Küng in *Concilium*, vol. 34 (New York: Paulist, 1968), 28–35; see also his *The Church* (New York: Sheed and Ward, 1968), 354–59.

[93] Edward Schillebeeckx, *Ministry: A Case for Change* (London: SCM Press, 1981), 33–37.

[94] "The Minister of the Eucharist," *Origins* 13 (September 15, 1983): 230–33. For the Latin original see *Sacerdotium ministeriale*, www.vatican.va/roman_curia/congregations/cfaith/doc_sac index.htm (accessed October 20, 2006).

apostolicity, sends the reader to Trent and to *Lumen Gentium* 20, and section 4.b, on the presidency of the Eucharist, refers us to *Lumen Gentium* 21 and *Presbyterorum Ordinis* 2. The modest and obvious point here is that the conciliar texts provide the basis for the rejection of such views as Küng's and Schillebeeckx's, not their starting point.[95]

That the council could be seen as their starting point, however, brings us to the broader context, a reformulation of the "two views." Schillebeeckx's concern is to understand ministry, including priestly ministry, in terms of the community's need, calling, and institution rather than in terms of one minister's empowerment of another through the rite of ordination. The two views are supposed to exclude one another. In the first, a community of apostolic faith needs pastoral leadership, which also suitably includes presiding at the Eucharistic assembly, and so there are priests; in the second, a hierarch ordains a priest, giving him power over the Eucharist, and therefore also over the community whose assembly the celebration of the Eucharist evokes. In the first, the priest says Mass because he is pastor of the community; in the second, he rules the community because he has the sacramental power to say Mass.[96] The first view Schillebeeckx sees in the first millennium of the Church, and in the prohibition of absolute ordinations. The second he sees in the theology of priestly character that developed especially in the thirteenth century and whose spirituality is found developed in the French School.[97] Now, did not the council begin a break with the second view? By reinserting priestly ministry into a fuller ecclesiological framework, by taking express note of the community to whom the priest is sent, by speaking of *munera* and *ministeria* rather than *potestates*, and by locating the foundation of jurisdiction in ordination, did it not take a first step in distancing the Church from the legitimacy of absolute ordination?[98]

The view of *Presbyterorum Ordinis* underlying Schillebeeckx's remarks is once again that the *Decree* is incoherent, that it took some steps in the direction of a ministry returned to the local Church, but did not complete the journey. This is clear even in one of his first comments on the *Decree*, in which he emphasizes the "pastoral" orientation of priesthood, obliquely refers to the issue of absolute ordinations, and regards the council as having desacralized the priest, taking from him the "aura of mystery" and

---

[95] See the remarks on Schillebeeckx of Herranz Casado, "The Image of the Priest."

[96] See Yves Congar, in his Préface to B.-D. Marliangeas, *Clés pour une théologie du ministère: In persona Christi, In persona Ecclesiae* (Paris: Beachesne, 1978), 13.

[97] For the "modern view" of the priest, see *Ministry,* 58–65, and for a summary statement of Schillebeeckx's view of the history, 66–74. The history is fuller and more nuanced in his subsequent *The Church with a Human Face: A New and Expanded Theology of Ministry* (New York: Crossroad, 1987).

[98] *Ministry,* 67; *Church,* 205.

regarding him as "a real human being."[99] Schillebeeckx's view has been very influential, especially in the United States.[100]

One can say that Schillebeeckx's view breaks the synthesis so artfully constructed by the council. It is not, however, that he takes one of the "two views" at the council, the "mission" view, and makes that architectonic. Schillebeeckx is faithful to neither of the views in play at the council.

We wish to say that the priest is sent empowered to say Mass, yes. He is sent by Christ, through the bishop, by ordination. He is sent to and for the sake of a community. Both things must be true. It is because he can say Mass that he rules the community, and it is because he rules the community that he can say Mass. There is no full and fully fit pastor of a parish who cannot say Mass. Also, there is no one who can say Mass (ordinarily speaking, and setting aside the question of religious priests) who does not have pastoral care of a community of faithful. But the community to whom he is sent and for whom he presides at Mass does not give him the wherewithal—the power— to represent Christ and act in his person in saying Mass. And the Lord who makes a man a priest through ordination at the hands of a bishop does not send him to say Mass in a vacuum, he does not send the man to *himself* (which is not to deny the value of Mass said without a congregation).

It is just here that the issue of the origin of apostolic ministry arises. For Schillebeeckx, an apostolic community, that is, a community of apostolic faith living by the Spirit, is the sufficient empowering principle of apostolic office. As already indicated, this stance undervalues the principle of succession in office, of historical connection to the apostolic age and to Christ. In addition, it misidentifies the needs of the community to whom the priest is sent. What the community needs is precisely an apostolic ministry, which is to say, a ministry from outside of itself. Just as salvation is from *extra nos*, just as grace is not produced by nature, just as the Gospel word is not the word that comes from within our heart but enters through the ears, so also the ministry the Church needs is a ministry that comes to it from above and from outside. It is just this that Schillebeeckx denies when he denies a "direct" Christological foundation for priestly ministry.[101] The candidate for such ministry may come from the community, but the ministry does not come from the community, even from a community instinct with the Holy Spirit.[102]

---

[99] Edward Schillebeeckx, *The Real Achievement of Vatican II* (New York: Herder & Herder, 1967), 42–43.

[100] See, for instance, Paul Philibert, "Issues for a Theology of Priesthood: A Status Report," in *The Theology of the Priesthood*, ed. Donald Goergen and Ann Garrido (Collegeville, MN: Liturgical Press, 2000), 1–42, at 24–24 and 38–40.

[101] *Ministry*, 67; *Church*, 206.

[102] See John Paul II, *Pastores Dabo Vobis* 16.

It is not, then, as if Schillebeeckx has developed or completed one of the views at the council at the expense of the other; he has abandoned both views. What is true of *Presbyterorum Ordinis* is that it inserts the understanding of priestly ministry into ecclesiology, and into a network of relationality, whereby the priest is related at once to other priests (number 8), to bishops (number 7), and to the baptized faithful in both their pastoral need and their own ministerial competence (number 9). The development of these avenues, however, is to be found not in what amounts to a plea for the abolition of apostolic ministry, but in the even richer development of the relations the priest is the center of and an ever more express realization of the Church, the context of the priest, as mystery, communion, and mission. These things, however, are in *Pastores Dabo Vobis* 12.

Representation and Gender

Perhaps the most contentious of the issues about ministry and orders troubling the postconciliar Church was the question of the ordination of women, where the issue was fought especially on the ground of the priestly representation of Christ.[103] What is the relation of priestly speaking in the person of the Church and priestly speaking in the person of Christ? *Inter Insigniores,* the 1976 statement of the Congregation for Doctrine of the Faith on the inability of women to be ordained, appeals to the second and thirteenth paragraphs of *Presbyterorum Ordinis,*[104] with its strong emphasis on the priestly representation of Christ (on acting in his person, especially in the Eucharist), in order to draw the conclusion that only men and not women can in the wholeness of their personal reality, which of course includes bodiliness, successfully carry out this representation of Christ.

In fact, hardly were the decrees of the council published before the question of the order and relation of the representations, ecclesial and Christological, was raised. In the highly influential Herder commentary on the documents of the council, Wulf wants the priest's priesthood to be a function of the priesthood of the Church. As already noted, he thinks the characterization of the priest in number 2, facing the Church as representing Christ the Head, is "one-sided."[105] The text forgets that the priesthood of priests represents the priesthood of the Church, and is "its organ of fulfillment." Further, while the powers of the priest are "given by Christ," they are "primarily powers of the Church."[106]

---

[103] That is, setting aside such considerations as dominical intention, the alleged cultural conditioning of the mind of Christ and the New Testament hagiographers, subsequent Church history, etc.

[104] There is appeal also to *Lumen Gentium* 10 and 28, and *Sacrosanctum Concilium* 33.

[105] "Commentary," 222.

[106] Ibid., 221.

A host of theologians tried their hand at so describing things as to counter the argument of *Inter Insigniores*. Edward Kilmartin has it that the priest represents the faith of the Church, and consequently Christ.[107] Similarly, Hervé Legrand holds that the priest's representation of Christ is indirect, through first representing the Church.[108] To which it might be replied that, although the priest exercises the faith he shares with the Church and, in the sacraments, with the assembly, for that very reason he need not represent either the Church or its faith as though they were absent things. It is rather Christ, ascended to heaven, who needs palpable representation in the Eucharist. David Power argued that the priest represents both Christ and the Church in the sacrament equally immediately[109] In this reconstruction, however, the assembly ends up as the instrument of consecration,[110] and the body signified by the consecrated elements is the body of the assembly.[111] In a similar way, Susan Wood has it that the priest represents Christ only in that he represents the *totus Christus*, Christ and the Church.[112] Wood thinks that since to say "head" makes us think also of "body," the priest in representing Christ the Head must also by that fact represent the body, as if one cannot say "head" without also saying "body." Indeed, she seems to make headship mean nothing more than representing the *body*.[113]

Such liturgical and sacramental convolutions urge a return to the simplicity with which *Inter Insigniores* 5 reads *Presbyterorum Ordinis* 2.[114] By speaking of the priest acting in the person of Christ the *Head, Presbytero-*

---

[107] Edward Kilmartin, "Apostolic Office: Sacrament of Christ," *Theological Studies* 36 (1975): 243–64; and repeating Kilmartin's view, see also Mary Schaefer, "Forum: Ordaining Women," *Worship* 63 (1989): 467–71, at 469.

[108] Hervé Legrand, "*Traditio perpetuo servata?* The Non-Ordination of Women: Tradition or Simply an Historical Fact?" *Worship* 65 (1991): 482–508, at 503–4.

[109] David Power, "Representing Christ in Community and Sacrament," in *Being a Priest Today* (Collegeville, MN: Liturgical Press, 1992), 97–123.

[110] Ibid., 101.

[111] Ibid., 104–10, 116.

[112] Susan Wood, "Priestly Identity: Sacrament of the Ecclesial Community," *Worship* 69 (1995): 109–27. See the replies of Sara Butler, "Priestly Identity: 'Sacrament' of Christ the Head,'" *Worship* 70 (1996): 290–306, Lawrence J. Welch, "Priestly Identity Reconsidered," *Worship* 70 (1996): 307–18, and his "For the Church and within the Church: Priestly Representation," *The Thomist* 65 (October 2001): 613–37.

[113] Wood, "Priestly Identity," 114–15.

[114] For further convolutions, see Dennis Ferrara, for whom the priest says the consecratory words both in the person of Christ and in the person of the Church; see his "Representation or Self-Effacement? The Axiom *In Persona Christi* in St. Thomas and the Magisterium," *Theological Studies* 55 (1994): 195–224, and "*In Persona Christi:* Towards a Second Naïveté," *Theological Studies* 57 (1996): 65–88, and the reply of G. Mansini, "Representation and Agency in the Eucharist," in this volume.

rum Ordinis means to say that the priest acts in the person or name of the Church only because he first acts in the person of Christ. This would reflect the original deployment of the language of headship in the Letter to the Ephesians and the Letter to the Colossians.[115] Is this reading of *Inter Insigniores* faithful to the conciliar decree itself?[116]

Presbyterorum Ordinis certainly seems to incline to the view of *Inter Insigniores* by speaking first and foundationally of the priest as representing Christ; the priest as representing the Church, acting in her name, is added only at the last, not before the final text, and toward the end of paragraph 2, in 2.d. Paragraph 2.a speaks of the mission of the whole Church; 2.b, however, speaks on the contrary of ministers, and does so quite consciously as of something distinct from the mission of the Church as such (see the introductory *vero*), in the line of Christ's own being sent and his sending, the line from Father, to incarnate Son, to apostle, to bishop and priest. Priests are therefore ministers of Christ *and not of the Church.* This is expressly the understanding of the text publicly stated at the council, just prior to the adoption of the final text.[117] On this basis, of course, priests act for and in the name of the Church. But as ministers of Christ they are instruments of Christ, not of the Church.[118]

Again, *Presbyterorum Ordinis* prepares for the position of *Inter Insigniores* by noting in number 2 that since the priestly mission is a mission from Christ (2.b), it therefore is conferred by a special sacrament, which, of course,

---

[115] This is so because the life and growth of the body is, for these letters, derived from the head. Heinrich Schlier, commenting on the term *kephale* in Eph 1:22f; 4:14; 5:23; Col 1:18; 2:10; 2:19, observes that Christ is presented as Head of the Church "in the sense that from this Head the body grows up to this Head." Moreover: "In this unity of Christ and the Church the Headship of Christ is manifested in the fact that He directs the growth of the body to Himself. The kephale determines not merely the being of the body but also the fulfilment of its life. . . . He is the effective "whence" of the activity of the body whereby it edifies itself though gifts given to its members. As the kephale He is thus the concrete principle of the bodily growth of the Church. He is the arche, Col 1:18." See Heinrich Schlier, s.v. "kephale," *Theological Dictionary of the New Testament*, vol. 3., ed. Gerhard Kittle, tr. Geoffrey W Bromiley (Grand Rapids, MI: Eerdmans,1964–1976), 680. See also Markus Barth, *Ephesians: Introduction, Translation and Commentary* (Garden City, NY: Doubleday, 1974), 190–91.

[116] This is also the reading of the *Catechism of the Catholic Church*, 1553.

[117] See the Response to Modus 35, *AS* IV/7:123–24: To the suggestion in 2.d that priests be said to act *ut Ecclesiae ministri* in joining the sacrifice of the faithful to the sacrifice of Christ, the Commission replied that the text already has it that priests act in the name of the Church, and that anyway, "presbyters act, not as ministers of the Church, but as ministers of Christ," with reference to *Lumen Gentium* 10.b and 28, where priests act *(agunt)* in the person of Christ.

[118] As in theory, the prime minister of England is the agent and instrument of the queen, not the people of England. This precision seems to rule out Power's view of things.

like all the sacraments, is the action of Christ, and by construing the mission in 2.c as a mission to the "nations" so that the people of God may be assembled. The priestly mission must be seen, therefore, as mission *to* the Church, not *from* the Church, which it is rather the function of the mission to constitute. Even apart from the final *relatio*, therefore, the text itself substantially answers the question as to priority of the representations.

In other words, *Presbyterorum Ordinis* simply presupposes the position of *Mediator Dei* but without drawing attention to the position the Church has consistently rejected; *Mediator Dei* for its part did not fail to do, appealing to the Council of Trent, the Decree on Orders, chapter 4. So, in paragraph 83 of *Mediator Dei*, the idea that the "priest acts in virtue of an office committed to him by the community"—which is only another way of saying that the priest represents first the community and only so Christ—is reproved; in paragraph 84, we read that "the priest acts for the people only because he represents Jesus Christ insofar as *[quatenus]* Christ is Head of all his members and offers himself in their stead."[119]

Presbyterorum Ordinis, in fact, includes the remarkable argument of paragraph 93 of *Mediator Dei*, and does so in 2.d, only without explicit reference to *Mediator Dei*, which has it that the people offer the sacrifice of the Mass "by the hands of the priest," and according to which this is evident "from the fact that the minister at the altar . . . represents Christ, the Head of the Mystical Body." The people offer, but not because like the priest they perform the rite. Were that true, they would not need the priest to represent them, and, were that true, and they did not need the priest to act for them because able to act on their own here, then the priest could indeed represent the people independently of representing Christ. But no, the people offer because they "unite their hearts in praise, impetration, expiation and thanksgiving with the prayers or intention of the priest, even of the High Priest himself." *Presbyterorum Ordinis,* for its part, says exactly the same thing, but without the contrast to the counterposition. So, in paragraph 2.d, "the spiritual sacrifice of the faithful," in union with the sacrifice of Christ, is offered "by their [the priests'] hands" and "in the name of the whole Church" *(per manus eorum, nomine totius Ecclesiae)* And this happens, quite evidently and even though the text does not remark the error of reversing things, because, as the beginning of 2.d says, priests are "ministers of *Jesus Christ*"—that is, not ministers of the people—and ministers of Christ, again and quite evidently, on the ground of the conclusion of 2.c, that priests are in the first place conformed to *Christ* and act in *his* person.

---

[119] See also paragraph 40: The priesthood of the priest "is not a delegation from the people." And "prior to acting as representative of the community before the throne of God, the priest is the ambassador of the divine Redeemer." And note that the priest is an ambassador of Christ as Head.

In this light, we can take *Pastores Dabo Vobis* as the authentic development of *Presbyterorum Ordinis* 2 on the question of representation.[120] In number 12.d, the Holy Father notes that the priest's relation to Christ is "primary," and in numbers 13–15 he treats the priest's relation to Christ as Head and Shepherd as "fundamental." Paragraph 13 deals with Christ the Priest, who makes a priestly people; number 14 notes that the ordained priest exists for the sake of this priestly people; and number 15 tells us that the service he brings to it is precisely the representation of Christ the Priest. Then in number 16a, the priest's "sacramental representation" of Christ "serves as the basis and inspiration for the relation of the priest to the Church." Again, number 16.d speaks of "the relation of the priest to Jesus Christ and in him to his Church." That is, once again, the relation to the Church is a function of the first, foundational relation to Christ. This ordering of things, moreover, is a sign of the priority of the grace of Christ to the Church (number 16.f):

> And so the priest, on account of his very nature and sacramental mission, appears in the structure of the Church as a sign of the absolute priority and gratuity of that grace which is conferred by the risen Christ on the Church. And through the ministerial priesthood, the Church acquires an awareness of herself in faith, that she has her origin not from herself but from the grace of Christ in the Holy Spirit. The apostles and their successors—since they exercise an authority which is not their own—but one which has been received from Christ the head and shepherd, through their ministry occupy a position facing the Church. And this ministry is nothing but the sign, as well as the sacramental and visible continuation, of Christ himself, who faces the Church and world as the one author and source of an abiding and always new salvation, since he alone is himself the savior of the body.[121]

---

[120] See also the explanation of the priest's acting in the person of Christ in the Eucharist in the Holy Father's letter of 1980, *Dominicae Cenae,* which speaks in no. 8 of the priest's "sacramental identification" with Christ the High Priest.

[121] We have reworked the official English translation of this passage because it does not accurately convey the meaning of the Latin original. For example, the official translation renders "Apostoli autem eorumque successores, cum potestatem non suam sed a Christo Capite et Pastore receptam habeant, locum coram Ecclesia occupant" into: The apostles and their successors, inasmuch as they exercise an authority which comes to them from Christ, the head and shepherd, are placed with their ministry—*in the forefront of the Church*—(italics ours). "In the forefront" does not capture the sense of the Latin original *(locum coram Ecclesia occupant)*, which tries to express the nature of Christ's headship in distinction from the Church, and hence the ministry of the apostles and their successors as involving an authority that addresses or faces toward the Church. Elsewhere, at 16.b and 22.c the text has *erga Ecclesiam* as equivalent to *coram Ecclesia*, and *erga* is "toward" or "in relation to." "In the forefront"

This perception of the order of the relations, first to Christ, then to the Church, perfectly reflects theological tradition. So, for instance, for St. Thomas, the priesthood of Christ is treated before Christ's mediation in the *Tertia pars* of the *Summa*. For St. Thomas follows an explanatory order, where causes and principles are treated before effects and things derived from principles. Therefore, although both priesthood and mediation suggest a double relation, God to man and man to God, Thomas treats first the consequence of the hypostatic union for Christ's relation to the Father, and second of the consequence for his relation to us, for the very good reason that his relation (as a man) to the Father is the *foundation* of his relation to us. And the relationality of the ordained priesthood mirrors this structure, for the relation to Christ is first and the foundation of the priest's relation to the Church.

We see here also the strength of de La Soujeole's observation, comparing the conciliar texts to previous magisterial anathema, that positive statements of the council provide for less theological freedom than the negative, condemnatory ones typical of past conciliar canons.

> [P]ositive language is much more restrictive for the theologian. When the magisterium undertakes to formulate catholic doctrine for itself and on such or such a point, it deploys a certain number of affirmations bound together with one another, and that become the obligatory framework of theological reflection.[122]

Had the council been content to note the difference ordination makes in terms of incapacity to be reduced to the lay state or, for a bishop, to that of simple priest, there would have been no strong assertion of the priestly and episcopal action in the person of Christ. But in fact, the fathers chose to state the difference orders makes in terms of an episcopal and presbyteral capacity to act comprehensively and across the board, in all ministerial functions, in the person of Christ. And this plain and positive statement of the council is not well interpreted by the convolutions of relations and representations envisaged by those who wish to obscure the

---

suggests not an addressing or facing toward the Church but a position of facing with the Church and addressing something else. For the Latin original of this passage see *Acta Apostolicae Sedis* 84, (August 3, 1992): 682. For the official English translation see *Origins* 21 (April 16, 1992): 718–59. The official French translation available on the Vatican website has "face à l'Église."

122 452: "le langage positif est beaucoup plus exigeant pour le théologien. Quand le magistère entreprend d'énoncer la doctrine catholique pour ell-même sur tel ou tel point, il déploie un certain nombre d'affirmations liées entre elles et qui deviennent le cadre obligé de la réflexion théologique."

simple meaning, that the priest represents—immediately—Christ the Priest to the Church, and does so insofar as Christ is distinct from the Church, as is a head from a body, a bridegroom from a bride.

Celibacy

The priestly representation of Christ is at the same time a representation of Christ precisely as bridegroom relative to the Church. This, too, has been resisted in the postconciliar age for sake of the ordination of women. This, too, is present if not prominent, in *Presbyterorum Ordinis*, but in connection with another issue involving gender, celibacy.

For all that it recognizes the perfect legitimacy of the practice of the Eastern Church, paragraph 16 indicates the suitability of celibacy for priests in very strong terms. Celibacy "is at once a sign of and a stimulus for pastoral charity and a special source of spiritual fruitfulness in the world" (16.a). But these reasons are not foundational. The suitabilities of celibacy for priesthood are indeed both personal and pastoral, but the foundational one is the relation that celibacy gives the priest to Christ. Celibacy consecrates priests to Christ "in a new and exceptional manner," so that they may "more easily *(facilius)* cling to him with singleness of heart" (16.b), just as St. Paul told the Corinthians (1 Cor 7:34). Celibacy, a consecration to Christ, is thus suitable for a minister who is to be consecrated to Christ also by ordination; it links the priest in another way to the consecration for mission that is constitutive of priesthood.[123]

The council was most express about this foundational aspect of celibacy, which entered the text only before its final version. The Commission observed that it is not sufficient to say that celibacy is a sign, or testifies to the kingdom, and so on; rather, its value is first of all to unite the celibate to Christ, whence the sign value follows.[124]

Everything else is built on the foundation of consecration, beginning with pastoral effectiveness. The consecration of celibacy as of orders, in other words, is for mission, and being undividedly devoted to the Lord is at the same time being devoted to the things of the Lord, taking care of the Lord's people in his name. This is spelled out in the clauses following the fact of consecration, which detail, as it were, its intended result. Consecration is said

---

[123] For a brief history of the work leading up to paragraph 16, see Frisque, "Histoire," 172–76.

[124] *AS* IV/7:212, Response to Modus 21: "[T]he theological justification of celibacy cannot be adequately drawn uniquely or principally from its sign or witnessing value. The more profound reason for celibacy, rather, consists in a more intimate consecration to Christ, from which its value as a sign flows as a consequence." And the Commission directs us to *Lumen Gentium* 44.

in the first place to be for union with Christ, but immediately following we read also that celibate priests more freely *(liberius)* dedicate themselves to God *and* men, that they serve the kingdom and the work of human regeneration with greater ease *(expeditius)*, and that they are better fitted *(aptiores)* for paternity in Christ (see 1 Cor 4:15; 1 Thess 2:11), a paternity they accept more openly *(latius)*.

Last, "by this state" *(hoc modo)*, that is, by enacting their ministry in the aforesaid ways and so fulfilling the pastoral purpose of celibacy, priests are also a sign. First, they "make an open profession before men" of their undivided dedication (see again 1 Cor 7:34) to the task of betrothing Christians to Christ. The *first* meaning or sign value of celibacy the council mentions is therefore that it shows a will to consecrate oneself wholly to the task of betrothing Christians to Christ the Spouse (2 Cor 11:2), and in this way it is a sign of the eschatological wedding of the Lamb.[125] Also *(insuper)*, in a *second* way, celibacy is a sign of the eschaton, where there is no marriage or giving in marriage, as the Lord says in the gospel (Lk 20:35–36).[126]

In insisting that celibacy must in the first place and foundationally conduce to holiness, the council makes the structure of celibacy the structure of the priesthood itself: first Christ, conformity to Christ and union with Christ, and on that basis, ministry and sign value. Priestly celibacy has, as it were, the same structure as priestly identity. Just as the priest is consecrated to Christ for mission, and just as he represents Christ and on that basis represents the Church, so celibacy is also, in another way, consecration to Christ, and on that basis there is erected pastoral zeal and the further service of eschatological witness. Moreover, it is to be noted that the "better" way that celibacy is as compared to marriage is not simply a matter of being a clearer sign of eschatological blessing, but enters into the objective good of the person, holiness itself. It enters, doubtless, as a more efficacious means to the holiness of the kingdom of God; it is not that

---

[125] The text refers us to *Lumen Gentium* 42, where continence for the sake of the kingdom is a spur to and a source of spiritual fruitfulness, to no. 44, where observance of all the evangelical counsels bears witness to the eschaton and is an imitation of Christ, and to *Perfectae Caritatis* 12, where the chastity of religious leads to greater love of God and man, readies one for apostolic work, and is a sign of the wedding of the Lamb.

[126] The council's theology of celibacy is nicely reprised by Max Thurian in his "The Theological Basis for Priestly Celibacy," in *For Love Alone: Reflections on Priestly Celibacy* (Middlegreen, UK: St. Paul's, 1993), 53–65. This article is also available at www.vatican.va/roman_curia/congregations/cclergy/index_en_giub_presb.htm (last accessed October 24, 2006).

non-celibates are not called to perfection,[127] or do not cling to Christ; it is that the celibate "*more easily* clings to Him."[128]

Notwithstanding the careful avoidance of an appeal to ritual purity in expressing the value of celibacy, however, the postconciliar charge was that celibacy, like the restriction of orders to men, is a function of some kind of anti-body fear of sexuality, driving it underground, where it spoils and leads to perversion and immorality and abuse. So Nadine Foley, writing also after *Sacerdotalis Caelibatus* (1967) and the *Letter to Priests* of John Paul II (1979), says that "if a non-celibate state is inappropriate to sacred priesthood, despite the tradition of the eastern Church, then something definitive is being said about women and about marital relations with women. Women are unfit to approach the realm of the sacred."[129] At the same time, the very fear and repression of sexuality is said to be an ecclesiastical instrument of political power.[130]

---

[127] *Lumen Gentium* 40 "Thus it is evident to everyone, that all the faithful of Christ of whatever rank or status, are called to the fullness of the Christian life and to the perfection of charity."

[128] *Presbyterorum Ordinis* 16. The straightforward sense of 1 Cor 7 and of the tenth canon of the twenty-fourth session of the Council of Trent is therefore upheld. It would not be sufficient to say that celibacy or virginity is always better relative to marriage only insofar as it is a sign, as does Karl Rahner, "On the Evangelical Counsels," *Theological Investigations,* vol. 8, trans. David Bourke (New York: Herder & Herder, 1971), 133–67, at 147 and 163. The greater sign value of celibacy or virginity in comparison to marriage is of course to be recognized, as does for instance John Paul II, *The Theology of the Body: Human Love in the Divine Plan* (Boston: Pauline, 1997), 273–75 (general audience of April 7, 1982). But also, celibacy and virginity are to be affirmed as more expeditious as means to holiness as compared with marriage. For this traditional affirmation, beyond St. Augustine's reproof of Jovinian, see St. Thomas, *De perfectione spiritualis vitae,* cc. 6, 8. As to the traditional nature of the council's teaching here, see Avery Dulles, "Vatican II: The Myth and the Reality," *America* 188 (2003): 7–11, at 10. See too Pope John Paul II, *The Theology of the Body,* 274, where he speaks of a greater human fulfillment through continence, and 277, which denies that continence in itself constitutes a state of perfection, since of the counsels it is rather affirmed that they (only!) "*help* us to achieve a fuller charity" (italics added). At the same time, the pope therefore affirms that it is possible for someone who has not taken a vow or made a promise of perfect continence to reach a superior degree of perfection, whose measure is charity "in comparison to the person who lives in the state of perfection with a lesser degree of charity."

[129] Nadine Foley, "Celibacy in the Men's Church," in *Women in a Men's Church* (*Concilium,* vol. 134), ed. Virgil Elizondo and Norbert Greinacher (New York: Seabury, 1980), 26–39, at 35.

[130] See Ferdinand Menne, "Catholic Sexual Ethics and Gender Roles in the Church," *Women in a Men's Church,* 14–25, at 20, for whom celibacy is a constituent of the Church's political power. Menne relies in part on the work of Michel Foucault.

We think that it can be readily acknowledged that the distinction of the sexes as well as marriage and the renunciation of marriage enter inextricably and powerfully into both the structure of revelation and the polity—the Church—that revelation calls into being. The disagreements in evaluating this fact have to do more with whether one enters into its intelligibility with faith or not, with confidence in the Catholic tradition or not, and we cannot deal here with the enormous differences of hermeneutical, anthropological, and theological principle involved. Of course, while maleness is a necessity for the sacramental representation of Christ, celibacy is not. Nonetheless, it can be understood as furthering the likeness to Christ, and in this way linked to the capacity of the priest to act *in persona Christi*. This implication in *Presbyterorum Ordinis* is not in fact hard to unfold, if indeed it can be said to be merely implicit at all. Furthermore, as we shall see, the postconciliar reception of the council's reaffirmation of celibacy makes of it ever more clearly a form of the affirmation and salvation of sexuality, and in its male form, not its denial or repression.

We take for granted, first, that sexual differentiation is ordered to the nuptial gift of embodied persons; second, that this mutual gift is itself further ordered to fruitfulness; and third, that the ways in which men and women compass both these things are distinct. Adding the issue of likeness to Christ, there are therefore four themes to watch for in the *Decree* and its reception in subsequent magisterial statements and theology: likeness to Christ, the gift of the person, fruitfulness, maleness. Likeness to Christ is, ideally, to be verified in all the other three things, not just in maleness.

If we return to the text of the *Decree*, we can note that insofar as it is a sign of the eschaton, priestly celibacy is not proper to priests, but something shared with religious. But the *Decree* says also that the priest's celibacy enables and shows him to be dedicated wholly to the service of betrothing Christians to Christ (2 Cor 11:2). And this meaning of celibacy *is* something proper to priests. In this way, as a celibate, a man's fecundity is, as it were, turned over to that of Christ and the Church; one's bodily fecundity is suspended at the straightforward bodily level, and directed to spiritual fruitfulness, the spiritual fruitfulness to which priestly ministry is already dedicated.

The pursuit of spiritual fruitfulness is predicated, however, on the prior gift of self to the service of God and man, the devotion of self "with greater freedom" that paragraph 16 says celibacy enables; indeed, it is predicated on the prior consecration to Christ that is the first moment of priestly celibacy, according to the council.

In the priestly pursuit of spiritual fruitfulness, moreover, in priestly celibate service to God and man, the celibacy in question is that of a man, a male, and this is clear from the text the council adduces. For in presenting himself as betrothing the Corinthians to Christ, the apostle Paul puts himself in the place of the *paterfamilias*, the father of the bride, whose office it is to betroth his daughter to her husband.

Celibacy for the sake of this spiritual fruitfulness therefore likens one at least to Paul, the apostolic minister par excellence. More than that, however, it likens the priest to Christ. For if the apostolic minister is in the place of the father of the bride, who would the mother be? She would be the Church herself, as we read in Galatians of the Jerusalem above, our mother, whose spouse, quickening the womb that is the laver of baptism, is Christ. So, Paul is here, in a sort of transitive symbolic way, in the role of Christ, the spouse of the Church (Ephesians). That is, the apostolic minister functions in the place of Christ the Bridegroom, and this joins up with the idea of paternity in Christ, also evoked by the council (1 Thess 2:11; 1 Cor 4:15).[131]

Of course, it might be argued that to say that the priest acts in the person of Christ the Head, as the *Decree* does in number 2, is already to say that he acts in the person of Christ the Bridegroom. In Ephesians, after all, Christ the Head is both and inclusively head relative to the body, and head relative to the Church his bride.[132] In any case, both Paul VI and John Paul II complete the inference the *Decree* suggests. Paul VI:

> "Laid hold of by Christ" (Philippians 3:12) unto the complete abandonment of one's entire self to Him, the priest takes on a closer likeness to Christ, even in the love with which the eternal Priest has loved the Church His Body and offered Himself entirely for her sake, in order to make her a glorious, holy and immaculate Spouse (cf. Ephesians 5:25–27). The consecrated celibacy of the sacred ministers

---

[131] Ignace de la Potterie, "The Biblical Foundation of Priestly Celibacy," in *For Love Alone*, 13–30, esp. at 21–25, finds another connection of 2 Cor 11:2 to the priestly celibate representation of Christ. The phrase "one husband," referring to the Christ to whom Paul says he betroths the Corinthians as a pure virgin, is recalled in the pastorals by the requirement that apostolic ministers be "a husband of one wife" (1 Tim 3:2; 3:12; Tit 1:6). The requirement follows from the symbolic character of the minister, as representing Christ the Bridegroom, a character recognized by both St. Augustine and St. Thomas. The representation is more perfect, however, according as the minister practices continence, for the marital love of Christ and the Church is virginal. As de la Potterie puts it, "the representational role of the monogamous priesthood also entails the call to continence for the married minister, and consequently, for the unmarried ones, the call to celibacy" (24). De la Potterie's article can also be found at www.vatican.va/roman_curia/congregations/cclergy/index_en_giub_presb.htm (last accessed October 24, 2006).

[132] It can be argued that it is the nuptial relation of Christ to the Church that makes the Church his body; see John Paul II, the catecheses given in the general audiences of August 18 and 25, 1982, in *The Theology of the Body*, 312–18, and Sara Butler, "The Priest as the Sacrament of Christ the Bridegroom," *Worship* 66 (1992): 498–516, at 510, who appeals to these catecheses.

actually manifests the virginal love of Christ for the Church, and the virginal and supernatural fecundity of this marriage, by which the children of God are born, "not of blood, nor of the will of the flesh" (John 1:13).[133]

And this text of *Sacerdotalis Caelibatus* sends us to *Presbyterorum Ordinis* 16.[134] And here is John Paul II:

> The will of the Church [legislating celibacy for priests] finds its ultimate motivation in the link between celibacy and sacred ordination, which configures the priest to Jesus Christ the head and spouse of the Church. The Church, as the spouse of Jesus Christ, wishes to be loved by the priest in the total and exclusive manner in which Jesus Christ her head and spouse loved her. Priestly celibacy, then, is the gift of self in and with Christ to his Church and expresses the priest's service to the Church in and with the Lord.[135]

It is the celibacy of a man that the priest brings to the priesthood and the representation of Christ, and this is very important for the psychological and spiritual integrity of priestly life that the *Decree* addresses in paragraph 14.[136] If it is precisely as a man that the priest's celibacy is important, then he can say not that he is leaving his sexuality and his masculinity behind, but that he is bringing them forward and offering them for the service of a higher fruitfulness.[137] Given the symbolic register that their own virginity or celibacy sounds, women can say, "It is precisely because we are women that our virginity and celibacy is religiously important; it is our celibacy, womanly celibacy, that we bring to the representation of redeemed humanity, of the Church, of the bride." So also for men, celibacy is the redemption and consecration of their own distinct sexuality. This is especially manifest, moreover, in the priest's presidency of the Eucharist.[138]

---

[133] *Sacerdotalis Caelibatus* 26.

[134] As it does also to *Lumen Gentium* 42.

[135] *Pastores Dabo Vobis* 29; see also the Congregation for the Clergy, *Directory on the Ministry and Life of Priests* (January 31, 1994), no. 13 and no. 58, for the same connection.

[136] See on no. 14, Ratzinger, "Life and Ministry of Priests."

[137] *Pastores Dabo Vobis* 29: "For an adequate priestly spiritual life, celibacy ought not to be considered and lived as an isolated or purely negative element, but as one aspect of a positive, specific and characteristic approach to being a priest."

[138] See Roman Cholij, "Priesthood and Celibacy according to Recent Church Teaching," in *Priesthood: A Greater Love*, who has it that, at the Eucharistic sacrifice, the priest "lends his chaste flesh to Christ, his continence now becoming an integral constituent of his iconic relationship with Christ who offers the sacrifice of a total self-oblation to the Father on our behalf."

John Paul II sounds this note both magisterially and more privately as a theologian. Magisterially, again from *Pastores Dabo Vobis*:

> In virginity and celibacy, chastity retains its original meaning, that is, of human sexuality lived as a genuine sign of and precious service to the love of communion and gift of self to others. This meaning is fully found in virginity which makes evident, even in the renunciation of marriage, the "nuptial meaning" of the body through a communion and a personal gift to Jesus Christ and his Church which prefigures and anticipates the perfect and final communion and self-giving of the world to come: "In virginity or celibacy, the human being is awaiting, also in a bodily way, the eschatological marriage of Christ with the Church, giving himself or herself completely to the Church in the hope that Christ may give himself to the Church in the full truth of eternal life."[139]

There is too much material in the "theology of the body" to canvass in this essay, but at least we can recall the catecheses on the Resurrection and on virginity. In the first, sexuality is seen to be fulfilled in the resurrected body, which is to say that the nuptial meaning of the sexually determined bodiliness of human persons is fulfilled in heaven, where deification makes the gift of self perfect.[140] From the catecheses on virginity, we have this:

> [I]f continence for the sake of the kingdom of heaven undoubtedly signifies a renunciation, this renunciation is at the same time an affirmation. It is an affirmation that arises from the discovery of the gift, that is, at the same time from the discovery of a new perspective of the personal realization of oneself "through a sincere gift of oneself" (*Gaudium et Spes* 24).[141]

Celibacy integrates male sexuality into priesthood. First it is self-gift, and precisely as involving (by way of renunciation, to be sure) sexually characterized bodiliness. Second, it keeps the specific finality of sexuality, fecundity, but orients it to a higher, spiritual fecundity. We should notice that here as for marriage, there is an inseparability between the union effected by self-gift and fruitfulness.[142] As the exclusion of one or the other destroys the

---

[139] *Pastores Dabo Vobis* 29; the quotation is from *Familiaris Consortio* (1981) 16.

[140] Catecheses on the Resurrection, *Theology of the Body*, 233–61, esp. at 238–40 (December 2, 1981), 240–43 (December 9, 1981).

[141] Catecheses on virginity, *The Theology of the Body*, 262–303, at 286.

[142] Ibid., 277–78 (general audience of April 14, 1982); see also Cholij, "Priesthood and Celibacy," for whom the priest's "conjugal debt is now not towards his wife, but towards the Church through frequent celebration of the Eucharist. His paternal responsibilities are first and foremost towards his spiritual progeny."

integrity of the marital act, so the exclusion of one or the other in priestly celibacy would destroy its way of affirming and redeeming sexuality.[143]

Also, the very way of being sexual as a male is affirmed and redeemed in priestly celibacy, though this is hard to put into words that will not be misunderstood. Sara Butler, relying on *Mulieris Dignitatem*, says that the feminine mode of loving is characterized "by active receptivity, a welcoming love which meets, accepts, and responds to the husband's gift with its own gift of self," and is careful to point out that "active receptivity" is not passivity.[144] By contrast, we can say that if the feminine welcomes, the masculine knocks; if the feminine meets, the masculine seeks; if the feminine accepts and responds, the masculine initiates and begins. And these harmonics, too, are sounded in the priestly initiative in gathering the Church by the initiative of evangelization and preaching, by the offering of word and sacrament to the welcoming, active receptivity of the faithful.

The orientation of sexuality to a higher goal occurs, *mutatis mutandis,* both in Christian marriage and also, and in another way, with a married clergy, as in the Eastern practice. If one sticks with the council, it cannot be said that celibacy flows from the nature of the priesthood, else a married clergy impedes the working out of nature of the sacrament.[145] Nor can it be said on the basis of the above argumentation that married priests unworthily celebrate Mass, or that they do not give themselves fully to the fulfillment of their charge.[146] But it can be said that with a married clergy, the integration of sexuality into priesthood does not happen as unambiguously as with celibacy, for sexuality finds its ordinary finality in procreation; it is not *exclusively* integrated into the symbolic register of priesthood, of the priestly representation of Christ, and indeed, the earthly Christ, nor is it uniquely integrated into the spiritual finality of the priesthood. Still, a married clergy does not of itself militate against either the symbolic harmonics or the finality of priesthood. Were it so, of course, the practice of the Eastern Church could not find the praise and approbation the council rightly gives it.[147]

---

[143] See here Michele M. Schumacher, "An Inseparable Connection: The Fruitfulness of Conjugal Love and the Divine Norm," *Nova et Vetera* 1 (2003): 381–402.

[144] Butler, "Priest as Sacrament," 511; see *Mulieris Dignitatem* 25.

[145] *AS* IV/7:209, Response to Modus 16.

[146] *AS* IV/7:211, Responses to Modus 18 and to Modus 20.

[147] On the other hand, those who want a female priesthood make of sexuality something indifferent to priesthood, irrelevant to priesthood, something that cannot, as such, be integrated into priesthood. Whether someone is male or not is wholly accidental to priesthood. Likewise, those who want homosexual "marriage," at the same time as they destroy the nature of marriage, also make of sexuality something indifferent to priesthood because incapable of speaking a relation to the finality of priesthood in (spiritual) fruitfulness. Here, sexuality is denatured because stripped of its ordination to procreation; it cannot therefore bear any special relation to spiritual fruitfulness, which could no longer justly be called spiritual "paternity."

Conclusion

Above, in the introduction to Part II, we asked where the legacy of *Presbyterorum Ordinis* is to be found. This depends very much on whether its view of the nature of priesthood is coherent, a true synthesis of the two dominant views with which the council started, or whether it is a juxtaposition of pieces that cannot go together. In the latter case, the legacy is a choice between two unsynthesizable pieces. As one popular hermeneutic of the council would have it, we could pursue a reconstituted post-Tridentinism, a sort of resupernaturalizing and resacerdotalization of ecclesial ministry (bad things), as some claim to see in the 1971 Synod and the Letters to Priests of John Paul II. On the other hand, still according to this hermeneutic, the course is forward, to the democratic and declericalized, egalitarian, charismatic, and collaborative style of ministry toward which the council took but a few hesitant and indecisive steps.

A seemingly more moderate hermeneutic, and one critical of the foregoing, would see the *Decree*, as it sees the production of the council generally, as a juxtaposition of views, but a not incoherent one. Rather, according to this view: "Fidelity to the Council requires that both juxtaposed theses be taken seriously and that an attempt be made through a more penetrating theological reflection and a renewed ecclesial praxis to reconcile them in a synthesis that will allow further advances."[148] So, the council bequeathed to the Church and theology the task of working for a synthesis that the council itself could not or did not effect.

We believe that neither of these approaches is helpful for interpreting *Presbyterorum Ordinis*. The textual history of the *Decree* and the speeches and discussions that are part of that history show that it was certainly not the intention of the council fathers to do nothing more than juxtapose two theses or viewpoints. The October 16, 1965, *relatio* of Archbishop Marty gave voice to that intention, accepted by the fathers. Further, we think it is no great feat of interpretation to see the fulfillment of this intention in paragraph 2 of the *Decree*. Interpreting *Presbyterorum Ordinis* therefore cannot be a matter of weighing or balancing two masses of material, the theses of a progressive council majority on one side and of a conservative council minority on the other. We are to see, rather, that consecration is for the purpose of extending the mission of Christ, whose own end is the glory of the Father in a redeemed humanity. The priest-presbyter is sent forth as one consecrated *in persona Christi capitis* authoritatively to proclaim the Gospel to the world, to extend the offer of salvation in the sacraments, and to build up the Church.

---

[148] Pottmeyer, "A New Phase in the Reception of Vatican II," 39.

Determining the legacy of *Presbyterorum Ordinis* depends also on whether the *Decree* is read against the background of prior Catholic tradition, the great democracy of the diachronic voices from Scripture, itself read as *Dei Verbum* 12 teaches us to read it, to the Fathers, from the Fathers to the theologians of the twelfth and thirteenth centuries, and very much including past conciliar and papal teaching. This way of interpretation was urged by the Synod of Bishops on the twentieth anniversary of the council.[149]

We think that, if read in that way, the synthesis of the views and the adequacy of the one view arrived at become manifest. If the priesthood was framed in the theology of mission, it remained the ministry that culminated in the Eucharistic sacrifice, where the Christian's sacrifice of life passes over sacramentally into the eternal sacrifice of the Lamb. Precisely because it was framed in the theology of mission, both its historical institution by Christ and its sacramental enablement, now, by Christ through the Spirit, were affirmed. If the priest was not hailed as an *alter Christus*, he was described as acting *in persona Christi capitis* no longer merely at the Eucharist, but across the length and breadth of his ministry. The *Decree* put it that the priest was to find holiness within the very exercise of his ministry—teaching, sanctifying, ruling. Still, that's what he was to find—holiness. The relation of the priest as minister to bishop, to fellow priests, to the laity, and including to the laity in their own apostolic labor—in other words, the concrete ecclesial context into which the priest is inserted—was affirmed expressly and in detail. Still, he remained a "man apart," both by reason of his consecration and in order to have something to bring to the people in whose midst he lived and worked.

If it is read in this way, furthermore, where the truly synthetic character of the *Decree* becomes manifest, then it is possible to answer the question of its legacy, which would appear to be the 1992 apostolic exhortation, *Pastores Dabo Vobis*. This is true for the ecclesiological presuppositions of the priesthood, spelled out by the Holy Father as the mystery, the communion, and the mission of the Church; it is true for the centrality of the priest as representing Christ the head; it is true for the priority of this representation relative to priestly representation of the Church; and it is true for the clarity with which the celibacy is also linked to this representative character of the priest. All these things, some more or less developed by the council, are brought fully to expression by Pope John Paul II, especially in relation to the human and ecclesial situation, the signs of the times, at the beginning of the third millennium. In this way, *Pastores Dabo Vobis* shows us a privileged way forward in the task of receiving the synthesis of *Presbyterorum Ordinis*.

---

[149] See "The Final Report," no. 5, "A Deeper Reception of the Council," *Origins* 15 (December 19, 1985): 444–50, at 445–46.

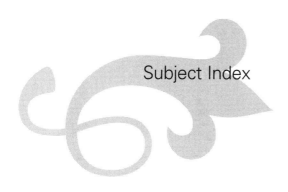

Subject Index

abbots, concession to ordain granted
 to, 169
Abelard, Peter, 98
AC (Apostolic Constitutions), 163
actuation *vs.* act, 49*n*15
Albert the Great, 164*n*22, 184*n*9, 189
Alfaro, J., 59*n*41, 60*n*48
d'Almeida Trindade, Bishop, 191,
 207*n*103
Anciaux, Paul, 74*n*7, 75*n*9
Anelli, G., 89*n*69
Anselm of Canterbury
 Balthasar
  critique of Anselm's soteriology,
   99–100
  on monastic origins of *satisfactio*
   doctrine, 73–74, 91
 Rahner
  compared to Anselm, 25
  critique of Anselm's notion of
   satisfactio, 95–96
  reclaiming soteriological tradition
   of, vii, viii
  satisfactio and monastic
   consciousness of. *See under*
   satisfactio
Apollinaris, 6
Apostles and apostolic succession
 episcopal orders, character and
  munera of, 162–63

male priesthood, dominical
 intention of, 130, 133, 134–35
relationship between priesthood
 and community of the faithful,
 237–41
relationship of particular/local
 Churches to universal Church,
 121–22
Apostolic Constitutions (AC), 163
Apostolic Tradition (AT), 163
Apostolicam Actuositatem, 222*n*40
Aquinas, Thomas
 Balthasar and, 28*n*2, 34, 39–41
 change, Aristotelian analysis of, 42
 on Christ's self-knowledge. *See*
  Thomist account of Christ's
  human knowledge of his
  divine nature
 episcopal orders, character and
  munera of
  relationship of character to
   munera, 161, 164, 165–68,
   169, 171–75, 178, 179
  sacerdotal character, 184*n*9,
   187, 194*n*54, 198, 208–9
 on *esse secundarium* of Christ, 16
 on implicit faith, 139*n*18

nature and person of Christ,
relationship between, 3–7,
111–12
problem of science of, 9–14
Trinity
distinctness of Persons in, 54
Logos as only Person of Trinity
that can be incarnated, 15,
19–20, 21–23, 25
Peter Abelard. *See* Abelard, Peter
Philibert, Paul, 240*n*100
Philip the Chancellor, 164*n*22, 184*n*9
Philippe, Bishop, 196*n*67, 197, 198,
203
Philippians
humility and obedience of Christ
in, 5
Philips, Gérard, 183, 184, 189–92
philosophy
Balthasar on theology's
measurement and confinement
by, 43
Christology as *scientia* in tradition
of, vii, 9–14
Thomist approach to, 9*n*1, 10,
43*n*60
pistis in New Testament, 60. *See
also* faith
Pius XII, 225*n*54
Plantinga, Alvin, 62
Plato and Platonism, 63*n*55, 123
Plourde, Bishop, 202*n*93, 210*n*120
Portillo, Alvaro del, 225*n*53
Poschmann, Bernhard, 74*n*7
Potterie, Ignace de la, 251*n*131
Pottmeyer, Hermann J., 220–21,
255*n*148
Pouchet, Jean-Marie, 74*n*5
Power, David, 242, 243*n*118
preaching. *See* teaching and preaching
Presbyterorum Ordinis, viii, 213–56
celibacy of priesthood, challenges
to, 236*n*89, 247–54
doctrinal novelty of Paragraph 2,
230–35

on episcopal character and *munera*.
See under episcopal orders,
character and munera of
history of, 213–14, 219
legacy of, 255–56
Lumen Gentium and, 214, 215,
225, 231–32, 234
male priesthood, challenges to,
236*n*89, 241–47
munera of priesthood, 218–19,
221–24, 231–34
relationship between priesthood
and community, 237–41
representative view of priesthood
in, 229–30, 231–35, 241–47
*Schema Propositionum de Vita et
Ministerio Sacerdotali*, 195,
196–97, 214
synthesis of views of priesthood in
juxtaposition *vs.*, 219–21
muneral approach to, 218–19
Paragraph 2, 225–30
second and third parts of text,
230
two views on priesthood at council,
215–21
priesthood. *See also* orders
celibacy of, 236*n*89, 247–54
Eucharist, ministry ordered to,
221–23
gender issues regarding. *See* male
priesthood
munera of, 218–19, 221–24,
231–34
post-conciliar challenges to,
235–37, 241–47
presbyteral ordinations, *Lumen
Gentium* avoiding discussion of,
185
Presbyterorum Ordinis on. *See
Presbyterorum Ordinis*
relationship to community, 237–41
representational role. *See*
representation, priestly role of

in *Theo-Drama. See under*
Balthasar, Hans Urs von,
Christology of
Christ's knowledge of, 63
distinctness of Persons, 54
ecclesiology of communion found
in, 117
episcopal character and *munera,*
Trinitarian view of, 189
invisibility as property of the
Father, 21
Rahner on
Logos as only Person of Trinity
that can be incarnated, 15,
19–20, 21–23, 25
Trinity, The, argument of, 22–23
universal Church's ontological
precedence to creation and,
119–20
Tromp, S., 189
Turbanti, Giovanni, 217*n*18
typos, 12

understanding
of Christ, 63–64
infinity of divine understanding,
40–41
universal Church. *See* ecclesiology

Vaillancourt, Raymond, 160*n*2,
170*n*49
van Roo, William, 99*n*25, 177
Vanhoye, Albert, 224*n*50, 227*n*61, 229
Vatican I, 230
Vatican II. *See also Lumen Gentium;*
Presbyterorum Ordinis
different understandings of
priesthood at, 196, 215–19
on episcopal orders. *See* episcopal
orders, character and *munera* of
post-conciliar challenges to
priesthood, 235–37

Veritatis Splendor, 223*n*41
Vincent de Paul, 217
Vio, Thomas de (Cardinal Cajetan),
168
Vogüé, Adalbert de, 82, 83–84
von Balthasar, Hans Urs. *See* Balthasar,
Hans Urs von, Christology of
von Speyr, Adrienne, 36, 37
Vorgrimler, Herbert, 160

Walgrave, Jan H., 137*n*17
Walsh, Liam, 49
Wasselynck, René, 195*n*61, 196*n*65,
197*n*71, 198*n*73, 199*n*77–78,
214*n*1, 215*n*5
Weber, Bishop, 200, 202, 203
Weinandy, Thomas G., 19*n*16,
110*n*70
Welch, Lawrence J., viii, 141*n*21,
155*n*48, 213, 242*n*112
wergeld and *satisfactio,* 74–75*n*9
William of Auxerre, 164*n*21
women
ordination of. *See* male priesthood
sexuality and priestly celibacy, 249,
250, 252–54
Wood, Susan, 242
world's importance to God, 30–31,
33, 35, 38–39, 43–44
Wojtyla, Karol, 4. *See* also John Paul II
wrath of God
in Balthasar's soteriology, 95,
101–2, 109, 111
Rahner on, 94
Wulf, Friedrich, 220, 221*n*38, 241

Scripture Index